D1067232

Gospel Light's

SPECIAL NEEDS

SMART PAGES

advice, answers & articles about ministering to children with special needs

created by joni and friends

★ Love and teach children affected by disabilities

★ Create Bible lessons designed to meet their needs

★ Help children discover and use their unique gifts to serve in the Body of Christ

DVD & CD-ROM included

reproducible

✺ **Gospel Light**

Guidelines for Photocopying Reproducible Pages

Permission to make photocopies of or to reproduce by any other mechanical or electronic means in whole or in part any designated* page, illustration or activity in this book is granted only to the original purchaser and is intended for non-commercial use within a church or other Christian organization. None of the material in this book, not even those pages with permission to photocopy, may be reproduced for any commercial promotion, advertising or sale of a product or service or to share with any other persons, churches or organizations. Sharing of the material in this book with other churches or organizations not owned or controlled by the original purchaser is also prohibited. All rights reserved.

* Do not make any copies from this book unless you adhere strictly to the guidelines found on this page. Only pages with the following notation can be legally reproduced:

© 2009 Gospel Light. Permission to photocopy granted to original purchaser only. *Special Needs Smart Pages*

Editorial Staff

Senior Managing Editor, Sheryl Haystead • **Senior Editor,** Deborah Barber • **Contributing Editor,** Patricia Verbal • **Major Contributing Writers,** Arlyn Kantz, Barbara Newman, Rachel Olstad, Kathy Weltner • **Minor Contributing Writers,** Cynthia Berry, Debbie Salter Goodwin, Dr. Kathy McReynolds, Chonda Ralston, Linda Weddle, Amy McMullin • **Art Director,** Lenndy Pollard • **Designer,** Annette M. Chavez
Founder, Dr. Henrietta Mears • **Publisher,** William T. Greig • **Senior Consulting Publisher,** Dr. Elmer L. Towns • **Senior Consulting Editor,** Wesley Haystead, M.S.Ed. • **Senior Editor, Theology and Biblical Content,** Dr. Gary S. Greig

About This Book (Symbol Key)

The following symbols are used in this book as signposts to help locate various kinds of disabilities.

Autism Spectrum Disorder

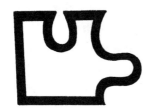

Physical Disabilities

Emotional/Behavioral Disorders

Speech and Language Impairments

Developmental/Cognitive Disabilities

Visual and Hearing Impairments

Learning Disabilities

Quick Start to Disability Ministry

1) Begin with the basics. Read the articles on pages 39-40, 43, 65-66, 69 and 72.

2) Add these articles for more depth: pages 13, 17, 121, 151, 182 and the small-group Bible studies starting on page 234.

3) Use the index for extensive and specific information about disabilities and disability ministries and resources.

What Children with Special Needs Wish You Knew

I'm Just "Me," and That's Okay

I Need Friends Along the Way

I Want to Know God's Word

I Like It When You Talk to Me

I Won't Give Up – Don't You

I'm Not Sick – I Have a Disability

I Mess Up – Like Any Other Kid

I Know God Can Use Me – No Matter What

Contents

Section 7: I Mess Up—Like Any Other Kid! (Behavior Issues)

Section 8: I Know God Can Use Me—No Matter What! (Spiritual Growth and Service)

Section 9: Hearts in Motion (Bible Studies on Disability Awareness) 234

Section 10: Real Kids (Read Aloud Stories) 253

Joni's Story

For years, my family and I enjoyed playing tennis, riding horses and hiking. That changed one hot afternoon in July 1967 when my sister, Kathy, and I went swimming in Chesapeake Bay. I didn't bother to check the depth of the water when I hoisted myself onto a raft anchored offshore. Positioning my feet on the edge, I took a deep breath and plunged into the murky water. To my surprise, my head hit the hard bottom and snapped back. A strange electric shock zapped the back of my neck. Floating underwater, I felt myself drifting and unable to surface.

My lungs screamed for air! As I gasped for breath, I felt my sister's arms around me, pulling me upward. Looking at my lifeless arm slung over her shoulder, I sputtered, "Kathy, I can't feel my body!"

A sunbather nearby rushed into the water with his raft. Another called an ambulance. Within the hour, ER nurses were cutting off my wet bathing suit, my necklace and my rings. As I began losing consciousness, I heard the sound of a drill buzzing above my head.

My diving accident thrust me into a strange and frightening world filled with antiseptic smells, plastic tubes and life-giving machines. For months, I lay on a Stryker frame, facing up for hours in the canvas sandwich-type sling. Then I was flipped facedown to prevent pressure sores. It didn't help. I lost so much weight those first months that my bones literally began sticking to my flesh, which resulted in more operations and more time in the Stryker frame.

A deep, dark depression came over me, and I questioned my faith. "God, how could You have allowed this to happen to me?" I asked. "I'm a Christian. I prayed for a closer walk with You, and if this is Your answer, how can I ever trust You again?"

Little did I realize that people were praying for me around the clock. As the weeks passed, I began to sense a difference. My anger subsided, and my depression

slowly lifted. God was lovingly wearing down my resistance through the precious prayer covering of my church family and friends.

I soon noticed a change in my occupational therapy. Weeks earlier, I had stubbornly refused to learn how to write with a pencil clenched between my teeth. That was before I met Tom, a young ventilator-dependent quadriplegic, who was more paralyzed than I was. When he enthusiastically asked the therapist to put the pen in his mouth, I stopped grumbling and complaining.

God used the prayers of my friends and Tom's example to show me the truth of Romans 8:28: "In all things God works for the good of those who love him." God's idea of my "good" seemed not to include getting me back on my feet. Perhaps it included a flexible attitude, an appreciation for small things, and a character that reflected the kind of joy that did not depend on circumstances.

I can't say that the past 40 years have been easy, but I *have* experienced my Savior's power and strength along the way. Jesus always knew exactly how I felt because He suffered, too. He turned His cross into a symbol of hope and freedom. When I realized that, I could do no less. My wheelchair has become the prison God used to set my spirit free.

What Is Joni and Friends?

For over a quarter of a century, Joni and Friends (JAF) has been dedicated to extending the love of Christ to children and adults with special needs and their families. Through the mission of Joni and Friends, the gospel has been communicated worldwide, and Christ-honoring churches are now equipped to evangelize and disciple all those affected by disability.

A diving accident in 1967 left founder, Joni Eareckson Tada, with quadriplegia and confined to a wheelchair. After two years of rehabilitation, Joni emerged with new skills and a fresh determination to help others in similar situations. Mrs. Tada wrote of her experiences in her best-selling biography, *Joni*. With the book's distribution in many languages, Joni's name soon became recognized around the world and was followed by her full-length feature film, *Joni*.

Having been propelled onto an international stage, Mrs. Tada launched Joni and Friends in 1979. In 2006, Joni and Friends grew to become the Joni and Friends International Disability Center, which ministers to thousands affected by disability around the globe through four flagship programs:

- *Joni and Friends* **Radio Ministry**—A daily five-minute radio program broadcast over 1,000 outlets and heard every week by a million listeners. In 2002, it received the Radio Program of the Year award from National Religious Broadcasters.

- **JAF Family Retreats**—Five-day summer programs provided for families affected by disability. In 2007, Joni and Friends served over 1,000 special needs families in 19 family retreats hosted across the United States.

- **Wheels for the World Wheelchair Outreach**—A program designed to provide wheelchairs to the disabled throughout the world and to share Jesus' love. To date, over 35,000 wheelchairs have been collected nationwide, refurbished by inmates in over 15 correctional facilities and donated and custom fit to a needy child or adult with a physical disability in a developing nation.

- **Disability Ministry**—A movement to equip churches to include people with disabilities and their families. The Joni and Friends' Field Service's staff and volunteers provide training and resources to equip churches in ministry to those affected by disability, and they also host regional Disability Ministry summits.

In 2007, the Joni and Friends International Disability Center took two giant steps of faith. First, the Christian Institute on Disability was established as a communications and training center to address disability-related issues in our culture. Second, a new TV series, *Joni and Friends,* was produced to proclaim God's victorious plan for all families affected by suffering and disability. This unique program is broadcast nationwide and internationally (see www.joniandfriendstv.org for your local broadcast schedule).

While JAF focuses on influencing the church on disability-related issues, Mrs. Tada's impact is felt beyond the Christian community. Her role as a disability advocate led to a presidential appointment to the National Council on Disability for three and a half years, during which time the Americans with Disabilities Act became law. In 2005, Mrs. Tada was appointed to the Disability Advisory Committee of the United States Department of State to advise Dr. Condoleezza Rice on policies and programs that affect disabled persons in the State Department and around the world.

Mrs. Tada and her husband, Ken, married in 1982 and minister together around the world. Both are permanent members of the International Board of Directors of Joni and Friends.

A Word from Joni

We're all richer when we recognize our poverty, we're stronger when we see our weaknesses, and we're recipients of God's grace when we understand our desperate need for Him. I'm confident that as you partner with us to love and serve families affected by disability, you, too, will be blessed.

Joni and Friends
INTERNATIONAL DISABILITY CENTER

I'm Just Me, and That's Okay!

This little light of mine,
I'm gonna let it shine.

This little light of mine,
I'm gonna let it shine.

This little light of mine,
I'm gonna let it shine,

Let it shine,

Let it shine,

Let it shine.

Awareness: Children with Disabilities Are Valuable to God

We know that in all things God works for the good of those who love him, who have been called according to his purpose. Romans 8:28

In the beginning when God separated the light from the darkness and created day, how bright that first light must have been. The contrast of an early sunrise against a black backdrop can still take one's breath away. We witness this same sort of contrast in the lives of children with disabilities. The depths of their struggles can make their smallest success glow with heavenly light. And those of us who are fortunate enough to know these amazing children experience the warm rays of God's love shining through their smiles.

All children remind us that **God is good**. According to Romans 8:28, He promised to share that goodness with us. Yet when Katie was born with a neurobiological disorder, the doctors said she would be mentally retarded, with all that such a pronouncement implies. One day, however, the toddler looked out of the car window and read a street sign. Then her parents gave her a book, which she also read. Katie was hyperlexic, meaning she had an exceptional, untaught reading ability at a very young age. As a fourth grader, Katie, who was diagnosed with Asperger's syndrome, taught herself Japanese. She continued to amaze her family and friends with God's perfect plan for her life.

Children remind us that **God is faithful**. From his wheelchair, Cole feared the rough neighborhood where he and his mom lived. He often cried himself to sleep because bullies made fun of him. But through his faith in Jesus, Cole learned to pray for bad people and to trust God for protection. He even requested prayer at church for his neighborhood, leading members to faithfully reach out to the bullies and share Christ with them.

These children show us that the image of **God is within us**—not outside us. Christy discovered this concept when she cared for Elliot at camp. Locked in a twisted body racked by multiple physical and mental disabilities, Elliot sat almost motionless in his wheelchair. He never spoke, made eye contact or responded to her touch. Early in the week, Christy watched with Elliot as the other campers swam, made crafts and giggled. By midweek, she felt content to push Elliot's chair down quiet paths under the trees, where she would stop and read poems to him or sing simple songs. She came to appreciate the serenity of their times together and was sad to say good-bye. When that time came, Christy patted Elliot's right hand, which lay in his lap. To her surprise, he slowly lifted her hand with his, drew it to his mouth and gave it a soft kiss. Christy's eyes filled with tears. Later, she described it as a kiss from God's own heart—the sweetest she'd ever felt and one she would never forget.

The Bible speaks of our need for childlike faith—a faith that surrenders our grown-up efforts to fix things. As you minister to these extraordinary children, you'll slam head-on into Romans 8:28. You may even question God's goodness and power to make all things work for good for children like Katie, Cole or Elliot. And that's when children with special needs will become your teachers!

Awareness: The Problem with Labels

Walking into a high school, a person might be strongly tempted to sort the students as "athlete," "brain," "geek," "loser" or "cheerleader"—all terms one may use to describe teens. These descriptors, or labels, however, are often misleading. They categorize students by emphasizing only one aspect of complex individuals. At a 25-year high-school reunion, how many of those descriptors would still be true?

Psalm 139:13 refers to God as a crafter and states, "For you created my inmost being; you knit me together in my mother's womb." With God as our master designer, only God's labels and designations should hold legitimacy and truth. The Bible is rich with descriptors that each one of us displays. "Handmade by God," "image-bearer of God," "significant," "honored," "dearly loved child" and "secure in God's hand" are just some of the words that describe us, God's handiwork.

There are no problems with God's labels for us; His words are declarations that honor and bless. Some of us, however, acquire man-given labels that are less than complimentary. For example, a child with an identifiable disability often wears some sort of limiting, derogatory descriptor that can obscure the vision of God's words for that child. While it may be true that a child has cerebral palsy, autism or Down syndrome, it is also true that an onlooker may mistakenly see only that characteristic. A child with a disability may appear to be "deficient," "incompetent," "unpresentable" or "totally incapable." Covering up God's labels for a child with these words that limit, degrade and hurt is sinful and offensive to the Creator.

Ephesians 2:10 affirms that "we are God's workmanship, created in Christ Jesus to do good works, which God prepared in advance for us to do." The Bible is clear that each child who attends your church is hand-knit with an individualized pattern by God. That pattern beautifully displays God's image in some form. Each child is created specifically to be able to fill a prepared spot in God's kingdom and an honored place in the Body of Christ. First Corinthians 12:12 declares, "The body is a unit, though it is made up of many parts; and though all its parts are many, they form one body. So it is with Christ."

Make it clear to peers, parents and volunteers that your church rejects all hurtful labels. While disability labels are needed for communicating useful information, always remember that God's perspective is much truer. Aggressively peel away the negative labels associated with disabilities. Focus on children's gifts, and give *all* children an honored place in your church community. While some children may require specialized equipment or techniques in order to meet their needs, you have the joy of seeing the participation of those children enrich the lives of others. "And this is his command: . . . to love one another" (1 John 3:23).

Join God's line of sight!

People may see	God sees
Cerebral Palsy Cindy	Cindy, handcrafted by Himself before she was even born. Part of her unique knitting pattern is her love for animals and gifted singing voice. She also happens to have cerebral palsy.
Down Syndrome Adam	Adam, image-bearer of Himself, who displays passion for prayer and care for the people in his life. He also happens to have Down syndrome.
Autistic Sam	Sam, honored and significant member of the Body of Christ, who is a gifted servant as he joyfully organizes the toy shelves at church. He also happens to have autism.

Awareness: Exposing Myths About Special Needs

"I can't serve children with disabilities because I don't have any formal training."

Have you considered that children with disabilities are born into families with no training? Parents, grandparents, aunts and uncles do what comes naturally. First they love these children; then they get to know them. God simply asks their church family to do the same. As a new volunteer, you'll be trained and educated and maybe even partnered with an experienced "buddy," and you'll be surprised by how quickly your confidence grows.

"Aren't children with mental retardation spiritually innocent before God?"

While some children with special needs may not understand God's grace, they can all experience His love in amazing ways. Many churches are confused about how to meet these children's spiritual needs and often wonder, *Are these children sinners? Or do they have a free ticket to heaven?* What we believe concerning their salvation is not critical to how we minister to them. And we don't need to figure out their age of accountability or their mental capacity to introduce them to Jesus.

"We don't need a disability ministry because the church downtown has one and does a great job."

Do your own research. For example, there are about 2,600 churches listed in the *Dallas Yellow Pages.* Bible studies, youth ministries, recovery programs and outstanding choirs are featured in many of the ads. And in some ads, churches brag about their sports ministry, and one even offers a "cappuccino ministry"; but not one ad lists a disability ministry. Yet school districts nationwide estimate that children with special needs make up from 15 to 25 percent of their student body. Your church should exist to serve your community.

"I guess I should volunteer because God sent these children to teach me to count my blessings."

"This myth defines a person's life solely in terms of his or her effect on others," says Rev. Dennis D. Schurter, retired chaplain at the Denton State School in Denton, Texas. "It is a rationalization in the face of a negative experience that says the person is 'sent' by God to test one's faith or teach one to love, etc. To place one on a pedestal is to dehumanize. Each person has equal value. . . . Each person can be a blessing to others, whether handicapped or not."*

"Aren't parents the best caregivers? Can't they just take turns at church?"

Sure, parents could take turns, but *you* would miss God's blessings. *You* would miss building wonderful relationships with some of the most terrific children you'll ever meet. And the fruit of the Spirit in *your* life will be less ripe on the vine. Why should parents have all the fun?

"I'm afraid of the legal responsibility of caring for someone with a disability."

There are legal responsibilities involved in serving in the nursery, in youth activities, in the church kitchen and on the parking lot. But we don't neglect those ministries. The church carries insurance for accidents. On occasion, a child with a disability may experience a medical condition that requires the intervention of a parent or a call to 9-1-1. But you can rest assured that you will always have a supervisor for support.

*Dennis D. Schurter, D. Min., *A Ministry Manual* (Denton, TX 2003), p. 16.

Ministry Is Messy!

God plops people with disabilities in the midst of a congregation—a hand grenade that blows apart the picture-perfectness of the church . . . The "uncomely" parts are critical to the life of the body. . . . We want the church to see some of these disenfranchised folks as the "indispensable" part of the body.
—Joni Eareckson Tada

Awareness: Disability Is a Family Affair

Same Morning, Different Households

Sunday Morning in the Browns' Home

It was 5:00 A.M., and Dylan Brown was up. *How is this possible?* thought his mom, Madge. She had spent half the night giving her three-year-old breathing treatments. Madge rolled over to poke her husband, indicating it was his turn to check on Dylan; but when she extended her arm, she found nothing. She wondered if he had fallen asleep on the downstairs couch or if he had bothered to come home at all.

After their son had been diagnosed with autism six months ago, Paul started going out with his friends, drinking heavily. He began missing work and, with his wages being docked, money was tight. The stress only caused Paul to drink more in spite of Dylan's escalating treatment costs. Madge worried about how they were going to survive. That morning, she tried deep breathing to calm her nerves and prevent another panic attack. It was hard to control her fear and rage. Marge felt trapped, with no one to turn to for help. She had little hope for her marriage, her son's life or her own dreams.

Sunday Morning in the Smiths' Home

It was 5:00 A.M., and Sarah needed to be "burped." To support her weight gain and growth, she was on a feeding pump most of the night. Melody looked at her husband sleeping peacefully beside her. Stan had taken the first shift to care for Sarah last night. He was happy to do it. He loved his daughter but didn't get to see her much due to his working overtime. Melody softly hummed a praise tune as she opened the G-button attached to Sarah's stomach, connected the appropriate tubing and gently pressed on her tummy. Melody smiled to herself, thinking about the many changes in their lives in the last year, including their new church.

The Smiths left their last church because people acted as if they didn't have enough faith to heal Sarah. But Stan insisted that church was a part of their lives, so when a neighbor invited them to visit her church, they went. They were good neighbors with strong family values, who drove the Smiths to church and sat with them during worship. Over the next few Sundays, Melody and Stan made new friends and felt accepted for who they were: parents of a child with special needs.

Unique Family Challenges

The diagnosis of a child with a special need can be a challenging and life-changing event for a family. It raises a multitude of difficult questions, many of which cannot be answered. The diagnosis impacts immediate family members as well as the extended family. When a congregation acknowledges these challenges and extends grace to these families, it is a tremendous blessing.

Impact on Parents

Parents of children with special needs may walk through your church doors with a variety of church experiences—some good, some heartbreaking. Their basic question is, "Are we welcome, just as we are?" Many parents are looking for a much-needed break, while others seek a religious education for their children or they feel the need for friends and fellowship. These are the most basic ministries every church should offer. But if your church is willing to learn, grow and make a few correctable mistakes, you can embark on a journey together that will reap rich rewards.

Impact on Siblings

Not all siblings handle having a brother or sister with special needs in the same manner. Some siblings compensate well and actually become more well-rounded, caring individuals. Others experience embarrassment or frustration, or they begin to initiate aggressive behaviors. The support and reaction of the Church can greatly influence these often-fragile sibling relationships.

Impact on Grandparents

Besides grieving the loss of not having a typical grandchild, grandparents often have great concern about the predicament their children are experiencing. Most grandparents do not have the training, physical strength and agility necessary to help care for a child with special needs. Support and understanding from the Body of Christ will make a world of difference.

Church-Family Support

In addition to simply understanding a family's stress and their child's unique difficulties, churches can provide support in a number of areas.

Provide Financial Aid

Having a child with special needs can drain a family's resources. Medical treatments and various therapies can be costly. Often at least one parent quits his or her job or sharply cuts back on work hours to become the child's primary caregiver. Church members can help relieve this stress by becoming a safety net when an occasional financial emergency occurs.

Supplement Needed Care

Parents work to provide exceptional care but fear that no one else would be willing to take care of their child as they do. Parents also realize their child with a disability may never become an independent, self-sufficient adult. This can cause enormous concerns about what the future may hold. As these families build strong relationships within the Body of Christ, however, their fears are alleviated because they see that people outside their family can love and enjoy their children.

Show Unconditional Love

Taking a child with special needs out into the community can be challenging. People may stare, make cruel comments or fail to understand obvious physical differences or strange behaviors. This stress can prevent a family from accepting an invitation for dinner at a friend's home after church or staying for a church social. By showing unconditional love, church members can help families overcome fears of embarrassment or rejection.

Some children may not be able to clearly express their basic wants or needs. This frustration may lead to aggressive or self-injurious behaviors that threaten a child's safety and the safety of others. Language differences like volume, pitch and unintelligible noises can draw misunderstanding and unwanted attention. A loving hand from a friend can keep a family from feeling isolated in their church community.

Share Grief

Although raising children with special needs brings many joyful experiences, parents must accept grief and sorrow as their companions along the way. They grieve over developmental milestones that their children miss, failed treatment plans, and dreams that will never come true. The success they hoped for is mixed with the powerful emotions of denial, anger, fear and shame.

Promise Hope

While the world might focus on cost, inconvenience and wasted energy and lay blame at the feet of parents or the medical establishment, the Church must speak out with an alternative message:

> But [God] knows the way that I take; when he has tested me, I will come forth as gold (Job 23:10).
>
> [God] was despised and rejected by men, a man of sorrows, and familiar with suffering (Isaiah 53:3).
>
> All your sons [and daughters] will be taught by the Lord, and great will be your children's peace (Isaiah 54:13).

God calls His people to proclaim hope to families affected by disability.

As Christians, we must commit to accept and help families dealing with special needs. Each child's differences must be understood and his or her strengths and gifts celebrated. As insight is gained into each unique situation, we discover how remarkable these children are and how easy they are to love.

Awareness: Autism Spectrum Disorder— The Growing Epidemic

Merriam-Webster defines the word "epidemic" as "affecting or tending to affect a disproportionately large number of individuals within a population, community, or region at the same time."* When one compares current numbers to past trends and statistics, it is clear that there is an epidemic in the area of autism spectrum disorders (ASD).

According to a report by the Centers for Disease Control Prevention in 2007, "autism is the most common of the Pervasive Developmental Disorders, affecting an estimated 1 in 150 births. Roughly translated, this means as many as 1.5 million Americans today are believed to have some form of autism. And this number is on the rise."** Twenty-five years ago approximately 1 child in 10,000 was diagnosed with autism; it was known as a relatively rare condition. Twenty-five years ago, a church would not expect to have a child with autism in Sunday School. Today, a church should expect to have multiple children with ASD in children's programs. Volunteers must have basic information and strategies to support the needs and to value the gifts of children on the autism spectrum.

What is autism spectrum disorder?

When attending a family reunion, it soon becomes apparent that people resemble one another in physical features, personalities, reactions and actions. When psychologists classify different conditions, they group similar disorders into families. Autism is currently under a family category called pervasive developmental disorders (PDD). Autism is one of five relatives in this category that also includes Rett syndrome, childhood disintegrative disorder, autistic disorder, Asperger's syndrome and pervasive developmental disorder-not otherwise specified (PDD-NOS). While the current heading for these five related conditions is PDD, many professionals suggest using the term ASD. Some professionals think of all five relatives as ASD; others would include only autism, Asperger's syndrome and PDD-NOS in that category.

While researchers can describe ASD and note neurological differences on the spectrum, vast amounts of effort and study still have not shown what causes a person to develop ASD. Without a cause, a cure is difficult to discover. Professionals have, however, developed many techniques and strategies to support children with ASD.

What should a church know about ASD?

While professionals continue to think about categories, causes and possible cures, church volunteers should know how to support and include a child with ASD. If a parent brings a child to Sunday School and says, "My child has Asperger's syndrome," the leader should be able to recognize that name. That name recognition should link to a set of differences that may be seen in this child. Knowing those differences will allow the leader to support that child's needs while also understanding that child's strengths.

(*Note:* While knowing basic information about ASD is helpful, remember that each child is a uniquely crafted being of God. No two children are alike. It is far more important to become an expert on Johnny or Sue than it is to become an expert on ASD.)

What differences might you notice in a child with ASD?

Areas of difference are important because they point us to strategies and techniques we can use within our children's ministry programs. Although each child is an individual with unique gifts and needs, a child with ASD will typically show differences in the following areas: social skills, language, and range of interests or behaviors.

Social Skills

Social interactions can be a challenge. Many instant and simple social decisions that you make are often laborious and mystifying for a child with ASD. While typical children understand when to be quiet and when to speak, a child with ASD might need individualized instruction in this area. For children with ASD, reading facial expressions, understanding another person's point of view and accurately estimating another person's emotions can be difficult. Some children prefer to avoid the confusion of multiple people in one place. Others enjoy being with a group but may make social errors. Instead of knowing, for example, when to ask a question, a child with ASD may interrupt a large group and talk to the pastor in the middle of a sermon. This is not intended to be rude; it is simply unknown territory for that child.

Language

Some children with ASD develop speech at 1 to 2 years of age, and then speech disappears. Those children may never regain the ability to use spoken words while others develop speech in later childhood. You may encounter a child who will use pictures to communicate, while others may be able to use some sign language.

Some children need to practice patterned speech before using original words or phrases. Some children who are unable to crack the speaking code may borrow speech from movies or books. These children might have a difficult time answering a question, but reciting large amounts of text from memory is an effortless task.

Other children with ASD speak very well with impressive vocabularies but struggle to comprehend conversations or figures of speech. The interpretation of a question or phrase might be very literal. For example, singing a worship song that speaks about Jesus "living in my heart" could be very confusing or upsetting for a child with ASD, because the child may interpret those words literally.

Range of Interests or Behaviors

"Repetitive" or "restricted" themes and behaviors can also be a unique area for a child with ASD. A girl with ASD may have a motion or phrase that she repeats frequently. A boy may have a topic that consumes his thoughts and conversations. Although such a narrow focus might look like an obsession, such an action or thought often calms and brings pleasure to a child with ASD. Rocking, lining up toys, talking about trains or reciting portions of movies can make life seem more comfortable and predictable. Although many times these actions and topics can bump into your lesson plan or activity for the day, there are ways to turn those bumps into a good situation for all involved.

Why "differences" and not "deficits"?

It seems most appropriate to call these areas "differences" instead of "deficits". As you work with a child with ASD, you will notice that sometimes an area of difference becomes an area of strength. A child who can focus on one topic often becomes very proficient in that area. For example, if a boy with ASD thinks exclusively about computers, he can develop amazing technology skills. If a girl with ASD cares passionately about telling other people about Jesus, she can become a powerful evangelist. God specializes in making individual patterns as He creates and builds children before they are even born. Remember to delight in that unique pattern for the children with ASD. God does. "I praise you because I am fearfully and wonderfully made; your works are wonderful, I know that full well" (Psalm 139:14).

Want to learn more?

Make sure you read about these and other sensory differences in "The Sensory Factor" (p. 78). To understand this topic in depth and to read about many strategies to try at church, read *Autism and Your Church* by Barbara J. Newman.

Merriam-Webster's Collegiate Dictionary, 11th ed., s.v. "epidemic"; www.merriam-webster.com/dictionary/epidemic.

**"What Are Autism Spectrum Disorders?" *Autism Society of America,* January 23, 2008. http://www.autism-society.org/site/PageServer?pagename=about_whatis (accessed May 24, 2008).

Physical Disabilities: Discover Their Unique Strengths

Jim and Janet Slaight and their four children were headed for a long-awaited vacation in their van when the unthinkable happened. An oncoming car crossed into their lane going 92 miles per hour, hitting them head-on and rolling their van. Their four-year-old daughter, Hope, was killed. The other family members—all with life-threatening injuries—were rushed to four different hospitals. That's when their close-knit church sprang into action, providing round-the-clock care for the children until Jim and Janet fully recovered. After everyone's hospital stay, five-year-old Joey and six-year-old Hannah were left with permanent paralysis. Life would never be the same again.

Eliminate Misconceptions About Children with Physical Disabilities

None of the following "facts" are universally true.

- Children with physical disabilities are slow learners.
- Children with physical disabilities don't like talking about their disability.
- Children with physical disabilities have emotional issues.
- Children with physical disabilities have difficulty making friends.
- Children with physical disabilities face many failures.

Learn the Causes of Common Physical Disabilities

Some of the more common physical disabilities are caused by birth defects, muscular dystrophy, multiple sclerosis, cerebral palsy, spina bifida, stroke and injuries to the head or spinal cord (see "Common Disabilities Among Children," p. 33).

Spinal cord injuries are what put Joey and Hannah Slaight in wheelchairs for life. The higher the location of the injury on the spinal cord, the greater is the loss of bodily function. Some of the associated problems include paralysis, bowel and bladder dysfunction, impairment of sensation, and susceptibility to infection. Joey and Hannah are paraplegics because they are paralyzed from the waist down. A quadriplegic has paralysis in all four limbs,

as actor Christopher Reeve did. Each year, almost 8,000 people in the United States suffer injuries to their spinal cord.

Joey and Hannah shatter the misconceptions about paraplegics. Children with physical disabilities can have other impairments; but for the most part, they are average students who make friends and have as many successes as they do failures. They try hard not to draw pity from others and do as much for themselves as they are capable.

The Slaight family admittedly didn't originally have a clue about what "getting back to normal" meant. They'll now tell you, however, that they had to learn a "new kind of normal."

Hannah was a rock through the whole thing. She never got bitter or angry, and she continued to praise God. She is a good student who wants to go to college someday and have a family. Joey is a little quieter but loves sports and knows that he and Hannah can talk about anything because they understand what the other is going through.

"God said He would never put us through more than we could handle," says Hannah. "I've met some amazing people that I would have never met. I've also learned that trauma doesn't change who God is!"

Joey has goals too. "I try to always look at the bright side," he says. "I want to be happy and make the best of things."

Accept Children for Their Uniqueness

We all want to be free of stereotypes and to feel accepted. We don't know what happened to the 17 people who suffered from a physical disability—including blindness, deafness, paralysis, a withered hand and leprosy—whom Jesus healed. But we do know that they were each unique and that they had spiritual gifts that were given to them to bless the kingdom of God. The grace and compassion that Jesus showed revealed the heavenly Father's love and personal care for them. Christ made people with disability a priority in His ministry, and so should we.

Include Wheelchair Users and Others with Limited Mobility

Your church building and facility may have some limitations that make accommodating wheelchair users difficult. By making the changes below, your church can meet those needs and show that you value *all* those who want to contribute to the Body of Christ.

- Reserve parking spaces for those with mobility difficulties.

- Make level or add a ramp to all internal and external doorways.

- Keep a few seats reserved near the entrance to the worship center as an easy-access section for families who have a wheelchair-using member and who wish to sit together. But do not put all the wheelchair users in one area because this highlights their disability.

- Provide wheelchair users with printed copies of slides used during worship services (displays of lyrics, the pastor's message, etc.). Screens used to display these sorts of things are often hidden from the view of wheelchair users.

- Ensure that wheelchair-accessible restrooms have space to maneuver and are never used for storage.

- Sit down or crouch so that you are on the same eye level when talking with anyone in a wheelchair. This will make eye contact easier.

- Do not lean on someone's wheelchair, and never attempt to move it without the user's permission. Remember, the wheelchair is part of the user's personal space.

- Teach other children not to push a wheelchair unless the user asks them to do so.

Meet the Needs of Children with Physical Disabilities

Children with physical disabilities need what we all need: love, acceptance, fellowship, instruction in the Word, an opportunity to know Jesus and the chance to use their spiritual gifts. Remember, they are more like us than unlike us!

It was through the care and acceptance of their church that Joey and Hannah Slaight came to accept their physical disabilities. Their story is about accepting—not coping, adjusting, submitting or resigning oneself to problems, but truly accepting that God is in control. A riveting story of tragedy turned to triumph!

You can view the Slaight family's inspiring story on a *Joni and Friends* TV DVD entitled *From Tragedy to Triumph* (order "Episode 3" at http://www.joniandfriends.org/tvstore.php).

Speech and Language Impairments: Encourage Their Efforts

Many children in our church families have speech and language impairments, and these can stem from physical, mental or psychological disorders. Speech problems are often also an early sign of learning disabilities. No matter the cause, all of these children can have trouble fitting in with peers and meeting the expectations of their teachers and other adults.

Children with speech and language problems may have average or above-average intelligence; but because they do not verbalize well, they may appear to be mentally slow. If they hesitate to ask questions or to express themselves, they may struggle to follow the teacher's directions.

- Susan does not answer questions in class. When the other children are all talking, she is very quiet. She has difficulty understanding verbal instructions. She feels isolated and sad.

- When Mary is asked a question, she sits quietly and does not answer. She has trouble finding the correct words to respond verbally, and the children in her class call her stupid. She knows the answer to the question but is unable to get her words together. She is quiet and withdrawn, and she feels isolated but desperately wants to be part of the group.

Some children with special needs are very developmentally delayed in speech ability. They may have trouble controlling their rate of speech or stumble with language, often calling objects by the wrong name. Fortunately, many of these students receive speech therapy regularly at school.

- Four-year-old Tony speaks only in two-word phrases rather than sentences. Other children say he is just a baby. He feels sad and left out.

- Six-year-old Ben refuses to answer even simple questions. He is not ignoring the teacher but is unable to express himself in sentences.

- Sam does not have the ability to speak plainly and is frustrated when he is not understood. He becomes angry when the other children tell him that he is wrong.

Children who have receptive language problems have trouble making sense of certain sounds, words or sentences. It's as if their reception of speech is poor because their brains are set to a different frequency. They may seem inattentive and tuned out.

- Alicia was asked to pick up the box and, instead, picked up a ball. She was not trying to be funny or insolent; she simply has trouble understanding verbal instructions.

Sometimes children are not able to "switch gears" swiftly in social situations or when class activities change. Such children may be focused on a craft project and not able to instantly change to another mode of thinking.

- Mary was working on her picture of Noah's ark and became angry and hostile when the crayons were collected and the table cleaned off. She didn't understand that the class was ending. She felt as if she had done something wrong and was being punished.

Some children, such as those who have autism, have problems processing spoken language and may seem defiant, refusing to follow directions. In reality, however, they are overwhelmed by too many words, and they are often confused about what is expected of them.

- When Julie was told not to put her feet on the table but to sit in the chair properly, she didn't move. She was not challenging the teacher but was unable to mentally process so many words. If she had been told "Feet down," she would have been able and willing to comply.

It is important for teachers to understand that speech or language difficulties can be the ultimate source of a child's inappropriate behavior—whatever form it takes.

Nonverbal Cues with Verbal Messages

An important component of language is not verbal but physical, and when this fundamental understanding is missing, the real message that is being communicated is not understood. Many children with special needs cannot decipher body language; they cannot accurately read facial expressions, nor understand verbal nuances such as jokes. Their behavior may seem totally inappropriate, but they desperately want to fit in with their peers, not cause problems.

- John came to class, happy to see his friends. He ran up to Henry and gave him a tight hug and kiss. Then he ran to Nancy and did the same. He was not trying to be offensive but has trouble understanding appropriate displays of affection and honoring other people's personal space.

A Caution About Correcting a Child's Speech

Take time to talk to the parents of the children with special needs, and ask them how to best communicate with their child. Let the parents and the child know that you value the child and want to help integrate him or her into the class so that he or she can be friends with the other children.

- It's natural to want to correct a child's words. That approach can appear to be controlling and cut off dialogue between you and the child. Instead, smile and ask open-ended questions. "Do you want the box or the ball?"

- Use playful phrases and patiently encourage the child to correct him- or herself. "Wait a minute, my friend! Can you show me more?"

- Compliment every effort the child makes to respond and engage in discussions with you or classmates.

All children want to be accepted by their peers and have friends. You can explain to the other children that the child with special needs has the same feelings and likes the same things that they do. When the children understand this, they are usually willing and happy to help the child with special needs become a happy participant in your class.

Essentially, the more students communicate, the better their behavior will be, and thus their achievements and overall quality of life will be greater. When the most basic communication occurs, the community benefits from being more connected to the child with special needs. The subsequent reduction in problem behavior alleviates frustration for everyone involved. When the church helps all children participate to their fullest capacity, church becomes a place of safety and healing.

Emotional and Behavioral Disorders: Determine Their Preferences

Imagine an adult saying to a child, "Sit in the corner! It's time-out for you! Go and think it through. If you tried harder, I know you could get your body under control. In fact, I am starting a new sticker chart. If you produce enough insulin today all on your own, you can have a sticker."

What an absurd treatment for a child who has diabetes. No parent, teacher or church leader would dream of responding that way. The fact is, insulin production is not a "won't," but a "can't." The child's body *cannot* produce insulin on its own and needs some support. The child's will is not involved.

There are a whole series of unique special needs that we need to look at in a new and similar light. Children with emotional or behavioral disorders often encounter adults who see their issues as a "won't," not a "can't." Some believe that if these children would only try harder, pick themselves up by the bootstraps or develop some self-discipline, then their unique needs and behaviors would disappear. The truth is, while we all need to take responsibility for our behavior and actions, most emotional or behavioral needs have some sort of physical root cause.

Definition of a Child with an Emotional or Behavioral Disorder

In order to better understand what constitutes an emotional or behavioral disorder, think of an imaginary line. Every child gets down or depressed at times and temporarily drops below the imaginary line. These bouts often last a short time, and the child bounces back above the line and again begins to enjoy life. When the depression continues for a long time, however, and begins to impact schoolwork, friendships and family relationships—when the child crosses the line and stays there—the child may require medical attention. When the highs and lows become persistent cycles that impact all areas of life—when the child rises high above the line and then falls far below the line in a repetitive pattern—the child might have bipolar disorder. For that child, the issues of anger, aggression, posttraumatic stress, depression, anxiety or other needs are a daily, significant and ongoing challenge. All of these needs are defined as emotional/behavioral disorders.

In a few cases, these conditions can arise from circumstances in a child's life. Perhaps a parent has died or the child experiences ongoing failure in social relationships; such situations certainly can trigger a bout of depression. But most of the conditions in this disorder category stem from imbalances in brain chemicals. Therefore, many children take medication to help relieve some of the symptoms that accompany these areas of special need.

Importance of a Child's Preferences

If in your church you have a child who fits in this category, it's critical to get to know the child. Use some of the forms in this book to help you better understand that child's unique gifts and needs. Find out what settings, people or events make this child most content. Find out what might trigger a bad day for this child. Find out what a good day and a bad day might look like and what you might expect to hear, see or feel in a church setting.

Once you get to know the child, develop a partnership with the child's parents or caregivers. What allows that child to be successful in other settings? If the child is supported by a consistent behavior plan that entails specific responses to certain actions, find a way to implement that same plan in your children's ministry setting. It's far easier to use an established plan than to embark on your own ideas for a setting that typically meets once or twice a week. With the permission of the child's parents, you may also be able to visit the child's school to get some advice from the staff there.

Surround the young one with understanding adults and peers. While some of these disorders are not outwardly apparent, the behavior of certain individuals with one of these disorders could mystify or frighten peers and leaders. With parent permission and with great respect and honor for the individual, you may wish to say, "God created each one of us with things we are good at and things that are more difficult. For me, I am really good at _____, but _____ is more difficult for me. You all have your own pattern. For example, our friend Joe is really good at _____, but it's more difficult for him to keep the way he is feeling inside his head. Sometimes it comes flying out of his mouth. [Substitute the observable weaker area of the child without giving them the technical term or diagnosis.] I am excited to see how God is helping Joe learn to talk to God about how he is feeling so that he is less frustrated or angry." Highlight other children in the group as well.

You may want to supply your fellow staff members with detailed written information about any child with an emotional/behavioral disorder in your class. But make sure you obtain parental permission before such information is given to anyone (children or adults).

Expectations in Terms of Growth

As you interact with the child, constantly keep in front of you the model of therapy: growth over time. We would not expect a weak muscle to instantly get strong after only one therapy session. Growth over time is the goal of therapy, and it's an important point to remember for everyone working with an individual with an emotional or behavioral disorder. Be patient. Expect good days and difficult days. Put everything in the context of seeing someone made in the image of God, entrusted to your church. Identify and use the gifts of that child while you surround the individual with understanding, consistency and respect.

Family Support Is Imperative

Many parents of children with emotional or behavioral needs feel judged. Other adults may have given them callous advice or critical stares. Still others may have sent them the message that poor parenting is the cause of the child's misbehavior or condition.

Parents need support, not judgment. Remember, your interaction with that child lasts for one to two hours. The parents are always on duty. Put yourself in their place and imagine supper time or bedtime in that home. Parents need understanding encouragers who will walk beside them. Many of these families would benefit from a church G.L.U.E. team—individuals trained to support people experiencing long-term special needs (see "Creating a G.L.U.E. Team" on p. 139).

Jeremiah 29:11 encourages us, "'For I know the plans I have for you,' declares the Lord, 'plans to prosper you and not to harm you, plans to give you hope and a future.'" It's often easy for a caregiver in the trenches to lose sight of this hope and promise. Remind the parent of the strengths and gifts you see woven inside their little one. Talk about the God-given labels that surround this child—"valuable" (Matthew 6:26), "loved" (see Ephesians 2:4), "embraced" (see Mark 10:16), and "an image-bearer of God" (see Genesis 1:26-27). Remember God's promise to the caregivers as well: "Let us not become weary in doing good, for at the proper time we will reap a harvest if we do not give up. Therefore, as we have opportunity, let us do good to all people, especially to those who belong to the family of believers" (Galatians 6:9-10). Join caregivers in persevering and looking for the harvest.

Developmental Disabilities: Recognize Their Challenges

There is an old children's story that features two animals preparing for a race. The tortoise, obviously a slow and steady creature, is facing off against a hare, an energetic sprinter. All bets are on the hare to win the race. In the end, it's the tortoise that finishes first. His slow and steady progress pitted against an overly confident sporadic hopper gives a surprise ending.

That beautiful characteristic—slow and steady progress—often typifies a child who has a developmental disability (DD), a term that describes a large number of children and wide areas of disability. If a child experiences some sort of intellectual or physical disability before the age of 22 and is unable to develop independence in language, movement, learning, self-help or living, the term "developmental disability" might be used to describe that child. A child with cerebral palsy, for example, who needs special support to get dressed, eat and learn, would fit the category of developmental disability. A child on the autism spectrum who has difficulty learning to speak and can't take care of him- or herself could also be called DD. Any physical or cognitive disability that prevents a child from becoming independent and able to complete daily tasks could be described as DD. It is also possible to have cerebral palsy or autism and not be considered DD. The issue is one of independent living.

Learn the Causes of Developmental Disabilities

Some children experience differences even before parents lay eyes on their little one: A child may have a genetically caused DD such as Down syndrome. Before birth, a child may have experienced trauma—such as maternal drug use or an accident—that injured the development of the baby. An extra or missing chromosome may have caused one of the baby's body parts to develop differently, causing blindness or a spinal column abnormality. The possibilities are numerous. Through the use of medical tests, some of these causes are picked up before the baby's birth, so parents are aware of the baby's developmental differences. In other cases, the parents don't find out until the child is born.

Some causes for DD happen at the time of childbirth. Although medical advances have dramatically reduced these causes, certain children experience trauma coming into the world. Some babies arrive too early and struggle to survive. Other babies might be injured during the process of birth and develop differences that last a lifetime.

Sometime between birth and before the age of 22, a child who is developing normally may also experience something that causes DD. A child may have an accident or contract a disease. A child might suffer abuse or neglect. The cause might even stem from poor nutrition or some other sort of outside agent. Whatever the cause, the effect will result in a child who is unable to develop the independence necessary to live without the support of caregivers.

People often use the words "mild," "moderate," "severe" or "profound" in order to suggest to what level a developmentally disabled person will need care and support. Obviously, the needs of a child with mild DD will look very different from the needs of a child with severe DD. But whatever the level or needs of the child, it is important to look at the whole picture.

Look at the Beauty and Gifts of that Child

While it is tempting to look only at the gifts exhibited by the hare in our children's story, it is also important to consider the beauty and giftedness presented by the tortoise. The slower creature was actually quite amazing in his approach and endurance with the task. Likewise, make sure you put the needs of the DD child in context. Each hand-crafted boy or girl of God deserves our admiration and attention. Look at the complexity and beauty of that child. How is God using that little one in the family or church? See the whole picture—a beautiful child with gifts and needs. When all is given over to God, He can use that child for His glory and purposes. Now that's a pretty picture!

Measure Growth and Success in Tortoise Time

Many people make the mistake of comparing a child with a developmental disability to his or her peers. While that child should spend time with peers and enjoy that setting, measure growth and success on that child's unique timeline. For example, it's true that most children in second grade speak in complete sentences, so a child who speaks in two-word phrases would be very much behind—in the back of the line, so to speak. If, however, that child had been speaking only one word at a time and then started to combine those words into small phrases, the leaders and peers should celebrate. On that child's timeline, a huge accomplishment has just taken place.

Look for growth over time. Expect to see steady movement in one direction. When that is the focus, others will be able to see God's faithful hand in that child's life.

Determine a Good Track for the Child

While the tortoise and hare went head-to-head on the same trail, think about the path you have in mind for your DD child. Parts of the route might be the same as others experience at your church. Other portions of the track might be individualized, based on the gifts and needs of that particular child.

- **Set appropriate expectations.** Make sure the child is challenged at his or her level of development. Use materials that match the child's understanding and interest. Many times, that can be done within the context of the room and time frame of peers, but individualized touches should be added to better meet this child's needs.

- **Respect both the child's chronological age and mental age.** The child's chronological age represents how old that child is in physical years. The child's mental age represents the age level at which the child understands. It's important to respect both of those ages. Include the child in a group close to chronological age level. This is where the furniture, size of friends, and room items will be most appropriate for the child. Bring in materials that honor the child's mental age. While others may enjoy reading a passage from the Bible, this child may enjoy pictures and a Bible storybook about the same passage. While a child's level of understanding may be younger, expect that child to act and interact with peers in an appropriate way. If you treat a child like a baby, you will get baby-type behaviors. If you meet the child's level in materials and understanding while expecting behavior more typical of his or her peers, you can capture the beauty of both worlds.

- **Develop sensitivity in others.** It's important to give others who are in contact with a DD child the information they need to offer acceptance and appropriate support. Prepare written materials, so others know the child's unique gifts and needs. Using ideas from this book or other sources, allow peers to embrace their DD friend, having been honestly and positively informed. Consider using *Helping Kids Include Kids with Disabilities* by Barbara J. Newman as your guide.

Make it your goal to remind others to gaze on the beauty of that tortoise, and allow God to use each child's gifts in the life of your church.

Visual and Hearing Impairments: Adapt to Their Needs

When students with visual or hearing impairments attend your class, it is helpful to have as much information about their disabilities as you can. Talk with parents about children's strengths and needs. Ask how best to adapt your room and teaching methods to their learning styles. Invite parents to introduce their child to other students, educating them about the disability and etiquette.

Visual Impairments

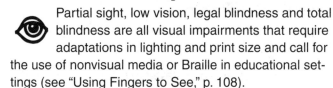 Partial sight, low vision, legal blindness and total blindness are all visual impairments that require adaptations in lighting and print size and call for the use of nonvisual media or Braille in educational settings (see "Using Fingers to See," p. 108).

Extra Assistance for Visually Impaired Children

- **Guide Dogs**—Specially trained and certified animals to assist those with visual impairments. While working, dogs wear identifying vests and harnesses. Teach children not to pet or play with these animals while they are working. If dogs are off duty, children should ask permission before touching them. Federal law gives access to working dogs in all public places.

- **White Canes**—Specially colored walking sticks that are essential tools for independence. With canes, children can navigate curbs, steps and furniture, and find walls and doors. One red stripe at the tip denotes blindness; two red stripes show the user to be deaf and blind. Some canes can be folded when not in use. It is against the law for a person who is not visually impaired to use a white cane. Make sure your students know not to touch or grab canes.

- **Personal Navigation Devices**—Global positioning systems that enable confident travel. Older students might learn to use them to navigate your city.

- **Other Senses—Normal faculties** (smell, touch, hearing and even taste) that enable greater perception of the environment. Keep these senses in mind as you plan lessons and activities, using at least one each time.

Etiquette for Serving Children with Visual Impairments

- Speak in a normal voice, directly to the child.

- Greet children by name, so they know you're speaking to them.

- Identify yourself when talking to a child with visual impairments, especially in group settings. Say the names of other students while speaking to them, so everyone understands whom you are addressing.

- Indicate when you're finished talking to the child or when you're leaving the room.

- Never grab a child. Instead, offer your arm if he or she desires assistance, walking a bit in front.

- Use verbal and audible cues when giving directions. For example, say, "Here is the chair"; then pat the seat several times.

- To provide a sense of orientation, after guiding a student, leave him or her by a physical object instead of in an open space.

- Tell students when the classroom is rearranged. Leave doors completely open or shut to avoid injury.

- Use a calm voice to warn students if they are in danger.

- Do not avoid using words such as "see," "look" and "watch." These words are fine to use.

Adaptations for Teaching Children with Visual Impairments

- Record Bible memory verses.

- Dance and move with students.

- Bring in varied textures during stories (a lambskin, a palm branch, etc.).

- Provide adequate lighting and enlarged print if necessary.

- Use Wikki Stix reusable wax-covered yarns. This material sticks to almost any smooth surface and can be used for art projects and/or to outline pictures for students to feel.

- Create pictures on large pegboards.

- Provide magnetic construction toys.

- Provide balls with bells inside for games.

- Play games that limit the vision of the other students (Break the Piñata, Pin the Tail on the Donkey, etc.).

- Cups Full of Water (an awareness activity for students without visual impairments): Challenge each student, while blindfolded, to fill a cup full of water. Have plenty of towels ready for spills! Notice if anyone uses his or her finger to feel when the cup is getting full—just how a person with a visual impairment might do it.

Hearing Impairments

Hearing impairments include any type of hearing loss as well as deafness. Deafness refers to hearing loss that is severe enough to impair a child from processing information through hearing, with or without hearing aids.

 It is important to be aware that some people in the deaf community *do not consider deafness to be a disability* and dislike the term "hearing impaired." They view themselves as a culture with its own language. Because of this, oral communication and cochlear implants can be controversial.

Extra Assistance for Hearing Impaired Children

- **American Sign Language (ASL) and Finger Spelling**—Methods of communicating that use specific movements of the arm, hand and/or fingers. Most children with hearing impairments learn to communicate with one or both of these methods. Make sure your church provides ASL interpreters for all events your student attends. Some children will learn oral communication: the use of lipreading, residual hearing and speech. Total communication is the combination of oral communication and sign language.

- **Hearing Aids**—Electronic devices used to amplify and/or clarify sound. Hearing aids, usually the behind-the-ear kind, can be fitted to children as infants. In the classroom, hearing aids can sometimes connect to assistive listening systems, which allow the teacher's voice to be heard directly by the child through the child's listening device. Ask parents how this is used and if it would be beneficial to use at church.

- **Hearing Dogs**—Specially trained and certified animals to assist those with hearing impairments. They wear a designating vest while working and are legally admitted entrance to any public place. Teach children not to pet, feed or play with these animals while they are working. If dogs are off duty, children should ask permission before touching them. Federal law gives access to working dogs in all public places.

Etiquette for Serving Children with Hearing Impairments

- To get a child's attention, lightly touch his or her arm or shoulder, flick the lights or wave your hand.

- Make eye contact and speak directly to the child, not the interpreter.

- Speak clearly and in a normal tone of voice.

- If you don't understand a response, ask the child to repeat it or write it down.

- Give interpreters periodic breaks.

- Provide written materials to interpreters in advance.

- Make every effort to learn sign language.

Adaptations for Teaching Children with Hearing Impairments

- Use ASL with all students during singing and memory verse times.

- Use an ASL video Bible (available at http://www.ASL Bible.com, along with other Christian ASL resources).

- Provide front-row seats for your student and interpreter.

- Create good lighting.

- Keep your face and mouth visible, and don't stand right in front of a window.

- Show movies that have subtitles.

- Provide handouts in advance.

- Keep background noise to a minimum.

- Rephrase something if the student doesn't understand what you've said, and check for understanding often.

- Use facial expressions.

- Point to students who are speaking.

- Do not abruptly change topics of discussion, which can be confusing; use transitional phrases such as "Let's talk about Moses now."

- ASL "I Love You" Artwork (an awareness activity for students without hearing impairments): On colored paper, students trace one of their hands and cut paper hand out. Students fold down the middle and ring fingers of paper hand and glue hand onto a different-colored paper. Students write "I love you" below the hand, identifying it as the ASL shorthand for saying "I love you."

Learning Disabilities: Believe in Their Abilities

When making a batch of chocolate chip cookies, the baker begins by selecting a recipe. Most recipes contain a list of common, or standard, ingredients. Many recipes, however, also have a list of optional or alternate choices; these might include adding walnuts to the mix, substituting butter for margarine, or making giant-sized or small-sized tasty treats. Whatever the outcome, the process of baking the cookies involves a decision to stick with the original recipe or try out one or more of the options.

Our children's ministry programs should have a similar recipe. There is a standard recipe for our meetings, presentations and children's responses that works well for most members of the group. For example, fourth-grade children might listen to the leader read from the Bible and then be asked to write an answer to a question on a piece of paper. For most children in fourth grade, that format can work well.

There are other children, however, who need the leaders to select from the optional or alternate ingredient list in order to successfully complete the task. In other words, there might be one fourth grader who is able to listen well to the Bible reading, can construct an excellent answer to the question but finds it very difficult to write that response. While the child may be able to answer verbally, writing an answer might be a painful task. To express the answer, that child will benefit from an alternate ingredient in the children's program—either a laptop computer, a "buddy" writing plan or a picture option. By the leader's making this substitution, the child is able to more fully participate in the children's program. While all children are unique individuals and deserve access to options that best fit a learning style or gifted area of expression, children with learning disabilities need support for an area of need to allow expression in areas of strength.

What are learning disabilities?

Learning disabilities may perhaps better be expressed by the term "learning differences." A child who has a learning difference will have a typical IQ. The child has the same potential for intellectual success as the other children in the room. For a myriad of possible reasons, however, that child is unable to be successful in one or more areas. That difference could be in the way the child takes in, remembers or expresses information. A child may have a specific learning disability that primarily impacts reading, math or writing. When reading is involved, a child may have a condition known as dyslexia. When math is involved, a child may have dyscalculia. Dysgraphia may describe a child who struggles with writing. Sometimes children who are able to hear well struggle with processing words and understanding them; these children may be described as having an auditory processing disorder. A child with a visual processing disorder may struggle to make sense of what he or she sees, despite having good eyesight.

Whatever the learning difference, school-type settings often create the most vibrant background to highlight that difference so that it's noticeable. As children age, vocational choices and family settings can often best display the individual's gifted areas.

Is a learning disability more about school or about church?

A child with a learning disability will need accommodations and support to be successful in a school setting. Some church programs, however, ask children to do similar tasks. Children in church often need to take in, remember and express information. While we don't ask them to calculate math problems, we do ask them to listen to Bible stories, follow directions, memorize Bible verses or Christmas play lines, and read aloud in a group or write down answers. If a child needs support in school to be successful, a child in a church program will need a similar understanding and supporting environment.

How can a church program support a child with a learning disability?

Going back to our chocolate chip cookie example, a church needs to have a list of alternate ingredients and options. The most important ingredient is getting to know the child with the learning disability. What gifts does that child have? While writing may be a struggle, that child might have an excellent ability to draw. In what area does that child have a learning difference? How might that difference bump into the activities you do in church?

From the moment the child walks through the church door, notice what activities may clash with the child's areas of difference. If the child has difficulty remembering more than one verbal direction at a time, limit the number of times a child may get a verbal list of instructions. For example, the pastor may call children forward for a children's message and tell them where and how to sit. Obviously, all leaders involved with the care of a child with a learning disability need to be informed about that child's differences. Make sure each person knows the recipe and plan for the day.

- **Find out what supports are helpful for the child.** The child's parent or school will have a list of ways to bypass or address the area of concern. With parent permission, talk with the child's teacher about the areas you discovered at church that might be difficult. Write down a list of those ideas.

- **Create an alternate recipe.** Using your knowledge of the child, understanding all areas of church where there could be difficulties and gathering a list of ideas to try, put together that child's recipe for the children's setting. While many things may remain the same, you may need to alter expectations for Bible memory activies, have a child practice reading aloud at home before coming to church or use a buddy system when writing or reading.

- **Include time for strengths in your recipe.** No child wants to be in a setting where everything is a struggle. Imagine running into a roadblock at every turn. Make sure the child has an opportunity during each session to enjoy using his or her God-created gifts. If the child is nurturing, have him or her help the younger children. If the child is artistic, create multiple opportunities to draw or paint. Use the child's gifts.

- **Be sensitive to the child's desire to fit in with the group.** While a pencil grip may be an excellent idea, the child may prefer to use it when you offer pencil grips for several in the group to use. A slant board might work well, but the child may not want to be singled out. Have two slant boards for the group to use. Be discreet about accommodations and make them available to more than one child.

Create an environment where all chocolate chip cookies are treasured! While our children's programs need to have alternate ingredients, we also need to remember that God is the master baker. He designed each person's recipe and stamped Himself on each unique blend. Learning differences don't alter or change the worth of a child. Leaders and peers need to celebrate and affirm the beauty of each and every person.

Awareness: Common Disabilities Among Children

Autism Spectrum Disorder—A broad term of diagnoses for autism, pervasive developmental disorder (PDD), Asperger's syndrome and Rett syndrome. Children with this condition may have delayed and/or limited social skills and language; they also may be overly sensitive to sound and light and be resistant to change.

Behavioral Disorders—A broad term for conditions that generally arise from chemical imbalances. The most common behavioral disorder is attention-deficit/hyperactivity disorder (AD/HD), which causes constant movement and an inability to focus on a task. An older term for AD/HD but one still often used is "attention-deficit disorder," or "ADD."

Bipolar Disorder (BP)—An emotional disorder marked by manic-depressive swings, anxiety and anger issues that interfere with positive interaction with peers or family. BP can be detrimental to a child's self-esteem, success and academic achievement; and a child with BP can become dangerous to him- or herself or to others.

Cerebral Palsy (CP)—A condition characterized by the inability to control muscular movements due to either damage to or faulty development of the motor controls of the brain. This is not one specific disease; rather, it is a group of disabling conditions that all contribute to lack of muscle control. CP can cause uncontrolled movement of limbs, head and eyes and can cause poor balance.

Developmental/Cognitive Disabilities—A category that includes mental retardation, slow learners, Down syndrome and fetal alcohol syndrome. Difficulties in basic thinking and learning may be moderate, severe or profound.

Dyslexia—A learning disability involving reading, writing and spelling. Children with dyslexia confuse sounds and see words backwards or in the wrong order. Many are gifted in other areas such as art, music or athletics.

Emotional Disorders—*See* behavioral disorders.

Epilepsy—A condition of the brain characterized by recurrent seizures. It affects 2 percent of the population, but the prognosis is good when children adhere to prescribed treatment.

Head Injury—Damage to the brain caused by sudden trauma. It can be mild with no lasting effect to so severe that a person may be left in a vegetative state. The severity and location of the injury and the age and general health of the individual will determine if the individual will have any lasting disability.

Hearing Impairment—A condition that prevents full use of the sense. It can be partial or total in degree and may occur at birth or later in life. Causes include birth defects, disease, trauma, accident and aging.

Language Impairment—*See* speech and language impairments.

Muscular Dystrophy (MD)—A disease in which the voluntary muscles gradually weaken and degenerate. The muscles appear normal, but internally, they are wasting away. In the disease's early stages, a child with MD uses crutches; eventually a wheelchair is needed and ultimately, the person with MD is confined to bed. MD strikes children during early childhood and shortens life spans.

Speech and Language Impairments—A category of conditions of delayed oral motor function ranging from simple sound substitution to the inability to understand or use language.

Spina Bifida—A condition in which the bones that cover and protect the spinal cord fail to develop fully, causing difficulty with walking and an inability for lower extremities to sense pressure, friction, heat or cold; also results in an inability to control bladder and bowel function.

Spinal Cord Injury—A condition caused by a fracture or compression of the vertebrae that results in paralysis. A paraplegic is a person who is paralyzed from the waist down. A quadriplegic is a person who has paralysis in all four limbs.

Stroke—Sudden damage to the brain due to a lack of oxygen because blood flow to the brain has been interrupted. Strokes range from being so slight that they go unnoticed to so severe that they result in death. A child who has suffered a stroke may exhibit a wide range of needs, depending on the stroke's severity and the side of the brain injured.

Visual Impairments—*See* hearing impairment.

U.S. Children (Ages 3–17) Need A Hand Because . . .

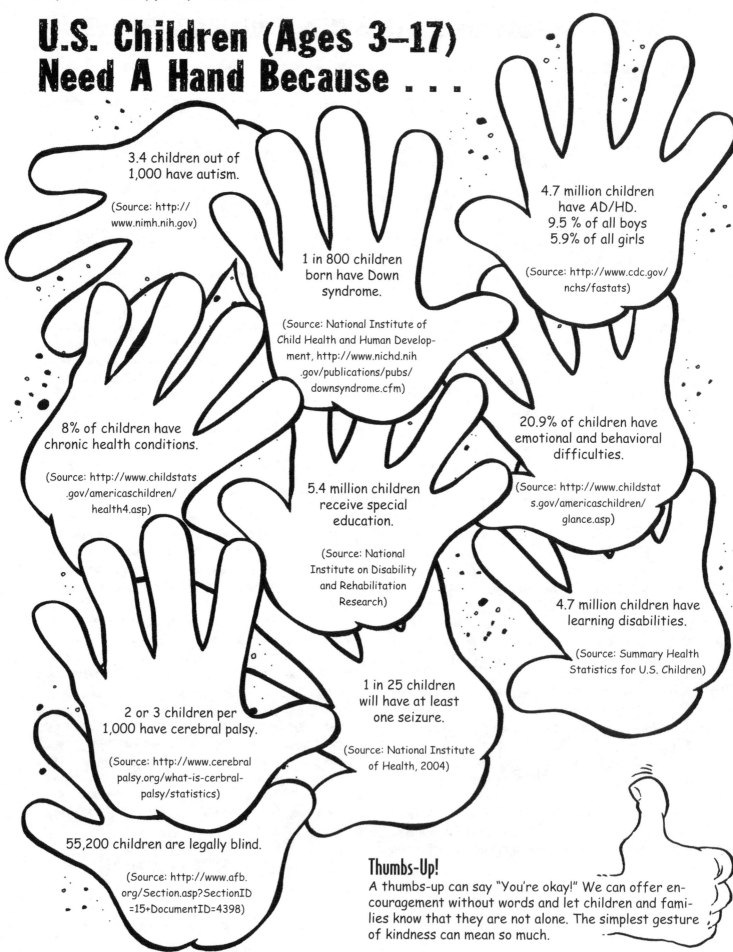

3.4 children out of 1,000 have autism.

(Source: http:// www.nimh.nih.gov)

1 in 800 children born have Down syndrome.

(Source: National Institute of Child Health and Human Development, http://www.nichd.nih .gov/publications/pubs/ downsyndrome.cfm)

4.7 million children have AD/HD. 9.5 % of all boys 5.9% of all girls

(Source: http://www.cdc.gov/ nchs/fastats)

8% of children have chronic health conditions.

(Source: http://www.childstats .gov/americaschildren/ health4.asp)

5.4 million children receive special education.

(Source: National Institute on Disability and Rehabilitation Research)

20.9% of children have emotional and behavioral difficulties.

(Source: http://www.childstat s.gov/americaschildren/ glance.asp)

4.7 million children have learning disabilities.

(Source: Summary Health Statistics for U.S. Children)

2 or 3 children per 1,000 have cerebral palsy.

(Source: http://www.cerebral palsy.org/what-is-cerbral- palsy/statistics)

1 in 25 children will have at least one seizure.

(Source: National Institute of Health, 2004)

55,200 children are legally blind.

(Source: http://www.afb. org/Section.asp?SectionID =15+DocumentID=4398)

Thumbs-Up!
A thumbs-up can say "You're okay!" We can offer encouragement without words and let children and families know that they are not alone. The simplest gesture of kindness can mean so much.

I Asked the Little Boy Who Cannot See

I asked the little boy who cannot see,

"And what is color like?"

"Why, green," said he,

"Is like the rustle when the wind
   blows through

The forest; running water,
   that is blue;

And red is like a trumpet sound; and pink

Is like the smell of roses; and I think

That purple must be like a thunderstorm;

And yellow is like something soft and warm;

And white is a pleasant stillness when you lie

And dream."

-- Anonymous

I Need Friends Along the Way!

A friend loves at all times.
Proverbs 17:17

Director: Breaking Down Barriers to Inclusion

*In him the whole building is joined together and
rises to become a holy temple in the Lord.
And in him you too are being built together to
become a dwelling in which God lives by his Spirit.*
Ephesians 2:21-22

Are families affected by disability part of the building blocks of your church? Or do they feel isolated and set apart? How can you create a church body that honors God's picture in Ephesians 2:21-22?

Before the church can effectively begin this construction project, some existing walls to inclusion may need to be destroyed. The best ways to discover these barriers is to look deeply into the heart of children and adults with special needs. Discover how they process information, and mimic that perspective. Survey the physical, developmental and emotional needs of people in your congregation. Then pretend to put yourself in that special needs person's body, and go through your church to discover the walls that need a demolition crew.

Physical Barriers

Some church facilities, particularly older buildings, present physical barriers. Step into the body of a child with a disability, starting at home. Is there a transportation barrier? Some children may have limited access, particularly on weekends and evenings, to getting to church. Are there medical barriers to attending a germ-infested environment? If church is not a building but God's people, is there a way to bring church into that home? Continue in the church parking lot. Are all the areas of your building physically accessible to that child? The child should be able to go to the bathroom and get a drink of water while at church. Hallways and aisles should be clear of clutter and wide enough to accommodate tools that help a child walk or move. Individual rooms must accommodate the child's physical needs. Assume the child's physical perspective, and make a list of obstacles that must be removed.

Content and Materials Barriers

Step into that child's mind, body and learning style. Each person needs to enter into a conversation with God during worship time. If a child is not able to speak, how can he or she sing God's praises? If a child is not able to read, how can he or she participate meaningfully in that activity through discussion? There are liturgical and program barriers to discover for each individual. Simply getting in the building is not enough. Creatively think through taking down the walls of participation.

Congregational Vision Barriers

Look into the heads and hearts of your congregation. Many times people will ask, "Who is in the inclusion program of this church?" They expect to hear that Frank, Sue and Kim are the children who are included. If one considers the wording, however, it's a laughable question. "Who is in the inclusion program?" The answer is "Everyone." That's the nature of inclusion. While significant time must be spent on disability awareness, it's important to balance that with an equal dose of inclusion awareness. Imagine how many individuals will meet that child during a typical activity time. Greeters, ushers, volunteers, paid staff, church members and peers all need a chance to catch the vision.

There needs to be a clear congregational-sized effort to recognize inclusion as a highly valuable goal for your church body. Each member and attendee needs to see that God blesses and enriches your church family by bringing in those with varied gifts and needs. Each person God sends will be considered an honored gift to the community—no exceptions. This message must be shared repeatedly in different ways. Sermons, written materials, newcomer training, volunteer training, children's lessons and paid-staff training need to include clear instructions on the intent and practices of your church. Inclusion awareness will emphasize the interconnections and mutual blessings we receive from one another within the Body of Christ.

Fear and Misperception Barriers

Inclusion awareness needs to offer opportunities to learn. While we can spend a great deal of time talking about one sort of disability or another, that disability is only one facet of a complex individual. Our time is much better spent becoming an expert on Sue or Peter or Melanie. If Sue is unable to speak and uses a communication device, the other children need to be taught how to interact with Sue. Once the other children—and the adults—learn that lesson, Sue has a voice in the church. Without that, Sue is isolated and the group misses out on learning from one of God's intended gifts.

If Peter needs to use a device that props him up and allows him to stand in his Sunday School class, the children in that room need to know about that device. If left uneducated, the children may wonder if it's safe to sit by Peter or if he is somehow contagious. With a basic lesson, the other children can understand that some people need a chair and some people need a stander. Either way, all are welcome and honored in the room.

If Melanie is sensitive to loud noises, the congregation may want to know this before the microphones screech the fact that there are technical difficulties in the system. Some basic information to the whole group about the pain Melanie experiences will allow the community to better understand and sympathize with her screaming that day.

Accurate information is the best antidote to fear and misperceptions. Make sure, however, that you have permission to talk about a specific child. You must have the consent of the parents or guardians before giving out information. Barbara J. Newman's book *Helping Kids Include Kids with Disabilities* may be a great help because it contains ideas for teaching accurately and positively about individuals with different special needs as well as about differences in general.

Personal Barriers

It's important to examine your own heart. Do you agree that you are responsible for the spiritual growth and nurture of all the children God sends to you? Jesus said to His disciples, "Let the little children come to me, and do not hinder them, for the kingdom of heaven belongs to such as these" (Matthew 19:14). Picture that line of children. Could it have included children who had limited vision or hearing? Would a parent of a child with Down syndrome have come to Jesus that day? Was a child using crutches? The Bible does not specifically describe each of the children, but there is no disclaimer stating that each child had to have a specific IQ or ability level. Simply being a child qualified for a touch from Jesus. Simply being a child qualifies every child for a spot within your church and community. Let the Word of God invade your own personal perspective. Be fueled by God's Word. Let His picture of community be the hammer of destruction to your own personal barriers. As the director, you will need to clearly choose your role—a locked gate to Jesus or open and embracing arms. May God bless your open arms.

Director: How to Begin a Special Needs Ministry

As you begin a special needs ministry, remember that a giant oak tree grows over a period of years, even decades. It starts from a small acorn and develops a root system that sustains the tree through all sorts of weather during its many seasons of growth. Each season is important and leads to great stability. So start small and build well!

Start Small and Build Well

As you identify the needs of children with special needs, pick one or two programs to focus on initially, such as including children in regular classrooms. After you see needs met and stability develop, add another activity such as a sibling support group. This may take a year or two. Slow, steady growth will avoid burnout. Soon your church will become known as a place where children and families affected by disability come to know the Lord.

Learn the Definition of Disability Ministry

Disability ministry is an activity of Christians with and without disabilities working together to reach children, youth and adults affected by disabilities with the Gospel, to integrate them into the church and to meet their needs in a way that witnesses to the community. As you catch the vision for developing this ministry, consider the following three goals that will reap enormous benefits for the church and, ultimately, for the glory of God:

1. A disability ministry opens the door to share the Gospel with families affected by disabilities and to introduce them to a personal relationship with God (see Romans 3:10,23; 5:8; 6:23; 10:9-10; 2 Corinthians 5:21; 1 John 4:8).

2. A disability ministry integrates those with disabilities into the life of the church and gives them the opportunity to have active roles in serving God (see 1 Corinthians 12:7, 21-26).

3. A disability ministry enables the church to serve as a witness or model to the community in meeting the spiritual, physical and social needs of families affected by disabilities (see Acts1:8).

Let the Lord Direct You to the Best Program for Your Church

No single disability program is perfect for every church. The Lord knows which is best for your church and your pool of volunteers. Simply pray for God's wisdom to love the families He sends to your church. Update your prayer team throughout the planning stages and as the new program is launched. Your work delights the Lord, and He wants to direct you in the following steps:

1. Build a leadership team.

2. Survey church members.

3. Consider facility and liability issues.

4. Decide on a program.

5. Involve the congregation and community.

1. Build a Leadership Team

Your initial group may consist of only two or three people with a passion for this new ministry. As you take the first step, God will call others. These leaders will determine ministry strategies, such as how to survey the church, recruit volunteers, plan the intake-registration process and communicate with the community. The group should include a pastor. Other team members might include the children's directors, special educators, parents, and church members who share this vision.

2. Survey Church Members

Every congregation has silent needs. Good leaders find ways to discover and meet those needs. The survey form included in this book is designed to seek out information about individuals with disabilities who might benefit from intentional church programs (see p. 42). It will also help you identify church members with helpful skills in planning, training and implementing a disability ministry.

After you evaluate the church survey, form several subcommittees to efficiently work on the best ministry models for your church.

- **Intake Committee**—Professional teachers, occupational therapists, speech therapists, physical therapists and nurses who can meet with families, observe children and suggest classroom adaptations. These specialists can offer advice and carry on-call beepers when kids with special needs are in the building.

- **Welcome Committee**—Individuals with warm smiles, strong handshakes and big hearts. They greet families, make them feel comfortable and guide them to the appropriate classes.

- **Staff and Training Committee**—Those who recruit, coordinate and train volunteers to minister to children with disabilities (see "Building a T.E.A.M.," p. 43).

- **Program Committee**—Individuals who will evaluate the effectiveness and accessibility of existing practices and design new programs.

- **Outreach Committee**—Individuals who will consider ways to reach community families who do not attend church anywhere.

3. Consider Facility and Liability Issues

Evaluate your church building for accessibility to those with special needs. What facility spaces are currently in use? Is there room to start new classes on Sunday morning? Do outside groups use rooms during the week? When are rooms available for respite events, support groups or fellowship gatherings? Use this checklist to evaluate your facility.

> ❏ Individuals in wheelchairs have easy access to classrooms and recreational spaces.
>
> ❏ Restrooms are equipped for wheelchair use.
>
> ❏ Room doors can be secured to keep children from slipping away from caregivers.
>
> ❏ Breakables are removed from rooms being used by children.
>
> ❏ Rooms have sufficient electrical outlets for communication and media devices.

For the safety of our children, each state has unique laws regarding church liability. Speak with your church's legal counsel and insurance agent before beginning a new program. These professionals can help you create a liability release form for signature by parents who leave children in your care. Forms should include an authorization to seek medical care and a release from liability for injuries that might occur. (*Note:* Sample forms are not included in this book because liability forms must reflect the specific laws of the area your church serves.)

4. Decide on a Program

The church survey will suggest ideas for serving families in your initial programs. Those families will bring in others by word of mouth. If you plan church respite care, sibling support or support groups for parents, be sure to advertise these programs at local schools and therapy centers.

Create a Special Needs Hub, a location at your church where families can obtain information, complete forms and meet buddies (caregivers). The Hub might feature a lending library and entertainment area for kids as parents meet with leaders or complete paperwork.

Programs and schedules may be driven by your availability of volunteers. For instance, you can't offer a weekday morning program if you're counting on using high-school students as volunteers. But if you have volunteers working in disability classes on Wednesday night, they may also be willing to serve at a monthly parents' night out. Volunteers with experience can train recruits. Some people will feel comfortable working together at large-group events, while others may prefer working as one-on-one helpers in the classroom.

5. Involve the Congregation and Community

Be sure to keep church leadership informed at each stage of your program development. The congregation is more likely to get involved if they know the ministry is close to their pastor's heart. You'll gain better access to classrooms, materials and financial support when church leaders are excited about the program. A copy of this book or a copy of *Special Needs Special Ministry* would be an excellent gift book for your pastor(s) as you pray together (see the JAF website store, http://www.joniandfriends.org/store). Once the church staff is hooked, consider ways to keep the congregation interested in your disability ministry:

- During worship services, make announcements about disability ministry events.

- Send invitations and reminders in church bulletins or newsletters.

- Print or e-mail a quarterly disability newsletter to publicly recognize families and volunteers.

- Create a disability web page linked to the general church website.

Displaying photographs of children with special needs adds a compelling personal touch to announcements, posters and websites. Create videos and PowerPoint presentations that show children and volunteers having fun together. Be sure to include pictures of nondisabled children making friends with children who have special needs. For security reasons, never put a child's name with photos on a website. And always ask parents for written permission to use their child's photograph (some churches include a publicity release form in registration packets; see the sample form on p. 42).

Create a Mission Statement

Marketing professionals tell us that people must see or hear a message 16 times before they grasp its contents. Maybe you've tried many things such as announcements during worship, flyers sent to home with students, bulletin inserts, e-mails and booths at ministry fairs. Okay, let's face it—communication is tough! Everyone wants to be part of a winning team, but we can't get there without a finish line. An inspiring mission statement is that banner waving at the finish line, drawing us onward. Create one for your special needs ministry (see samples on p. 41).

Sample: Mission Statements

All Children, All Families, Always Welcome!

The heart of *Free2Fly Ministries* is modeling Christ's ministry here on Earth by bringing freedom and purpose to people with disabilities and their families, freedom to live victoriously and an opportunity to use their God-given gifts for the edification of the Body of Christ.

Our children with special needs teach us that wheelchairs are not obstacles to playing in God's house, that communication disorders do not prevent us from talking to God, and that learning differences do not keep us from being students of the Lord.

Caring Heart Ministry

Our mission is to serve the Lord by providing a valued time of teaching God's Word and providing a safe, loving, accepting environment. We value ALL children and seek to help them use the gifts and talents God has given them.

SonShine Zone

Our mission is to identify and break down barriers that keep children with disabilities and their families from being able to fully participate in the community of the church. We believe every child can know and serve Jesus. Our Special Friends are a blessing to the body of Christ and we embrace them by God's grace.

Every child will be called by name.
Every child will be affirmed in some way.
Every child will hear about the mighty love of Jesus.

Form: A Church Survey of Special Needs

1. Are any member(s) of your family disabled?
   _____ Yes _____ No

2. If yes, what are your family members' disabilities?
   _____
   _____
   _____

3. Do these family members attend church regularly?
   _____ Yes _____ No

4. How could our church better support this person or persons?
   _____
   _____

5. If one or more of these family members are children, do they regularly attend Sunday School or worship?
   _____ Yes _____ No

6. What could be done to make the children's classes more accessible for your child(ren)?
   _____
   _____
   _____

7. What could be done to better support your family?
   _____
   _____
   _____

8. If your family member(s) would like to attend our church, what changes (if any) should be made?
   ❏ More accessible parking
   ❏ Large-print Bibles
   ❏ Better lighting
   ❏ Better sound equipment
   ❏ A sign-language interpreter
   ❏ Wheelchair space that does not obstruct aisles
   ❏ A special class for adults with developmental disabilities
   ❏ Special care for children while other family members attend the worship service
   ❏ Better accessibility (please specify) _____
   ❏ Other (please specify) _____

Getting Involved . . .

Our church would like to give everyone full access to our programs. Please indicate your willingness to become involved in our disability ministry.

❏ I would be interested in helping with the planning team.
❏ I would be interested in learning more about being a buddy.
❏ I would be interested in helping with weekend respite events.
❏ I am a special education teacher, speech pathologist, occupational therapist, physical therapist, nurse or doctor, and would be interested in helping with training or intake of those with special needs.
❏ I have further questions. Please call me at _____
❏ No, I am not interested in helping at this time.

Thank you for taking the time to complete this survey.
Please return it to:
[Include your contact information here.]

Your Name _____ Phone _____
Address _____
City _____ State _____ Zip _____
Name of Each Family Member (include age if a child)
_____
_____
Additional comments _____
_____
_____

- -

Form: Publicity Release

[Church Name]
[Church Address]

I have agreed voluntarily to appear or I agree for members of my family to appear without compensation in a brochure, film or videotape produced by the church. The church shall have the right to distribute, exhibit and televise said brochure, film or videotape. All copies thereof and all rights therein shall be the sole and exclusive property of the church.

I hereby release and discharge the church and its respective agents, employees, successors, assigns and licensees from any and all claims, liabilities and obligations of any kind or nature which may arise from my appearance or participation in the brochure, film or videotape or any exhibition thereof.

I agree that the church has no obligation to exhibit or televise our performance or otherwise use us in its brochure, film or videotape.

Signature _____
Date _____
Printed Name_____
Address _____

Director: Building a T.E.A.M.

Special needs ministry is no place for the Lone Ranger. In the early days of black and white TV, this mysterious cowboy rode into town wearing a mask. He fought for justice, won single-handedly and escaped on his trusty steed, Silver. And no one knew his true identity except his Native American friend, Tonto. This leadership model is too common at church.

If you're that lone cowboy on the road to creating a disability program, you're on the wrong path. Heroes in this ministry learn to work with people and not for them. In his book *Doing Church as a Team*, Wayne Cordeiro reminds us the church is not an organization but a living organism. "If I cut off my arm and planted it in dirt, that arm would not grow into a new body; it would die!" Cordeiro warns. "So it is with the Body of Christ. Each of us has an individual assignment and role, but apart from the rest of the Body, we are useless. God created us that way. That is His design, not ours."*

The first thing Jesus did after His temptation in the wilderness was to build a ministry team by calling on the first 4 of 12 men (Matthew 4:18-22). He handpicked a diverse group and lovingly molded them into a family. You can follow Jesus' model in your special needs ministry by selecting a recruiting team. Remember to include special education teachers, grandparents, business leaders and people with disabilities who share the vision.

T–Training Coordinator

Volunteers will come into this ministry with a variety of experiences. Some have taken a Spiritual Gifts Inventory and found they have strengths in this area. Others grew up with a sibling who had a disability and can help train new volunteers. The training coordinator doesn't need to know everything about every disability (no one does), but this people person should be skilled at matching volunteers with special needs children and with providing training resources.

E–Events Coordinator

Everyone wants to be part of an exciting, well-managed program. When planning a Disability Awareness Sunday, Fall Fun Fair or Parent Night Out, this team member will display happy pictures of children, parents, siblings and caregivers having fun together. He or she should be skilled in creating informative flyers, brochures and movies (video or digital) that invite people to get involved.

A–Ask in Prayer Coordinator

Jesus urged us to ask God for workers for our ministry. This prayer leader will encourage others to pray for the

special needs ministry by (1) writing simple prayer guides with Bible promises, (2) visiting small groups in your church once a quarter to encourage them to pray, (3) leading children in praying for adult caregivers, and (4) praying for needed volunteers as well as those currently serving.

M–Managing Coordinator

Volunteer screening is a must! This team leader will assist volunteers as they complete an application that gives permission for a background check. (A number of websites provide screening for a history of child abuse or endangerment.) This team member will keep volunteer records protected and stored in a locked cabinet. He or she may also manage weekly volunteer/teacher schedules and provide substitutes as needed.

The team's goal is to remind the whole congregation that recruiting is everyone's job as we "spur one another on toward love and good deeds" (Hebrews 10:24) and to correct misconceptions people have about children and adults with special needs.

*Wayne Cordeiro, *Doing Church as a Team* (Ventura, CA: Regal Books, 2001), p. 176.

Director: Blessing the Whole Body of Christ

[Each child] is a God-created package of gifts and needs.
Barbara Newman, "Our Spiritual Keys"

Jesse and Jordan are friends. Jesse loves to play guitar. He is an avid reader and enjoys going to movies. Jesse, although large enough to be recruited for the football team, does not excel in athletics. Math is a struggle. Jordan enjoys video games and frequents movie theaters. He is forgiving and eager to be with friends. Jordan struggles with diction in speaking and has trouble learning complicated concepts. Jordan happens to have Down syndrome. Jordan and Jesse have been friends at church and at school since they were young.

The Inclusion of Everyone

We were created to be part of the Body of Christ where each person uses his or her gifts and receives support for his or her needs. Jesse and Jordan's friendship is one of giving and growing together. Now that they're both in high school, it is evident that their friendship has shaped both of their lives. Jesse spends enough time with Jordan to understand his limited language, serving as an interpreter. Jesse also has a driver's license, which comes in handy when they go to the movies together. Jordan supports Jesse by praying for him by name every night before going to bed, something he's done since first grade. He shows Jesse forgiveness and dedication.

It's possible that along with Jesse's driver's license came an army of angels urged by Jordan's faithful and daily prayers. It's clear to see that the relationship with Jordan has impacted Jesse's character over the years.

This friendship has been a powerful tool that God has used in both of their lives—the blessing of relationships goes both ways. One person is not the only giver and the other person only a receiver. God's plan was that we grow by interacting with one another.

Jesse's dad told him, "Son, I am so proud of you. I love watching you continue your friendship with Jordan. He may not be a friend like all your others, but it's good that you include him." Jesse was angered at his father's words, and said, "Dad, don't ever say that about Jordan. He knows how to be a better friend than all my others. He is always glad to see me, and we get along great. He is one of my best friends."

Through their years together, Jesse understands that this friendship has been mutual. They need one another. While he has offered his gifts to Jordan, Jordan has of-fered his gifts to Jesse. They are more complete together as a team than they would be apart.

This true story is one example of what comes from an inclusive church community. Living together, learning together and serving God side by side, children have the chance to benefit from one another.

A Word About Pity

One of the greatest barriers to inclusion is the notion that those not yet experiencing a disability will be the givers, and those who have special needs will be the receivers. Out of pity and expecting nothing in return, a congregation pours out services and showers a child with care. This is not a Biblical perspective.

While the Body of Christ is called to respond to others with compassion, we are also to expect that each member has a gift to give. There will be times when we minister to a child's area of need, but we should also expect to receive a gift from that child. That child will minister to you. This is a gift exchange system, and God's purposeful design is to empower each one to bring a gift to the party.

Get off the pity horse, and experience the joy of mutual ministry within your church.

Director: Job Description for Teachers

Fear of the unknown can be the greatest deterrent to volunteering. People often think that in order to work with special needs kids they need to have special education or training. While that can be helpful, the most important qualification is to have a heart that is willing to learn how to help any child that God has created. Clear guidelines and ongoing support will help to alleviate a volunteer's apprehensions. Below is a sample job description for a special needs Sunday School teacher.

Special Needs Sunday School Teacher

Task: To prayerfully build relationships with special needs children and guide them in life-changing Bible learning

Term: One year, beginning in September

Supervisor: Special Needs Ministry Director

Qualifications

- Church membership.

- Personal recommendation and background check.

- A heart for children. Eager to love and help any child that God has created.

- Teachable. Ready to learn the unique needs of students in order to integrate them into the classroom.

- Flexible. Willing to alter routines and schedules to accommodate the unique needs of each student.

- Patient. Glad to alter own expectations to reflect God's will. Knows that progress may be slow but has patience to wait to see God at work.

- Able to see beyond the disability. Looks beyond what students can't do and sees what they can do.

- Displays integrity, sensitivity and confidentiality. Treats each child and family with respect.

Expectations

- Attend worship services weekly, maintaining a growing personal relationship with Christ.

- Pray regularly for each student and member of the team.

- Attend quarterly training sessions for the special needs ministry.

- Communicate regularly with the director, special needs buddy and parent to ensure a successful experience for the child.

Teaching Responsibilities

- Teach to the student's strengths and abilities, making appropriate adaptations in the lessons, schedules, games and activities.

- Offer at least one learning center that meets the unique needs of each special needs student.

- Maintain the physical classroom setup so that it is accessible to each child.

- Assist classmates in interacting with special needs children.

- Work as a team with special needs buddies.

- Be ready to be blessed!

The job description is a helpful tool for both the volunteer and the director. Mike knew that God was calling him to work in the special needs class. Even though his heart was ready, he was unsure of what to expect. Mike contacted the director who sent him an application. They scheduled a meeting to talk through the job description. Mike and the director were able to discuss his concerns and clarify the expectations. They discussed whether he possessed the necessary qualifications and if he would be able to follow through with the responsibilities. He felt reassured knowing that ongoing training and support from the director would be available. Throughout the year, the director was able to use the job description to remind Mike and the other teachers of their responsibilities and commitments. During annual recruitment drives and training sessions, the director again referred back to the job description to affirm and redirect teachers.

Director: Job Description for a Special Needs Buddy

Special Needs Buddies play an invaluable role in special needs ministry. They provide assistance, support and friendship to children with disabilities, so the whole family can participate as valuable members of their church congregation. Buddies (also sometimes referred to as Pals, Shadows or One-on-Ones) can be assigned to students in typical classrooms, special needs classrooms, large-group settings or special events. Assign a minimum of two buddies for each student so that responsibilities can be rotated and families will not be without assistance in the case of illness or vacations. Below is a sample job description for a special needs buddy.

Special Needs Buddy

Task: To provide assistance, support and friendship to a child with a disability

Term: Two Sundays per month for one year

Supervisor: Director of Special Needs Ministry

Qualifications

- Church member aged 16 or older.

- Personal recommendation and background check.

- Good role model.

- A heart for children.

- A desire to assist a child in knowing and serving God.

- Dependable.

- Teachable. Willing to learn the unique needs of students and ways to appropriately assist them.

- Able to see beyond the disability. Looks beyond what students can't do and sees what they can do.

- Displays integrity, sensitivity and confidentiality. Treats each child and family with respect.

Expectations

- Attend worship services weekly, maintaining a growing personal relationship with Christ.

- Pray regularly for assigned student and student's family.

- Attend quarterly training sessions for the special needs ministry.

- Communicate regularly with the director, teacher and parent to ensure a successful experience for the child.

Responsibilities (These will vary depending on needs of student assigned.)

- Provide necessary physical assistance for mobility, seating, game playing, and learning activities.

- Assist with self-help skills such as eating, wiping mouth, or toileting, according to church guidelines (men will not be assigned toileting duties).

- Use appropriate behavior management techniques specific to the student. Training will be provided.

- Learn how the child communicates and assist in his or her communication with others.

- Encourage social interaction among classmates.

- Be a friend to the student—someone that he or she looks forward to seeing each week.

Although each buddy is recruited for a year, this length of time actually may vary. Sometimes a buddy will be required indefinitely; at other times, a buddy will be needed only temporarily, to provide assistance as the student becomes acclimated to his or her surroundings.

When Max, who has autism, first attended church, he required the help of a buddy in his special needs class. The buddy learned specific skills to help him with his behavior and communication for a few months, until he adjusted to the class routine. As Max progressed, he was ready to be mainstreamed into the children's worship with a buddy who assisted him with social interactions and took him on walks when the noise level became overwhelming. Eventually, Max graduated from needing an adult buddy to having peer buddies who were eager to learn how to help Max cope in their group. Each of these buddies was a tremendous blessing. Their ministry permitted Max and his family to worship and serve the church. His classmates and buddies were also blessed and learned how to communicate and be friends with those who are different from themselves.

Director: Make It Easy for Volunteers to Say Yes!

Let us consider how we may spur one another on toward love and good deeds.
Hebrews 10:24

Ministry to children with special needs can seem overwhelming. It's a commitment that requires a willingness to embrace the world of disability. As you pray for volunteers, trust God to work in their lives. For it is in saying yes to His Spirit that they find true joy in serving. "I think people would volunteer if they realized that special needs children are no different than other children," says Lisa, a faithful Life Guard. "They may look different, drool a little, walk differently or wear diapers when they're 10, but they're all God's children. When you get to know them, you don't see the difference." (For a sample volunteer application, see p. 49.)

A Call to Kindness

You can spot the best volunteers by observing people who display the fruit of the Spirit in their lives: "love, joy, peace, patience, kindness, goodness, faithfulness, gentleness and self-control" (Galatians 5:22-23).

"A disability ministry is made up of many small and ordinary acts of kindness," says Joni Eareckson Tada. "It is people ministering to people in simple ways. It's opening a door for a young boy with crutches. It's holding a hymnal for a girl who is a quadriplegic. It's going for a walk with a boy who is blind and describing to him what you see around you."

Ask God to show you the right time to contact potential volunteers. Begin by affirming the wonderful qualities that you see in their actions. Be specific about what you're asking them to do and realistic about the task. Remember, you are not only challenging them to obey God's call, but you are also inviting them to build new friendships. You can approach volunteers with the confidence Paul described in 1 Corinthians 15:58:

My dear brothers, stand firm. Let nothing move you. Always give yourselves fully to the work of the Lord, because you know that your labor in the Lord is not in vain.

A Call to Grow

Some leaders feel guilty about asking people to serve. They think people are too busy and their approach says, "Please, just help for one Sunday. We really need your as-

sistance." These leaders fail to understand that Christians desperately need to serve to grow up in Christ. Immature Christians struggle because they focus too much on themselves. The opening on your volunteer schedule exists so that someone can become Jesus to a family. This kind of passion and vision will draw volunteers to your mission statement.

A Call to Missions

Volunteers want to make an eternal difference, not just show up to serve. But one senior pastor admitted that he found his mission the hard way:

I'm the senior pastor of a large church. As much as we like to think we care, our church's attention to special needs ebbed and flowed for years. At times, we focused on creative solutions to nurture these families. In other seasons, we turned them away because we couldn't provide what they needed.

Finally, the situation hit too close to home. One of my best friends—a prayer partner and golf buddy—left our church simply because we were not consistently serving his son's special needs. It broke my heart that it took losing a friend to another church to make me give prayerful attention to sustaining an effective disability ministry. I no longer lament that loss. It taught me that the cries of those with disabilities will always land close to home, and now our church is ready!

Imagine the joy that awaits uninvolved adults in your church, and determine to make it easy for them to say yes to special needs ministry.

Yes to the Call

Volunteers say yes when called to work in special needs ministry when certain conditions are met:

- The mission matches their own values and beliefs.
- They receive proper training, supervision and support.
- They are constantly learning new things.
- The work is rewarding and satisfying.
- They enjoy their coworkers and feel appreciated.

Director: Recruiting Ideas

Some Leaders Just Don't Get It!

Sometimes sharing your vision for a ministry to children with special needs can be disheartening, as revealed in the e-mails below.

To:	
Cc:	
Subject:	Disability Ministry

Dear Pastor James,

A ministry to children and families with disabilities is no longer optional for the church. Seventeen percent of today's children have a disability and their numbers are growing. Many of their families have been hurt by a community of faith and need support. The divorce rate among couples dealing with disabilities is 80 percent. Churches that reach out to this mission field will be blessed.

Sincerely,
Pat

Subject:	RE: Disability Ministry

Dear Pat,

We have dealt with special needs children, but we don't do it very well. One day we hope to be able to offer this ministry. Unfortunately, we have a lack of volunteers willing to participate. We need parents to "donate" time if their children are involved in church programs.

Sincerely,
Pastor James

Subject:	RE: Disability Ministry

Dear Pastor James,

I feel your pain. These are challenging days for volunteerism. Our church started a ministry to children with special needs four years ago. Pastor Eric hired a part-time director but limited the program to 20 children. He understood the demands and lack of trained helpers. Now, the church ministers to 50 special needs families each week.

Food for thought,
Pat

Some Leaders Know a Secret

Although both Pastor James and Pastor Eric saw the need for a special needs ministry, Pastor James's focus on a lack of volunteers paralyzed him. With so many obstacles, are you wondering why Pastor Eric's church succeeded? How did they recruit and train so many volunteers? They knew the following secret about children with disabilities. Remember it, and you too *can* recruit today's fast-paced volunteers:

Adults, who will *never* volunteer to teach a classroom of kids, *will* step up to love *one* child!

Wasn't that Jesus' method—building one-on-one relationships? Volunteers who serve as Buddies, Life Guards and Angels often move up the grade levels with their assigned child. Why? Because these children grab hold of your heart and don't let go—that's how God created them. It is part of the rich blessing these precious kids give back so freely. It is core truth of recruiting volunteers.

Some Leaders Get It

Fortunately, sometimes sharing your vision for a ministry to children with special needs can be uplifting and affirming, as revealed in the e-mails below.

"Our special needs children are integrated into regular classrooms with volunteers to oversee them. The volunteers rotate, so each child has four assigned to them. Parents communicate with volunteers regarding which service they'll attend. The volunteers know the children and take them to a special needs room when necessary."
—Walter, a community pastor

"We assign a child the same volunteer all the time. Parents share the child's background information and what special care is required. We discuss parent's goals for their child at church and work together to reach them. This is most successful and makes a huge difference in the confidence level of our volunteers."
—Ronda, a special needs pastor

"Most parents want their children mainstreamed. So we include them in a regular classroom or small group, if just for a short time. We also provide a Life Guard Room for children whose actions could injure themselves or others. It's a happy space where volunteers share Bible stories and learning activities."
—Bobby, a minister of children and families

"We do everything in teams in our special needs ministry. We have a special needs class with a volunteer ratio of one teacher per two children. There is a buddy team for children who attend children's worship and small groups. All special needs volunteers join our monthly children's ministry meetings for ideas, fellowship and support."
—Karen, a children's pastor

Form: Volunteer Application

[Church Name and Address]

_____

_____

Department Assignment: Special Needs Ministry

Date _____

Name _____

Home Phone _____ Cell _____

E-Mail _____

Address _____

City _____ Zip _____

Sex _____ Date of Birth _____

Marital Status _____

Spouse's Name _____

Number of Children _____ Ages _____

1. How long have you attended this church? _____
   Are you a member? _____

   Do you agree entirely with our church's doctrinal
   statement of faith? (See attached copy.) _____ If
   not, which statement(s) do you disagree with?
   _____

2. How and when did you become a Christian?
   _____
   _____

3. What other ministries, adult fellowships and classes
   are you involved in?
   _____
   _____

4. Do you have a family member or friend with a
   disability? Explain.
   _____
   _____

5. Have you taken a spiritual gift class or survey? What
   are your ministry interests?
   _____
   _____

6. Have you ever been abused or neglected? _____
   If yes, would you prefer to discuss this privately?
   _____

7. Have you ever been convicted of physical or sexual
   abuse of a child? _____

8. Have you ever been convicted of any sexual
   misbehavior? _____

9. Have you ever been convicted of possession or sale
   of controlled substances or of driving under the influence of alcohol? _____

10. Have you ever been convicted of child pornography,
    domestic violence or any other crime against a
    person? _____

11. Is there any other information that would call
    into question your ability to work with children or
    adolescents? _____
    _____
    _____

12. Please list two people who have known you for five
    years and who we can contact as your personal refer-
    ences. Please include one pastoral reference, and do
    not include immediate family members.

    a) Name _____
       Relationship _____
       Day/Cell Phone _____
       E-Mail _____

    b) Name _____
       Relationship _____
       Day/Cell Phone _____
       E-Mail _____

Your signature on this form also confirms that you understand and agree to the following:

- You have answered all questions honestly.

- You will support the guidelines in the attached memo
  of integrity and mission.

- You understand that the church may do a confidential
  criminal background check that requires your social
  security number.

- You will fully cooperate with the church's inquiry into
  any allegations that may arise in your conduct at
  church or in the community.

Social Security Number _____

Print Name _____

Signature _____

Date _____

Please return this application to
[Fill in with appropriate information.]

_____

_____

Director: Interviewing Volunteers

No two gold nuggets are shaped exactly the same, but each has a distinct value. In Romans 12:6-8, Paul lists some of the unique gifts that God gives Christians to continue His work in the world.

> We have different gifts, according to the grace given us. . . . If it is serving, let him serve; if it is teaching, let him teach; if it is encouraging, let him encourage; if it is contributing to the needs of others, let him give generously; if it is leadership, let him govern diligently; if it is showing mercy, let him do it cheerfully.

So what qualities, or gifts, should you look for in a volunteer? Some parents of children with special needs answered that very question.

Faithful—Can they stick by the task?

"The best thing about our church's special needs ministry is Beth, our son's Life Guard," said Kevin. "She's there for him each week and even moved with James to his new class. You can't imagine how much this benefits him. James never liked Sunday School until Beth volunteered to be his Life Guard. Now, he loves it."

Understanding—Can they see past a child's disability?

"Sidney's caregiver knows what she wants and can make her happy," said her mom, Melissa. "I go to worship with the assurance that Sidney is in good hands. She is also learning how to fold her hands in prayer."

"Our son Josh really likes Alan. They talk about sports and cars and what Josh will be when he grows up," said his mom. "Alan also helps Josh interact with the other kids. He's a real blessing."

Relational—Can they share joys and sorrows with the heart of a friend?

"Marty not only takes great care of our twins who are both autistic, she takes care of the whole family," said Joseph. "The twins play soccer on a Miracle League team, and Marty is usually there to cheer them on. She even watched the girls on our anniversary. That's really going the second mile."

Flexible—Can they accept children just as they are?

"Jack is truly an Angel," said Martha. "Austin has poor impulse control and gets frustrated when things don't go his way. Jack uses Austin's love of art and music. Sometimes they review Bible verses by drawing cool picture cards or just listen to CDs by Christian artists."

Persistent—Do they display high energy and patience?

"I know there are days when Sue feels like giving up on Julie," said Pam. "She is a challenge. Her attention span is so short, and some days all she does is throw things. But Sue rarely calls me out of the worship service, and I'm so grateful for her patience."

You'll find that people who volunteer for a special needs ministry have *big* hearts and *tender* spirits, but you should approach interviews prayerfully. Ask about their faith in Jesus Christ and why they want to serve. If you detect a questionable attitude or misconception they may have about disabilities or personal faith, be ready to address your concerns. If potential volunteers are members of your church, they should have taken a doctrinal class. If not, tell them that's a great place to start. Or you may encourage them to meet with your pastor.

Director: How to Match Buddies with Students

Special buddies may be the key to successfully bridging the gap that allows children with disabilities and their families to attend church. Before matching students with buddies, it is important to interview the parents and determine the needs of each child with special needs as well as how that child relates to other people.

- Does the child require special medical attention?

- Does the child use or understand sign language? If so, is the language used American Sign Language, Signed Exact English, self-made signs or a combination of these?

- How does the child communicate? Does the child use eye gaze, gestures, or picture cards? What do we need to know to better communicate with the child?

- What type of self-help skills (toileting, eating, etc.) does the child need assistance with?

- Does the child relate better to men or women?

- Would having a peer buddy (same age) make the child more comfortable?

- Would an older junior-high or high-school student be appropriate, or is an adult needed?

- Does the child require physical help such as being lifted or transferred?

- What behaviors might we encounter, and what is the best way to handle them?

- What goals do you have for your child while the child is at church?

Once you understand a student's needs, you can match him or her with a peer buddy, a student buddy or an adult buddy.

Buddy Choices

Peer Buddies

Peers make great buddies when a student with special needs requires simple help. Classmates often like to take turns pushing a wheelchair or helping with a craft. Sometimes special needs students just like to know they have a friend. Anna, who has some physical malformations, was hesitant to go to Sunday School because people always stared at her. Then Anna's classmate Holly volunteered to be her buddy. Holly and Anna always sat together, talking and playing. Holly even stood up for Anna when she got teased. Anna told her mother that she didn't mind if people stared at her as long as she had at least one friend.

Junior-High and High-School Buddies

An older student can be a great choice when the child needs help with minor behavioral or physical issues. Student buddies can also serve as role models for children with disabilities, because they look up to teens. They will also feel less singled out than if they had an adult hovering over them. Jimmy, a fourth grader, is hard of hearing and has mild developmental delays. He does fine in his small group, but when Jimmy is in a large group, he gets confused and often wanders off. He has two junior-high helpers who take turns being his buddy. They help Jimmy stay focused by explaining what he needs to know and making sure he does not get lost. His parents feel comfortable leaving Jimmy because they know he is being watched, and Jimmy loves his cool friends.

Adult Buddies

An adult buddy is often necessary when a student's behavioral issues or medical needs are fairly serious. Parents are more at ease knowing an adult is nearby if their child is prone to emotional outbursts or is medically fragile. For example, when Bradley becomes agitated, he responds best to a man. Frank volunteers as his buddy, and they have developed a respectful relationship. Leanne has complicated medical issues. Several nurses in the congregation take turns staying with Leanne in class, so her parents can enjoy going to worship.

Safety First

Before placing a buddy with a student, make sure background checks and/or fingerprints have been cleared according to your church policy. All buddies should also submit personal references. A good source for recruiting junior-high and high-school buddies is youth leaders and pastors. They know the students that demonstrate the maturity and responsibility needed to handle the assignment. All buddies must be trained on how to handle the behavior, communication and physical needs of their specific students as well as how to follow church policy and emergency plans.

A Get-Acquainted Meeting

Once a director has chosen a prospective match, it is time to set up an initial meeting, so everyone can get acquainted. The child, parent, buddy and ministry director can share needed information to help the buddy understand and communicate with the child. Here are a few discussion starters to ask the child at the meeting.

- What do you like to do just for fun?

- What don't you like to do?

- What things can you do by yourself, and what do you need help with?

During this meeting, observe how the prospective buddy and the child interact. Are they at ease with each other? Is the buddy trying to decipher the child's communication style? Is the buddy overwhelmed by the child's needs or does the buddy seem willing to learn whatever might be necessary? Everyone should feel that the match is a good fit.

Regular Checkups

After a match has been made, check in with the both the family and the buddy after one or two weeks. The buddy may have new questions for the parents, and parents will be eager to know if the match is working well. Continue to schedule checkups at regular intervals. If the family is uncomfortable with the situation, they may stop coming to church. If the buddy has difficulty with the student, he or she may give up.

It takes time for special needs students and their buddies to know and trust each other. At first, Allison didn't warm up to her new buddy, Janet. Although Janet did everything Allison's parents told her to, Allison remained withdrawn and quiet. It was a mystery, until Allison's mother realized that Janet looked very similar to a person with whom Allison had a bad experience. Over time, Janet won Allison's trust, and they became friends.

Problem Solving

When problems occur, it is important to address them quickly. Many issues are the result of misunderstanding, miscommunication or the lack of a better plan. Jill was unhappy whenever it was Sue's turn to be her buddy. Jill would get angry, but she couldn't articulate what bothered her. After Sue talked with the director and other buddies, they realized the problem was quite simple. Sue sat Jill on the "wrong" side of the room. Jill liked the consistency of sitting in the second row near the windows. When Sue started sitting with Jill on the "right" side of the room, they both got their smile back!

Veronica's buddy was about to give up because Veronica constantly interrupted the teacher with vocal outbursts and showed no desire to behave. The buddy felt frustrated and inadequate. The director, teacher and buddy got together and developed a plan in which Veronica earned a smiley face for every five minutes she sat without a vocal outburst. After she received five smiley faces, she got a reward. Veronica's behavior improved and her buddy came to enjoy working with her.

As much as we'd like the match between every buddy and special needs child to work out satisfactorily, there will be times when a match does not work. We all respond to certain people better than others. Sometimes the best solution is to make a different match. This can relieve stress for both the child and the buddy. A match that doesn't work out well should never be considered a failure but rather a step in the process of doing what is best for all concerned.

Director: Disability Training 101 and Beyond

As great teachers seek to discover each student's learning style, great directors understand that today's volunteers are drawn to a variety of learning experiences: books, DVDs, seminars, podcasts, conferences, newsletters, discussion groups, in-service opportunities, etc. But before you get overwhelmed, remember that training is ongoing, and quality volunteers are not created in a day. With the help of your disability ministry team, plan a training calendar using the articles in this book.

Sample Training Calendar

August Disability Ministry Orientation for New Volunteers	Loving Children with Special Needs (Awareness)	Creating Disability-Friendly Classrooms (Curriculum, Schedules, Activities)
November Keeping Children with Disabilities Safe	Good Health Practices at Church (Policies)	Preventive Discipline and Play-time Safety
February Reaching Out Beyond the Special Needs Classroom	Becoming a Child's True Friend (Evangelism, Discipleship)	Supporting a Child's Extended Family (Prayer)
May Discipling Extraordinary Kids	Discovering Each Child's Unique Gift	Planning Service Projects for Your Class

How to Conduct Successful Trainings

- **Have fun.** Create an atmosphere where volunteers feel welcome, get their needs met and want to hang out. That's when volunteers will stick—and grow in their desire to serve and lead.

- **Be consistent.** Schedule regular meetings where they know they can get helpful suggestions, share ideas and request supplies. Follow through with what you say you'll do or get or ask about. And follow up. Make it clear that you can be depended on. "I meet with my special needs team on a monthly basis to brainstorm ideas for their lessons," says Steve, a special needs director. "This gives me the opportunity to guide their preparation and to tell them they're great. And after the meeting I can round up needed supplies. I want to walk alongside them and give them tools."

- **Respect their time.** Set up a group e-mail list, so you can easily update volunteers on small details that don't warrant a meeting. Use it to remind them of events and to share praises and prayer requests.

- **Provide child care.** If you had to pay for your volunteers' time, you couldn't afford a special needs ministry. Reward their valuable service by budgeting for child care during your training meetings. It pays!

Where to Find Training Help

Seminars and Local Agencies

Watch for disability training opportunities in your area, and invite volunteers to go as a group. Or host training workshops at your church for parents, teachers and caregivers. Invite knowledgeable speakers such as authors, doctors, special education teachers and pastors. (For a list of Joni and Friends Regional Disability Summits, visit www.joniandfriends.org.)

Online Training

Direct your tech-friendly volunteers to the Web for sites offering training tapes, books and seminars. Here are several to get you started:

- http://www.disabilitytraining.com
- http://www.eparent.com
- http://www.specialtouch.org
- http://www.joniandfriends.org
- http://www.cec.sped.org

In-Service Training

In your community, there might be a chapter of one of the national organizations (such as the ARC—an organization for people with intellectual and developmental disabilities—or the Special Olympics) that serve children and adults with disabilities. There also might be local group homes, schools, churches and support groups who serve people with special needs. They provide a wealth of information and training for volunteers willing to get involved. Look through your phone book and talk to community leaders to find out what's close to your home.

Continuing Education at Colleges and Universities

Courses at Johnson Bible College in Knoxville, Tennessee, are taught by experts in the field and offer excellent insights into how to minister to and with the disability community. This is one of a growing number of Christian colleges that award a B.A. or B.S. in disability ministry.

Biola University in California requires all undergraduate students to complete a course in the theology of suffering and disability.

Reformed Theological Seminary, Charlotte, North Carolina, offers courses in disability ministry for personal enrichment, for certification and for a master's degree. These courses are designed to help equip churches to minister to those with special needs and to help people with disabilities take their places in the Body of Christ.

Training Resources Available from Joni and Friends

- *The Father's House: Welcoming and Including People and Families Affected by Disability,* a DVD, uncovers for viewers the most common fears, myths and misunderstandings that churches face when they begin a disability ministry. The DVD also includes 10 practical tips for becoming a disability-friendly church.

- *Through the Roof: A Guide to Assist Churches in Developing an Effective Disability Outreach* by Joni

Eareckson Tada and Steve Miller discusses the hows and whys of disability ministry and how to determine what your congregation needs. The book also includes a training course and a list of recommended resources.

- *Exceptional Teaching: A Comprehensive Guide for Including Students with Disability* is a book by Dr. Jim Pierson. In it he describes each disorder along with teaching tips, discipline ideas and suggestions for classroom management.

- *Let All the Children Come to Me: A Practical Guide to Including Children with Disabilities in Your Church Ministries* by Malesa Breeding, Dana Hood and Jerry Whitworth is an excellent book for teaching methods in special education. Topics include modifying instruction to teach to strengths, dealing with difficult behavior, and teaching strategies.

- *Autism and Your Church: Nurturing the Spiritual Growth of People with Autism Spectrum Disorders* by Barbara J. Newman offers practical ways to welcome and include individuals with ASD into the full life of the congregation.

Build a Scrapbook Reference: Collect inspiring magazine and news articles about children and families with disabilities. Store them in plastic pages in a colorful notebook (or in file folders). These will be a tremendous source of encouragement and current information. As volunteers ask questions, lend them the scrapbook, and soon they'll be bringing you clippings to add to the collection.

Director: A Special Needs Handbook

A well-crafted handbook is a reference tool that can answer many questions for volunteers and all others who need to be informed about the ministry and is a simple way for all volunteers and other staff to have the same information. The handbook can be brief, providing the most basic information (programs, policies and procedures; staff list with contact information; schedules; training opportunities, etc.), or it can be extensive with articles and training materials. The handbook should be updated and distributed at the beginning of each term of service and to new volunteers as they join during the term. Here's a sample of what to include:

Concerning Volunteers and Mission Statement

- Welcome letters from senior pastor and special needs director
- Church mission statement

Concerning Staff and Programs

- People (staff, leaders and teams)
- Programs (schedules, and curriculum)
- Volunteer opportunities and job descriptions
- Volunteer orientation and training events

Concerning Policies and Procedures

- Keys to a disability-friendly classroom
- Check-in and parent's notification procedures
- Disability etiquette and language
- Curriculum, resources and class schedules
- Behavior management guidelines (parent conferences)
- Substitute policy (phone numbers to call)

Concerning Health and Safety Issues

- Child wellness policy
- Medical guidelines (foods, allergies, swallowing, seizures, etc.)
- Restroom policy
- Emergency procedures and accident/illness report form
- Playground rules
- Child abuse policy and reporting

Concerning Training and Resources

- Volunteer development and growth
- Special needs classroom forms
    - Child profile—"All About Me"
    - Sunday School and church sign-in
    - Parent support and respite sign-in
- Supplies and equipment needs

After you give a person a handbook, have that person write the date and their initials next to their name on a master list of everyone who should receive a copy of the handbook. In this way, you'll have a record of who received the book and when they received it.

Teaching: Disability-Friendly Language and Manners

Remember the childhood chant "Sticks and stones . . ."? Well, the end of it should be revised because words *can* hurt!

The world of people with disabilities has its own evolving language. Terms that once reflected certain disorders have been replaced in favor of ones that focus on the individual rather than on the disability. This is called "people-first" language. Even using the word "the" in regard to people in a disability category lumps them together in a negative classification, such as "the blind" or "the disabled." To eliminate negative stereotypes, here is a list of preferred expressions collected from various national disability organizations:

Negative Expressions	Positive Terms
"The autistic boy."	"The boy with autism."
"The handicapped (or disabled) girl."	"The girl with a disability."
"The deaf mute (or hearing impaired or blind child)."	"The child who doesn't talk and is hard of hearing (deaf or blind)."
"The deformed (cleft lip or hare lip) child."	"The child with a congenital disability."
"Lame," "crippled," "paralytic," "spastic" or "gimp."	"The girl is a wheelchair user" or "the girl with cerebral palsy."
"The dyslexic boy."	"The boy with a learning disability."
"Crazy," "maniac," "demented," "psycho" or "schizo."	"The girl with an emotional (or mental) disorder."
"The hyperactive boy."	"The boy with an attention disorder (or AD/HD)."
"The brain-damaged child."	"The child with a brain injury."
"The burn survivor."	"The boy with burns."
"The epileptic girl."	"The girl with a seizure disorder."
"Victim," "suffers with," "stricken" or "afflicted." (These terms imply patients with diseases.)	Focus on their abilities and achievements.
"Normal children," "healthy children" or "able-bodied children."	"Nondisabled children."

Teaching: Helping Children Accept One Another

Imagine every child in a group holding a single puzzle piece. That puzzle piece represents a child's areas of strength as well as areas of need. In an accepting group, each one of those puzzle pieces will fit snugly together. Each individual will hold a spot that is critical to the completed puzzle. It's important in our children's groups to create exactly that kind of environment—one in which each child belongs, including the child with a puzzle piece of unique gifts and special needs.

Acceptance begins at the top. Leaders constantly send messages to children. If you have an accepting attitude toward each child in the group, the other children will see that by your physical proximity, eye contact, discussion and informal interactions. If you have an attitude of confusion or fear, children will take note. Sometimes a child with special needs has a one-on-one mentor, so the group leader doesn't ever interact with the child. The other children may accept this as their model for also not interacting with the child. You can influence your group to accept each child's piece of the puzzle as a gift to the group.

Notice how the children interact with one another. Listen to the words they use. Observe where they sit and if everyone is welcome as part of the group. Watch for facial expressions and gestures. Children communicate acceptance in a host of different ways.

When you notice positive interactions, be specific in pointing them out to the children. "I noticed that everyone has a buddy next to them in our floor circle. That's great." "Gavin, smart thinking! You noticed that Brad has a hard time lifting his right hand, so you gently put your hand on his arm during circle prayer." You can also write a note or card to a child at home, so the observation is done privately. Either way, point out the positive interactions and be specific in your praise.

When you notice negative interactions, deal with them immediately. Each child deserves a place of safety and respect within the church setting. When you hear or see a negative behavior, state the standard for your room. For example, if a child is sitting all alone at a table, you can say, "We can continue when everyone has a friend at the same table." Usually, children will figure it out from there. If you notice a child shoot off a nasty look to someone, teach the class about how we send messages with different body parts. "When we wave, we are communicating something with our hands. A nod also gives information. We can also send signals with our eyes. The eye signals we use in this room for one another will be ones that say, 'Good job' or 'I like you.'" Give the children a chance to practice these positive hand, head and eye messages. Bullying and put-downs must be outlawed in your group—no exceptions.

Use each person's gifts. As you examine each puzzle piece, make sure everyone gets a chance to offer strengths to the group. Collecting the offering, choosing a song, setting out napkins for a snack, passing crayons or drawing a picture all contribute to the group. Use the gifts of each puzzle piece while using the whole group to help support the areas of need in one another.

A Note About Peer Questions

Asking a question in order to get information about a peer is very different from bullying. Don't run away from questions or hush the child. Information about the gifts and needs of another group member allows the children to be supportive and helpful.

Teaching: Disability Awareness Activities

Disability awareness activities are a fun way to promote understanding and compassion. Children are often afraid of what they do not understand, but once educated, they begin to view people with disabilities as individuals created in God's image. Make sure that activities presented to your class are done in a positive, knowledgeable way, avoiding the creation of pity or condescension for people affected by a disability. Use one activity a week or use all during one class for a Disability Awareness Fair.

Understanding Sign Language

Display a chart of the manual sign language alphabet. Have students practice the letters that spell their name. Teach sign language to a song, looking the signs up in a book from the library or online in a visual sign-language dictionary.

Understanding Learning Disabilities

Create a lower-case letter "b" out of construction paper. Hold the "b" up to the children and ask them to name the letter. Then show it as the letter "d" and again ask children to name the letter. Continue by holding it as the letters "p" and "q" and as the numbers 9 and 6. Explain that for some people with learning disabilities, the brain twists around what the eyes see, which creates difficulty in reading and writing.

Understanding Quadriplegia

Challenge your class to create pieces of art just as a mouth artist would, using pens or pencils gripped in their teeth. Tape paper to a wall or table for stability and provide new golf pencils for this project. Suggest students draw simple pictures such as hearts, flowers or smiley faces, and have them sign their name to their artwork.

Understanding Wheelchair Use

Provide a wheelchair for your class to use, and let them discover how accessible your facilities are. Make sure they check out doorways, table heights, sidewalks, entryways, drinking fountains and bathrooms.

Understanding Blindness

Pair students with partners and blindfold one of them. Go on a trust walk with the blindfolded student following the verbal directions and physical cues of his or her partner.

Understanding Autism

To help your class understand the sensory overload that many with autism experience, seat one student on a chair in the middle of the room. Assign other students different tasks such as turning lights on and off quickly, blowing a fan into the seated child's face, tickling the seated student with a feather, etc. Any children without assignments can be directed to loudly sing "The Star-Spangled Banner." While all of this chaos is going on, ask the seated student to recite a familiar Bible verse such as John 3:16. Ask the child if he or she had any difficulty concentrating on the task while all of his or her other senses were being over-stimulated.

Understanding Down Syndrome

Arrange the pieces of a simple puzzle on a table, adding an extra but similar piece to the mix. Then ask your class to assemble the puzzle. When the children discover there is an extra piece, explain that people with Down syndrome have an extra chromosome that creates the distinctive physical features and developmental disabilities that characterize this congenital disability.

Understanding Those Without Speech

Some people without speech or voluntary movement can communicate by blinking their eyes once for yes and twice for no. Play an old-fashioned game of Hangman using yes-or-no eyeblinks to answer the class.

Understanding Deafness

As students enter the classroom, do not speak to them but use motions and facial expressions (and sign language if you know it) to communicate to them a task that you would like them to complete (rearrange the chairs, write their name on a piece of paper, etc.). Require students to remain quiet and communicate without using their voices.

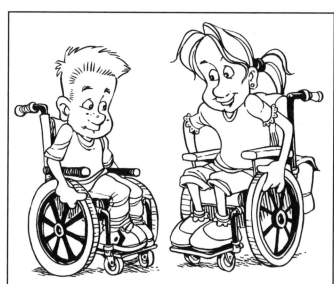

Volunteers: Becoming a Child's True Friend

We can't do this alone anymore, Marge thought as her alarm clock signaled another day of caring for Stephanie, who has autism. *Lord, help us find someone who will love our daughter as much as we do.*

Marge and her husband couldn't even enjoy church, because Stephanie's special needs teacher had moved out of state. One of them constantly had to take their child out of the sanctuary because of her agitation. And it broke their hearts when she kept asking, "Where's my teacher? Doesn't she want to be my friend anymore?"

When a child has a friend, life is good, especially if that child is one with special needs. Stephanie's teacher obviously had a calming effect on her and made her feel important at church. As a caring mentor, you, too, can fill an enormous role in a child's life—comforting, sharing and directing, and always modeling Jesus Christ.

Some children with disabilities do not easily make friends due to their lack of understanding social responses. They can easily and unconsciously drive away peers and adults who aren't sure how to respond to their unique abilities. Loneliness is a constant struggle for these children and often for their families as well. Even their siblings' friends may not want them around. But when they do connect with a mentor, they're furiously loyal and generous with their affection.

Some mentors get involved because they have had extended family members with disabilities. Their mentoring inspires others because their actions say, "My friend Stephanie is okay! I enjoy her company, and you should get to know her!" They can also pray with families, assuring them that they know of similar situations that were difficult, but other parents prevailed with God's help.

You can mentor a child in a formal role as a regular teacher or as a buddy. But you can also come alongside a family and befriend their child with notes in the mail, visits on birthdays and holidays, and trips for ice cream or simply by sitting with their child for a few hours. Mentors are good listeners, and that's a skill that comes with a promise:

> If you do away with the yoke of oppression, with the pointing finger and malicious talk, and if you spend yourselves in behalf of the hungry and satisfy the needs of the oppressed, then your light will rise in the darkness, and your night will become like the noonday (Isaiah 58:9-10).

Stephanie eventually found a new mentor and friend in Mrs. Jefferson, an elderly woman who filled her purse with surprises each week. After 54 years of sitting next to her husband in church, Mrs. Jefferson was alone after he died. Over time, a strong bond grew between Stephanie and Mrs. Jefferson. Her parents once again enjoyed worship, and their daughter relaxed so well next to Mrs. Jefferson that she often fell asleep. This was a friendship forged in prayer and made in heaven.

You Do Make a Difference!

It's a big world out there that needs changing. It's a small world near you that needs changing, too. People are desperate for help and hope. But take heart! Your prayers and practical action make a dent in your world—a big dent in your small world and a small dent in the big one.
—Joni Eareckson Tada

Volunteers: Visiting a Child's Weekday World

Mrs. Jennings was having difficulty understanding Jonathan's behaviors in her Sunday School class. But when she visited him in his home, she gained a whole new perspective on interacting with him and on understanding his needs and abilities. This short visit translated into better teaching and improved learning experiences for everyone.

Obtain Permission

When setting up a visitation at the child's home, therapy session or school, always first obtain parents' permission. Most parents will be excited about your interest in their child. Let them suggest the appropriate time and length of your visit. Therapists and schools also need to grant permission. Some may require you to have a background check and sign paperwork guaranteeing confidentiality. It's best to visit when parents can accompany you.

Build a Relationship

Let the child learn more about you during your visit. Play with the child, read aloud a story or sing a song to or with the child. Let the child guide the play with his or her own toys and set the tone and pace of your visit. As you join in the child's favorite activities at home, during therapy or at school, the child will become more comfortable with you in the church setting. You will be a familiar friend whom the child recognizes, and the child will know that you care about him or her.

Make Visits Outside of Class

- **Home**—If possible, visit the child in his or her home and watch the interaction between the child and the parents, siblings and any other caregivers. Observe how they communicate with and respond to this child. Watch how they deal with various issues, from discipline to encouragement. Find out what equipment and adaptations are used to meet the child's needs as he or she participates with the family. Think about how you could make similar adaptations in your classroom. Observe the child's medical and feeding routines to gain perspective on what daily family life is like, and think of ways your church program could help support the family.

- **Therapy**—It can be beneficial to visit the child during a therapy session if the child uses speech, occupational or physical therapy. Therapists are invaluable resources, answering questions regarding specific issues that have arisen at your ministry. Therapists can also make suggestions about physical adaptations that allow the student to better participate in class, such as recommending special scissors or a slant board for written work. They can give ideas for interactive language and social skills or help problem solve how best to involve the child during arts and crafts time. Make use of their expertise and knowledge of the child.

- **School**—Observing the child at his or her school or early intervention class can also give you valuable information. Watch the teachers' responses and the way the child interacts with his or her peers. The school might be willing to lend special equipment for use at your church or allow you to use their resources to create individualized materials. They may also be willing to visit your church in order to help create a consistent program for the student.

- **Extracurricular Activities**—Attend a school play or music program in which the child is performing, or attend his or her sports games. Not only will this enable you to view more of the whole child, but also it will show the child and his or her family that you love and care about the child.

Now Mrs. Jennings is one of Jonathan's biggest cheerleaders and encouragers. Getting to know him outside of class has helped her see his strengths and abilities, and she no longer focuses on his disabilities. Jonathan responds well in her class and enjoys learning about how much God loves him.

Volunteers: Serving as a Short-Term Missionary

A short-term missionary (STM) serves families at Joni and Friends Family Retreats and Camps so that parents and children alike can take full advantage of the fun and activities of the events. These trained STMs extend the love of Christ by serving each family in practical ways and, as a result, are equipped to take disability ministry back to their church. Consider inviting your disability ministry volunteers to receive training as short-term missionaries.

An STM's Story

Hanna Powers served as a STM for Mia Boatright. Her story is repeated by the 1,200 youth and adults who give a week of their time each summer to serve families affected by disability.

I wake up staring at bite marks on my shoulder. The bruises match the arc of Mia's teeth. I remember the previous night's ticklefest and Mia's head thrown back in delight. At breakfast she greets me with her head bobbing, her ponytail flying and a vacant smile. An enveloping T-shirt bib must precede any breakfast food coming near Mia. Severe autism and mental retardation result in meals resembling a cafeteria food fight. We both look a bit ragged following the group of seven-year-olds to their first camp activity.

On a good day, the craft resembles an object someone would recognize when Mia is finished. We watch the camp skits calmly and an entire team of volunteers helps Mia jump off the diving board. The good days sustain me through the hard days. A meltdown can last 20 minutes or 20 hours. Mia lies on the floor, screaming and biting, turned inward as she punishes her own skin in frustration.

As Mia's caregiver, I play a role of crisis manager. When my short assignment ends, I return to life without edible hair accessories. Mia's family lives with the highs and lows of disability every day. But I love Mia for her humanity. Her happiness comes from something as simple as bouncing a ball. She dances unfettered; she knows no masks. I join Mia's family in celebrating her worth and value.

I love Mia for who I am because of her. I reject the default judgments of my culture as I engage others. I push to arrive at understanding, even when opinions are diverse or communication is muddled. Mia makes group projects at school look easy! For me, loving human beings well means a commitment to stay whether days are hard or easy, whether actions are kind or harsh. Loving well means patience is rewarded with a small hand resting in mine.

The lesson of Mia comes with me into life. Diversity allows the hues of humanity to enrich our lives. We learn to give each other grace to be as we become. Because of Mia, I can teach my friends how to eat water. Who knew that was even an option?

An STM's Benefits

- Educational resource CD-ROM and *Field Guide* to prepare for the week

- Experiential, on-site disability-awareness training and team building

- Five days of education, a T-shirt, new friends, and fun

- The opportunity to make a difference in the life of a family affected by disability

Family Retreats and Camps offer an enriching and inspiring week where families and STMs can build new friendships and make lasting memories, all while renewing hope and trust in God. (For retreat dates, locations and online registration, visit http://www.joniandfriends .org/pg_retreats.php.)

Volunteers: Working with Local Disability Organizations

Should a church or Christian organization work or partner with secular disability organizations? Is there a dual value in it for the church and the local organization? Is it worth all of the effort? The answers to these questions are yes, yes and yes!

When your church disability ministry partners with a secular disability organization, you may have opportunities to share the Gospel with people who otherwise might not darken the church door. The church has opportunity to minister to hurting families and to share the love of God in very practical ways. The church becomes known in the disability community as a disability friendly place, the place to naturally turn to with questions, hurts or needs.

Here are some ways to partner with disability organizations:

- Make your building facilities available for use by local disability programs.

- Let support groups and school parent programs meet in your building.

- Open your gym for after-school program use.

- Invite organizations to hold dinners and recreational events in your fellowship hall.

- Display literature that details your disability ministry so that families will learn that your church is disability-friendly.

- Advertise community disability events within your own ministry, as long as these events meet moral, ethical and spiritual standards set by your church. Display event literature alongside your own. Advertise your own events through local disability organizations' newsletters and Web pages.

- Participate in community events involving people with disabilities. For example, if the Arc (an organization for people with intellectual and developmental disabilities) is hosting a picnic, offer to provide dessert. They will be thrilled to have the help and support. They might give your program some free advertising and include your logo on their T-shirts or include you in their list of sponsors.

- Invite others to present their programs or expertise at your workshops or other events. A special education teacher can lead a workshop on autism for your Sunday School teachers. The Down Syndrome Association can tell your group what they have to offer. Be available and willing to present your ministry at local support groups and disability organizations as well.

- Participate in disability fairs. Besides offering your facilities for the event, make sure your ministry is represented as an exhibitor. Offer to provide volunteers to help out during the event. (See "Hosting a Disability Fair" on p. 135.)

- Attend local school-district or government meetings that deal with the topic of people with disabilities. Not only will this keep you informed about current policy and ideology, but it will also let others know that you are interested in issues that affect them.

- Adopt a program from a local organization for your church to serve, such as a group home. Provide the residents with gifts for Christmas, cards on Valentine's Day and/or an egg hunt on Easter. The organization will appreciate it and will respect your ministry for reaching out.

- Provide work opportunities for special education students. Teens enrolled in special education classes often look for work during high school and transition years (ages 18 through 21) through their school program. These may or may not be paid positions, and a job coach is usually provided. Jobs might be found around the church in custodial service, the office, yard maintenance, or the nursery and day-care program.

Secular disability organizations strive to meet emotional, physical, financial and educational needs but may forget spiritual needs. In many cases, if the organization accepts government funding, the group simply is not legally able to address the spiritual aspect. Your church ministry can partner to help meet that need. One church that has adopted this model is seeing growth, not just in its disability ministry, but also in its entire church body. They are successfully impacting their community for Christ.

Tips: Ideas from Special Needs Leaders

"Sadly, the Church cannot claim exemption from the neglect and abuse of children. The Church may have avoided overt sins of commission, but we are equally guilty of the covert sins of omission. Few gifts on Earth are as wondrous as the love of a child. Advocates for children know deep in their hearts the truth of the saying, 'You never stand as tall as when you stoop to help a child.'"

—Dr. Wess Stafford, President of Compassion International

"Work with the person, not the disability."

—Dr. Jim Pierson, author of *Exceptional Teaching: A Comprehensive Guide for Including Students with Disability*

"One volunteer who has grown the most in our disability ministry is my friend Chris. He came in with a willing spirit to serve God in this way. He has such a compassionate heart for those with special needs. He is always willing to help wherever he can. Now Chris and his wife even mentor couples in our parents' support group on Thursday evenings while continuing to serve as a Life Guard."

—Susan, Seattle, WA

"Our people are most comfortable when they get hands-on training. We have a student that can get violent and be extremely hard to handle. The volunteers who respond best to him are those who have witnessed his outbursts and observed how others handled him. It is not so scary when you have seen an episode unfold to the end and know that there is an ending."

—Pastor George, Atlanta, GA

"We did various things to recruit volunteers such as worship bulletin inserts, Sunday School flyers and booths at the ministry fair, but with little results. So we created a video series to use during worship announcements that makes the entire congregation aware of our ministry needs. We introduced the children and their parents who shared how volunteers bless their lives. These videos helped people see that they shouldn't be afraid because they don't have a medical or educational background. God can use them to serve children with disabilities."

—Mary, Fort Worth, TX

"One of the unique gifts that God has given my family is the ability to laugh at ourselves. God has used the entrance of disability into my world as a refining fire that has profoundly changed how I view and value others and myself. It has caused me to be deeply convicted by my need for grace, and at the same time it has encouraged me to embrace God's grace and 'lighten up.'"

—Stephanie O. Hubach, author of *Same Lake, Different Boat: Coming Alongside People Touched by Disability*, and mom of Timmy, who has Down syndrome

I Want to Know God's Word!

The Lord is my shepherd;

I have everything I need.

He gives me rest in green pastures.

He leads me to calm water.

He gives me new strength.

Psalm 23:1-3, *NCV*

Director: Keys to Disability–Friendly Classrooms

First impressions are always important. The classroom environment answers a lot of questions for the child with disabilities. *Am I wanted? Will I fit in? Is there a place for me? Will I be comfortable? Am I safe?* A classroom that doesn't have room for a wheelchair or is overstimulating may be saying "Go away." When children in wheelchairs enter a room and find tables high enough to fit their chairs under with room to maneuver, they can begin to feel welcome. It is important to look at your room from the perspective of all those who will use it.

Inclusive vs. Self-Contained Classrooms

Most churches will be able to start a special needs ministry by including children with disabilities in their existing classrooms. These are called inclusive classrooms and should be inviting for children with or without disabilities.

As the ministry expands, you may want to add (or convert) a classroom designed specifically for children with special needs. Including children with their peers is a priority; however, some children have unique behavioral, physical or emotional needs that make inclusion, or mainstreaming, difficult. Their families feel they can't worship because there is no place for their child. Creating a special room designed to meet specific needs allows many families the freedom to attend church. Many of the ideas listed below apply to all classes while some specifically refer to the self-contained special needs classroom.

A Child's Point of View

Am I welcome?

When children have physical disabilities, their families need to know that the room provides a safe and inclusive environment.

- **Wheelchair accessibility** is a must. There also should be large clear areas for wheelchair navigation, and tables high enough to roll underneath.

- **An ADA-approved bathroom** should be close to the classroom and changing areas for older students.

- **A designated parking area** for wheelchairs, walkers and adaptive devices is necessary.

- **Adaptable furniture and equipment** should be available as necessary, including cube chairs, beanbags, "feeder chairs" and floor mats.

Will my senses be on overload?

Children who have hypersensitivity to sights and sounds need an area free from sensory distraction.

- **Create a safe, quiet retreat.** Designate a small area of the room that has a blank wall as a place for a child to withdraw for a time. A small pup tent or even a table with a blanket over it works well

- **Use nonfluorescent lighting** if flickering or noise from fluorescent lighting is troublesome. Table lamps or dimmer switches on nonfluorescent lighting may be good alternatives.

- **Check the room for bothersome noises.** Is the heating or air conditioning creating annoying noise? Use either unit sparingly if it is bothering the child.

Am I safe?

Parents will be willing to leave their child if they are sure safety concerns have been addressed.

- **An inside gate or door** is a helpful deterrent for children who have a tendency to run.

- **A two-way radio or phone** is needed in case of emergency.

- **Pagers** given to parents assure them that they can be reached immediately if necessary. If pagers are not available, make sure you know exactly where to find the parent.

- **Locks on all cabinets and drawers** are necessary.

- **A two-way window** in a self-contained special needs room allows a parent (without being a distraction to the student or class) to observe a child and offer suggestions about how to handle behavior.

Is there a place for me to learn and have fun?

Classrooms should have several learning areas that create unique experiences that are adaptable to individual needs.

• Circle Time or Lesson Area—Include only what is necessary for the lesson. A flannel board for stories or a pocket chart for attendance and Bible memory verses may be necessary, but the area should be free from other visual distractions, so the child can focus on the lesson.

Appropriate seating should be available to suit each unique need. Lizzie, who has cerebral palsy, sits in a beanbag chair. Brianne needs a space for her wheelchair. Anthony does best in the cube chair, but David likes a regular chair.

• **Sensory Exploration Area**—An inclusive classroom should have a sensory learning center. Rotate items for the children to explore using vision, hearing, smell and touch. Have available such things as bins of rice or sand; or small containers with cotton balls soaked in perfume, spices, fish oil or extracts.

A self-contained classroom will want a permanent sensory area. It may include a sensory wall that has attached to it different textures such as fake fur, packing bubbles, corrugated paper, or leather. A safety-glass full-length mirror can be fastened to the wall. A water table or small inflatable pool makes a great place to play with feathers, cotton balls or packing popcorn.

When creating a sensory environment, safety is a key issue. Be aware of small items around children prone to put things in their mouths, and make sure the students don't have allergies to certain smells. Supervision is vital.

• **Gross-Motor Skills Area**—A minitrampoline is often a favorite for children with special needs as well as nondisabled students. It may provide a calming, effective release of tension or frustration and a great reward after achieving a goal. Those who can't jump on their own can lie on it while a volunteer gently bounces them.

Other items to provide include floor mats, therapy balls, an indoor basketball hoop, scoot boards or an indoor swing. An inclusive classroom may only be able to include one or two items due to space constraints. Choose items that will be beneficial to the student's needs while encouraging interaction with their peers.

• **Quiet Area**—When students on sensory overload feel that they are losing control of their emotions, they need a quiet, safe place to go. This area may include a small pup tent, blanket or body sock (see "Creating a Small, Safe Space," p. 191).

Do you care about my unique needs?

When you provide items that uniquely benefit a child with a disability, you show that child that he or she is valuable and important.

• **Sensory Toys**—These include vibrating, musical or light-up toys.

• **Switch Toys**—These are motorized or animated toys that have been adapted to be operated by a simple switch.

• **Fidget Toys**—These include water-filled balls, Koosh® rubber balls with soft spikes, tangle toys, Silly Putty® plastic clay, bendable figures and Slinky® coil-shaped toys.

• **Rocking Chair**—This sort of chair might be used by the child alone or by the child with a volunteer.

• **Computers and Adaptive Technology**—These include specialized devices, some of which are customized for an individual, depending on his or her needs. For example, a child with a speech impairment might have a touch-screen computer that voices what the child wants to say.

• **TV and DVD Player**—These devices are very helpful in the classroom setting, either to show simple animated Bible stories or sing-along DVDs.

• **Water Table**—For water play, a water table is essential. Other sensory items might also be included.

Every classroom will vary depending on the unique needs of the students. A classroom specifically designed for special needs students will look different from a classroom that is mainstreaming a child with autism. The key is to look at the room through the eyes of the child and see if it is a place the child looks forward to coming to again and again to learn and make friends.

Director: Create a Cheerful Classroom

Remember that the classroom should be neat, organized and free from clutter at all times.

Also provide table and floor lamps, 2 or 3 lockable cabinets, round table with four chairs, kidney-shaped table, toy shelf with plastic bins labeled "I See," "I Hear," "I Touch," "I Smell" and "I Taste", wide doorway with half door and a two-way mirror on one wall, so parents can view classroom

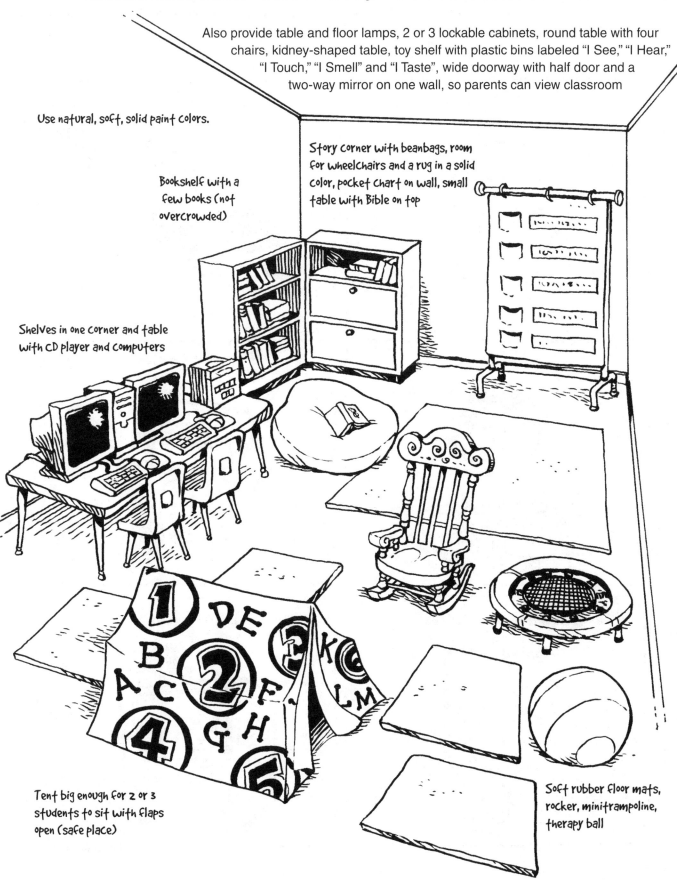

Use natural, soft, solid paint colors.

Story corner with beanbags, room for wheelchairs and a rug in a solid color, pocket chart on wall, small table with Bible on top

Bookshelf with a few books (not overcrowded)

Shelves in one corner and table with CD player and computers

Tent big enough for 2 or 3 students to sit with flaps open (safe place)

Soft rubber floor mats, rocker, minitrampoline, therapy ball

Sample: Visuals for Special Needs Classrooms

Symbols help communicate expectations for a cheerful classroom. Post these cards at an age-appropriate height in the room. Don't assume children understand the pictures. Carefully demonstrate for the children what each picture means. Review cards regularly, and make the review fun.

Raise your hand.

Walk-Don't run.

Sit down.

Please be quiet.

Teacher's turn to talk.

Cleanup time.

Director: To Mainstream or Not to Mainstream

Young children enjoy playing with a shape sorter. Each shape has some sort of corresponding hole. Slip the piece through the correct hole, and it fits inside the shape sorter. It appears that choosing the best fit for a child with special needs in church is a lot like that child's toy. One needs to first examine the child and then decide how best to have that child fit into the children's church community.

It's important to have a flexible shape sorter for your children's ministry. Become a student of that child. What delights that child? Think about individual strengths and needs. Once you have a good understanding of that child, construct a good fit within your children's program. Churches that assume there is only one type of child have only one option. Churches that understand each child as a unique creation of God will become creative in designing ways for every child to be successful at church.

Preserve the Body

It's critical that no matter the details of the specific plan, contact with peers must be preserved. Remember, the blessing of inclusion goes both ways, so to withdraw an individual completely from the group will cut off that blessing. One child may be able to spend all of his or her time with peers while leaders and classmates are trained to use a communication device. Another child may need the support of an extra adult in class for specific activities. Another child might enjoy a portion of the time with the group but would also benefit from having one-on-one instruction in the Bible story that day. When these options are not realistic, a child might be present with peers for very little of the time, but the whole group devotes prayer time to the child and gets to know more about that friend through prayer requests.

Build Options Around People

It's not helpful to construct several holes for your shape sorter and then jam every individual through only one of those holes. Concentration only on building a program often misses the mark for a child. If, for example, you only have the typical class or a special class as your options, the opportunities for children to connect with one another are limited. A child who may have several physical needs but is able to process information at the level of his or her peers would not be well served in either place. However, that child would be able to participate with peers if leaders put some physical supports in place. So individualize your placements based on the child's gifts and needs.

Begin with Same-Age Peers

As you look to create a good fit for each child, begin with looking at what is offered for children that age. Work from that base. Then prepare and add what best fits the child's unique pattern. While always maintaining some form of connection with those peers, the child needs a plan that allows for both social interaction and spiritual growth.

Take, for example, the story of Kendra, who has autism. She is six years old and enjoys sorting money. She loves to look at books. Loud noises upset her, and a schedule is very important to her. In church, Kendra enjoys children's worship time in the hallway with a trained teen helper. They dance and sing where the noise level is less intense. Kendra goes to the room with her kindergarten peers for Bible story, snack and craft times. The teachers put together a picture schedule that hangs up in the room, so Kendra knows what will happen each day. She uses her money-sorting gifts to help count the offering each week.

Director: Reverse Mainstreaming

While there are many individualized options for children, reverse mainstreaming is one overall idea that deserves consideration. For a variety of reasons, the church planning team may decide a child needs some time away from a larger group of peers while at church. It's also possible that a church already has some kind of small group set up to educate children with special needs. While a portion of time away might be necessary, reverse mainstreaming is a way to preserve peer interaction while giving opportunity for spiritual growth.

Reverse Mainstreaming Defined

The word "mainstreaming" refers to the practice of placing a child with a disability into the "mainstream"—the place where every other child that age participates and grows. Reverse mainstreaming, then, opens the separate, segregated environment and offers placements to some typically developing peers. These peers might be permanent residents of the group, or the children may rotate through those spots offering opportunities for all age-mates to participate.

One Age Group, Two Options

It's possible to set up reverse mainstreaming in a variety of ways. Basically, the church decides to match up two environments—a particular class or group and a child in a separate room or group, preferably at a similar age level. Each time the groups meet, representatives from the larger group attend the small-group environment. Some churches keep membership in these groups the same for the year while others rotate 2 to 5 peers into that setting each week or month. Either way, you create two learning and social environments for the children involved.

One Leader, Many Children

While it might be tempting to have the leader of the small group imagine the peers as additional teachers for the day, that notion is incorrect. The leader of the small group is the instructor for all of the children. While peers can be helpful in many ways, it's important for the members of the group to see themselves as equals with varied gifts and needs. The leader must create different levels of learning so that all of the children can grow from using the same materials. The leader can offer times of prayer and fellowship that place all participants on equal footing. While the group members will certainly support one another's needs, the children must clearly understand that the child with the disability is *not* the "taker" while the peers are the "givers." This is destructive to building the Body of Christ. Work to promote a place where each child can use his or her God-given gifts while receiving support for the needs in his or her life.

Building Relationships, Learning Together

A small group is an excellent place to support and appreciate one another. Be specific in setting up peer activities in which each group member has an important task. Share prayer requests, and create bonds around better understanding one another's joys and concerns. Create group art projects that involve each person's playing a role in the process and product. Many times you can use the same materials from the large group while adapting them to the varied levels represented in the group. For example, while the small-group leader may tell the Bible story as written, a peer can then read the story from a children's Bible storybook. Instead of creating individual papers, the group can create a wall mural depicting the story. One child may draw a house, another member colors it, and another child rips brown paper to glue on the house roof. That picture represents the beauty of reverse inclusion—a small group in which each member works with others and values the contributions of others.

Director: Choosing Curriculum

Children have unique strengths, abilities and learning styles. A teacher's goal is to present God's Word to children in ways that allow for understanding and life application. So any curriculum under consideration must be evaluated with the students' abilities in mind. Jessica is blind and mildly developmentally delayed; but more importantly, she can hear, feel, smell and taste. She loves to sing, listen to short stories and play with her friends. In this case, the curriculum that is chosen for Jessica and the other students must have lesson components that speak to Jessica's capabilities as well as the capabilities of the nondisabled children.

Most students with physical, visual, hearing or minor learning disabilities are able to use existing children's ministry curriculums with minor adaptations. James who is hearing impaired benefits from picture symbols that illustrate the story's sequence. A large-print Bible allows Dustin, who has low vision, to participate during the Bible reading.

Children with developmental, cognitive or multiple disabilities need curriculum that is modified to their levels of learning and understanding.

Usually, the biggest obstacle many teachers face is the belief that all students need to work on the same thing at the same time and in the same way. This sort of thinking does not allow for learning differences.

Simplify and Repeat

Choose one lesson goal or concept to emphasize, and repeat it in each activity. When one teacher chose to emphasize the concept of obedience with the story "The Fishermen Who Obeyed Jesus" (see Luke 5:1-11), she knew students with cognitive delays might have difficulty with the word "obey." So as a girl with Down syndrome entered the classroom, the teacher asked her to hang up her jacket. The child complied, and her teacher said, "Thank you for obeying; you put your jacket on the hook." She easily introduced an example of obedience and repeated similar examples throughout the students' time together.

Adjust and Accommodate

Expectations must be adjusted to meet students' needs. Some activities require more time; others need to have requirements altered. For example, while most of Susan's classmates memorized the verse "Obey the Lord your God and follow his commands" (Deuteronomy 27:10), Susan memorized two keywords: "Obey God."

Multiple learning opportunities accommodate a child's strengths. Because of Jessica's vision impairment, she can't visualize the fish, net or boat in the story. Keeping Jessica's strengths in mind, her teacher picked out activities that were based on Jessica's abilities to hear, feel and smell. As a CD of ocean sounds played in the background, the students played with toy boats and fish at the water table. During the story, Jessica was able to hold a fishing net and smell a piece of cotton dipped in fish oil to help her imagine what it would be like to be on the boat.

Modify

Sometimes students with disabilities and nondisabled students can do the same activity at the same time if minor changes are made to it. Can a child do the same activity with different materials or a simplified process? Would the child benefit from hand-over-hand prompting? The activity of cutting out fish shapes and gluing them onto a paper net was modified for several students. Lisa pressed fish stickers onto the paper. Joey is tactile defensive and needed help with the glue. Aaron played with the fish net and plastic fish while the others did the craft.

Choosing Appropriate Curriculum
for the Special Needs Classroom

The students in a self-contained special needs classroom often have more severe cognitive disabilities. You may choose to use curriculum for a younger age level, but augment it with age-appropriate pictures. Select specific lessons to meet the goals of your students, or develop lessons around simple Bible stories or topics. Repeat a lesson for several weeks. You can vary the activities while teaching the same topic over and over. *Repetition is the key to learning.*

Director: A Basic Guide for Curriculum Adaptations

Goals	• Simplify the lesson aim to one biblical goal that can be repeated throughout the lesson (Jesus loves me, God wants me to obey, etc.). • Apply the lesson to something the child can relate to in his or her everyday life.
Lesson/Story	Modify the lesson to accommodate the student's strengths. • Use sign language or picture symbols. Make sure your face is visible when talking. • Supply a large-print Bible or stories written in Braille. Explain what is happening in the classroom so that the child is not left out. • Provide instruction verbally and visually. Some students with learning disabilities have better auditory processing, while others are visual learners. Don't require this student to read aloud unless he or she volunteers. Simplify projects that require reading or writing. • Adjust length, minimize words, use visual props, and arrange for active participation to illustrate the lesson.
Memory Verse	• Have children memorize a part of the Bible memory verse or choose key words. • Use word cards, picture symbols or sign language.
Sensory Learning	Include the senses in the lesson or activities. • **Visual**—Pictures, felt figures, light-up toys, videos, flashlights, large print, Braille • **Auditory**—Musical instruments, songs, tapes of sound effects • **Tactile**—Shaving cream, rice, beans, sand, play dough, corrugated paper, feathers, cotton balls, packing materials, fidget toys, fur, real objects from lesson (fish, wood or water) • **Smell**—Perfume, spices, potpourri, extracts, fish oil
Arts and Crafts	• Simplify or reduce steps. • Provide precut craft items, stickers or shapes in place of cutting or drawing. • Tape down paper for coloring or writing. • Use hand-over-hand activities to help fine-motor skills. • Provide an alternate but similar activity. • Be aware of sensory sensitivities. For example, use markers instead of finger-paint if the child is sensitive to touch.
Games/ Activities	• Adapt rules. The child who walks with braces will be allowed to get to first base without being tagged out. • Simplify expectations. It is okay for some students to take more time or to accomplish fewer tasks. • Alter equipment. Use a beach ball in place of a softball when playing catch. • Provide assistance. The child in a wheelchair can participate in the parachute activity with a buddy's help.

Director: Leading Children with Special Needs in Worship

While there are thousands of lengthy books dedicated to better understanding worship, there is only one purpose for worship: Worship is an opportunity to have a conversation with God. While there might be other people present, the style might be traditional or contemporary and there might be a variety of tempos and volumes, the core of every worship service is the same: it provides the chance to direct our hearts to God and communicate some simple truths. Boiled down to basic language, worship communicates heartfelt phrases such as "I love You," "Thank You," "Bless You," "I'm sorry" or "Use me." As leaders, it's important to give each child present a chance to focus on God and talk to Him.

That conversation with God, however, might involve creativity on the part of the leaders when a child has some type of special need. While many children may sing words of worship, other children may need to communicate with sign language. One child might be able to call out in worship while another points to a picture that represents his or her heart. Whatever the unique areas of gifting and need, music often brings delight and a chance to join with friends and leaders in bringing praise, honor and glory to God.

Get to Know the Children as Individuals

Before you can help guide children with special needs into a conversation with God, you will need to better understand each child. What does he or she like? What areas and movements are strengths? Find out what is difficult for that child. Remember to look for strengths within areas of limitations. For example, a child may have limited movement with one hand but still be able to move the other hand in a way that allows the child to clap or tap sticks together. Find out how a child interacts with music at home or school.

Find Out What Children Do During Worship Time

Once you have spent time understanding your worshiper with special needs, examine the activities you use during worship. Don't look at what the leaders do; look at the activities and responses of the children in that setting. The list of activities and responses might include choosing songs, listening to the leader, playing rhythm instruments, doing hand motions, singing, danc-

ing, clapping, stomping, bowing, following directions, waving streamers, praying aloud, praying silently, giving prayer requests, reading words or music, holding songbooks, choral reading, watching a drama, taking part in a drama, saying Scripture, memorizing Bible verses, shaking hands with friends or playing a game. To best make this list, have someone carefully observe your worship time and list exactly what the children do as they do it.

Decide How Each Child Will Participate in Worship

Once you know the child and the worship activities, begin to think about how that child will participate in worship. Perhaps much of what happens during that time will require no modifications. Some of the activities, however, might need to be altered in a way that encourages the child's participation. Remember, you are helping to facilitate a conversation with God. This is important.

- **Preteach songs and motions.** Send a recording of the music home with the child. This allows the daily repetition of the songs and words, and the child will become very familiar with them. If you have a standard list of movements, signs or gestures, make copies of those so that a parent or volunteer could help practice or modify those actions with the child. Repetition is often very important, and building a child's storehouse of songs and motions is a benefit that lasts a lifetime.

- **For a child who is nonverbal, look at what the child *is able* to do.** Can the child point to a picture, wave a streamer or use sign language? Can the child clap, dance, play a rhythm instrument or hold a word or picture card? The book of Psalms is rich with varied ways to bring praise to God. Think about how that child may be able to communicate love and adoration to God without using words. Make those objects and opportunities available. Remember, it might be fun for other children to also enjoy other ways of conversing with God. Consider teaching all of the children some basic signs or having a bin of praise streamers, so several children can praise God in this way. Use this child with special needs to expand and grow the creativity with which the whole group can bring glory and honor to God.

- **For a child with limited language ability, participating with some of the words is an option.** A powerful technique in music is leaving out words in familiar songs. For example, an adult or group of peers can sing, "Yes, Jesus loves me. Yes, Jesus loves me. Yes, Jesus loves ____." At that point, the leader or whole group stops and the child with special needs can fill in the word "me" or point to him- or herself. It may take a few seconds, but it's worth the wait. This is also a creative way to allow a child to have a meaningful part in a program while creating sensitivity in peers. Leaving out words may also support learning partial Bible memory verses or memorized prayers or litanies.

- **If children often choose songs, it's possible for a child with limited speech or mobility to also choose favorites.** One way to do this is to draw a picture that represents a song on each face of a large six-sided cube. Have the child toss the cube to choose a song for the group to sing. Another way is to display picture cards or word cards that represent some favorite songs. Ask the child to choose or look at the picture of the song the group will sing.

- **Make use of pictures.** While others in the group may be able to read words, it's possible the child with special needs will need picture cues. Not only can you use these to help communicate words to sing, but also consider picturing prayer requests, phrases that honor God or cues for the memory verse.

- **Be aware of children who have sensitive ears.** Many children with special needs also have a different way of processing sensory input. A sound that is not loud to you may cause excruciating pain for a child with auditory sensitivity. For such a child, wearing sound-blocking headphones or worshiping with a volunteer in the hallway outside the worship room are options to consider. Some children can tolerate noise as long as they know it's possible to leave for a short break if the noise becomes too painful. Offering a quiet retreat area for this child might help support times of participation. If you see a child cover his or her ears in response to a buzzing microphone or an unexpected loud noise, consider looking at the issue of sensitive ears. This is very common, particularly for children on the autism spectrum.

Remember, two heads are always better than one when coming up with creative solutions and alternatives. As you look at the child with special needs and at the standard children's activities, remember God's command in Psalm 150:6: "Let everything that has breath praise the Lord. Praise the Lord." As the worship leader, it's a privilege and responsibility to lead each breathing child into a conversation with God.

Director: Why Learning Centers Work for Young Children

Learning centers offer opportunities to engage children in active learning experiences that are easily adapted to suit many needs and purposes. The centers consist of several areas or tables that are set up with a variety of activities designed to use a multisensory approach to enhance the aim of your lesson. Centers may include music, art, books, sensory activities, games and/or imaginative play.

Learning centers encourage exploration for young children who are discovering and giving meaning to their environment. A wide range of modalities, or methods, should be used in their setup, including auditory, visual and tactile senses and gross- and fine-motor skills.

Developmental Benefits of Learning Centers

- **Knowledge**—Children gain information by interacting with objects and people in their environment. Children with special needs require assistance in exploring their world. Most children who see a feather on the ground will pick it up, look at it, touch it and even smell it. The child in a wheelchair needs someone to help him or her have the same opportunity. Exploring is essential to learning.

- **Communication**—Young children are learning the names and meanings of objects, people and feelings. They're also figuring out how to express what they learn as each new experience introduces new words. Learning centers create an environment for language interaction. The child who has difficulty acquiring language may need adaptations such as sign language or picture symbols.

- **Working with Others**—Learning centers help children discover appropriate social interaction. Playing, taking turns, and understanding the feelings of others are important steps in development. Children with autism or developmental delays need assistance from an adult in acquiring these skills.

- **Gross-Motor Skills**—Large-muscle activities that use the whole body include walking, running, climbing, jumping, throwing and catching. Gross-motor activities develop fitness, balance, coordination and the foundation for building fine-motor skills. For some children with special needs these activities are challenging. Fun activities created to encourage movement help students develop strength and endurance.

- **Fine-Motor Skills**—Development of the muscles in the arms, hands and fingers will eventually allow children to cut, write and draw. Opportunities to develop fine-motor skills include playing with clay, stringing beads, tearing paper or building with small blocks. The special needs child may need adaptations such as spring-loaded scissors, puzzle pieces with knobs glued on or hand-over-hand assistance.

Special Needs Benefits of Learning Centers

- **Choice**—Learning centers give children the opportunity to choose activities based on their specific interests, preferences or abilities. Some students will rotate through all activities while others may choose only one. Students with special needs may need help in making choices. Make a picture card that represents each center—Blocks, Music, Art, Water Table—and place Velcro hook-and-loop fabric tape on the back of each card. Give the child a choice of two or three appropriate activities. Have the student put the Velcro card on his or her own picture schedule or on a card with his or her name and picture on it. Sometimes too many choices can be overwhelming. For some students, you will want to start by only giving one possible activity and increase the number of choices as they become comfortable with the routine.

- **Predictability**—Routine and predictability are important to young children, regardless of ability. Make centers available at the same time each week. The locations of specific centers should change as little as possible. For example, have the art center at the small table, the listening center by the bookcase, and sensory play at the water table. Expectations for changing centers and cleanup should be clear and consistent.

- **Transitioning**—Changing activities can be especially difficult for the special needs child. Use a consistent signal such as a bell or song to indicate the time to clean up centers and be ready for the next activity of the day. Students will quickly become accustomed to the signal and automatically start preparing for the next activity.

- **Visual Boundaries**—Clearly defining the area of a center helps the students keep items in the right place as well as know where they (the students) are to stay. Use small bookcases, tables and masking-tape lines to help define areas.

Types of Learning Centers

Learning centers offer a broad range of experiences that can vary from week to week. One of the benefits of having learning centers for children with disabilities is that you can always arrange to have at least one center that meets the needs of that child.

- **Arts and Crafts**—Activities in this center could include coloring with crayons, chalk or colored pencils; painting with brushes, eyedroppers, sponges or paint rollers; cutting or tearing paper; and using stamps or stickers.

- **Music**—At this center, playing musical instruments, singing on toy microphones or learning Bible songs from CDs or sing-a-long videos could take place.

- **Reading**—This center would be a place to explore picture books, board books, books for beginning readers, picture albums, books with tactile pages, books on tape, large-print Bibles or books in Braille.

- **Pretend Play**—At this center could be a play kitchen or living area with dress-up clothes, puppets, dolls, stuffed animals, play medical kits or plastic tools.

- **Sensory**—Items used in activities at this center could include shaving cream, goop, pudding or salt to draw in; and tubs of feathers, cotton balls, fabric swatches or packing peanuts. A water table filled with rice, beans, sand, pebbles, funnels, buckets, sieves, spoons and small shovels could also be placed here.

- **Fine-Motor Skills**—Activities in this center could include the use of puzzles, pegboards, sorting items, dressing boards, beads for stringing, clay or play dough.

- **Gross-Motor Skills**—Activities here may include playing with therapy balls, foam balls, ribbon sticks, scarves, a small parachute, a minitrampoline, hula hoops or tunnels. Depending on the size of your room, this center may need to move to an alternate playroom or take place outside.

Adaptations at Learning Centers

 Provide appropriate positioning to allow the child to participate in the activity. A child may be able to play with blocks on the floor if he or she is placed on an incline board. A chair insert may allow a child with balance problems to sit at the table to finger-paint. Tape papers to the table to keep them from moving when the child is writing or drawing.

 Label items in centers with words or picture symbols. Provide picture sequences in addition to verbal directions for activities.

Avoid clutter. Children with autism may be sensitive to visual and auditory clutter. Take away any unneeded items in the center. Sunglasses or noise-reducing headphones may reduce over-stimulation.

Students with cognitive delays do better at centers that involve sensory exploration such as at a water table, listening to CDs, playing musical instruments or molding clay. A peer buddy can help assist the child with more difficult activities such as making a craft or playing a game. Give clear, simple directions, and make appropriate modifications.

Children with visual impairments have an easier time seeing bright and high-contrast colors such as black, white, red and yellow. Use bright-colored tape to help identify items. For example, put bright-red tape on the handle of the shovel in the sand bin. Provide activities that involve touch and sound, such as would be found at a listening or sensory center.

Teaching: Creating Predictable Schedules

Feeling anxious about a new job or class is normal. When we understand the routine and expectations, we relax and feel more at ease. Children with disabilities are the same, but difficulty processing information can add to their anxiety and confusion. A consistent and structured routine will create a more secure environment.

Knowing What to Expect

The classroom routine should remain consistent from week to week. And it is good for students to be engaged in an activity as soon as they arrive. Jana knows that when she enters the classroom, she will be able to color pictures. She heads right to the table where crayons and paper are ready. This makes the process of separating from her mother easier. Here's a sample schedule:

- 9:00 Learning Centers
- 9:15 Circle Time
- 9:45 Outside Play
- 10:00 Snack
- 10:15 Parents Pick Up Children

Remember, the predictability of the schedule provides comfort for students.

Using Picture Schedules

A picture schedule, illustrating your timetable, allows students to see instantly what is expected of them without having to process language. Display a poster-sized schedule that is visible to all students. Attach pictures of each activity with Velcro. Here's an example:

Craft · CircleTime · Playground · Snack · Home

As each activity begins, the teacher or a student removes the appropriate picture card and places it in a container. When it's time to switch tasks, the student is easily able to identify the next activity and knows where to go.

Some students benefit from their own individualized schedule. The activities are similar to those for the group but may be customized for the child's specific needs. Here's an example of a customized picture schedule:

Clayton · Story Time · Fish Crackers · Color · Parachute · Parents

Clayton's schedule shows the activities that he likes to do. It is about 4x10 inches (10x25.5 cm) and has small pictures attached with Velcro with an envelope at the end where he places the pictures of completed activities. Physically taking off the picture and putting it in the envelope helps him transition to the next activity. Clayton loves goldfish crackers and usually starts asking for them as soon as he arrives. By having a picture of them on the schedule, he knows that he will get goldfish crackers after he plays outside.

Picture schedules can also be used to prepare a child for a new activity, a change in routine or a special event. For example, if it is Chloe's first time to come to church, you may want to give her a picture schedule before she arrives. Her parents can discuss the things she will be doing while at church. The last picture should be of the parents or home, which assures Chloe that Mom is coming after playtime. When Joseph goes to the church picnic, his mother gives him a schedule with pictures of a car, people eating, a swing set and home. Joseph eagerly hangs on to his schedule and anticipates his favorite thing, the swing set.

Making Picture Schedules

The computer programs, Boardmaker or Picture Exchange Communication System, are helpful in creating pictures and schedules. However, if you do not have access to those programs, drawing pictures or taking photographs works well. Make a base out of cardboard or poster board. Glue pictures onto card stock, laminate all parts and attach Velcro. The schedules may be vertical or horizontal with an envelope attached to the end. Sizes will vary depending on the number of pictures you want to attach and the needs of the students. Larger pictures work best with children who have visual or fine-motor impairments.

Teaching: The Sensory Factor

While some clothing claims to be "one size fits all," that is certainly not true for our sensory systems. Each one of us has a brain that takes in and processes information from our senses in unique ways. The way we process sound, touch, taste, smell, sight, movement and pressure allows us to organize our environment and learn in unique ways. God-designed, unique sensory systems give us differences as well as preferences. As a children's leader, it's important to consider the sensory factor when planning children's activities and environments.

Sensory Differences

Most mature sensory systems look like a piano keyboard focused on middle C. That's a comfortable place for an individual. Middle C allows you to take in the input you need from each sense while blocking out unimportant information. While walking in a crowded mall, for example, one can tune out the extra noises while allowing a familiar voice to penetrate the auditory channels. When putting on a new shirt, one can block out any sensation from the small collar tag rubbing the skin, but the slight touch of something hot causes an immediate reaction. Middle C lets a person accept and reject sensory information and allows the environment to be comfortable and safe.

Some individuals, however, have one or more senses set above or below middle C. For those with a sense or two above middle C, only a small amount of stimulation is necessary for that sensation to register. A slight noise might seem loud, and a loud noise might create great pain. A light touch could seem like a slap, or an uneven surface could tip a person off balance. On the other hand, for those individuals who have one or more senses set below middle C, a lot of input is necessary for a sensation to register. Sounds might need to be loud before the brain begins to process them. Spicy foods register while mild foods are tasteless.

Several children with special needs have sensory differences in one or more areas. It's important to know this information about each child so that you can best understand daily actions and reactions.

Sensory Preferences

Just as children have unique sensory systems, children also have different sensory preferences. One child may learn and remember best when given a visual diagram or picture. Another child will relate to information that enters through touch or smell or movement. While many learning activities cater to children who learn best by hearing, it's important to plan activities that appeal to the sensory preferences of all the children in the group.

One way to determine sensory preferences is to be a good observer of the children in your care. If given a set of free-choice activities, a child will often gravitate to a preference area. Notice which children tune in during a Bible story told with words, which children come to life when you show them a book that has a picture that illustrates the story and which children engage the most while holding and moving figurines that accompany the Bible story. The chances of having a child relate to and remember information presented through a sensory preference area will be very high.

Limited Senses

There are times when a child with special needs has one or more senses that are limited, not through preference or difference, but through the area of disability. For example, a child with limited vision will always need input through an alternate channel. A child who is unable to hear will need to have communication through a different sensory system. While it's important to offer sensory options to children based on preferences, it's critical that we offer alternatives for those children who have one sense completely or partially blocked.

Teaching: Storytelling Is More than Just Words

Tell me, I forget. Show me, I remember.
Involve me, I understand.
—Chinese Proverb

Jesus was the master Storyteller. His listeners were drawn to His simple language and vivid word pictures, like the story about the man who built his house on the sand only to have it smashed by the storms. As you choose stories for your class, use these questions to evaluate your choices:

- Does the story have one main point that my students can relate to their daily lives?

- Can my students picture the scenes and understand the vocabulary used in this story?

- Will this story provide sensory experiences and discussion?

- Is this story fun to tell and entertaining for students?

Tell Age-Appropriate Stories

Parents often observe teachers at church giving their fourth graders crayons and coloring pages or showing them preschool movies. This is upsetting, even when the student acts younger than his or her age. It takes a little extra work, but always interact with a student according to his or her chronological age, and include activities that can be done with a little help. For example, if your story takes place in the forest:

- **Grades 1-2**—Give students green construction paper and tell them to cut out large leaves. Tape leaves to their hands and let them hold up their arms to become a forest of trees.

- **Grades 3-4**—Let students create a forest by drawing chalk-art posters of trees and displaying them behind actors as you tell the story.

- **Grades 5-6**—Give students instant cameras and let them take pictures of trees outside. Put photos on a color copier and enlarge them to create a wall mural of trees.

Plan the Story Sequence

1. **Setting**—Where does the story take place? How can you help your students relate to that location? Show pictures, maps and books about that area. Find information about it and/or pictures of it on the Internet.

2. **Characters**—Who is the main person in the story? Age? Occupation? What is special about him or her? Can you dress up like the character or carry an object used by that person?

3. **Beginning Event or Problem**—What happens to the main person? Is there a problem or need the character must overcome?

4. **Action**—What does the main person do in response to the problem or need? If the story is too long, simplify the action steps for children with short attention spans. A general rule of thumb to keep in mind is that a child's attention span is roughly one to two minutes for each year of age; i.e., a story for six-year-olds should be about 10 to 12 minutes long.

5. **Result**—What happened as the result of the main character's decisions? Children need satisfying conclusions—"Hooray! We did it!" moments.

Use Story Props

Look at how many sensory experiences you can pull from the story. Try talking a little faster and then slower. Maintain good eye contact, and vary your facial expressions. Ask students to show you a surprised face, a mad face, happy face, etc. Are there sound effects or songs you can add that are specific to the story? How about odors or textures?

When telling Bible stories, remember that there are many things mentioned in Scripture that children may be unfamiliar with (shepherd, altar, temple, caravan, pitchers, etc.). Props can help children relate to these items.

Costumes are fun, but use caution when using them with children with special needs. Some children will not want to put on hats or head coverings. Others may not like the textures of a fabric or simply prefer to wear only their own clothes. Children may also fear that others will make fun of them if they dress up. Never push a child to do anything he or she doesn't feel comfortable doing.

Use picture signs to represent people, places and things. Most children are happy to hold up a sign and stand in place while you tell the story.

Try a Pop-Up Book

Pop-up books have paper cutouts that unfold as the story is told. There is a wide variety of these available, but look for pop-up books that have simple cutouts. Karyn Henley has created several such books (visit her website at http://www.karynhenley.com).

Involve the Students

Skits, dramas and puppetry are great ways to involve students in storytelling. The rule is to never do for students what they can do for themselves, so depending on their age and disability, include students in preparing and telling the story. They can come up with some amazing ideas.

 Children with limited mobility may enjoy narrating the story while others act it out. Or they can hold video cameras that capture the action.

  Students with learning disabilities or speech and language impairments probably won't want to read parts, but they can work sound equipment, CD players or video or digital cameras.

 Many students with developmental/cognitive disabilities or emotional/behavioral disorders enjoy puppets and can follow a story or song sound track with practice. Challenge them to spend several weeks preparing to perform a story for a younger class. They'll be so proud to serve others.

 Some students with high-functioning autism or Asperger's syndrome are very creative and may enjoy writing their own stories. They can enter

stories into computer programs to create and publish storybooks to give as gifts to family and friends.

Serve Appropriate Snacks

If characters in the story are from a different country, let children taste foods from that country during snack time. (Always be aware of food allergies.) Or as one of the learning activities for that day, let children make a snack to share with another class or to take home and retell the story. Here are a few examples:

- **Fishers-of-Men Nets**—Place fish crackers in net bags and tie with ribbon.

- **Noah's Ark**—Fill a pita bread with animal crackers, and spread jelly on the edges to seal it.

- **Food of the 5,000**—Make tuna sandwiches on small rolls.

- **The Prodigal Son's Party**—Make a traditional Jewish snack with hummus and matzos.

A good story well told is worth a thousand pictures. If you feel a little inadequate as a storyteller, keep practicing and trying. Also consider inviting a guest storyteller to your class and learn from the guest's example. Your skill and confidence level will grow over time.

Storytime Dos	and Don'ts
Speak clearly.	Speak too loudly.
Talk up to listeners.	Talk down to listeners.
Use your Bible.	Use unfamiliar vocabulary.
Be dramatic.	Move in inappropriate ways.
Accept students' comments.	Cut off students' comments.
Change the story if needed.	Complicate the story with detail.
Plan the ending.	Ramble at the end.

Teaching: The Magic of Music

Children with special needs are reached in amazing ways by the power of music. Through dance, a child's movements become controlled, fluid and purposeful. Playing with musical instruments enhances a child's range of motion and handgrip. While singing helps children with oral motor skills and pulmonary (lung) function, it also improves breath control, articulation and pronunciation. For students with severe needs, music time may be the only time we witness signs of their involvement through their displays of pure joy and exuberance.

Teachers must not shy away from music because they don't possess a good solo voice. Children don't care about a teacher's level of talent. Though live music offers more adaptability, all you really need to engage your students in the magic of music is a good CD player.

Use Simple Instruments

Buckets of instruments are available at toy and teacher stores. They might include tambourines, egg shakers, triangles, castanets and wood blocks. Plastic horns, kazoos and whistles are fun, but they require sanitizing between uses. Dried beans in a plastic container or oatmeal box with a secure lid make useful homemade shakers and drums. For kids who are unable to hold an instrument, sew small sleigh bells to pieces of elastic to create wrist or ankle bands of bells.

Show children how to play an instrument and then let them try. Play instruments in different ways: loudly, softly, with a fast tempo and a slow one, and with short sounds and long ones. Compare the different sounds of each instrument.

Give each child one instrument, line up with the children in a marching band, and turn on the music. March and push wheelchairs enthusiastically. Even the children with hearing impairments will feel and see the rhythm in the other children. Children with vision problems can hold another's hand or be guided by the shoulders. Let the children take turns conducting.

Start with Basic Rules and a Warm-Up

- Each child receives only one instrument at a time.

- Everyone remains quiet while instruments are being passed out.

- Playing does not start until directed by the teacher.

For a warm-up activity, ask children to pretend they're listening to the beginning of a rainstorm with the drops of water tapping gently. Challenge them to use their instruments to imitate what they think they might hear. Then let them increase the sound as they imagine the rain coming down harder and harder. Peak the intensity with cymbals clashing to represent the thunder and lightning. Then tell the children to play progressively more quietly until the rain fades away.

Use Music to Teach Listening Skills

Playing music can benefit children's listening skills because each child will learn when his or her rhythm is out of sync. Encourage children to tune in to the sounds around them and try to mimic them by using their hands, feet, voice and instrument. Play "Follow the Rhythm" by helping them copy a simple rhythm that you or another child plays. As a starting point, beat out the rhythm of a familiar song. Make up guess-what's-making-the-sound games by using sounds from different things in the room, musical instruments, children's voices, etc.

Use Music to Develop Language Skills

A child's heightened response to music allows teachers to encourage the growth of language skills through songs. Children who struggle to communicate need an expressive outlet that will not only improve their self-esteem but also improve other's opinions of them.

If a child is very familiar with a song but part of the song is suddenly missing, he or she will be compelled to fill in the missing part. For example, if "Jesus loves the little children. All the children of the _____" is sung, everyone in the room suddenly wants to hear the word "world." This urge for completion can be increased by leaving out the last two words, the last three and so on. In this way, a child who normally does not speak may participate in longer and longer sections of the song.

Apply Music to Memory Verses

Children who struggle with language can participate in reciting Bible verses much more easily if the verses are put to music. You can shorten Bible verses to their most essential words and teach them in a rhythmic, singsong way that can be quickly mimicked. This allows children with special needs to participate and receive the same recognition as their classmates. For example, suppose the class is learning Luke 18:27: "Jesus replied, 'What is impossible with men is possible with God.'" This could be shortened to "With God, all things are possible." This shortened verse can then be sung to the first line of "Here We Go 'Round the Mulberry Bush."

Use Visuals

As often as possible, use visuals to illustrate songs. Seeing what they hear helps children derive meaning in concrete ways. Whether a child's favored mode of taking in information is hearing or seeing, presenting both helps the child connect the two channels and gain better understanding. Pictures are invaluable, especially if new concepts are being taught.

Add Fun and Variety

Choose a variety of recorded music with drastic changes in rhythm, style and tempo. Vary your selections from classical to pop, nursery rhymes to spirituals. Choose different instrumental tunes as background music to pantomime different Bible stories. Lumber like the elephants walking into Noah's ark; crawl like the serpent weaving through the Garden. Let children pretend to be Elijah riding a chariot up to heaven (great for wheelchairs), Zacchaeus balancing in a tree, or Jesus walking on the water. Add props like branches, sheets, mirrors or clothing for costumes.

Students love physical movement added to music. While praise music is playing, call out different parts of the body for the children to move. To include a child with physical disabilities, purposely call out to the whole class something you know he or she can easily move. "Move your chin! Move your thumb! Move your eyebrows! Nod your head!" You can also request that children move their whole body and include children with disabilities by exploring movements around their physical restrictions. The goal is to encourage any movement while being sensitive to those with physical disabilities.

To gain individual interest, substitute the child's name in a song: "Jesus loves Bill! This I know." Record the class playing and singing, and let them dance to their own music.

Another way to add variety to music time is to invite guest musicians to your room. Many talented church members are willing to give a few minutes on a Sunday morning to stop in and play an instrument or sing a song or two. When your guest sees the level of enthusiasm and appreciation of your children, getting him or her to do a repeat performance is usually not a problem.

Bring Music Time to an End

Before beginning any musical activity, think about how and when it will end. When several children dance, march or play instruments all at once, the activity can turn to noise and chaos. Think ahead, set a timer, and ask the children to stop playing or dancing when they hear the buzzer. Or play a game to see who can be quiet the fastest when you say "Stop!" Make sure everyone can see your face and see what you are saying. Also remember not to end music time too abruptly. Instead, wind down gradually from faster to slower and louder to quieter songs.

Teaching: The Tactile Toolbox

Imagine a plumber who arrives at your home with only one tool. He examines the problem with the bathtub and then drives back and forth to the store, making multiple trips for the needed tools. Most plumbers would find that ineffective and arrive in a van stocked with a variety of tools, repair kits, and pieces and parts most needed to fix bathtub problems. They come equipped to handle multiple issues and circumstances.

Our children's programs also need to have a toolbox stocked with a variety of items. A plumber with one tool is laughable, and a church program with only one tool will miss opportunities to meet the needs of all those gathered. Look at the model of Jesus Christ: He offered teaching and intervention with a whole host of options. Some of His teaching was to a large group; other times he met with small groups or individuals. He used stories to teach, and He used examples from everyday life—whatever would allow people to relate and understand. Jesus interacted uniquely with those He met, giving a stern lecture or a compassionate comment based on the setting and needs of the individual or group involved. Using Jesus as its model, a church should begin to grow the children's program toolbox so that every child is included in the learning and social opportunities of the group in the best way.

Visual Tools

Many children benefit from visuals; these children need to see something in order to comprehend it. While a leader should use pictures, charts and diagrams, here are a few other tools that might support the needs of visual learners:

- **Make the schedule visual.** Use pictures or words to show what the group will do that day or month. It's best to use a schedule that shows the sequence of activities. Add specific times only if they are completely accurate. Make the picture or word pieces moveable so that any necessary changes can be easily made.

- **Make time visual.** Many children struggle to understand "in a little while" or "in five minutes." Consider using a visual timer, which displays time with a red color dial that disappears over time (see such timers available from Time Timer on the Web, http://www.timetimer.com).

- **Make a picture file.** Have a volunteer or teen begin a folder file (or a scrapbook with plastic pages) to which pictures can be continually added. Include pictures of schedule items as well as pictures of Bible characters or favorite songs. Having all needed pictures in one place will save time.

- **Consider making a welcome story.** Sometimes it's helpful to write out ahead of time a story of what you are going to do during church and then give each child with special needs a copy of the story at least a day before the class will gather. This gives the child information in advance and let's the child practice the day before arriving. Barbara J. Newman's *Church Welcome Story,* available from the CLC Network, could be used as a sample to follow.

Writing Tools

Writing can be a difficult area for many children with special needs, so get to know what a child is using at home or school to help support writing needs. The following list contains some of the more common things to consider:

- **Seating**—While our churches often have small children's heads peeking above oversized tables, remember that 90-degree angles are best for writing. Feet should be flat on the floor with knees and elbows at 90-degree angles to the writing surfaces. Don't expect a child to write if his or her body is not stabilized.

- **Grips and Pencils**—Many times, it's helpful to have pencil grips or writing tools that support weaker hands. Try breaking crayons or pencils into smaller pieces. Larger pencils or crayons as well as writing utensils shaped like triangles can also help give support. Trial and error usually help decide what will work.

- **Adapted Tools**—Check with parents to find out if the child uses any adapted tools. Sometimes a special scissors or glue bottle will allow a child to participate in an activity. Or a child may have a laptop computer or slant board to facilitate writing tasks.

- **The Amount of Writing**—For a child who struggles with writing, decrease the amount of writing that is required. Have the child fill in just one word or answer only two questions.

- **A Scribe or Buddy**—Remember, the object of church is not to teach writing, but church often uses writing to help a child learn. Therefore, have two children work together on one paper while talking about each question, or supply a scribe or buddy for the child who needs writing support.

Reading Tools

We often ask children to read as part of a lesson. Here are some ideas for struggling readers:

- **Add color.** Highlighting text with color can often help support readers. Consider copying a passage onto colored paper. Consider purchasing E.Z.C. Readers to highlight text one line at a time. Highlighting tape is also a great option; this can safely be placed over text in a book and will peel off after use. (See products available at http://www.reallygoodstuff.com.)

- **Preteach the reading passage.** Consider sending home the verse or portion of reading ahead of time. Let the child practice reading a section that will be used the following day or week.

- **Limit the amount of reading**. If other children are reading a page, perhaps ask the struggling reader to read a paragraph or a sentence.

- **Use a buddy or a recorded voice.** Remember, the goal of church is not to teach reading but to use reading as a tool in learning. Consider having a peer read to the struggling reader, or provide the child with a recorded version of the passage.

Sensory Tools

It's critical in the area of sensory tools to know what specific tools a child uses to help create a more comfortable sensory environment. Talk to parents, and learn how and when to use those tools. The following list contains some of the items commonly used to help children adjust to their surroundings:

- **Movement Supports**—Some children need to rock or move in order to focus or stay calm. Examples of helpful items that could be available in a classroom include a rocking chair, an indoor swing, an inflatable seat cushion or a minitrampoline.

- **Weighted Items**—Some children need heavier items for periods of about 20 minutes at a time in order to be comfortable and at rest. Providing a weighted blanket, vest or lap pad can support those needs. Some children wear weighted wrist and ankle weights or use weighted pencils. It's important that these weighted items be used properly so that children won't adjust to the weight, making the exercise ineffective. Talk to parents to get clear instructions for the use of these items.

- **Sound Blockers**—Some children need ways to restrict noise. Sound-blocking devices like construction workers use, large headphones or earmuffs can help, or a child may have a specially designed system. Making these available can allow a child to be much more at ease in a noisy environment.

Whatever tools you choose to use, remember to explain them in such a way as to make all the children comfortable. Let the group know, for example, that some people need eyeglasses in order to read and others need to highlight reading with color. Having two of each item allows other children to try out the items so that no one child is singled out. Enjoy finding other ways to grow your tool box, but this is a great place to begin your set (see also "Adaptive Products and Product Sources," p. 178).

Inclusive Centers Work for All Children

"Be doers of the word."

James 1:22, NKJV

Teaching: Building Inclusive Learning Centers

Learning centers are a wonderful way to allow younger children to explore new materials, enjoy making choices of interest to them and interact with others in the learning process. Learning centers are also an excellent way to offer opportunities to *all* of the children in your group, including those with special needs. Making some simple changes in the materials and activities will allow children to better access each center and build relationships with others. Such changes will help support children who may either excel or experience need in a particular area. Choose supports that make sense for the children in your group. The ideas listed here and on the charts are given to get your own creative juices flowing (see also "I See; I Hear; I Touch" on p. 87 and "I Taste; I Smell; I Move; I Giggle" on p. 88).

Ideas for Setting Up Learning Centers

- Use simple words to label items in your centers.

- Store learning-center items in cardboard file boxes in a closet or resource center for easy rotation and setup.

- Collect safe props and visual display boards of photos of children using centers. These also make a wonderful display when recruiting and training teachers.

Ideas for Setting Up a Bible Times Learning Center

Bible terms and objects are foreign to today's children. But a Bible Times Learning Center will help children relate to everyday life in Bible times and better understand how people lived and worked in the past. Children with disabilities often have great imaginations, and hands-on Bible centers give Bible stories new meaning. Here are a few examples of Bible stories and the items you could make available at the Bible Times Learning Center:

- Martha's and Mary's House—Fruit bowls, pitchers of water, towels, pillows, Bible-times clothes (sandals, lengths of fabric for robes, etc.), etc.

- Jesus by the Sea—Boats, nets, sails, sand, shells, water, play fish, etc.

- Peter in the Marketplace—Tables with baskets of vegetables or fruits, play coins, bowls of grains, etc.

- Jesus at the Temple—Scrolls, string instruments, Passover foods, pictures of temples, a stone altar, pictures of Jesus as a boy, etc.

Traditional Learning Centers	Unique Learning Centers
Home Living Center	Pet Shop Center
Book or Block Center	Big and Little Center
Art Center	In and Out Center
Water Center	Doctor's Office Center
Puzzle Center	Bakery Center
Nature Center	Computer Center

Tips: I See; I Hear; I Touch

Ideas to Support Children Who Benefit from Visuals

- While it's helpful to give verbal instructions, consider giving picture or word instructions at each center to help remind children about what to do.

- If appropriate, include a few samples of a finished product or start one of the projects for children to continue and finish.

- At each learning center, have a classroom helper who can do the activity, creating a good visual model to follow.

- Consider making bold outlines around or highlighting the portion of the page children will color, or make an outline of how to place the blocks to form, say, a temple replica.

- Consider offering strong color contrasts. Setting boldly colored objects on a white or black surface allows the objects to better stand out to children.

Ideas to Support Children Who Benefit from Auditory Input

- Provide clear verbal directions, and offer one step at a time.

- Control background noise, so children can focus on verbal input. Some children benefit from a sound system that pipes the leader's words into headphones the children can wear. If children use these in other settings, borrow them for church times, too.

- Leave a tape recorder at each center and make a tape of instructions and directions for children to listen to.

- Appoint a peer to read a set of instructions one at a time to children.

- Tell children what you want them to do. If a child has limited language understanding and you say, "Don't touch the paint," the child may have only registered the second and fourth words: "touch" and "paint." By instead suggesting, "Fold your hands," the child knows exactly what to do until instructed to paint.

Ideas to Support Children Who Benefit from Tactile Input

- Provide actual figurines for children to manipulate; these will bring to life many Bible stories for children. Flannel-graph pieces are also great items to touch and move at a center.

- Hide story items in a tub of sand or rice. Let children dig for items that connect with the theme for the day.

- Put together a guessing station where children can reach in a box without looking and try to guess what's inside the box. This allows children to explore with touch and put language to that exploration.

- Cover items with materials of different texture (flannel, cotton, sandpaper, etc.) at a craft center. For stories concerning shepherds, put cotton on paper lamb cutouts. For the story about Moses in the basket, make a blanket out of scraps of various materials.

Tips: I Taste; I Smell; I Move; I Giggle

Ideas to Support Children Who Benefit from Oral Input

- Allow children to have water bottles. Not only is water good for children, but also it's an appropriate item to put in the mouth and enjoy repeatedly. Some children listen more attentively while drinking water.

- Make a tasting center that illustrates the story for the day, and then enjoy eating the food with the children. Make the wall of Jericho out of cheese crackers. Put animal crackers two by two on a folded paper plate to mimic the story of Noah. Use bottled cheese to decorate round crackers with happy faces and sad faces to remember the stories about Good Friday and Easter.

- Use cereal or other small snacks to help count out important parts of the story. Count out the 10 lepers and then eat the number who did not come back to thank Jesus. Set out one piece of cereal for each disciple. How many children did Jacob have? Cereal counting and sorting can be a lot of fun—as well as tasty.

- Have children form pairs to make a food treat to share. Put out a recipe and allow pairs to make and enjoy one treat. It might be a no-bake cookie recipe, a smoothie made in a baggie, or trail mix. This allows the children to work together and enjoy a treat as well.

A Note of Caution: Before offering foods to the children, it's important to know about any food allergies or sensitivities to food that children in your group have.

Ideas to Support Children Who Benefit From Olfactory Input

- Consider beginning a story by introducing a smell. Some Bible stories or holidays lend themselves well to scent containers. Have the children guess what might be in the container.

- Consider setting up a center with several scent containers, and have the children match each scent to a picture of the object associated with the scent.

- Create a partner activity in which the children work in pairs to make a scent container for others to guess. Set out choices, and let children pick a favorite scent to capture in a bottle or small vial.

A Note of Caution: Watch out for children who may have allergies to scents. Hay, grass, nuts, perfumes and scents from other items can irritate certain children.

Ideas to Support Children Who Benefit from Motor Input

- Consider seating that moves gently. Add a rocking chair, an inflatable seat cushion or a small hammock for children to use in book centers or other quiet areas.

- Add a center where children can act out the story. Find a few standard props to start with (a small wooden rocking boat, some nets for casting into pretend water, dress-up clothes for Bible-times costumes, etc.).

- Provide an area for dance and worship. If no leader is available for this center, try getting some worship DVDs and letting children move with the leaders on the TV screen.

Ideas to Support Children Who Benefit from Good Old-Fashioned Fun

- Tap into the creativity of others. You may have a church member, for example, who works with clay and a potter's wheel. What a wonderful center to offer the children as you talk about God forming us from the dust of the earth.

- Turn a center into an area that better describes the friend with special needs. If that child uses sign language, consider an area where children will learn some signs and perhaps use those movements in a song or poem.

- Expect messes as part of the day, and then be surprised if cleanup is minimal.

- Create centers where children can play and laugh together. It's a common language for all children.

Teaching: Every Child for the Kingdom

Children with special needs and their families are the largest unreached mission field in America. Children's ministry specialist and author Karyn Henley says, "The gospel is not a rote message. It's the passionate overflow of who you are!"* Does that passion overflow in your church to reach every child for the Kingdom?

Children with Disabilities Need Salvation

Some people act as if children affected by disabilities shouldn't be burdened with spiritual things. When their time is spent with doctors, physical therapists, counselors and speech therapists, going to church can seem like just another appointment. Their parents also ask pressing questions: "Why does my child have to be different? If Jesus has the power to heal, why doesn't He heal my child? How can my child possibly comprehend God's ultimate plan?"

Sadly, many Christians are baffled by these questions, too. Some churches provide physical care for children with special needs so that adults can attend worship, yet they miss their true mission of partnering with parents to introduce the children to Jesus Christ as Savior and Lord. But before church leaders and teachers can create an effective evangelism plan for their special needs ministry, the church must understand and affirm three basic truths:

1. The Great Commission is for all.

2. All children need faith.

3. All children are God's treasures.

1. The Great Commission Is for All

When Jesus commanded His followers to go and make disciples, He made no exceptions. According to Matthew 28:19-20, Jesus said, "Go and make disciples of all nations, baptizing them in the name of the Father and of the Son and of the Holy Spirit, and teaching them to obey everything I have commanded you." The church's mandate is to reach every child for the kingdom of God. Children come to know God by believing in His Son, Jesus Christ, and by growing through the power of the Holy Spirit, who indwells each believer. We can depend on the Holy Spirit to know and reveal a child's spiritual capacity. As we prayerfully preach the good news, children will believe God's promises and share their faith story as they are able.

2. All Children Need Faith

What we believe concerning a child's salvation is critical to how we minister to him or her. Are children with disabilities still sinners in need of God's grace? Or do they somehow have a free ticket into heaven? In Romans 3:23 we're assured that "all have sinned and fall short of the glory of God." Does a child's salvation depend on each child's level of functioning and understanding? What about the "age of accountability"?

All children are capable of experiencing God's love in amazing ways, even if they are severely disabled. Yet many Christians seem confused about how to meet these children's spiritual needs. In Ephesians 1:5 (*NLT*), Paul tells us that "[God's] unchanging plan has always been to adopt us into his own family by bringing us to himself through Jesus Christ." We don't need to know each child's age of accountability in order to introduce him or her to Jesus. God sees every heart, and He will be faithful to bring forth spiritual fruit from the seeds that we have planted through our teaching and our love for each child with special needs.

3. All Children Are God's Treasures

Jesus said, "Whoever receives one little child like this in My name receives Me" (Matthew 18:5, *NKJV*). In the heart of a child, we see the humble, teachable spirit that is so treasured by our heavenly Father. Children with special needs model the values of the kingdom of heaven, where the innocent and pure hearted are treasured and their weaknesses reveal God's strength.

All children are capable of experiencing God's love in amazing ways, even if they are severely disabled.

*Karyn Henley, "Presenting the Salvation Message to Children" (Children's Pastor Conference, Dallas, TX, 2002, tape 501), quoted in "Be a Hero, Lead a Child to Christ," *International Network of Children's Ministry,* http://www.incm.org/MinistryTools/ChildrensMinistry GreatIdeas/ChildrensMinistryChallenges/31629.aspx (accessed May 29, 2008).

Teaching: Assessing a Child's Understanding of Truth

Children relate to life from their own limited set of experiences. They quickly learn to make their needs known, and they ask a multitude of questions beginning with "why." When children receive kind and loving responses, they develop trust-worthy relationships. They see the character of God through the actions of faithful Christians in their lives. As children hear their parents, grandparents and teachers pray in the name of Jesus, they begin to ask what knowing Jesus means.

God speaks to kids! Dr. James Dobson, founder of Focus on the Family, says he clearly recalls praying with his mother at the age of three. What are your earliest memories of the Lord's presence in your life? When did you realize that God loved and cared for you?

Most children with physical, emotional or learning disabilities have the same capacity to accept or reject Christianity as any person. "Students with mental retardation will have the most difficulty with religious concepts," says Dr. Jim Pierson. "Of this group, 85 percent can be taught the facts about faith on a twelve-year-old level."* And in cases where a child cannot comprehend basic facts, we can confidently trust that God covers that child with His love and mercy.

If you feel inadequate to talk about Jesus, first ask the Holy Spirit to guide you. Pray that He will be so evident in your life that children will see the fruit of His Spirit and desire it for themselves (see Galatians 5:22-23). The Holy Spirit is the only agent of effective change in our lives. Below are four ways that the Holy Spirit works in the heart of a child:

1. The Holy Spirit prepares a child's heart to hear the gospel (see Acts 11:24; 13:1-2; 16:6-7; Ephesians 4:11).

2. The Holy Spirit gives a child the desire to turn away from sin (see Luke 15:20-21; John 16:8; Acts 11:18).

3. The Holy Spirit leads children into a new life (see John 3:5-8).

4. The Holy Spirit helps children grow to obey Jesus as Lord (see 1 Corinthians 2:4-5).

Your changed life is another powerful witness to children in your ministry. John encourages us to tell "that . . . which we have heard, which we have seen with our eyes . . . and our hands have touched" (1 John 1:1). Share with children what you thought about God before you knew Him personally. Explain that God helped you recognize your need for Jesus and understand His forgiveness. Show them the difference that serving Christ has made in your life.

If you're unsure of a child's level of comprehension, talk with him or her using God's Word as your guide. It's been said that the whole Bible is summed up in John 3:16 because it contains the three foundational truths about salvation. Use this verse as a basis to ask the children questions and comment on salvation:

- **"For God so loved the world that he gave his one and only Son"—Do you believe that God loves you?** (Assure children that they can't do anything to earn or to lose God's love.)

- **"That whoever believes in him shall not perish"—Do you know what doing wrong, or sinning, means? Sin hurts everyone and breaks God's heart.**

- **"But have eternal life"—Do you like gifts? Jesus is a gift from God. He is better than any gift you could ever get because He gives us God's wonderful love.**

As your relationship with a child grows, you'll sense the child's response and know when to invite him or her to pray a simple prayer:

Dear God,
Thank You for sending Your Son, Jesus, to die for me. I'm sorry for my sins and for living for myself. Please forgive me. I give You my life to use in Your kingdom. Help me to love and serve You every day.
In Jesus' name, amen.

With some children, you may need to simplify a bit more by omitting one or more phrases. For example:

Dear God,
Thank You for loving me. Please forgive me and help me to love You every day. Amen.

*Jim Pierson, *Exceptional Teaching: A Comprehensive Guide for Including Students with Disability* (Cincinnati, OH: Standard Publishing, 2002), p. 211.

Teaching: Four Ways to Present the Gospel

1. Salvation Road

Cover an 8-foot (2.4-m) table with green butcher paper and tape the ends under the table. Draw a winding road down the center with a brown marker. Block the road off into 12 squares and add one small toy car per child. On index cards, write the references to age-appropriate Bible verses about salvation. Include some cards with simple questions about the verses for discussion. On each card, write a "1," "2" or "3" to indicate the number of squares a child can move his or her car forward. On toy road signs (available at toy stores), write the following Bible verses, and place the signs along the road.

STOP: Romans 3:23

U-TURN: Romans 6:23

YIELD: Romans 5:6

ONE WAY: Romans 10:9

GO: Romans 8:16

Say to the children, **Have you ever been on a vacation? Where did you go? Where would you like to go that you have never been before? This road represents the highway of life. We're all on a journey toward heaven. The Bible is our map and gives us clear road signs. You may pick a car to represent your life. Then we'll take turns choosing a card and following the directions to answer questions and move along the path**

2. Basic Gospel and Childhood Songs

Songs are wonderful evangelism tools. There are powerful truths in old hymns like "Amazing Grace," "Just As I Am" and "Jesus Loves Me." And childhood favorites can be sung with new words. For example, any child can sing to Jesus to the tune of "Frère Jacques":

I am sorry. I am sorry.
I was wrong. I was wrong.
Will you please forgive me?
Will you please forgive me?
Let's be friends.
Let's be friends!

(Words by Linda Smith)

3. Gospel-Truth Card Game

To help children memorize Bible verses about salvation, create a matching card game. Cut 10 large index cards in half. Write half of the Bible verse on one half of the card and the other half of the verse on the other half of the card. Symbols may also be substituted for words.

God will

forgive our sins (see 1 John 1:9).

Jesus died

for my sins (see 1 Corinthians 15:3).

Jesus promised

eternal life (see John 3:16).

You can be a member

of God's family (see John 1:12).

Mix the cards up on a table and lay them faceup, so the children can see the verses. Ask a child to pick one card and read it. Ask another child to point to the matching card. Let the children take turns matching the cards and looking up the verses in their Bibles. Some children enjoy being timed to see who can match and say the verses the fastest. Everyone is a winner in this game, because they're learning God's Word.

4. Skits

Jesus told dramatic stories about God's love and plan for His people. As you read together, encourage students to act out each story, paying attention to what the characters saw, heard, touched, smelled and felt. You'll be surprised how your students will add their sensory experiences to get deeper into Jesus' message.

- The Wise Man Builds on Rock, and the Foolish Man Builds on Sand—(see Matthew 7:24-27; Luke 6:47-49)

- The Lost Sheep (see Matthew 18:12-14; Luke 15:4-7)

- Jesus Talks with a Samaritan Woman (see John 4:5-26)

- Preparing for the Last Supper (see Mark 14:12-16; Luke 22:7-13)

- The Resurrection (see Matthew 28:1-8; Mark 16:1-8; Luke 24:1-12; John 20:1-10)

Teaching: Ten Ways to Teach Memory Verses

I have hidden your word in my heart that I might not sin against you. Psalm 119:11

Think creatively, and you can teach almost anyone God's Word. Never underestimate your students or limit them based on what you think they can or can't do. The key to memorizing Bible verses is repetition and using a combination of hearing, vision, touch and movement.

1. Pocket-Chart Matching Game

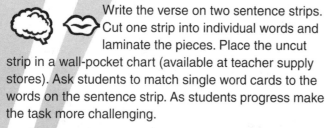 Write the verse on two sentence strips. Cut one strip into individual words and laminate the pieces. Place the uncut strip in a wall-pocket chart (available at teacher supply stores). Ask students to match single word cards to the words on the sentence strip. As students progress make the task more challenging.

- Hand word cards to students, and ask them to match the corresponding words on the sentence in the pocket chart.

- Mix up the word card order, and repeat the above activity.

- Remove the sentence strip, and have students place word cards in order.

2. Sign Language

 Combine vocal language with signs for keywords. This allows students to use multiple modalities of learning—auditory, visual and kinesthetic.

3. Verse Songs

 Students with speech problems are often good singers, and they find it is easier to remember words set to music. Have children sing the verse to the tune of a familiar childhood favorite.

4. Picture Pairing

 Create picture word symbols to increase meaning. Place each picture on a card. Ask students to put pictures in order or match pictures to appropriate words. Using pictures or symbols helps students understand word meanings. Computer programs are available that allow you to type out words with picture symbols (see "Creating Predictable Schedules," p. 77).

5. Magnetic Letters

 Hide magnetic letters for the verse in a bucket of rice, beans or sand. On a metal tray, place a written copy of the verse. Let students find the letters and match them to the words on the tray.

6. Sensory Writing

 Write keywords of the verse in shaving cream, finger paint, pudding or salt. The sense of touch makes a lasting imprint on the brain.

7. Cut and Paste

 Cut out words of the verse from magazines or newspapers. Paste the words in order on a piece of construction paper. For students who need help, write the words on the construction paper for matching.

8. Computer Writing

Many students with limited verbal skill are able to use computers. Write a verse on a small index card and Velcro or tape it to the monitor, so students can copy as they type.

9. Beanbag Game

Attach small plastic bins to a piece of plywood or heavy cardboard measuring 4x4 feet (1.2x1.2m). In the bottom of each bin, place a keyword and/or picture from the verse. Challenge students to throw a beanbag into the appropriate bin as they recite the verse. This game encourages dialogue and uses sight, movement and language.

10. Velcro Bible

 Laminate a piece of black construction paper; fold it in half like a Bible cover. Inside, attach one strip of Velcro to the left side and four horizontal strips of Velcro to the right side. Write the memory verse on a small index card, apply Velcro to the card and attach the card to left side of the folded paper. Write each word of the verse on individual pieces of card stock. Laminate and attach Velcro to each card-stock piece. Ask students to place the words in verse order, using the verse on the index card as a guide. For a greater challenge, remove the index card. To the back of the folded paper, attach an envelope for storing cards.

Teaching: Adapting Games for Various Abilities

For many of us, our best childhood memories come from playing games with our friends. Games provide a way to increase physical skills, learn how to interact with others and have fun. The child with special needs, however, often feels left out or unsure of how to participate.

As James keeps score for the baseball game, he longs to run around the bases like his friends. James feels trapped in his wheelchair, so instead of playing, he just keeps score. Danny always feels sick to his stomach right before activity time. He has difficulty with coordination, and most children don't want him on their team. He'd rather hide than face rejection one more time. Susan's hypersensitivity to sound and her inability to read social cues make playing games almost unbearable, so she usually doesn't want to play games.

Our job as teachers is to find ways to help all children feel wanted, included and safe.

How do I adapt games so all children can participate?

Including James in the baseball game only takes a few adaptations. Being in a wheelchair limits James's range of motion, so instead of the ball being pitched to him, he can use a baseball tee. James can have a runner push him around the bases. Some students with physical disabilities may need to have the distance between bases shortened, while others may need to use a larger-sized plastic bat and ball. Think of individual needs while still making the game appropriately challenging—not too easy, not too hard. Identify the elements of the game that need to be modified.

- **Equipment**—Do adjustments need to be made for weight or size? Can adaptations be made? Sam's class had a small golf-putting game. To enable Sam to hold the handle of the plastic club, his teacher made a Velcro strap that wrapped around the club and Sam's wrist. Sam also used a larger-sized plastic golf ball, which would be easier for him to hit.

- **Distance**—Should variations be made in length, space or height? Lower the height of a basketball hoop, lessen the distance of a race or shorten the space between bases.

- **Time or Repetitions**—Does the student need more attempts to complete the task? Should the time requirement be shortened or lengthened? Give the student the opportunity to succeed without becoming frustrated.

- **Rules**—Should rules or expectations be simplified? Students were participating in a relay in which they held spoons in their mouths, placed a marshmallow on the spoon, walked 10 feet (.3m) and transferred the marshmallow to another team member's spoon. Several adaptations were made: Jana held the spoon in her hand instead of her mouth. Jason didn't use a spoon; he carried the marshmallow to his team member in his hand. Lisa has multiple disabilities, so her buddy placed the marshmallow in Lisa's lap and pushed her wheelchair to the other side. All the students were able to participate, but the expectations for each were different.

How do I make game playing fair so that the child with special needs won't feel singled out?

Danny's anxiousness about playing games resulted from too many experiences of being singled out as different or always being chosen last. Students like Danny can benefit from games that don't have winners or losers or games in which teams work together in groups.

- **Balloon Corral**—Students stand in a large circle and are given a color. Balloons of corresponding colors are scattered in the circle. When the teacher calls a specific color, each student with that color runs into the circle and tries to kick out all the balloons that are not their color. Because several students are in the circle at the same time, no child is singled out. A child in a wheelchair can have a buddy help push the wheelchair to move the balloons. Other students may be allowed to use their hands. (Check for latex allergies.)

- **Parachute Activities**—Students hold the edges of a large piece of cloth while lifting it up and down, throwing plastic or foam balls on it to bounce or taking turns hiding underneath it. This activity has no winners or losers and is easily adaptable for all students. Straps can be added to make holding easier, buddies can assist those who need it and students in wheelchairs can easily participate.

What do I do for the child who doesn't want to play games?

There are many reasons why children may be reluctant to participate in games. Students on the autism spectrum are often uncomfortable in social situations or have difficulties when rules are not followed precisely. Games can be painful for students with hypersensitivities to sound, light or touch. Other students may be fearful of trying something new. The better you know your students, the easier it will be to determine how to help them be included.

Susan is more likely to participate in an activity with only one or two other students in a quiet environment. She likes jumping on the trampoline and rolling on the therapy ball. Inviting one or two students at a time to join her helps Susan learn how to interact with others without causing her to become overstimulated.

Consider these options:

- Will the student do better in a smaller group?

- How can I change the environment in regard to sound, light and touch?

- Would having a buddy make it easier for the student to participate?

- Can I give the student a small game-related job that is not intimidating, such as timekeeper or game starter? (As the student becomes comfortable with whatever is going on, he or she will be more likely to join the game.)

What are the benefits of playing inclusive games?

When students with and without disabilities learn how to interact and play together, they benefit physically, socially and emotionally. Susan J. Kasser states in her book *Inclusive Games: Movement Fun for Everyone!*

Inclusive games, therefore, offer a supportive environment that enhances each child's self-confidence, regardless of physical ability. Inclusive games can teach children how to succeed, how to accept the strengths and limitations of everyone involved, and how to strive for improvement.*

God has given each person a unique role in His Church. He did not intend for any one person to stand alone or be isolated. He did intend for us to work together and learn from each other.

What are basic game adaptations?

- Adjust size, weight and height of equipment. Provide alternative equipment (for example, a beach ball in place of a volleyball). Let students use scooter boards instead of crawling or walking through an obstacle course.

- Provide a picture sequence for directions. Have a buddy be responsible for making student aware of any sound cues. Use a flag to indicate the beginning of a race.

- Give clear directions and explanations, letting the child know what is happening now and what will happen next. Describe the activity in progress. Allow the student to explore any equipment before using it. Put bright or contrasting tape on balls or targets.

- Use silent cheers—students cheer with their hands instead of their voices. Be aware of hypersensitive children who avoid touching, excessive noise or visual stimulus when necessary. Make rules and expectations clear and consistent.

- Simplify rules, model the expected action, and provide buddy assistance.

- Be creative!

*Susan J. Kasser, *Inclusive Games: Movement Fun for Everyone!* (Champaign, IL: Human Kinetics, 1995), p. 7.

AWANA Working with Special Needs Children*

The ABCs of Working with Children with Special Needs

A—Acknowledge the child's uniqueness and giftedness.

B—Believe that the child can accomplish good things.

C—Challenge yourself to develop tactics and strategies to help the clubber on an individual basis.

D—Dare to give yourself to make a difference in the life of the child and family.

E—Eternity is at stake. Always remember this.

F—Focus on the child, not the disability.

G—God can do great things. Grow in wisdom and stature with God and man.

H—Hearts will be blessed.

I— Involve the child in the club. Give intervention that allows the child to function at his or her true potential.

J—Jesus loves each child.

K—Keep working at it! Don't become discouraged.

L—Lead the child by your example.

M—Make adjustments and allowances.

N—Never give up. Never allow the child to say "I can't." At the same time, be aware of the child's ability level. Don't frustrate him or her.

O—Offer creative solutions to the family.

P—Praise and encourage the child. See his or her potential. Pray continually. Provide appropriate interventions.

Q—Quote and meditate on God's Word. He has a plan!

R—Reach out to the clubber and his or her family.

S—Shower the child with love, acceptance and support.

T—Teach the child in a way he or she can learn.

U—Utilize the child's talents.

V—Value each and every child.

W—Widen your vision of what God can do.

X—X-ray your motives.

Y—*You can do it!*

Z—This is not the end but just the beginning of what we hope is a great child/leader relationship.

Large-Group Time

Jenny's clear voice filled the room as she sang about God's love. No one moved; they didn't want to miss a note of the melody or a word of the lyrics. They understood that Jenny was singing her own words to music she had written herself. Applause exploded at the conclusion, and immediately five girls rushed out to the platform for the opportunity to wheel Jenny's chair off the stage. See, Jenny is a quadriplegic—she cannot use her arms or her legs.

Use Large Group Time to highlight the strengths of all your clubbers, but don't forget your kids with special needs. Many of them are talented. Provide opportunities for them to shine and contribute. Share stories of famous people who had special needs yet triumphed because of God. Take this time to share with the children how they can be kind to and considerate of one another, regardless of differences. God made them all, loves them all, died for them all, and has a plan for them all. In the most critical ways, kids with special needs are the same as all children. They are created by a loving God, and they are sinners in need of a Savior.

Social Considerations

- **Avoid distracting stimuli.** This is good advice for talking to any group of children. Arrange the children so that they're looking at a wall, not out a window or at the door to the hallway.

- **Make sure the room is uncluttered.**

- **Break up your lesson** so that the children aren't sitting for a long period of time.

- **Use a multisensory approach.** Vary your teaching. Involve the students with visuals, music and object lessons.

- **Incorporate various learning styles.** Ask clubbers to repeat verses or phrases in unison.

- **Seat a clubber with special needs next to you.** Use your hands, eyes and voice to guide. If appropriate, sit near the front of the room so that the clubber can experience what is happening.

- **Use verbal and nonverbal cues to count.**

- **Ask a clubber with special needs to help** erase white boards, pass out paper or hold song lyrics.

- **If a child is deaf, ask someone to sign the lesson.**

- **Write out the announcements, and send them home** with clubbers who may have difficulty understanding what you're saying.

Testimonies and Explanations

Ask a child with a special need to give a testimony, if he or she is capable. You could work with the child before the club meeting or ask a parent to help. Sometimes children with special needs feel comfortable explaining their disability to others. Other times they don't. Don't force a child to do something he or she doesn't want to do. Share testimonies or watch a movie about someone who has a special need (such as one about the life of Joni Eareckson Tada).

The Bible Lesson

- Make sure you have the child's attention. Vary your tone of voice, maintain eye contact, model excitement and enthusiasm, and ask questions to generate discussion and interest.

- Keep clubbers' attention by allowing them to participate repeating and retelling the story. Present your lesson well, with a minimum of down time.

- Be patient when waiting for a child to answer a question. The average time for a child to respond is 2.6 seconds.

- Use bright visuals with simple patterns, verbalizing what is pictured for those who are visually impaired.

- Use the Large Group Time lesson provided in *Awana for Me: A Guide to Working with Special Needs Children.*

Handbook Time

The leaders recognized that Susan had a serious learning disability the very first night she came to club. She played the games (although she didn't do well at them) and answered basic questions, but she didn't give out too much information. The leaders attempted to visit the parents but to no avail. The parents never seemed to be home, the phone number was unlisted, and Susan came to Awana with some neighborhood kids.

All year Susan attended club, patiently sitting through Handbook Time but accomplishing nothing. Periodically, leaders would find a few minutes to work with her, but she didn't seem to respond to their attempts. Near the end of the year, after one of the older clubbers had completed her handbook, a leader gave the older clubber a short and easily understandable verse and asked her to teach it to Susan. The leader promised that if the girl taught Susan the verse, both of them would earn shares. Susan *said* the verse! The helping clubber was proud, Susan was proud, and the leaders were elated. One-on-one attention from a peer was what it took!

Adapt the Work

Handbook Time can be the most frustrating part of club for children with special needs. The story of Susan is a true one, but some clubbers will not be able to recite an entire verse no matter who works with them. By adapting the work through modification, limiting the number of verses, giving the clubber more time to complete a task, and teaching organizational and memory skills, most clubbers with special needs will progress. A corollary goal of the Handbook Time is that the clubbers will develop habits and skills while taking responsibility for their work. The process will help them gain independence.

Remember your ultimate goal: You want to reach all clubbers for Christ. You want to teach all clubbers the good things God says in His Word. That's more important than finishing the handbook. Set high expectations, but do not cloud the real purpose of Handbook Time.

Remember Some General Things

- Become familiar with the strength(s) as well as the weakness(es) of each clubber.

- Utilize the clubber's strength as well as his or her preferred style of learning.

- Allow each clubber to do as much as possible by him- or herself.

- Explain the content of the verse. Ask questions to make sure the clubber understands what you're saying.

- Ask questions to make sure the clubber understands what you want him or her to do.

- Challenge two clubbers to race each other in saying the verse.

- Allow the clubber to share what he or she thinks and feels.

- Use sign language, music and illustrations to teach and help the clubber memorize.

- Put the verse on sentence strips. Challenge the clubber to place the words, pictures and symbols in sequence.

- Use stickers to reward small achievements.

- Encourage the use of colored pencils or felt-tip markers to underline or highlight.

- Use mnemonics or other appropriate memory devices.

Always enlist parent support. Encourage parents to provide a quiet workplace and make the appropriate supplies available. Parents also need to check the clubber's progress, provide a consistent routine and encourage the clubber to practice his or her verses at the same time and place every day.

The Goal of Awards

Jeremy happily bounded through the church halls. "I got my trophy! I got my trophy!" he screamed. Jeremy, diagnosed with AD/HD, had worked hard to concentrate on his verses, and now he was seeing the result—the reward for his effort.

The goal of awards is to encourage, motivate and reward the clubber. Clubbers with special needs enjoy awards just as all children do. Although, in some cases, awards may be a little harder to use with children with special needs, you *can* use them successfully. By keeping a few things in mind, awards can have the same impact on these clubbers as they do on any clubber. Motivation must be sufficient to maintain clubbers' efforts until goals are achieved. If the awards are too distant or seem impossible to achieve, motivation will be diminished.

What are some general things I need to know?

Make sure the clubber understands the expectations. For many children with special needs, these expectations are no different from what they are for other clubbers. On the other hand, some clubbers with special needs will not be able to do the work as it is laid out in books. Again, we encourage you to work with the parents in adapting the lessons to the child's abilities.

- Develop short-term goals and individualize the award system based on needs, behavior, ability and attitude.

- Develop graded, incremental awards leading up to a section or unit award. For instance, you may give a sticker when one verse is completed and then encourage the clubber to do the other verse(s).

- Build a relationship with the clubber, so you know what the clubber likes and dislikes and so you understand what motivates him or her.

- Remember that a nontangible word of praise can be just as rewarding as a tangible object.

- When possible, use awards that double as positive learning experiences. For instance, a bookmark that lists the books of the Bible could be an award for correctly saying a portion of the Bible books in order.

- Make sure that the bigger the incentive (the more desired by the clubber), the more important the task.

What does it mean to individualize the award program?

Ask the clubber for suggestions. What rewards does the clubber like? What rewards does he or she not like? Be aware of how often a clubber chooses a particular activity or thing. Identify the circumstances that reinforce positive traits, behaviors and attitudes. Always praise the child after he or she does a desired action.

What are nontangible awards?

- An appropriate touch, a gesture, a hug, a pat on the head or shoulder

- Words of kindness and a smile

- A thumbs-up signal or some other positive cue

What are tangible awards?

- A positive note sent home to Mom and Dad

- Regular achievement badges and seals

- Holding song cards during Large Group Time

- Holding the flag during the opening ceremony

- Shares

- Privileges for the clubber to choose from (leader's helper, first in line, choice of where to sit, choosing music, dinner with the leaders and their families, etc.)

- Stickers, small prizes, food, colorful pens and pencils

- Helping with a bulletin-board display or missionary report

- Playing an instrument or giving a testimony to the younger clubs

Whether you attend a large church with a special needs ministry or have just one or two children with special needs in your club, we hope these tips will help you.

* Modified from *Awana for Me: A Guide to Working with Special Needs Children*. Used by permission of Awana Clubs International. (www.awana.org)

Tips: Information and Resources on the Web

Achievement Products for Children—Source for therapy products, special needs exercise products and special education products to help children achieve their full potential (http://www.specialkidszone.com).

American Academy of Child and Adolescent Psychiatry—Professional association dedicated to the treatment of and improvement of the quality of life for children and families affected by emotional and behavioral disorders (http://www.aacap.org).

American Association on Intellectual and Developmental Disabilities—Professional association that supports people with intellectual and developmental disabilities (http://www.aaidd.org).

Anxiety Disorders Association of America—Nonprofit organization intent on preventing, treating and curing anxiety disorders and on improving the lives of people who have them (http://www.adaa.org).

Autism Society of America—Leading voice and resource of the autism community in education, advocacy, services, research and support. Has a free 30-minute online course on autism (http://www.autism-society.org).

Bethesda Young Life—A Christ-centered outreach ministry serving teenagers with physical and mental disabilities in the Dallas area (http://sites.younglife.org/sites/Bethesda/default.aspx).

Beyond Play®—A source for adaptive play and learning toys, equipment and furniture for children with special needs (http://www.beyondplay.com).

CARE Ministries, Inc.—A Christian resource that offers a variety of services for people who are blind or visually impaired (http://www.careministries.org).

Child and Adolescent Bipolar Foundation—Nonprofit Web-based organization of families raising children with bipolar disorder; has downloadable resources, including "Educating the Child with Bipolar Disorder," an excellent source of information (http://www.bpkids.org).

Children and Adults with Attention-Deficit/Hyperactivity Disorder—National nonprofit organization that provides education, advocacy, support and resources for individuals and families affected by AD/HD (http://www.chadd.org).

Christian Institute on Disability at Joni and Friends—Advocacy group that aggressively promotes a biblical approach to life, no matter what disabling condition might affect people; provides training for church leaders and others to empower people with special needs; offers internships and certification in disability ministry. (http://www.joniandfriends.org/institute.php).

Christian Church Foundation for the Handicapped—An independent Christian nonprofit ministry serving people with disability and their families through training, resources and partnering with churches and organizations (http://www.ccfh.org).

Enabling Devices—A company dedicated to developing affordable learning and assistive devices that help people of all ages with special needs (http://enablingdevices.com/catalog).

Evangelical Lutheran Church in America Disability Ministries—Assists congregations in inclusive ministry, resources, etc. (http://www.elca.org/Growing-In-Faith/Ministry/Disability-Ministries.aspx).

Faith Alive Christian Resources—A source for books, curriculum and other materials for children and adults with disabilities (http://shop5.gospelcom.net/epages/FaithAlive.storefront).

Friendship Ministries—A nonprofit international and interdenominational organization that provides information on ministering to people with cognitive impairments (http://www.friendship.org).

Joni and Friends International Disability Center—A ministry to spread the gospel and equip churches to disciple people and families with special needs (www.joniandfriends.org/intl_disability_center.php).

Key Ministry Foundation—A ministry that equips churches to welcome and include children and families affected by hidden disabilities (i.e., emotional, behavioral and developmental conditions) (http://www.KeyMinistry.org).

Lifeway—A source for books, CDs, DVDs, curriculum and other materials and information for people of all ages with disabilities (http://www.lifeway.com/specialneeds).

Lift Disability Network—A consortium of Christian people and organizations working to connect, educate and communicate with and for people with disabilities (http://www.lift disabilitynetwork.org).

Mayer-Johnson—Source for computer software to create symbol-based communication boards and lessons and for an array of other software and of communication devices (http://www.mayer-johnson.com).

National Dissemination Center for Children with Disabilities—Source of information on disabilities in children of all ages; on IDEA, which is the law authorizing special education; on No Child Left Behind (as it relates to children with special needs); and on educational practices (http://www.nichcy.org).

Nathaniel's Hope—An organization dedicated to sharing hope with children with special needs and their families by providing resources, practical assistance and educating and equipping the community and churches (http://www.nathaniels hope.org).

National Down Syndrome Society—An organization dedicated to benefiting people with Down syndrome and their families through education, research and advocacy (http://www.ndss.org).

National Organization on Disability—Organization that works to make it possible for all people with disabilities to participate in all aspects of life; provides much information and makes available many disability-related programs and publications (http://www.nod.org).

Online Asperger Syndrome Information and Support—An online source of vast amounts of information, articles and links helpful to those having or serving individuals with Asperger's syndrome and related disorders and their families (http://www.aspergersyndrome.org).

Presbyterian Health, Education and Welfare Association—A ministry network that serves the entire Church, seeking to ensure that *all* people are supported and affirmed; one of its 10 mission networks concerns people with disabilities; single copies of several resources are free to download; provides other disability resources as well (http://www.pcusa.org/phewa).

Special Child—Online publication dedicated to parents of children with special needs; has outstanding list of information about rare conditions and disabilities, along with other information on many other related issues (http://www.special child.com).

Special Touch Ministry, Inc.—Nonprofit interdenominational Christian organization that evangelizes and provides support services to people with disabilities and their families. Among other services, it holds disability awareness and training seminars for churches that are interested in having a disability ministry (http://www.special touch.org).

I Like It When You Talk to Me!

Whatever you say, Whatever you do,
Bounces off others And comes back to you!

See Matthew 7:12

Say what people need—words that
will help others become stronger.

Ephesians 4:29, NCV

Communication: Six Communication Milestones

Communication is vital to a child's development—mentally, physically, socially, emotionally and spiritually. We've all been delighted by the smile of a baby who responds to our voice. As months pass, babies begin to understand that their cries can cause positive (or negative) reactions from others. Thus, communication begins.

Children with certain disabilities, however, move through the stages of communication at a different pace from their typically developing peers. This slower approach can be unpredictable and requires the patience of everyone in their world.

When Susie was a preschooler, her family loved teaching her songs, which she learned by filling in a missing word. Due to her Down syndrome, she understood a lot more than she could verbalize. Everyone prayed that Susie's language would develop. But even after years of speech therapy, her limited vocabulary prevented her from functioning in a typical class at school. People outside of her immediate family found her still-limited vocabulary and mumbled speech difficult to understand. Susie had reached her limits of social interaction and two-way communication. She would remain profoundly disabled.

In their book *The Child with Special Needs: Encouraging Intellectual and Emotional Growth*, Doctors Greenspan and Wieder describe six milestones of communication that a child typically achieves as the child grows.* A child who has special needs, however, often remains stuck between milestones, as Susie did.

The Milestones

Milestone 1: Self-Regulation and Interest in the World

Initially, infants cry when they are hungry, wet or bored. Gradually, they discover the world around them. By about six months of age, they are able to make sounds that stimulate and calm themselves.

Milestone 2: Intimacy

Babies reach this point when they discover that their parents and caregivers are most important in their lives. Relationships begin to bring them joy. Touch, eye contact and snuggling are important skills that prepare children to think, move and talk.

Milestone 3: Two-Way Communication

At this point, babies discover that their actions elicit reactions from others. A smile brings a smile in return; a laugh causes others to laugh. This is essential to their sense of self and to the beginning of logic.

Milestone 4: Complex Communication

Young children who achieve this milestone have moved from acting out a sequence of behaviors to communicating thoughts and feelings by using an expanding vocabulary. Their personalities have begun to surface, and they have discovered patterns in their own behavior and in the behaviors of others.

Milestone 5: Emotional Ideas

When children play with toys such as dolls and cars, they begin to move from simply labeling objects to creating stories about them. These story ideas help them advance from concrete to abstract thinkers. They not only envision thoughts they want to communicate, but now they also can add more vocabulary words to express their needs and emotions.

Milestone 6: Emotional Thinking

At this point, children begin to observe contrasting feelings. Children who are happily playing can quickly become angry when something seems unfair. Children begin to predict emotions and understand time and space. They think, *If I don't listen to Daddy, he might get mad again.* This leads to higher levels of problem solving and a greater sense of themselves as separate individuals.

Many children with special needs easily achieve these six milestones. Others need careful evaluation and treatment programs to master the skills necessary to move from one milestone to the next. Some will never achieve all six due to their level of disability.

Ways to Promote Communication

There are things that parents and teachers can do to promote communication development in children with disabilities. Here are a few to keep in mind:

- When children are upset, comfort them with gentle words and soothing actions.

- Play with children. Let them lead, but observe their imaginative play and encourage interaction between the children.

- Build a caring relationship with children. Talk to them as friends. Tell them about your day and ask about theirs, even if their responses are limited.

- Read to children. From stories, they learn about emotions, and they imagine themselves as the characters.

- Give children opportunities to share their ideas. Ask them to describe their art. Present them with a problem and encourage them to consider solutions.

- Help them become leaders in small ways, even when very young.

- Respect their age level and show that respect with your words.

While some children with special needs will take twice as long in the maturation process, many do accomplish more than their parents anticipated. As Christian leaders and teachers, we should be the first ones to cheer them on and to celebrate each milestone with them and their families.

*Stanley I. Greenspan and Serena Wieder, *The Child with Special Needs: Encouraging Intellectual and Emotional Growth* (Reading, MA: Perseus Books, 1998), chapter 4.

Communication: Sign Language

Many people who are deaf do not consider themselves disabled. They prefer to be understood as people who use another language to communicate, much like speaking in French or Spanish. There is a church in the Dallas area where the pastor, who is deaf, preaches in sign language. Members of his congregation have someone in their family who communicates in sign, so they're comfortable with singing, praying and reading Scripture in sign language.

American Sign Language (ASL) developed from French Sign Language used by Laurent Clerc, the first deaf teacher in America. Clerc came to Hartford, Connecticut, from Paris, France; and in 1817, he and Thomas Gallaudet established the first Amercian school for the deaf. Clerc's early use of French Sign Language eventually led to the standardization of early and then modern American Sign Language.* In the United States, ASL is the primary language of an estimated half a million to two million people.**

Three Kinds of Sign Language

1. American Sign Language (ASL) is a visual language and speech reading skill used by some deaf children. ASL is a complete language that uses its own hand symbols to spell words.

2. Signed English, or Pidgin Signed English (PSE), is a popular communication method among deaf children and hearing people who work with them. It's a form drawn from ASL but shortened for quick, easy dialogue in signs.

3. Signing Exact English (SEE) uses ASL to create a beautiful, flowing style of visual language for a more colorful signing expression.

Children usually learn SEE first and move to ASL as they learn to read and spell. Sign interpreters also use ASL to communicate full sentences and content. Children who do not have hearing impairments can benefit from learning sign language, because it aids in memory skills and is a useful tool in ministry to the deaf community.

Sources for Further Information

Abundant resources on ASL research, evaluation, curriculum, literature, books and videotapes are available for students and teachers via the Internet. One website to start with is http://www.learnamericansignlanguage.net.

Tools to Learn ASL

- Sign Language Alphabet Wooden Peg Puzzles teach letter recognition and the alphabet.

- Sign language Pocket Flash Cards help users learn ASL.

- "Sign It!" is a board game that teaches sign in interactive ways for education and fun.

Teachers of ASL

Qualified ASL teachers are certified by a national professional organization, the American Sign Language Teachers Association (ASLTA). Many states have chapters of ASLTA, and there are state organizations affiliated with ASLTA. Check the ASLTA website for more information (http://aslta.org).

*Anna Mindess, "The Value of ASL and the Presentation of Deaf Culture," *Welcome to Sign Language Interpreting!* http://teachers.lps.org/sshacke/stories/storyReader$6 (accessed June 3, 2008).

**Tom Harrington, "American Sign Language: Ranking and Number of 'Speakers,'" *Gallaudet University Library*, May 2004, 2008. http://library.gallaudet.edu/deaf-faq-asl-rank.shtml (accessed June 21, 2008).

Activity Page: Crack the Sign Language Code

On the blank lines, write the letter for each sign.

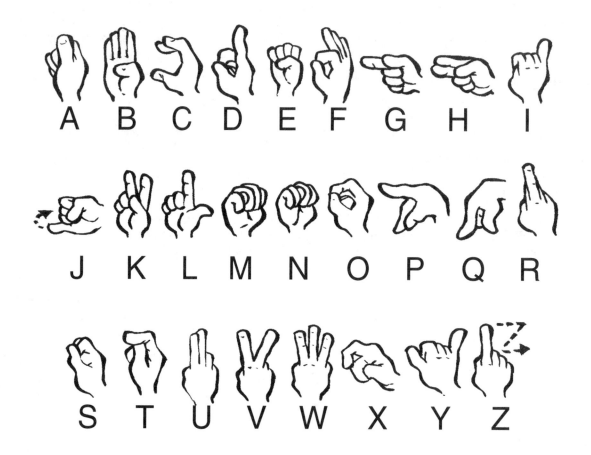

1. _____

2. _____

3. _____

4. _____

5. _____

6. _____

7. _____

The Manual Alphabet (Finger Spelling)

A B C D E F G H I

J K L M N O P Q R

S T U V W X Y Z

Communication: Visiting with Children Who Are Nonverbal

The game was exciting. You screamed and yelled until the tiebreaking score at the final buzzer. You eagerly anticipate telling your family about the event, only to discover that you now have laryngitis. You have no voice at all. Yet with such exciting news, you quickly discover that there are many ways to communicate that do not involve spoken words. As you interact with a child who is nonverbal, you will soon discover the same truth: Communication is so much more than speaking.

For a whole host of possible reasons, the link between the mouth and the area in the brain in charge of speech production is not connected in a nonverbal child. This connection may have been missing since birth or a child may have babbled until one or two years old and then lost the ability to speak. It's also possible that there was some type of injury to the speech area of the child's brain, and the loss of speech came after the injury. For most children, however, there are many other working channels that connect communication to other body parts.

Observe a Child's Communication Patterns

If talking is not an option, the child will have some other way of communicating. It's important to interview parents or caregivers to understand how the child interacts with others. Observe others using the child's system of communication with the child so that you are comfortable with it. Note in particular how a child indicates distress or the need for help. Also note if there are ways you can add to the system in a meaningful way so that the child can communicate in your setting. For example, can you add ways for the child to answer a question or choose a song? While there are many options, here are some of the communication systems children may use:

- Some children may talk by pointing to or handing you pictures or words. These pictures may be on a paper board so that another person can look at the icon, or they may be in some type of a notebook so that the child can pick it up and hand it to you. When this happens, repeat back to the child what was said. "Oh, you want a cracker for your snack today."

- The child may use a small computer to talk. Many of these computers have a flexible programming system so that when a child touches a word or picture, the computer speaks whatever is pictured. Some children need adults or peers to program the machines, while others can access and program the system on their own.

- Sign language and gestures are another way children may communicate. Many children learn individual signs, while some master the whole language system involved in signing. It's important to have an individual who can interpret what the child is saying. If a child has a limited number of signs, learn them. If a child speaks fluently in sign language, have an individual who can interpret for others. There are times when the child, due to physical limitations, develops his or her own gestures. Learn the meaning of each of those gestures.

- Many children have a way to communicate yes and no. This is very helpful. It might be an eye gaze or head movement. It could involve a different body part. It's amazing how much a person can communicate by using the words "yes" and "no."

- A child may use a paper and pencil to communicate, or the child may type words on a computer to communicate. Some computers can speak what a child types.

- Some children with very limited or controlled body movement have a communication system wired to the one body part that can be controlled and moved. With advances in technology, an individual who can choose when to blink can use that voluntary body part to scan and click on a customized computer system.

Relate to the Whole Child

Many people assume that a child with limited speaking ability also has limited understanding, hearing or intelligence. It's important to get to know the whole person. What does that child enjoy doing? Understand areas of gifting and areas of need.

Once you best understand the child, gear your own speech to match the child's level. It's not necessary to speak more loudly to this child unless hearing is an issue. Don't simplify your wording unless the child has limited ability to understand your words. Present information at the intellectual level of the child, not at the level of their speech production.

Most of all, remember that this individual is a child—like all other children of the same age. While the speaking system is unique to the child, this boy or girl probably enjoys thinking about many of the same subjects that interest the other children. If you are looking for topics of conversation, consider what this child enjoys watching or doing. It might be cartoons, the newest movie release, sports, pizza or friends. Just relax and enjoy the whole child.

Educate Other Leaders and Peers

It's important for others in the group to know how to communicate with the child. Share your knowledge with others. If the child knows some signs, teach them to the group. If the child uses a communication board—and it's okay with the individual—let the other children push one of the buttons or learn how it works. If the child has clear yes and no responses, teach others how to ask yes-and-no-questions, so they can play together and communicate with one another. Most importantly, model for others how to interact in a natural and positive way. If you notice another individual speaking loudly to that child, simply say, "I usually speak at a regular volume because Marie's hearing is great." Give information to others as needed.

Educate others about the child's likes and gifts. It will give peers ideas for topics of conversation. If the girl enjoys playing with dolls, let the other girls know this so that they can all play together. If the boy enjoys drawing pictures, let the class know this so that others can enjoy the activity with him. Pull in this child's gift of drawing when you need an artist to portray a Bible story scene. Remember to allow others to see that each person has a gift to bring, and each one has a need that others can support. That's the way the Body of Christ functions.

Be Creative with Participation

Once you know how a child best communicates, think of ways you might plug into that system so that the child can participate in worship time, prayer time, answering questions, reading the Bible and playing with peers. If the child uses pictures, develop a usable picture bank for church topics. Consider ordering one additional set of student materials so that you can cut up the pictures to place on a communication board or speech button. The child can then answer a question about the story or interact using materials from class time.

If the child uses signs or gestures, consider adding these movements to the songs you sing or the Bible verses you memorize. Children enjoy learning individual signs, and the whole group will have a great memory tool and expressive movement to add to the experience.

Hearing Impairments: Helping Children Tune In to Their World

Being deaf is much more than simply not hearing. It is like being a goldfish in a bowl, observing what is going on but not participating. A child's natural curiosity might perk up when he or she sees laughter, tears or excitement in other children, but he or she is unable to interpret what is going on. At most, the child might get a short summarized statement of the situation, a far cry from truly being a part of what's going on. In these situations, a child is unintentionally left feeling like an outsider.

Among the over 30 million Americans with hearing loss, the degree of impact varies widely. Hearing loss present at birth causes a child to be more disabled than one who loses his or her hearing later in life, after some language skills have been acquired. Depending on the degree of loss and age of onset, children cope and communicate in a wide variety of ways. Usually these methods combine speech, signing, lipreading and amplification of any remaining hearing.

Speech

Many children with hearing impairments can speak but have difficulty monitoring the tone and volume of their speech. This causes them to be difficult to understand. As you become more familiar with each child's speech pattern, your comprehension will improve.

Sign

American Sign Language (ASL) is the most common form of sign language. Thoughts are expressed through a combination of gestures and hand and arm movements. Intensity, repetition of movements, and facial expressions play a key role in conveying meaning. Finger spelling is used when there is no equivalent sign for a particular English word or concept.

One-on-One Communication

- Before speaking to a child, attract his or her attention with a cue such as a tap on the shoulder or a wave.

- Get close to the child at eye level with your mouth area clearly visible.

- Avoid standing in front of a light source like a window where glare from behind can make lipreading difficult.

- Speak naturally without exaggerated enunciation.

- Speak at a normal volume because yelling only distorts sound.

- Watch for comprehension. Often children will think

they understand but do not. Or they will say they understand to avoid unwanted attention.

Group Communication

- Quiet the environment. This includes fluorescent lights that hum and noisy air-conditioning units.

- Use visual mediums, especially when new concepts are being introduced.

- Show videos that have subtitles, and remember to use that option.

- Repeat what is said by others who are not in the child's range of vision.

- Prepare a child to interact through prompts. "Sarah, the next question is yours. Are you ready?"

Interpreter Etiquette

All communication should be directed toward the child with the impairment, not toward the interpreter. Also, the child and interpreter should choose the location in a room where they can best access information.

Facility System

A simple assistive listening system can be added to a church's sound system so that anyone with a hearing impairment can hear everything that happens. These systems transmit directly to headphones and separate out speech from background noise. Less technical adaptations that reduce noise and reverberation are sound-absorbing tiles, carpets and drapes.

Technology

Make an extra effort to get messages to families of children with hearing impairments, especially if caregivers have communication impairments also. In addition to e-mail, become familiar with teletypewriter (TTY) technology. TTY is a telephone device that enables individuals with a hearing impairment to make and receive telephone calls. A free nationwide relay network service (TRS) handles voice-to-TTY and TTY-to-voice calls.

The most important factor for including a child with a hearing impairment is the desire to reach out to the child and his or her family. Technology, which enables better communication, is important; but it's not as important as loving, teachable church members.

Visual Impairments: Using Fingers to See

History and Development

Louis Braille invented Braille at age 15 while attending a school for the blind in France. He became intrigued by a secret code involving raised dots on paper that soldiers could use at nighttime. Immediately, he wondered if it could be a way for people who are blind to learn to read and write. Braille eventually refined the code to a six-dot rectangular cell. Each cell represents a letter, number or punctuation mark. Frequently used letter combinations and words are contracted into cell patterns, and music and math can also be notated.

Braille is embossed onto paper and read with the fingertips moving across the dots. It is the only worldwide literacy method for people who are blind. Since the technology boom in the last half of the twentieth century, however, the Braille literacy rate has fallen from around 50 percent to about 10 percent, with many who are blind being mainstreamed (and not instructed daily in Braille) and many who are blind using different communication methods.* Braille books are large and often multivolumed (a Braille Bible has about 17 books!); and Braille/text books include printed words on the page opposite the embossing. Children's picture books use clear overlays embossed in Braille over pictures and text, so adults can describe the illustrations while helping children read.

Using Braille in the Classroom

There are a variety of technological tools available for children who read Braille. Find out what your student uses.

- **Embosser**—Braille version of a computer printer. Software is available so that you can enter lesson materials and print them in Braille.

- **Brailler**—Enables a student to type Braille onto a refreshable screen or onto paper. Although both electronic and manual versions are available, the electronic version has additional capabilities such as a synthesized voice and Internet access.

- **Slate and Stylus**—The least expensive and most portable method to write Braille. They operate in much the same way as a pencil and paper.

- **Handheld Braille Labeler**—An easy way to identify things in your classroom. With it, you can punch Braille onto a piece of plastic backed with sticky tape for a semipermanent sign.

Braille versions of most standard games you might use in your classroom are available. Dice, card and board games, blocks, and even a rag doll whose six buttons form letters of the Braille alphabet are also available for children who have visual impairments.

Many church denominations translate their own publications into Braille, so check with your denomination's main office to see if church materials are already available in Braille. There are printers who will accept customized embossing orders, but plan ahead, as it can take weeks to receive your finished materials. Two places to contact for price quotes on embossing are Bibles for the Blind and Visually Handicapped International (http://www.biblesfortheblind.org) and National Braille Press (http://www.nbp.org).

When Braille is not available or practical, there are other nonvisual ways to teach a child who is blind (see "Visual and Hearing Impairments: Adapt to Their Needs" on p. 29).

*John Faherty, "Proponents Say the Decline in Braille Instruction Is Leading to Illiteracy," *National Federation of the Blind,* 2007. http://www.nfb.org/Images/nfb/Publications/bm/bm06/bm0609/bm060905.htm (accessed June 23, 2008); article originally appeared in *Arizona Republic,* June 1, 2006.

Understanding Braille

(an awareness activity for students who are not blind):

Display the Braille alphabet (see p. 109). Write a riddle in Braille, and have children decipher the cells for the answer.

Braille cards with the raised-dot alphabet and 10 numerals on each card are available at the Joni and Friends Web store (http://www.joniandfriends.org/store.php).

Activity Page: Write with Braille

In the space below, draw one Braille cell for each letter of your name. (See "The Braille Cell" below.)

Braille Alphabet

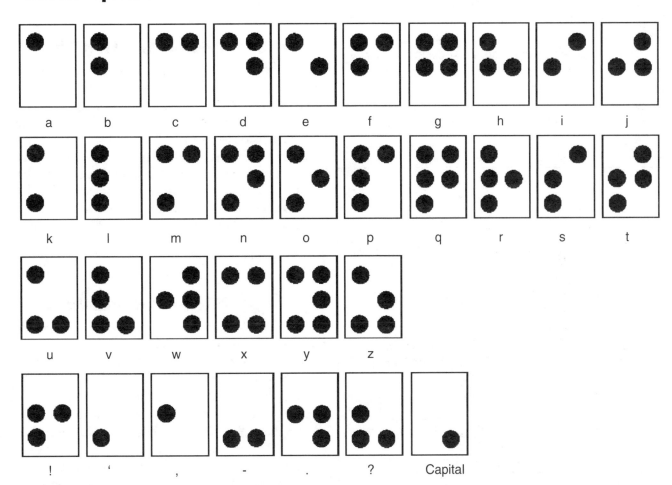

Numbers

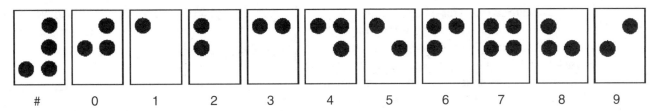

The Braille Cell

```
1 ○ ○ 4
2 ○ ○ 5
3 ○ ○ 6
```

Cognitive Disabilities: Simplicity Is Key

In years gone by, children with cognitive disabilities were called mentally retarded or mentally challenged. Sometimes these disabilities were even confused with mental illness. Parents preferred that their nondisabled children not be in the same class as those who could not perform at grade level.

Through better medical care and education, society has taken great steps in helping children with cognitive disabilities. Today, many of these children finish high school, live in group homes and hold jobs. How well these children do in regard to communication and other skills depends on their IQ range.

Give Simple and Concise Instructions

Much of your communication with children with cognitive disabilities will be to direct and redirect their activities. Without talking down to them, simplify your language. Give one instruction at a time, and follow up to see that they stay on task to complete it. If they don't, use a multisensory approach, such as a touch or a smile, to get their attention. Then restate the instruction. These children want to please you and will respond well to verbal praise.

Be firm and supportive as you draw them into the classroom routine. They can learn to sit at a table or in the story circle for lesson time. Many teachers require this of all their students. Be sure the lesson includes concrete examples and that there are as few distractions in the room as possible.

During discussion time, give these children time to think for themselves and share their thoughts. As you model patience, classmates will also learn compassion

and be more willing to work with these children on a small-group task.

When praying with these students, use short, simple prayers. Ask them to repeat each phrase after you.

Be a Sensitive Listener

Children with a profound disability may use basic signs to communicate. Their parents will help you learn what those signs are and how to respond to them. Many children will have speech problems. Look children in the eye when they are speaking to you, and listen to their voice as well as watch their body language. If you don't understand what they say, ask them to repeat what they said. Offer your hand, and ask them to show you what they mean.

Remember, these children have the same emotions as other children, even though they don't function at their chronological age. Their interests, however, will be closer to their mental age.

Create a *My Church* Book

Since children with low IQs have a difficult time adapting to new surroundings, make a booklet about coming to church. Take pictures of the parking lot, the front door, the hall, the classroom, the teachers and classmates. Label the pictures, and send the book home with the child to look at during the week. Create a new book for VBS, day camp, children's church or promotion Sunday.

These students enjoy being with classmates and teachers. And in their simple way, they can bring out the best in us and show us God's unconditional love.

Educable	IQ 51-70	Able to slowly learn to read, write and do math
Trainable	IQ 36-50	Can learn self-help skills and simple chores
Profound	IQ Below 35	Can learn limited self-help and social skills, and needs supervision

Physical Disabilities: The Art of Body Language

It was Samuel's job to anoint the next king over Israel. He was sent to the house of Jesse where there were many young men. Samuel laid eyes on one of the sons and was positive that that son was to be the next king over Israel. God, however, warned Samuel to align his eyes with God's vision: "Do not consider his appearance or his height, for I have rejected him. The Lord does not look at the things man looks at. Man looks at the outward appearance, but the Lord looks at the heart" (1 Samuel 16:7).

When working with children who have a physical disability, remember that your line of sight must align with God's vision, too. While those in the world might judge a person based on outward appearance, the focus for a Christian is very different. Instead of wearing sunglasses, perhaps a Christian wears "Son-glasses"—lenses that allow a Christian to see past the outer layer and into that place where God's image is reflected in His creation and so is honored and treasured as part of God's family. Son-glasses note that each individual, crafted uniquely by God's hand, has an important purpose and gifts to offer the Body as a whole.

Get to Know the Child

The area of physical need is only one part of this complex individual. It's important to get to know the child's likes and dislikes. What makes the child burst out into laughter? What kind of abilities and unique personality traits exist in this child? What areas are difficult? As you gather more information about this child, you will be better able to use the child's gifts in your church and community while you support the needs that exist.

Give Peers and Leaders Son-Glasses

The physical features of any individual are the ones that stand out to others. Therefore, you will need to be specific about passing out God's Son-glasses to the entire group. One way to do that is to have children think about individual skills or qualities that are easy for them and areas that are more difficult. From this base, children understand that each person has areas of strength and need. Share your own areas of strength and need, and then ask permission from the parent and individual to share specifically about the child with a physical disability. What activities or areas are easy for that person? What things are more difficult? Tell that child's story to the group—information is a powerful tool.

Many children with a physical need might use particular equipment. Other children might wonder if it's safe to touch that friend or play with him or her. If the child and parent are willing, let peers see and handle the equipment. Tell them what function it serves. If it's possible for children to take turns trying it out, do so. The more they touch and see the equipment, the more natural it will be to the peers, and they will begin to see past the equipment and see just another friend.

There are many excellent children's books that discuss or involve as characters children with disabilities and that explain some of those areas of disability. Read one to the group. Some parents of children with unique needs and gifts write their own story. Using real pictures and events, the parents talk about the child's story as well as areas of likes and dislikes. Such a personal story shows that a child may have a physical area of need, but it is wrapped around a boy or girl who is a lot like the peers. Consider writing that kind of story for the group.

Differentiate Friend Peers from Parent Peers

Sometimes peers can be helpful in managing some of the physical tasks of the friend with special needs. If the child needs a push down the hall, peers may enjoy helping. If the child needs help zipping a coat or putting on a shoe, a peer might be a great support. Children love to help one another. It's important, however, for peers to know the difference between being a friend and being a parent. The child already has a parent, so friends are more desired. Use exaggeration to show the group how a friend might invite someone to play. "Hi Joe. We are playing blocks. Do you want to play?" Then show the class how a parent might invite the child to play, saying in a baby voice, "Hi, honey, sweetie Joey. Do you want to come play blockies with me?" The group soon gets the message that even though a peer might be asked to help out at times, that help is extended by a friend—not by someone acting like a mom or dad.

It's also helpful to give peers good advice about what help that child needs and what help the child does not need. Many times peers want to help so much that the child with special needs is robbed of the chance to be as independent as possible. If the child can put on his or her coat and then needs someone to get the zipper started, so he or she can pull it up, let the peers know exactly what part they are to do—start the zipper. Even if the child has an assigned older buddy in the group, make sure you use the peers. This will be a great way for the children to interact with one another.

Be Prepared for Health Needs

Part of knowing the child also means knowing about medical needs and concerns. It's vital to the child's safety that you know signs of distress and the action plan you are to follow if you see those signs. This information is covered in more detail in another article in this resource book (see "Allergies and Treatment" on p. 165 and the "Allergy Action Plan" form on p. 166). The child's safety or even the child's life may depend on your staff having an action plan ready to follow for times of emergency and intervention. In some cases, a child may need food prepared very specifically. In other cases, a child may need to be moved or positioned in a particular way. Know this information, practice it with a parent until you are comfortable, and then make sure all leaders have the self-care and medical information they need to interact safely with this child.

Create Paths for Interaction with Peers and the Materials

Many of our children's activities involve movement on the part of the children. As you prepare your materials for the day's lesson, think specifically about how that child will be part of the group. Are there activities that require movement from a body part that is not available to that child? How can you modify that activity so that the child can participate? If your lesson requires a written response and the child is unable to write, you might have two friends work together to produce one final response—each one contributing to the discussion while one person writes the answer. If your lesson has a game that requires running, consider having a peer push the child's wheelchair, or place the child in a wagon that a peer can pull, allowing the two to be part of the game.

Be creative ahead of time. While some great ideas come on the spur of the moment, most come from creative planning and making sure you have the needed equipment before you start the lesson. Count on those Son-glasses to give you the vision and insight you need as a leader for that group.

Speech and Language Impairments: Using Communication Devices

Are you an individual who enjoys the inner and technical workings of a computer, or do you cower and pray every time you push the power button of that mystical machine? If computers are more of a mystery for you, having a child with a communication device will be a great opportunity to add a technology person to your children's team. If computers are a joy for you, then get ready to have some fun. Either way, adding the chance to learn and grow from a child with a communication device will be a great experience.

The Technology

Advances in technology have given a voice to some children who have been unable to use their own vocal cords. Children who may benefit from such a device usually go through an evaluation to help decide what might best support their needs and use their gifts. If a child is able, for example, to type and program a machine, that child might have a device that speaks in complete sentences to any question you ask. The child simply types his or her response to the question and then touches the screen; this signals the computer to speak the answer aloud. Another child may not be able to type but may be able to use a finger to push a picture on a touch screen. This child may use a computer that allows an adult to program it to spell certain words when the user touches a certain picture on the screen. Some children have multiple layers (or "pages") of pictures, accessing hundreds of programmed words and phrases; other children may have only two to eight pictures. The details and complexity of such a computer depend on the child's ability level.

There are other amazing advances in technology that allow a child with voluntary control over only one body part to use a computer. If a child has even one finger that responds on command or one eyelid that blinks under his or her control, that child can use a computer that can links to that body part. For example, a child can use an eye gaze to scan a set of words or pictures and blink to select the desired word or picture.

Whatever device is used by the child with a speech and language impairment, learn how the device works. See how the child uses the device in multiple settings to better understand what kind of tool it can be in your setting. If possible, learn how to program the machine so that you can use it as part of the children's activities.

While it's impossible to describe all of the types of machines and how they work, it *is* totally possible for you or someone on your team to become an expert on one child's communication device. There are several companies that make communication devices, and they all provide training and follow-up of some sort. One such company is Mayer-Johnson. It offers many communication devices and an excellent computer program that will allow you easy access to pictures for several popular devices. Various computer software programs, like Boardmaker, allow you to not only print out a large variety of pictures but also create a layout of pictures that matches different devices. Whether it's a DynaVox, Tech/Talk, Macaw or some other new communication device, it can help the child be an active participant at church.

Church Use

The best place to begin to figure out how a communication device can be used at church is to understand how all of the children participate verbally at church. Children might sing, choose songs, give prayer requests, read Scripture, answer questions, tell jokes, play games or have informal conversations. As you look at each setting and the way children speak in each setting, consider how that communication device might be used in the same or a similar way. Although each device is different, any device might be able to be programmed to do a variety of tasks.

- Put song selections on the device. The child can choose or announce a song.

- Program the Bible memory verse on the machine. The child can recite the verse by touching a picture or a series of pictures.

- Put words of adoration and praise to God—words that are on the child's heart—on the device so the child can contribute to a worship time.

- Program the device with words associated with the weekly Bible story. This will allow a child to answer a question. For example, if you cover the story of David and Goliath, place "David," "Goliath" and numerals 1-5 on the device. Ask the child questions at his or her level. "Which person got killed in this story?" "Which person follows God?" "How many stones did David pick up?" "How many stones did he use?"

- Put the names of people important to the child and possible prayer requests on the individual's device.

- Some children have a great sense of humor. Consider programming a weekly joke on the computer so that the child can interact with peers. It could become a great weekly event!

- Need to make an announcement? Put the announcement on the machine, and allow the child to give that information to the group.

- Be creative. The more you enjoy the device, the more ideas you will form about how that child may take a speaking role in church services, Christmas programs, choral readings, skits and weekly events.

Preparation

While technology is a gift, the more complex the device, the less simple it is to use. Ask a question of a child who signs the answer and you'll usually get an immediate response. Asking a question of a child who uses a device that needs to be programmed ahead of time takes planning and thought. Waiting for a child to scan and blink through a series of pictures is worth the wait, but it takes patience on the part of the listener. Advance preparation is key.

It might be helpful to appoint one person to be in charge of "thinking" for the communication device. While the leader in charge might be a good choice for this position, a teen or helper in the group may enjoy that task and may be better suited for it. Of course, some children with a device may be able to completely program the device on their own, but having an individual think of how that person might be involved from week to week still helps.

Peer Involvement

Make sure peers take part in understanding and using the device. Getting to know that piece of equipment is critical to interaction. With parent and child permission, consider introducing that child and piece of equipment to the group. Peers will want to know about their friend. What is easy for the child? What is the child's story? What common interests do they share with the child? This is a great time to talk about the many similarities they share as well as celebrate the unique ways in which God has made each person. As part of this celebration, consider showing the children how the communication device works and why the child needs it. Depending on the situation, a peer might even be able to put some information on the device, allowing the child to tell parents about what happened in the group time at church. Perhaps peers could have some input about what information the device needs to be programmed with that might be helpful as the children play together. Involved and informed peers will often be able to have the most natural and caring relationships.

Emotional/Behavioral Disorders: What to Say, How to Listen

"Are you having a good day today?" It's a logical question—most of us have an ebb and flow to our good and bad days. One day we might feel giddy and excited while another day we're more somber or serene. Good and bad days are natural as we wade through the expectations and events of life. For a child with an emotional or behavioral disorder, however, this ebb and flow will likely be more obvious from week to week or moment to moment at church. The child will display signs of good times and difficult times, and it's important for leaders to expect that to happen.

Be Educated and Understanding

When an individual gets a master's degree in a specific area, people understand that he or she is an expert in that field. Seek your "master's degree" in knowing your students with emotional/behavioral disorders. Educate yourself about the child as an individual as well as about his or her particular area of special need. Know what each child enjoys and what areas might cause distress. What people are important to the child, and in what areas is he or she gifted?

When you read and research about a particular area of need, remember that it's important to search for information related to the childhood version of the disorder. Bipolar disorder, for example, looks different in a child than in an adult. It is helpful to read general information, but it is more important to find out what a particular disorder looks like in a child of the age you're dealing with.

Understanding a child's good and bad days is easier when it's clear that the issues often stem from brain chemicals. In general, the child is not creating his or her response on purpose; there is a physical cause for the emotional or behavioral response. It's also important to keep in mind that many children take medication for these areas of need. While medication is a lifeline for many, medication can also have side effects. A child may be sleepier than normal, have appetite changes or display other side effects. Realize, too, that some parents choose to give their child certain medications during schooltime only, often resulting in the child exhibiting a different personality in the evenings and on weekends. Becoming an expert on this child will allow you to be more understanding as you lead him or her to grow spiritually.

Create Understanding Peers

While it's important to protect confidentiality for the child and family, it's also critical to create a group in which peers are understanding and helpful. Children with behavioral and emotional needs are often the most difficult for peers to embrace. As the leader, create an environment in which everyone is welcomed and embraced.

One way to cultivate that atmosphere is by using the story of Moses found in Exodus 17:8-13. Talk with the children about Aaron and Hur coming alongside Moses to hold up his hands:

> On his own, Moses would not have been able to keep his hands steady and in the air. His friends, however, came alongside Moses to allow him to complete his job. As friends in the children's group, we also need to help one another. Someone might need a friend to pray for him or her. Someone might need a friend to help read some difficult words. Another person might need us to be patient when a friend gets angry and upset. That's like the job Aaron and Hur did for Moses.

Describe to the children what they might see or hear, and be specific about how each of them can be a friend to that individual. "Even Moses needed some good friends, and we will all have those times here at church, too." Using this kind of analogy with the children allows you to revisit the story as needed throughout the year. It allows you to explain some of the child's specific behaviors without giving an exact label for the disorder.

Develop a Good Offense

A sports team usually has two different types of plays—offensive and defensive. When on the offense, the team has control of the ball. It's a time to be proactive and score some points. Likewise, there are many things a children's ministry leader can accomplish with a good offense. Here are some strategies you can implement while being proactive, setting up a successful environment in which *all* of the children can grow:

- **Be prepared.** Have each time block and transition in your group structured and ready. Letting children sit unoccupied for a stretch of time creates pockets of opportunity for disruptive behavior. Have a plan, and be ready to start putting it into action as soon as children hit your environment.

- **Create realistic expectations.** Know what the child with special needs can accomplish, and then set up your expectations around that. For example, knowing a child can be engaged with the group for 15 minutes, prepare 15-minute lesson segments. Planning for the child to be engaged for 25 minutes will only bring disappointment and opportunities for difficult times.

- **Give advance information.** Go over the schedule for the day. Tell the group what you expect in terms of behavior. Consider writing these things out in words or displaying the information in pictures. When you describe your expectations for behavior, make sure you tell the group what you *want* them to do. A list of *don't dos* is often ineffective (see "Can-Dos for Children," p. 203).

- **Develop a relationship with the child.** Many children with emotional or behavioral needs require the support of someone they know and trust. Visit that child at home. Find a topic you both enjoy. Attend a ball game together, or go to the movies. Play a video game, or go eat ice cream together. Spend time together outside of the group, getting to know and appreciate one another. This relationship will often be a critical force in allowing a child to ride the storm of uncontrollable emotion or disruptive behavior.

- **Be positive, and notice the good.** As you relate with the child, make sure you point out the good

times. "I like the way everyone is using respectful language today." Those kinds of comments are important while setting up the offensive moves.

Develop an Appropriate and God-Honoring Defense

Along with a good offense, it is also important to develop a strong defense. A defense is a plan for action in response to what the other team is doing. When supporting the needs of a child with an emotional or behavioral disorder, creating a defensive plan is critical. While the child is certainly not your opponent, the child does need to know that you have a plan, even when life feels out of control.

- **Develop a plan of action.** Once you get to know the child, you can imagine what you might see in your church group. Be ready to respond with an action plan. Develop this plan from ideas that work in other settings. Schools are a rich resource in this area.

- **Be consistent.** Use the same action plan every time. Calmly and lovingly move to that plan each and every time it's needed.

- **Be respectful.** The child should never be put down in any verbal or physical way. Having a calm voice and pleasant face will communicate an air of respect to all involved. "You may walk in the hallway with Sue until you feel safe and calm." Tell the child the plan and at the same time communicate how the child will benefit.

Communication: Helping Children Relate to One Another

All human beings have a God-given desire to be a meaningful part of their community. Many disabilities hinder this desire, causing great heartache. When nondisabled children are taught how to befriend their classmates with disabilities, everyone finds out what being blessed by our unique differences means.

Breaking Down Barriers

Some children first react to friends who are different by avoiding them. Other children may imitate a physical disorder in a mocking manner. These defense mechanisms communicate what children fear but cannot verbalize. When fears are openly addressed, barriers are broken down.

Growing Relationships

If a child with special needs does *not* have trouble communicating, icebreaker games can help classmates get to know one another. The main focus of relating needs to be taken off of the disability and moved on to topics of interest to all (pets, favorite foods, sports, family life, movies, etc.). Older children with disabilities can answer personal questions ("What happened?" "Does it hurt?") that come up during casual conversation. However, if you sense questions are getting too personal, redirect peers to other topics.

If a child's communication is affected by his or her disability, explain to the other children that someone's speech is not necessarily a reflection of his or her intelligence. For children to understand how difficult language can be, have them complete a short exercise: Ask them to recite the Pledge of Allegiance. Commend them on how easily they did it. Then ask them to repeat the pledge without saying any words that have the letter *e*: "I . . . to . . . flag . . . of . . . of . . . and." Ask them how much effort it took and why it took them so long. Then say, "This is how much effort it takes for Sammy to say anything." This exercise in empathy allows peers to appreciate the hard work of their new friend.

When teaching a child with special needs how to socialize, avoid vague instructions like "Be nice." Instead, teach specific skills such as (1) listening to what others are saying, (2) responding with one comment that is on topic, and (3) asking one question about a classmate's day. Simple social skills like taking turns and asking politely for a desired item may require modeling, prompting and reminding. Lack of social skills is not a lack of desire for friendship. Instead it is the lack of know-how, vague rather than specific instructions and few opportunities to practice.

Helping Children with Special Needs Relate

- Use a timer or a watch with an alarm to teach taking turns. The child uses an object until the alarm goes off; then gives it to another child.

- Teach empathy by pointing out specific situations of need, hurt, happiness, etc. and discuss others' reactions.

- Make "please" and "thank you" high-priority vocabulary words. Model the use of these expressions.

Helping Nondisabled Children Relate

- Talk to the class about the disability without the child with special needs present.

- If a child uses sign language, make sure classmates know the signs for "please" and "thank you." Simple reciprocal courtesy goes a long way.

Have children take turns helping the child with special needs. Use a reward chart for encouraging children to be part of a helper rotation. Children earn stickers by modeling, prompting skills or helping their friend with tasks. A reward is gained after 10 boxes are filled with stickers. Allow helpers to choose something they wish to work toward.

> Children with disabilities enter a society that neither adjusts to their needs nor recognizes their abilities. Approaching these children without pity or patronization will empower their God-given desires to be full-fledged members of the church community.

Communication: Advances in Technology and Software

Assistive technologies are helping many children with special needs to become increasingly independent, allowing them to meet personal, social and educational goals. After home and school, a child's next step into the community is often their church. Any church with a working knowledge of assistive technology will easily make the child feel welcome.

Assistive Technology

Assistive technology is any tool that helps a child with a disability get through daily activities. The tool may be something as common as a walker, a hearing aid or a scooter; or the tool may be an extremely specialized computerized item. Specialized tools are becoming common and will allow many of today's children to attend college.

For the latest on assistive technology information, updates and resources, visit the "Assistive and Information Technology" page of DisabilityInfo.gov, the federal government's website for disability-related information and resources (http://www.disabilityinfo.gov/digov-public/public/DisplayPage.do?parentFolderId=187). Or attend a Closing the Gap annual conference on resources for children and adults with special needs (to find out where and when the next conference is, visit http://www.ClosingTheGap.com).

- **Orthotic or Prosthetic Equipment**—These are designed to compensate for a missing or disabled body part. They range from an orthopedic shoe insert to an artificial or mechanical limb. A child with an artificial arm can usually shake hands, but always let him or her take the lead. Classmates should use verbal greetings and be ready to shake a hook if it is offered.

- **Seating Aids and Wheelchairs**—Wheelchairs, motor scooters and modifications to regular chairs help children stay upright, get up and down unaided or reduce pressure on the skin. Other children need to be taught that wheelchairs, scooters and specialized chairs are not toys but crucial pieces of equipment—as important as arms and legs. Be sure to lower yourself when talking to a child in a wheelchair, and do not lean or hang on the equipment.

- **Sensory Equipment**—Many children with special needs are oversensitive or underinsensitive to light, sound, heat, smell or hard pews. Weighted vests, sunglasses worn indoors, and noise-blocking ear-plugs or headphones are some of the equipment a child might use in order to participate more fully.

- **Communication Equipment**—Anything that enables a person to send and receive messages is communication equipment. These devices include hearing aids, picture-exchange systems and a variety of talking computers. Cyrano2 Communicator, a new handheld device from One Write Company, uses a built-in camera and text for a personalized speech system (http://www.cyranocommunicator.com). Communication equipment also includes an assistive listening system that could be installed in the sanctuary.

Computer Access

Many churches now use computers for class projects. Special software has been designed for children with disabilities, giving them access through a modified keyboard or mouse. Other modifications include single-switch software and a keyboard with oversized and colorful keys. Over the last decade, computer software that transforms speech into electronic text has greatly improved in both usability and price.

The best ages for children to learn to use these new advances are in their preschool and elementary years. Ask parents to recommend or share software that their children are using at home. Parents will often be excited to share new resources and even help raise funding to purchase new technologies for the church.

Adaptive Switches

Adaptive switches are used to control the on and off functions of such devices as lights, radios, battery toys, elevators, doors, tape recorders and other types of equipment. These switches must be used with a device that has been adapted for switch access. Touch-sensitive switches respond to a very light touch. Air-pressure switches are activated by a sip or puff of air. Some switches are so responsive that they can be activated by the movement of a finger, an eyebrow, a cheek or a small muscle.

If your church desires to provide a Christian education for children who are dependent on technology, you must invest in equipment when it is appropriate. Remember that your willingness to learn about advances in technology and software will draw these families into church where they will learn more about Jesus.

I Won't Give Up—Don't You!

"For I know the plans I have for you," declares the Lord, "plans to prosper you and not to harm you, plans to give you hope and a future."

Jeremiah 29:11

Understand that God has individual and unique plans for everyone.
Olympian Jean Driscoll, with spina bifida, an eight-time winner of the Boston Marathon in the women's wheelchair division and winner of silver medals in the 800-Meter Women's Wheelchair Exhibition Event at the 1992 and 1996 Olympics

Activity Page: God's Word on "Keeping On"

These verses tell us how to keep on trusting God—no matter what happens! Draw a line to match the first part of the verse on the left side of the page to the correct ending on the right side. Look up the Bible reference in the second column if you need help.

He will have no fear of bad news;

The Lord himself goes before you and will be with you;

Be strong and courageous. Do not be terrified;

For he will command his angels concerning you

I tell you the truth, anyone who has faith in me will do what I have been doing.

Therefore he is able to save completely those who come to God through him,

do not be discouraged, for the Lord your God will be with you wherever you go (Joshua 1:9).

because he always lives to intercede for them (Hebrews 7:25).

to guard you in all your ways (Psalm 91:11).

He will do even greater things than these, because I am going to the Father (John 14:12).

his heart is steadfast, trusting in the Lord (Psalm 112:7).

he will never leave you nor forsake you. Do not be afraid; do not be discouraged (Deuteronomy 31:8).

Faith Steps: Helping Children Deal with Fear and Pain

I trust in God. I will not be afraid.
What can people do to me?
Psalm 56:4, NIrV

All children experience fear—that's normal. Children with special needs don't necessarily have more fears than their peers, but their challenges are unique. These children can become depressed because they constantly deal with their limitations and often experience painful treatments. They often feel lonely, because people may not take the time to get to know them. Sometimes people treat them as if they're not as smart as other children. Children with special needs fear they will never measure up. They need to be assured that Jesus understands their feelings and that He cares about their fears.

Questions You May Have to Answer

As you work with children who are worried or afraid, here are some of the questions they may have for you and some answers you can give:

Does Jesus know when I'm scared?

Jesus came to Earth as a baby. He was even your age once. Jesus knows how you feel when other children call you names like Cripple or Retard. People called Him Liar [see John 8:52-53] and Blasphemer, one who speaks against God [see Matthew 26:65]. Jesus also understands your fears because men nailed His hands and feet to a cross and stuck a spear into His side. Jesus understands your fears and loves you just the way you are. He will comfort you in hard times. He can also use you to comfort others [see 2 Corinthians 1:3-4].

If Jesus loves me, why doesn't He fix my disability?

That's a hard question to answer because of all the stories in the Bible about how Jesus healed people. He touched a blind man's eyes so he could see. He told another man to pick up his bed and walk, and the man's crippled legs became strong. It's true—Jesus healed people when He lived on Earth, and He still does miracles today. But Jesus didn't heal everyone He met. Only God knows why Jesus heals some people and not others. While we may not know why, we can be sure that Jesus knew that people are much more than their disability.

When Joni Eareckson Tada dove into a lake at the age of 17, she broke her neck and severed her spinal cord. She feared what would become of her if she could never walk or use her hands again. But today from her wheelchair, she leads a worldwide ministry to people with disabilities and to people who are nondisabled.

Maybe you don't need fixing, because you're more than your disability. Like He does for Joni, Jesus has a plan for your whole life. Think of all the ways He will use you and your disability. Jeremiah 29:11 says, "'For I know the plans I have for you,' declares the Lord, 'plans to prosper you and not to harm you, plans to give you hope and a future.'"

Is Jesus disappointed in me when I'm not brave?

You probably wish you never had to have another treatment or see another doctor. Maybe you are afraid that you'll have to stay in the hospital again. Jesus doesn't expect you to be brave all the time—everyone gets scared sometimes.

It's normal to be scared about serious health problems. It helps to talk to your parents and doctors about your concerns and to ask questions. You have a right to know about your condition. If you feel scared, you can also call friends and ask them to pray with you. Learning to quote Bible verses will also help. A good verse to repeat is Psalm 56:3: "When I am afraid, I will trust in you."

If I can't do very much, does Jesus still want me?

Jesus cares more about who you are than what you can or cannot do. He loves you, and He cares about who you are on the inside. Are you honest and kind? When someone takes time to help you, do you say "Thank you"? Are you grateful for everything you have, or do you envy others? Your disability doesn't give you the right to be rude or act out. Don't be afraid to try new things, and do what you're able to do. Jesus only expects you to do your best. Don't compare yourself to others; instead, encourage them. Colossians 3:17 says, "Whatever you do, whether in word or deed, do it all in the name of the Lord Jesus." And remember, you can always pray for your friends.

Does Jesus know when I'm going to die?

Yes! Jesus not only knows when you will die, but He also has already prepared a heavenly paradise for you. One day, all sadness and suffering will end for those who know Jesus as their Savior. There won't be any more pain or tears. In eternity, *every* child will get a perfect mind and body, and life there will be much better than it is here. Then you'll understand things that frighten you now. Best of all, Jesus will welcome you into His kingdom. You can read about it in the book of Revelation where John wrote, "I saw a new heaven and a new earth. . . . I saw the Holy City. . . . It was prepared like a bride beautifully dressed for her husband" (Revelation 21:1-2, *NIrV*).

Five Truths Children Need to Know About Fear

1. Fears are normal, and everyone has them.

2. Fears do not come from God.

3. Fears are temporary, and you can outgrow fears.

4. Fears don't seem so bad when you talk about them.

5. Fears can be overcome with faith and prayer.

Four Things Children Need to Know About God

1. God is in charge (see Daniel 4:25). He is in control of our lives.

2. God is our helper (see Psalm 33:20). He promised to be with us in times of trouble (see Psalm 46:1).

3. God is trustworthy (see 2 Samuel 7:28). All things work together for our good (see Romans 8:28).

4. God knows all things (see John 16:30). He is totally aware of our situation (see Psalm 139:16).

The apostle Paul was afraid when he faced evil. In 2 Corinthians 1:8-10 (*NIrV*), he wrote:

Brothers and sisters, we want you to know about the hard times we suffered in Asia Minor. We were having a lot of trouble. It was far more than we could stand. We even thought we were going to die . . . . But that happened so that we would not depend on ourselves but on God. He raises the dead to life. God has saved us from deadly dangers. And he will continue to do it. We have put our hope in him. He will continue to save us.

God wants to do the same thing for hurting children who feel fear and pain. When you serve in a special needs ministry, God will use you to help them learn to trust Him in times of trouble. What an awesome opportunity!

Outreach: Giving Parents a Respite

Respite events at church may be the single most effective way to reach out to families affected by disability in your community.

Most parents, whether their children have special needs or not, recognize the benefits of hobbies, clubs and sports programs in which their children can be taught by capable adults. In these settings, children make friends and learn new skills. Such programs also allow parents to enjoy a break from their routine. But parents of children with disability can't always find qualified caregivers or appropriate activities for their children. Without these options, parents of children with special needs have very little time for themselves.

To meet this need, many churches around the country provide respite care. Your church can make this exciting ministry available in your community, too. Providing a much-needed break for parents of children with special needs is extremely worthwhile and beneficial for all those involved, as evidenced by parent comments:

We get a break from autism. It helps us be more patient with our son.

Respite refreshes my soul.

It allows me and my wife to spend time alone to catch up on our relationship.

While our daughter was at respite, we had lunch, did errands and actually had a conversation! We were able to take a breath!

Site-Based Respite Programs

Respite programs provide a brief period of rest and relief for parents of children with disabilities. During respite, parents drop all their children off at church or another location and take a well-deserved break from the rigors of parenting to spend time doing things they enjoy. Trained volunteers run a three- or four-hour program at no charge to these families. (As volunteers become attached to families affected by disability, some may offer to provide in-home respite or overnight care.) Site-based respite programs typically run monthly or bimonthly on Friday nights or Saturday mornings. Churches with gyms or other recreational facilities may offer respite through day camps, a Vacation Bible School or various sports programs.

Events like these make it easier for families to participate in church activities without the pressure of embracing the church's beliefs. Through practical acts of love, respite care demonstrates the value the church places on these families. In turn, the families become more open to hearing the gospel.

Why do families need respite care?

- **The Fear Factor**—Many child-care workers are too intimidated to work with children who have a disability. Therefore, parents of these children have few options for getting help or relief from their constant care-giving duties.

- **The Protective Factor**—Parents are very protective of their children and need trustworthy caregivers.

- **The Time Factor**—Some parents of children with disability are responsible for their young children 24 hours a day, 7 days a week. Many of these children can't be left alone in a playpen or in front of the TV to watch a movie, even for a brief period of time.

Why is respite so successful?

Respite events are so successful for many reasons:

- Programs are easy to organize and fun for everyone involved.

- Respite meets a significant need for parents and volunteers: Parents get to spend quality time strengthening their marriages and renewing their energies. Volunteers see how happy parents are when they drop off their children and how grateful they are when they pick them up.

- Families experience a bit of God's perspective toward people affected by disabilities. They build relationships with church members and receive spiritual nurture.

- Volunteers build relationships with families who appreciate their care more than they can express.

- Volunteers enjoy the fellowship of serving together. New volunteers become comfortable caring for children with special needs when working alongside experienced friends. They feel less vulnerable stepping into unfamiliar situations and are more likely to volunteer again in similar settings.

- Siblings build friendships as they're encouraged to share their experiences. They feel valued, apart from their brother or sister, when activities are planned especially for them.

What resources are required to start a respite ministry?

Site-based respite programs that allow parents to drop off their children at church for a few hours are extremely easy to plan. They don't need to be elaborate or require expensive equipment. An event is successful in a child's eyes if it's fun and does not feel like school. Parents simply want their children to be safe and well supervised while at respite.

- **Schedule**—When to hold respite events depends on the families involved. Some churches offer respite once a quarter rather than monthly. Other churches join together and alternate offering monthly care, with each church hosting the event once every three or four months. The most common time schedules are 6:15 P.M. to 9:15 P.M. on weeknights or 9:00 A.M. to 1:00 P.M. on Saturdays. You may want to ask the parents in your church what times would be best for them. Active, ambulatory children would benefit from daylight hours spent playing outdoors. Young children would be best served in programs that don't run too late in the evening. Schedules may also depend on the availability of recreation rooms or playgrounds on your church campus. Once you determine the date, time and location of the event, you'll need to decide how families will sign up.

- **Applications**—Finding out ahead of time how many children to expect and what special needs will be represented is a must. Then you'll be able to better prepare for the event. Application forms should include space for parents to include details about their children (see form on p. 126).

- **Numbers**—Decide in advance how many children you can serve at the event. Many churches have more families wanting to attend respite than can be accommodated. Programs can only be as large as the volunteer pool and facility space allow. A typical program might include 15 to 20 children with disabilities, plus their siblings.

- **Promotional Flyers**—Create interest in your ministry and get word out to the community in a flyer distributed throughout your church and community. Attract attention by choosing a positive, upbeat name for your program: Break Out, Friday Night Fun, Breakaway, Fun Zone, Joycare, Parents' Night Out, Evening Stars, Take-a-Break, etc. Use the flyer to provide parents with clear application instructions, and ask parents to bring their own snacks if their child has food restrictions.

What volunteers are needed?

All volunteers should complete an application and attend a general disability-training workshop. The application should include a request for permission to run a criminal background check. Ideally, there should be one volunteer buddy for each child with special needs, and there should be extra volunteers to work with the siblings. In addition, the leadership team should include:

- **A program coordinator** to plan promotional, registration and event details

- **A volunteer coordinator** to recruit and schedule volunteers

- **Age-group leaders** to direct volunteers for nursery, preschool and school-age groups at the event

- **Activity leaders** to gather materials and supervise the activities or centers you choose to have (crafts, music, recreation, games, snacks, etc.)

- **A registered nurse** to be available on site for medical emergencies and to provide peace of mind for parents and volunteers

How should volunteers communicate during respite?

Every group leader, nurse and coordinator should carry a walkie-talkie or cell phone during each respite event. On the day of the event, volunteers should arrive one hour early. They may eat a meal together, pray together and discuss how they will meet the needs of the children they'll be serving. Leaders can review disability etiquette and give any needed instructions. Volunteers should look over the respite applications to become familiar with the abilities of the children, review the program schedule and ask any final questions before the event begins.

What happens at respite care?

In some churches, respite runs like a giant carnival with a theme for each event. Other respites are structured like a Vacation Bible School and use a published curriculum. Curriculum can easily be adapted to the talents and energy of your staff. To get a snapshot of what happens on the day of the event, here is a typical respite timeline:

2 hours before: The setup crew arrives to prepare the nursery, preschool rooms and large activity spaces.

1 hour before: Volunteers arrive to share a meal, pray together and receive assignments. Buddies review application forms and discuss strategies for success.

15 minutes before: The check-in team and nurse sit down at registration tables in a central location to greet the children.

As families arrive: Parents sign in on clipboards that will stay with each group. Sign-in sheets should include parents' names, children's names and disabilities, emergency contact numbers, siblings and ages. Parents complete a simple form that addresses changes that occurred since the initial application. Group leaders should be alerted to these changes. Buddies meet the children at a central meeting area and let parents know where to pick up their children after the event. The nurse collects and labels any foods or medicines brought by the parents. If appropriate, a food-allergy sticker is put on the child's name tag. If a child wears diapers, the diaper bag is labeled with the child's name and sent to class with him or her.

After check-in: The nurse distributes the sign-in clipboards to group leaders. Attached to the clipboard should be a copy of the informational sheet the parents filled out.

First 45 minutes: Children and buddies play in class or on the playground as everyone arrives. Be sure these spaces are well stocked with appropriate toys, therapy balls, books, play dough, bubbles, etc.

The next 2 hours: The time goes quickly as small groups rotate through activity centers on a set schedule or are allowed free choice between rooms and centers. Remember that children with sensory sensitivities or developmental/cognitive disabilities may hesitate to take part in some of the group activities. They should be encouraged to get involved in the activities they enjoy. Be sure to also give them the freedom to refrain from participating in any activity that they find uncomfortable. Siblings should be given the option to participate with their brothers or sisters or with other children their own age.

The **Recreational Center** can vary according to the creativity of your staff. Offer at least one large-group recreational activity, such as a parachute game or relay race, and also make a variety of individual activities available. For children who aren't comfortable in a large group or have sensory issues, provide bubbles, therapy balls and squishy balls for use in playing with a buddy. Scooter boards and beanbag toss games are also fun, especially on the playground.

In the **Craft Center,** children will love creating unique art projects using simple things like cups, blocks and sponge shapes dipped in tempera paint. Crafts should be easy enough to be done with minor assistance for children with limited dexterity. Avoid small pieces that could be swallowed, and be sure all paints and markers are nontoxic. If you have an artistic volunteer, ask him or her to paint faces; most children will enjoy this.

In the **Music Center,** provide an assortment of rhythm instruments and colorful ribbons for waving. Most children with special needs will light up with joy when given the opportunity to sing with a guitarist or help the pianist play a song. Use a CD player or music DVD to accompany a lively classroom parade. For praise and worship songs, check out the music of Mary Rice Hopkins at her website (http://www.maryricehopkins.com).

In the **Community Center,** children get short presentations from local public servants—firefighters, police officers, nurses, trash collectors, etc.—and others who hold jobs that the children might find interesting—utility workers, science teachers, magicians, dog trainers, etc. Many of these people will come free of charge and are delighted to see what the church is doing for children with disabilities. They usually enjoy meeting the children as much as the children enjoy their presentations.

45 minutes before pickup: Children return to their rooms for snacks and play. Be sure to furnish healthy snacks that do not present choking hazards. Some programs choose to serve gluten-free snacks and avoid all peanut products. Parents appreciate a calming-down period before they arrive for pickup. You can show a short movie, read a story or provide quiet table activities such as puzzles, drawing or playing with dough.

Pickup time: Make sure the children are where parents were told to pick them up, and make sure parents sign their children out. This is also a great time to ask parents about their time away. It's natural to focus on the children, but respite is for parents, too. You should celebrate their time alone as a couple or the long nap they enjoyed. Your interest will remind the parents that you care about them and will reinforce the important work of your volunteers.

One Special Needs Pastor said, "The key to success in our respite care is that it's not like going to school. This is a fun time for the children! They can't wait to come back next month. Our buddies truly personalize the program. If a child enjoys one station more than another, the child is encouraged to remain at that station a little longer. I can't brag on our volunteers enough!"

Form: Application for Respite Care

We are excited to learn more about your child, so we can match him or her with the right respite worker. Please complete this mandatory form. We also encourage you to create an optional "Who Am I?" profile of your child on the back of this application. Thank you!

Child's Name _____ Birth Date _____

Address _____

Parent's Name(s) _____

Home Phone _____ E-Mail _____

Cell Phone _____ Work Phone _____

Referral Source _____

What community agencies is your child involved with? _____

_____

Who should we call in case you cannot be reached? Name _____

Phone _____ Relationship _____

Primary Physician _____

Address _____

Phone _____

Any additional physicians or other clinicians and phone numbers? _____

_____

Medical Insurance _____ Policy Number _____

Hospital of Choice _____

Medical History

Diagnosis of Disability _____

Date of Diagnosis _____

Cause (if known) _____

Significant Medical History (hospitalizations, surgeries, chronic illnesses, injuries, etc.) _____

_____

Allergies (food, medicines, insects, etc.) _____

_____

Is your child prone to respiratory ailments? _____

If so, please describe. _____

Has your child had seizures in the last two years? _____

If yes, when? _____

Types? _____

Frequency? _____

Duration? _____

What is the preferred caregiver response? _____

What cues does your child give when he or she is getting ill? _____

_____

Prescription Drugs and Dosages

1. _____

2. _____

3. _____

How are medications given (whole, crushed, in fruit, etc.)? _____

Other Medical Problems _____

Mobility

Please indicate which of the following your child does:

_____ Sit unsupported

_____ Crawl, creep, scoot, roll

_____ Walk independently

_____ Walk on uneven terrain

_____ Use a wheelchair or stroller

_____ Move his or her own wheelchair? (Circle whether the wheelchair is motorized or operated manually.)

Equipment and Activities

What equipment is needed by your child while in respite care? _____

_____

What does your child enjoy? _____

What makes your child laugh? _____

Does your child prefer soft or firm things? _____

What smells does your child like? _____

Does your child have a favorite movement (rocking, spinning, jumping, walking, rolling, etc.)? _____

Does your child have any favorite sounds, or is there a sound your child likes to make? _____

Does your child like looking at or playing with anything in particular? _____

What activities (reading, singing/music, arts and crafts, coloring, puzzles, water, sand play, etc.) does your child enjoy?

_____

_____

What are your child's favorite books, stories, music, computer programs? _____

_____

Speech Communication and Sensory Impairments

Which methods of communication does your child use?

_____ Points to objects named

_____ Uses generalized gestures or sounds

_____ Uses sign language

_____ Uses pictures or icons

_____ Says single words or sounds

_____ Says phrases or sentences

Can your child follow simple directions? _____

Does your child understand abstract ideas? _____

Does your child have any sensory impairments?

_____ Vision

_____ Hearing

_____ Touch (sensation)

_____ Balance

Cognitive and Emotional Characteristics

Cognitive Function—Describe your child's general development level. _____
_____

Emotional Characteristics—Does your child have special behavior problems? _____
If so, what are the specific problems? _____
How are they handled? _____
_____

What things are likely to distract, upset or frustrate your child? _____
_____

How does he or she react when upset or frustrated? _____
_____

What works to assist or comfort your child? _____
_____

Does your child like to be cuddled or hugged? _____

Activities of Daily Living

Does your child need assistance with dressing? _____
Does your child eat independently or need assistance? _____
Can your child use a cup, spoon, fork and knife? _____
Is your child right- or left-handed? _____
What are your child's favorite foods or snacks? _____
Does your child have a choking problem? _____
Does your child need assistance with toileting? _____
Does your child have occasional or frequent accidents? _____
Please describe _____
How often? _____
Is your child in diapers all the time or use a catheter? _____
Are there particular positions or activities to be avoided? _____
_____
_____

Signature of Parent/Legal Guardian _____
Date _____

Use the reverse side of this page to create an optional "Who Am I?" profile of your child and to tell us anything else we should know.

Outreach: Making Memories at Camp

Church camp! Those words stir up memories of s'mores around the campfire and devotions with cabin mates. Children with disabilities can share those memories, too, when you include them in your camping program. An integrated camp (one that includes children with disabilities alongside nondisabled chldren) can serve as an outreach to boys and girls who might not be welcome elsewhere.

Inclusive Camps

Challenges involved in integrating a child with a disability can be overcome with careful planning and creativity.

- **Our campsite isn't wheelchair friendly.** Build temporary plywood ramps or sidewalks. Mobi-Mats, portable roll-out access ways useful for wheelchairs, are available for purchase or rental. Make a private restroom and shower available, or provide a portable commode. Recruit volunteers to push a wheelchair over rough areas. Whatever the difficulty, think of a solution. After viewing your efforts and success, campground administrators may be willing to make permanent changes.

- **A child with an intellectual disability needs individual care**. Provide one-on-one buddies to help navigate the time at camp. Integration with peers is usually the goal, but some friends with developmental disabilities may prefer to stay in a cabin with a counselor of their own while participating in the week's program.

- **The child needs a family member or caregiver to attend**. Provide an individual cabin for personal-care needs. If a helper is required but family members need respite, provide a caregiver (paid or unpaid).

- **The medical needs are too great for us to handle**. The camp nurse can interview the parents before camp. If a caregiver needs to be provided, provide one.

- **Winter camp or beach camp doesn't seem very practical for walkers, wheelchairs or crutches**. Use a sled on the snow or beach to access fun with other campers. Place plywood walkways over snow or sand. Beach wheelchairs can be rented, as can Mobi-Mats.

- **The camper is on a special diet**. Arrange for the kitchen to prepare individualized meals or allow parents to send food. Ahead of time, provide parents with a menu so that they can create comparable meals. Remind them to send snacks for free time.

- **The campfire and recreational activities are not accessible**. Create a portable fire pit in the parking lot. Adapt recreational areas to include all campers.

- **There's no way the facility we use will work.** Find a new one!

If your church doesn't have a camp, provide scholarships that will enable children with disabilities to attend Christian camping programs designed with them in mind. Throughout the United States, there are many camps that offer experiences for children with special needs. Research ones in your area. The Joni and Friends International Disability Center website lists many Bible camps that are accessible and inclusive (http://www.joniandfriends.org/resources.php). Teens with disabilities are welcome at all Young Life camps, and their Young Life Capernaum Ministries have camps specifically for young people with disabilities (http://www.younglife.org/Capernaum).

JAF Family Retreats

Joni and Friends Family Retreats are five inspiring days of summer camping for families affected by disability. Families are renewed, marriages restored, children motivated and souls saved. Tell the families in your disability ministry about JAF Family Retreats and encourage them to attend one of the many retreats held across the United States. Offer to assist parents in raising money to attend, because attendance is life changing and so worthwhile.

Disability impacts the entire family, and JAF Family Retreats address each member's unique needs.

- **Parents** participate in workshops specifically for them, listen to Bible teachers, attend praise and worship, and network with other parents. Married couples are treated to special times, and single parents are encouraged as they fellowship with one another.

- **Children impacted by disability** enjoy the week with short-term missionaries as buddies. They are encouraged to stretch themselves during activities designed with them in mind. They can hang out and be part of the crowd, gaining independence that might not be available to them at other times. Children and adults with disabilities can help one another progress, whether in trying new physical skills, learning to be more social, expanding language abilities, emotionally accepting situations or growing in their spiritual walks.

- **Siblings** enjoy the activities as well, gaining new insights from being with fellow siblings and other children with disabilities. They achieve a bit of normalcy at a family retreat, because everyone there is dealing with disability-related issues.

A week at a JAF Family Retreat is packed full of fun activities. Besides great Bible teaching and worship, campers are treated to a variety of opportunities and activities: a talent show, a square dance, swimming, fishing, a rock wall, horseback riding, a carnival, concerts, arts and crafts, sports and games, meeting old friends and making new ones, and making memories to last a lifetime (or at least until next year!).

The spiritual benefits of JAF Family Retreats are invaluable. Prayer times strengthen and encourage, whether they be corporate petitions or intimate, impromptu intercessions. Messages from God's Word, tailor-made for those affected by disability, change lives and attitudes. Often, people accept Christ as their Savior during a JAF Family Retreat, because the unconditional love given to them demonstrates a true picture of what the Body of Christ looks like. The retreats have even been described as a small taste of heaven, and families return home with greater vision for disability ministry in their churches and communities. Many families stay in touch throughout the year, praying for and encouraging one another.

Local Church Family Retreat

Consider hosting a retreat for families from your church. Model it after a JAF Family Retreat, coming up with your own ideas, too. Even a weekend away would be a treat, or if this seems insurmountable, hold a miniretreat day. Include fun activities for the children while the parents are treated to a day filled with teaching, fellowship and even pampering! Close your miniretreat with a celebration for the entire family.

Creating a family retreat for your church benefits your entire disability ministry. Volunteers receive hands-on training, advice, and encouragement as they serve families affected by disability. Camp is one place where they can truly "get" disability ministry, learning to understand it, embrace it, enjoy it and catch the vision to replicate it. Veteran volunteers will be the first to help in your special needs ministry, and most of their training will already have taken place! Encourage folks from your church to consider serving as retreat volunteers, and support them with prayer and finances. Your extra efforts will earn big rewards:

After being blessed by JAF Family Retreats for several years, Brent and Rachel were inspired to begin a Joni and Friends Chapter in their own community.

When Sable was brought to a JAF Family Retreat by her grandma, she heard the gospel for the first time. She accepted Jesus as her Savior.

Tim was bitter about being the brother to Bobby, who is severely disabled. He found forgiveness and acceptance at a JAF Family Retreat and now serves yearly as a short-term missionary.

Bryce lives for his annual week at retreat. It is his time to shine like the star he is. His first words when he gets in the car to go home are "What's the theme for next year's retreat?"

Outreach: Ministering to Siblings

When a group of people live together under one roof, relationships can get complicated. Their shared love provides a sense of security, and the status of their relationships also helps to uniquely shape each family member. Children are also affected by their birth order, environment, personality and passions. And while some children interact easily with their parents and siblings, others may be withdrawn, angry or feel misunderstood. The birth of a child with special needs further complicates the mix.

Understanding Their Unique Challenges

When a nondisabled child is born into a family, older siblings adjust to new routines and to receiving less attention from their parents, but they quickly return to activities they enjoy. When a child with special needs arrives, however, parents must work through their grief while researching medical decisions and taking care of their family at the same time. With one child constantly receiving extra time and attention, siblings often feel hurt and begin asking themselves some difficult questions:

- *Do my parents love me as much as my sibling?*

- *Why are my parents so cranky and stressed out?*

- *How can my friends understand me?*

- *Why do I feel so angry and lonely?*

- *When will our family get back to normal?*

Most parents of children with disabilities are very busy and often distracted by the day-to-day care the special needs child requires. They have less time for older siblings. Sometimes parents ask other children to stop taking music or dance lessons or to drop out of sports because the parents can no longer afford these activities or can no longer fit them into their schedules. Overworked, stressed-out parents may become easily irritated and seem insensitive to their other children's disappointments and accomplishments. Siblings of children with disabilities desperately want time with their parents and acceptance from their peers. At the least, these siblings need to be able to do the following:

- Focus on their own needs (to a certain extent)

- Understand their sibling's disability

- Learn not to be embarrassed by their sibling

- Find someone who understands their unique experiences

These children often carry heavy responsibilities at a young age and can become extremely mature and compassionate teens and adults. Without support, however, they may grow up feeling neglected and become bitter and angry. Your church can help by offering these children support activities and workshops.

Planning Sibling Support Activities

Earlier in this book, we discussed ways for families affected by disabilities to get acquainted at church, respite events, family camps or other church-sponsored activities. All of these events allow siblings to meet each other and explore their common experiences. As siblings grow comfortable with one another, consider offering fellowship activities and support groups designed with them in mind. Although Bible-based curriculum for sibling groups is still being developed, churches can pattern their program after the Meyer and Vadasy model developed by Donald Meyer and Patricia Vadasy and described in their book *Sibshops: Workshops for Siblings of Children with Special Needs.*

In 1999, Donald Meyer and Patricia Vadasy recognized the need for informal social gatherings for siblings of children with special needs, and they developed a national program called Sibshops. Sibshops are support groups designed to encourage siblings of children affected by disabilities. When children spend time with other siblings of children with special needs, they feel less isolated and vulnerable. A growing number of churches have started faith-based Sibshops in their communities, seeking to add a biblical perspective to these useful gatherings.

Running a Church Sibshop

A Sibshop should not be structured like a therapy session. It may be therapeutic, but from the beginning, it must be made clear to all concerned that only professional counselors are qualified to lead a therapy session.

Plan to meet in a relaxed setting so that siblings can discuss their joys and concerns. They need a safe place to learn how to handle the implications of a brother's or a sister's special needs.

Parent Meeting and Group Goals

Before meeting with siblings, hold a parent meeting to explain what your Sibshop group hopes to accomplish. You may want to suggest that each family order a copy of *Living with a Brother or Sister with Special Needs: A Book for Sibs* by Donald Meyer and Patricia Vadasy.

Then discuss the following goals for the children in your group:

- Meet together in a relaxed, recreational setting.

- Hear and understand that the church values the siblings as individuals and supports their unique family roles.

- Learn God's perspective on the value of all children—disabled and nondisabled.

- Have a forum for discussing the siblings' joys and concerns.

- Discover how others handle situations they experience at home and in the community.

- Learn more about the implications of the needs of each sibling's brother or sister.

Sibshop Discussion Topics

Here's a list of discussion topics for your Sibshop group, but don't be limited by this list. Create more topics as you get to know the needs of your group:
- How to Build Friendships
- How to Manage Anger
- How to Accept Differences in Others
- How to Handle Frustrations with Parents
- How to Overcome Guilt, Resentment and Jealousy
- How to Cope with Embarrassment and Pride
- How to Trust God with Loneliness, Isolation and Loss
- How to Handle Increased Responsibility and Change

Initial Meeting

At first, some siblings may be reticent about joining a Sibshop group. Although they recognize that their lives are different from those of their peers, they may not be in a hurry to talk about their experiences or to be singled out. They may not believe that other siblings could truly share their unusual experiences. They could be angry about their situation or afraid of sounding strange if they share their thoughts. For these reasons, any event planned on their behalf needs to be primarily focused on making friends and enjoying fellowship. Small doses of biblical teaching and self-evaluation can be mixed into a morning or afternoon of games, recreational and team-building activities.

Sibshop Scheduling and Activities

How often and how long a group meets and the number of children it serves will depend on the ages of siblings already in your community. Teaching and informational activities should be personalized to suit the dynamic of each group. You can use your own creative ideas and individual style to plan your group, but here are some popular activities for each gathering:

1. **Icebreaker Activities**—As children arrive, plan simple party games to help them learn each other's name, interests and background. Make these activities silly, lively and "connection" oriented. Adult volunteers should participate with the children, making sure that everyone is included and feels welcome.

2. **Lively Recreational Activities**—As you sprinkle games throughout your time together, keep in mind the size of your meeting room or outdoor space. Create variations on dodge ball or Duck, Duck, Goose. Most boys and girls enjoy running underneath a large, colorful parachute as someone calls out the color of their shirt or the first letter of their name. You may also check local bookstores or teacher-supply stores for party games that can be modified for your particular group. The key is to allow the children several opportunities to move around and to have fun.

3. **Team-Building Activities**—Challenge children to build giant towers with blocks of wood or pyramids with paper cups. Assign a team of children to prepare snacks or a meal together. Have the children work together doing some task that is difficult to do alone but is easy to do with the help of friends. As friendships grow, introduce activities like "trust falls" that require children to take turns falling backward into their partner's arms.

4. **Disability Simulations**—Although these children have watched their siblings face challenges, few have

actually navigated in the world of disability themselves. For example, one boy's sister, who has developmental delays, may use fewer than three words to communicate her needs. To help the children understand her frustration, pair them up and ask them to speak only three-word sentences throughout the meeting. As a result, the children will learn to ask simpler questions and give simpler responses. Here are some hands-on activity stations that work well with adults or children:

Visual Deficits Station

- Rub Vaseline on sunglass lenses to simulate blurred vision. Children take turns wearing the glasses while leading each other around.

- Children wear a blindfold to simulate complete blindness, and use a dowel as a cane to help feel around for objects in the room.

Physical Disability Station

- Children take turns sitting in a wheelchair and, without help, maneuver in and out of the room to simulate a person who has a spinal cord injury.

- Children tie their shoes while wearing oversized gloves or having several fingers taped together to simulate partial paralysis.

Deafness Station

- While everyone else speaks in a whisper, one child wears earplugs to simulate complete hearing loss.

- Children write down the words they understand by lipreading the words the teacher mouths.

Speech Limitations Station

- To simulate speech disorders, children use a straw as a pointer to spell out words on an alphabet communication board.

- Children spell their name and sign a five-word sentence using sign language.

5. **Bible Lesson Time**—At some point, you'll want to lead the children in a serious discussion about a Bible story and a Bible verse, and you'll want to engage them in prayer. Assure them that God created them, as well as their siblings, with value and purpose. Usually, a group must meet several times before the children feel comfortable responding to personal questions related to a Bible story. If several members' siblings share similar disabilities, talk about the causes and characteristics of these conditions. Discuss fears the children might have, such as the fear of catching the disability or the fear that they somehow caused the disability.

6. **Art Time**—Art provides a wonderful outlet for children to express their feelings. You might give each child a brightly colored piece of paper printed with the words "If I could tell the rest of the world one thing about having a sibling with a disability, I would say . . ." Leave plenty of room for a child to give a written answer and to illustrate his or her thoughts. If you work with young children, ask them to draw a picture of their family, and have volunteers available to assist them in putting their thoughts into words.

7. **Wrap-Up**—Close your gathering on a lighthearted, fun note. You may want to end with an upbeat sing-along or a humorous skit.

When churches help siblings of children with special needs, they grow to understand and welcome God's plan for these families. It's a high calling with rich rewards.

"Come on, Benny. You can do it!" shouted Andy from the stands at the Miracle Field softball playoffs. Benny rounded second base, furiously pushing his walker with the help of his buddy. He was biting his lip as he headed for home plate in front of his neighborhood fan club. "Wow! Your first home run, Bro!" screamed Andy. Benny pushed his hair off his sweaty forehead and looked at Andy in the stands. Then he pointed heavenward with one finger signifying God had helped him do his best. As Andy jumped over the bleachers to greet Benny, he realized that his old attitudes toward his brother were gone. Instead of embarrassment, Andy felt prouder of Benny than he ever had before.

— Andy's story about his brother

First Community Church
Special Needs Ministry

invites all brothers and sisters of children with disabilities to join us for

An Afternoon of Fun

Just for Siblings

We will go miniature golfing and return to the church to make a snack together, do some fun crafts and share a little about your unique role in your family. It will be a great chance to build new friendships and get to know other children in similar circumstances.

Date _____
Time _____
Please RSVP to _____

Meet in the church parking lot.

There is no cost for this event!

Outreach: Hosting a VBS for Children with Autism

The diagnosis of autism is growing in America. Fortunately, awareness and services are growing as well. A church prepared to welcome and teach children with autism will be on the cutting edge of ministry. Desperate, discouraged families will be uplifted and blessed when a caring church purposefully makes a place for these children who are often difficult to accept and include.

Place Children in Appropriate Classes

Autism impacts children in many different ways. Additionally, children with autism often pick up and mimic the behavior of those around them. For example, the behavior of a child only moderately affected by autism may actually regress if the child is consistently exposed to children who are more severely impacted. For this reason, church staff needs to be careful when determining appropriate classroom placement for each individual child.

Some children will be able to attend regular VBS activities that have had a little modification. Others are affected so deeply by autism that they need to be full-time in a classroom exclusively for children with special needs. Most children on the autism spectrum fall somewhere in between. One solution is to pair a child with a volunteer in a class with nondisabled peers and have lessons modified to meet the child's capabilities. Many students can join typical peers for crafts, music and recreation and then go to the special needs classroom during any lengthy sitting and listening time. Other options for these sitting and listening times are to involve the child in being a teacher's helper (showing pictures, handling props, etc.) or taking a walk with a buddy when needed. When students grow and change, their placement needs may also change. The higher the level of inclusion, the better for everyone involved.

If you decide that an autism-specific VBS classroom is necessary for ministry, be sure to provide thorough training for your staff.

Train Your VBS Staff

For volunteers who are unfamiliar with autism, serving in a special needs classroom can be a stretching experience. Preparation and training are key. Training materials are available in this book, through local autism societies and on the Internet. The Organization for Autism Research is an excellent source for inexpensive workbooks and other training materials (http://www.research autism.org). The movies *Autism Is a World* (DVD) and *Autism Every Day* (video) are excellent films to expose staff to common behaviors. Highlights of *Autism Is a*

World can be viewed online (http://www.cnn.com/CNN/Programs/presents/index.autism.word.html) and a 13-minute film version of Autism Every Day can be viewed online (http://www.autismspeaks.org/sponsored events/autism_every_day.php). The movies can be purchased in their entirety through Amazon.com or other online stores.

Recognize a Child's Abilities

Although autism may exist as a co-diagnosis with mental retardation, autism itself does not affect the intelligence of children. Language, perceptions of the environment, and the ability to socialize impact children with autism in varying degrees, but teachers are often surprised by these students' capabilities.

Understand the Physical Nature of the Task

Teachers of children on the autistic spectrum must realize that teaching children with ASD can be a physical job. There may be an occasion when physical restraint is needed to help a student regain self-control to prevent self-injury or injury to others. This may seem like a scary bridge to cross when relating to a child with special needs, but when done calmly, it actually builds behavioral boundaries and strengthens the teacher-child relationship.

Physical restraint is not about punishment but safety. For example, if a boy does not want to leave a play area to go to story time, he may throw himself down and bang his head on the floor. If the area is thickly carpeted, it is okay for teachers to calmly stand close by until he is finished and then guide him to story time. However, if the floor is tiled rather than carpeted, self-injury is clearly a danger, so physical intervention is a must. In this case, a teacher must be prepared to wrap the boy in his or her arms and hold him firmly against his or her body until the parents or appropriate staff is called or until the child is calm and indicates he is ready to move on to the next activity. A child may choose to lash out physically at a teacher or fellow student. If this were to happen, a teacher must be prepared to intervene quickly and calmly as described above. (Contact your local Department of Family and Protective Services, Educational Service Center, or Mental Health and Mental Retardation Center to get training in the appropriate use of physical restraint.)

With proper environmental preparation and classroom arrangements, most physical outbursts can be avoided; but it is unrealistic to assume they will never happen. If meltdowns are a pattern in a child's behavior, ask one of the child's parents to stay for the entire first session, so you can observe the interaction between child and parent and ask questions. Also be aware that some students with autism may react strongly and negatively to being touched, so getting to know your students beforehand is critical.

Learn About Students' Abilities and Needs

When ministering to individuals with autism, preparation and knowledge of each unique child is essential. Since first visits are critical, gather information ahead of time using a registration form. If at all possible, visit the child's home to get a feel for what makes the child comfortable. Call for an appointment, and keep the visit short. Leave a copy of the VBS schedule, so the parents can prepare the child for the first day of VBS.

As you preregister students, invite families to visit the church facility and classroom during the week prior to VBS. Family members can then help their child become familiar with the new environment—the route to class, restroom locations, etc. In this way, the child can become familiar with a new environment under the care of familiar adults. New classmates and teachers will then be introduced in an environment the child has already become familiar with, lessening the stress of change.

Establish a High Staff-to-Student Ratio

As your church plans a VBS for children with ASD, you should establish a ratio of one volunteer for every two students. When a child is new to the program, a ratio of one volunteer to one student may be best until that child is comfortable with routines and expectations.

Arrange the Classroom for Good Behavior

Give special attention to classroom arrangement. Remove unnecessary items that might distract the children. Arrange furniture to designate the different activities. You may set up a music area, a story circle and a craft table. Use bookshelves or other furniture to separate these areas, and put only the items necessary for that day's activities in each area. In the music area, for example, only hands-on instruments and a tape or CD player should be present. An excellent story area can be created with a circle of beanbag chairs in which children can sprawl and not be expected to sit up properly. Additionally, be sure to

block all but one exit and designate a volunteer to sit near that exit because some children with ASD are runners.

Choose a space where students who feel overstimulated can go to get their sensory needs met. And designate a separate room or area as a free-play zone geared to the five senses. It might include a net swing, a plastic pool filled with beanbags, an exercise ball, or any other type of toy. A small pup tent or a table draped with a blanket can also be a comfortable getaway.

Post a Picture Schedule

Most children with autism are visual learners. Hang a poster schedule on the wall, and illustrate the schedule with large icons representing each VBS activity you choose to offer (for example, music, story, craft, free play and snack). When children can see and comprehend the sequence of activities, there is much more order in the classroom.

Following a schedule may be difficult at first, but once it is established, it will curb problem behaviors in the long run. Children might display loud, physical protests when they are not allowed to spend the entire time in the free-play zone, but teachers should try to stick with the schedule. If necessary, lengthen the time of preferred activities and shorten the others. Following the schedule will communicate to the child that the child is not in control of the classroom and that activities come in a predictable order. You want the child to perceive that the church environment is not chaotic but orderly and safe. Simple adjustment of the schedule can solve transition problems as well. For example, moving students out of the free-play zone is much easier if free play comes right before snack time. Calm, consistent order will help protests fade considerably. However, always be willing to adjust to what works.

Use Music to Connect

Play soothing music as students enter the room. This creates a calm atmosphere and helps children feel at ease. Hands-on instruments such as maracas, bells and sand blocks will further engage the children. Playing familiar favorite tunes can establish a quick connection. Children may begin to request "I Love You" (a song sung by Barney, the purple dinosaur, on his television show), "Itsy Bitsy Spider" or "The Alphabet Song." Responding to these requests is an opportunity for teaching about taking turns and for interaction and bonding. Singing spiritual songs may seem important, but focusing on establishing relationships and structure are actually top priority. As students become familiar with their new environment, teacher-selected songs can be introduced. Later in the period, schedule music again in a more structured, lesson-specific format. If a teacher or volunteer is able to play an instrument, bring in live music as a special treat at the end of the period. This may be an excellent motivation to encourage good behavior and active participation.

Teach Visual Lessons

Whether teaching how to do a craft or the sequence of a Bible story, teach visually. This is usually the preferred way of taking in information for those on the autism spectrum. First *show* a child, and then *tell* a child, using short and simple sentences. If necessary, move a child through an activity bodily, decreasing your help gradually, because the goal is independence. Posting clear step-by-step pictures of the craft being assembled can be very helpful to some children. Their sense of independent understanding and completion instills a sense of pride and accomplishment that is priceless. All children deserve praise for even the smallest signs of participation.

A week of VBS may not allow you enough time to see changes in a child's life. The time needed for that may more realistically be months or years. But even a small investment of time can bless parents immeasurably and allow a child with autism to take the first small step toward understanding that church is a place of safety and love. More importantly, you and your church will learn the validity of an autism ministry, gain a better understanding of what is required, and understand how participating in such a ministry brings blessings in return.

Tips: Dos and Don'ts for Hosting a VBS for Children with Autism

DO

1. Educate others in your church and share your vision.
2. Make a home visit and get to know the parents.
3. Get to know each individual child before he or she attends class.
4. Have a high staff-to-student ratio.
5. Include students as much as possible in activities with typical children.
6. Treat children with respect.
7. Dress casually.
8. Communicate visually.
9. Follow a schedule.
10. Be sensitive to sensory issues.
11. Be in control of a single entrance and exit.
12. Post a picture schedule.
13. Use music to teach.
14. Have a sense of humor.
15. Expect the unexpected.

DON'T

1. Go it alone.
2. Wing it.
3. Assume if you have worked with one student with autism, you know how to work with another.
4. Automatically segregate students with autism from the rest of the children.
5. Assume students with autism are not intelligent.
6. Wear a suit and tie or hose and heels.
7. Have a cluttered room or fragile equipment.
8. Talk too much.
9. Invade personal space unless you know you are welcome.
10. Teach in a room with multiple or unattended exits.
11. Be a control freak.
12. Set rigid expectations.

Outreach: Creating a G.L.U.E. Team*

How many adhesives do you currently have in your home? What types of glue and tape are hidden in toolboxes and kitchen drawers? Certainly one needs tape for gift wrapping, electrical wiring, fraying carpet edges, painting jobs or displays. Glue bottles are also important for school crafts, wood projects, broken picture frames and delicate displays with a corner that just came loose. Whether hot or cold, sturdy or invisible, the right adhesive must be correctly matched to the job at hand.

Within the Body of Christ, it's clear from Scripture that everyone belongs and is a valuable member. What some churches need, however, is the correct adhesive to help certain body parts stick firmly within a local congregation.

G.L.U.E. teams enlighten the Body of Christ of its missing body part, those with special needs. Along with that, they assist the Body in finding the right adhesive that will ensure the person with unique gifts and needs bonds to that Body of Christ. . . . The mission of the G.L.U.E. team ministry is . . . including those with special needs, building the Body of Christ. G.L.U.E. teams help individuals or families belong. They encourage the Body of Christ to see those with unique gifts and needs as Christ sees them.**

The Need

There are some children with disabilities who will never need a G.L.U.E. team. Their families have the strategies and support they need to help surround that child. There are other families, however, who need planned church support to continue the daily tasks of raising their child in the Lord. As you get to know the child with disabilities, visit the child's home so that you learn what the child's daily home life is like and whether or not the home situation requires community involvement. Perhaps parents are never able to leave the house together because the child's care needs are so great. Caregivers may be getting little sleep at

night, a child may be isolated from the community or a family may not feel able to attend church. Whatever the situation is in the home, a visit there will allow you to determine whether the child could use some church arms wrapped around him or her in a trained and practical way.

The Glue

The letters *G, L, U* and *E* stand for the words "Giving," "Loving," "Understanding" and "Encouraging."

Giving

While many church ministries are set up to support short-term needs as they arise, a G.L.U.E. team exists to give support in situations where the needs will be ongoing. Raising a child with a particular area of disability often suggests that the child and family will need continued support over time. The church asks volunteers to obey God's command in 1 Corinthians 15:58 (emphasis

added): "Always *give* yourselves fully to the work of the Lord, because you know that your labor in the Lord is not in vain." A G.L.U.E. team offers volunteers a chance to give to the Lord by giving to an individual or family unit.

Loving

Loving a child with special needs as well as the child's family will be unique for each G.L.U.E. team, because the kind of loving, practical support given is based on the needs of the family and child. One G.L.U.E. team may support the family by providing transportation, while another set of volunteers focus on making Sunday worship a time when all family members can participate. Another G.L.U.E. team may be involved with providing respite care or supporting the family by helping with such daily tasks as meal preparation. The volunteers each have the chance to honor God's call for us to love one another within His family.

Understanding

G.L.U.E. team volunteers will understand better than most people the unique challenges and joys connected with the child who has a disability. The team will be well trained to offer desperately needed types of loving support. Each G.L.U.E. member will know the details connected with this child's life—procedures for feeding and clothing this person, allergies and sensitivities, likes and dislikes, challenges and joys, medical interventions and family preferences. This kind of specific information gives way to a deeper understanding and allows the child, family and volunteers to better see the beautiful portrait of community painted in 1 Corinthians 12:26-27: "If one part suffers, every part suffers with it; if one part is honored, every part rejoices with it. Now you are the body of Christ, and each one of you is a part of it."

Encouraging

Intimate understanding pours itself into encouragement. The encouragement happens in all directions. Not only can the volunteers encourage the family members, but also the child with special needs encourages caregivers—often teaching lessons no one else could ever offer. The family links with others in the congregation, freeing them all to minister to one another. Families who were unable to walk through a church doorway are now welcomed and enfolded by a team of individuals who are equipped to both suffer and rejoice with each other. A mom of a child with a disability can take her place as the church worship leader while teen and adult G.L.U.E. volunteers tend to the physical and spiritual needs of the woman's child. As others interact and watch, God uses the situation to grow the heart of all involved in the process. The Body of Christ is strengthened and offers

a fragrant sacrifice to God as they serve and encourage one another.

Brian's G.L.U.E. Team

Brian is 11 years old. He enjoys music, is able to give one-word answers to certain questions and is "all boy," needing a rough-and-tumble outlet for his maturing body. Brian also happens to have autism. Certain situations can upset Brian, and he can act aggressively with others but be unable to explain his behavior. Brian's family wanted to attend church together, but the parents decided that that was impractical, so they took turns staying home with him during worship services. Sometimes the parents ventured out to an evening dinner and praise service, but the family often left that setting exhausted and hopeless about Sunday attendance. They wanted each family member to grow within the local church body, but that didn't seem possible.

Noticing this family's desire, the church they belong to partnered with CLC Network to help launch a G.L.U.E. team for Brian. Using a set of interviews and other tools, volunteers got to know Brian—this was the most important first step. As part of this initial step, the family had a chance to describe the supports they thought would be helpful and to voice their greatest need. For Brian's family, church attendance on Sunday morning and Wednesday night was the greatest need. Then the congregation had a chance to respond.

At an informational meeting, congregation members had a chance to consider volunteering to be part of Brian's G.L.U.E. team. Those volunteers who stepped forward had an extensive training session. Each person knew exactly how to interact with Brian to solicit times of calm and to support times of need. Due to Brian's rough-and-tumble approach to life, the church placed a special call for "football player" type volunteers. Asking for males to do the direct care offered chances for other volunteers to come around the family in such areas as planning positive interaction with Brian's peers at church, designing an individualized curriculum that introduced Brian to Jesus, preparing occasional meals and making emergency calls during the week.

With the plan in place, the congregation devoted space in the church's newsletter and time in church to commission the G.L.U.E. team and give information to the entire community about Brian and the opportunities ahead. All church members learned that it's okay for Brian to stand on the side aisle and dance during worship time. They also learned that when the service becomes hard for Brian, two G.L.U.E. team members will take him to a well-designed room so that he can begin to learn about Jesus while enjoying time with his larger-sized male friends. Brian's peers learned about Brian and know that after church, he will be part of Sunday School for singing, snack and as much of the lesson as possible. At a certain point, his G.L.U.E. members for the day will go with him to a quiet room that has a door hammock swing for calming times.

The G.L.U.E. team also decided to invite Brian to some of the sporting events at the local high school. For the first time, the phone rang, and there were people asking for Brian. The family has marveled as older teens pick him up for an afternoon of fun. Well equipped to read Brian's mood, the teens understand that the fun may last an hour or three hours. These volunteers have embraced Brian, know him well and have given the family hope and a home for worship. The church as a whole now understands Brian, autism and the joy of opening their hearts and lives to a family affected by special needs.

The church correctly matched the right adhesive to the bonding job at hand.

G.L.U.E. Team Five-Step Process

The creation of a G.L.U.E. team is basically a five-step process.

Step 1: Read the Label

If you want to know what's inside, read the label. It's important to allow pastors, elders and other leaders to hear about G.L.U.E. teams, so they can understand and embrace the vision. Appoint a coordinator and then launch the remaining steps in the process of forming a team.

Step 2: Open the G.L.U.E.

Get to know the child and family. Offer the congregation the opportunity to join the team, energizing them with the vision and the needs of the family. Offer scriptural mandates for including and embracing each one within the church body.

Step 3: Select the G.L.U.E.

Collect the information you need from the child and family to form a plan for the team. Be specific about materials, facility issues, training, awareness and all facets of what needs to happen for the team to function effectively.

Step 4: Spread the G.L.U.E.

Make sure each individual on the team has the information and training necessary to be part of the plan.

Step 5: Secure the Bond

Perform needed tasks to maintain the team. Make sure that the G.L.U.E. team responds to changing needs within the family. Offer times to thank the team in an official way. Second Corinthians 9:12-14 speaks clearly to G.L.U.E. volunteers:

> This service that you perform is not only supplying the needs of God's people but is also overflowing in many expressions of thanks to God. Because of the service by which you have proved yourselves, men will praise God for the obedience that accompanies your confession of the gospel of Christ, and for your generosity in sharing with them and with everyone else.

You thank and honor God with your acts of giving, loving, understanding and encouraging.

*G.L.U.E. Team is a trademark of CLC Network. The G.L.U.E. Team Training Manual, which will guide you through the process of creating a team, is available from CLC Network (http://www.clc network.org).

** Kimberly Luurtsema and Barbara J. Newman, *G.L.U.E. Team Training Manual* (Wyoming, MI: CLC Network, 2007), p. 3.

Outreach: Breaking Bread at a Luke 14 Banquet

Pull out your Bible, and open it to Luke chapter 14. Read the parable of the great banquet, verses 16-24. This passage is what some involved in disability ministry call the Luke 14 Mandate: "Go out quickly into the streets and alleys of the town and bring in the poor, the crippled, the blind and the lame" (Luke 14:21). Why? "So that [God's] house will be full" (Luke 14:23). What an awesome way to reach out to the unsaved in your community: Literally, host a Luke 14 Banquet!

For your church's Luke 14 Banquet, invite children and families affected by disability to share a fabulous meal with the express purpose of showing them love and presenting the gospel. Many Bible translations say "*compel them to come in*" (Luke 14:23, emphasis added, *KJV* and *NKJV,* among others). By making your Luke 14 Banquet as compelling as possible, many will be attracted to God.

Invitees

Exactly who or how many should you invite? Start as small as you need to or as big as you have room and vision for! Invite one group home in your neighborhood or every individual affected by disability in your town. Find this population through local disability programs such as the Arc, the Down Syndrome Association or the Autism Society. Advertise in their newsletters, and send them invitations to distribute and posters to display. Extend invitations to caregivers and family members who may not live in the same home as the child with the disability.

Theme

Choose a theme around which you can build your event. The theme can be either a holiday (Christmas, Valentine's Day, etc.), a particular cultural event (Mexican fiesta, Hawaiian luau, etc.) or a motif of your own creation (a western hoedown, a cruise, etc.).

Welcome

First impressions are important, so think through what it will be like for those arriving at your church.

- **Provide adequate accessible parking.** Create additional temporary spaces if needed. Parking-lot attendants can direct cars, answer questions and help guests unload. Valet parking would add an elegant touch!

- **Take pictures as guests enter.** Print and place them in a cover with the logo of your event, ready to give each family at the end of the evening, or mail them later.

- **Have friendly greeters** welcome guests. The greeters can help with registration forms. In this way, you'll be able to obtain contact information for future events.

Dinner

Make your meal as extravagant and fancy as resources allow, demonstrating that God's love goes beyond what is deserved or justifiable. Invite volunteers to host tables, providing place settings and centerpieces. Servers can do the running back and forth from the kitchen. Your kitchen staff will be the behind-the-scenes heroes of the banquet.

Entertainment

Create an atmosphere that will make guests want to return next year or even next Sunday. Keep in mind your purpose in holding a Luke 14 Banquet—bringing people into God's kingdom. If possible, provide several types of entertainment:

- Magicians or clowns

- Choirs, worship bands or guest musicians

- A speaker and/or several testimonies (provide an interpreter for guests who are deaf)

Gifts

A gift basket or even one small item will shower guests with love. Recruit volunteers to gather, organize, wrap and distribute the gifts.

Extras

Offer a Quiet Room for guests who are overstimulated during the banquet and need a safe place to regroup. Ahead of time, think of any other necessities that should be available for guests.

And of course, cover your event in prayer from start to finish!

As you step out in obedience by holding your Luke 14 Banquet, "You will be blessed. Although they cannot repay you, you will be repaid at the resurrection" (Luke 14:14).

Twists to a Luke 14 Banquet

- Hold a Prom Night for teens and adults with developmental disabilities.

- Bless mothers of children with special needs with a luncheon and pampering. Hold a carnival for their children.

Faith Steps: Tools for Helping Children Deal with Loss

God keeps every promise he makes. He is like a shield for all who seek his protection.
Proverbs 30:5, *TEV*

As Pastor Matt drove to the Gonzalez home, he broke out in a cold sweat. He didn't have a clue about what to say to the two boys who had just lost their mother in a car accident. All the puppet shows he'd led in children's church seemed trivial at a time like this. Matt prayed for strength to keep his composure, because he really wanted to comfort Hosea and his brother, Felipe, who had multiple dystrophy and really had depended on his mom.

The Gonzalez children are part of a large number of children who experience loss each day. While losing a parent is the highest cause of stress, there are other losses that deeply affect children, especially those in families with disabilities. These include the loss of the family unit through divorce and the loss of a body part, a pet, a friend, a grandparent or a sibling. Children can also lose a sense of trust or confidence—even faith in God when their prayers seem to go unanswered.

Some people think children are resilient and adjust faster to a loss than adults, but much depends on the suddenness of the loss, the ages of the children and the degree of preparation the children have gone through. Regardless, children go through the same stages of grief as adults.

Stages of the Grieving Process

The five stages of grief are usually sequential and have distinctive characteristics. As with adults, though, children can get stuck in one stage for a period of time, or their grief can go underground and then resurface as they mature.

1. **Denial**—A time of confusion and disorientation that could include physical symptoms such as headaches, weakness and numbness.

2. **Anger**—A period of uncertainty, fear, panic, nervousness and/or changes in diet or sleep.

3. **Bargaining**—A time when attempts are made to change the situation by suggesting to God, "If I do this, will you take away the loss?"

4. **Depression**—A period when there is a sense of hopelessness and numbness and a fear of losing memories.

5. **Acceptance**—A time of understanding that this is not going away, relaxing with the change, adjusting to the reality and having hope for the future.

Children have a God-given ability to work through their grief and move toward healing. It is not up to us to talk them out of their feelings, but we can provide a safe, confidential place where they can move through the process.

Children younger than five years of age can't understand that loss is not temporary. Even older children may appear to be unaffected by loss. This may indicate that they're not ready to talk about their feelings. Never push the children to discuss their feelings, but let them know that you're there to listen and to pray with them. In cases of death, avoid words that might be confusing such as "passed away" or "went to sleep." Answer questions, but don't overload the children with information. And don't be surprised if children ask the same questions over and over. This is part of how they process their emotions.

Teach children that grieving can draw us closer to God, who wants us to put our hope in Him. First Thessalonians 4:13-14 (*NIrV*) says, "We don't want you to be sad, as other people are. They don't have any hope. We believe that Jesus died and rose again." To help children understand the partnership of loss and hope, Rabbi Marc Gellman and Monsignor Thomas Hartman wrote a wonderful book entitled *Lost and Found: A Kid's Book for Living Through Loss*. It begins with this great old hymn:

Amazing grace! How sweet the sound that saved a wretch like me.

I once was lost, but now am found, was blind, but now I see.

Gellman and Hartman write that their book will help children draw a hopeful conclusion about their world:

Each chapter is about something you might lose in your life and also about something you might find that will help you get on with your life. Every time something is lost, something can be found. That's the way life works here on planet Earth.*

In their discussion about losing a body part, Gellman and Hartman give children some great advice: Whether it is the loss of a body part through amputation or the loss of a body part's function (such as hearing):

How do you get comfortable with yourself if you have lost a part of your body? One way is to understand that you are not your body. Your body is kind of like a case for your soul, which is what you're really like. And even though you may have lost some parts of your body, you still have lots of parts left. By learning how to make your other parts stronger, you can overcome the loss of the parts you don't have. Have you ever seen the shoulder muscles of the people who use wheelchairs? Their shoulder muscles are usually stronger than those of people who have legs.**

This is a powerful message for children with disabilities.

Techniques for Dealing with Sensitive Topics

Here are several techniques that professionals use to address sensitive topics with children:

- **Help children preserve their memories.** Encourage the children to write letters or draw pictures describing their feelings and to share them with trusted friends. Some children plant a tree or make a scrapbook to honor the death of a loved one.

- **Read together age-appropriate books that provide examples of coping with difficult situations.** Stories enlarge a child's vocabulary for discussing loss. Books are available on the websites of many Christian publishers: ZonderKidz (Zondervan Publishing House, http:www.zonderkidz.com), David C. Cook Books (http://www.davidccook.com), Bethany Backyard (Bethany House Publishers, http://www.bethany house.com) and Tyndale Kids (Tyndale House Publishers, http://www.tyndale.com).

- **Help children return to their normal activities.** Encourage the children to enjoy hobbies, sports, favorite foods and spending time in nature. Watch their body language for clues on their general health, and if you have concerns, talk with their parents or caregivers.

- **Provide a support network of Christian friends.** Connect children who have experienced loss with children who are grieving. When the time is ready, ask friends to pray for them and reach out with phone calls. This is no time for children to feel they are alone, and their peers often are more effective than the adults in their lives.

As Pastor Matt sat in his car praying, he remembered a boy at church whose sister died the year before. He called David on his cell phone. David was more than happy to visit the Gonzalez boys with Pastor Matt. They also stopped to buy the boys a gift—a picture frame that was engraved with these words from Jesus: "I leave my peace with you! John 14:27." They would encourage Hosea and Felipe to put their mom's picture in the new frame, and they would pray with the boys. They also discussed starting a small group to help children in their community deal with loss. It was only the beginning, but they knew God was with them.

*Marc Gellman and Thomas Hartman, *Lost and Found: A Kid's Book for Living Through Loss* (New York: HarperCollins, 1999), pp. 13-14.

**Ibid., p. 68.

Faith Steps: Teaching Children About Heaven

All children have questions about heaven. Children with special needs are no different, though their experiences with disability may put a slightly different perspective on the questions. We can guide their faith by teaching them what the Bible says regarding heaven, and we can help them imagine and look forward to the glories of living with God forever.

Truths

God will one day heal all disease and disability. Tell the children that when Christians die, they immediately go to heaven to live with God (see 2 Corinthians 5:8). The Bible doesn't tell us what our bodies will be like then, but we can be sure they'll be perfect for us. At the resurrection, God will create "a new heaven and a new earth" (Revelation 21:1). God promises that there will be no more death or mourning or crying or pain in heaven, so we can be sure that disabilities and diseases won't be following us there (see Revelation 21:4). It will be awesome when we hear people who have never before spoken confess Christ as Lord, and when we see people who have never walked before bend their knees in adoration.

Compared to the glories of an eternity with Christ, suffering in this world will seem as if it was only for a moment (see 2 Corinthians 4:17). This truth may seem hard for a suffering child to grasp, yet it gives hope. Looking forward to a forever without pain and disability helps get children through daily hardships. Joni Eareckson Tada says, "Suffering keeps swelling our feet so that earth's shoes won't fit."* Teach children this eternal perspective so that they and their families can keep their focus on our glorious hope.

We can be excited about heaven! The Bible has all the information we need to help children look forward to eternity with excitement. Here are some typical questions they may have and the Bible-based answers you can give:

- **What will heaven be like?** There are many things we don't know yet, but we do know it's a real place, created by God. The new heaven and new earth will be like the Garden of Eden, only better. The New Jerusalem will be a beautiful city, without crime or pollution. It's the perfect place God is preparing for our perfect bodies. It's our true home.

- **What will be there?** God, angels, other believers, trees, rivers, animals, houses, food, cities and countless other things we can only imagine will be there.

- **What won't be there?** In heaven, there won't be sin and evil, Satan, darkness, sickness, disabilities, wheelchairs, hospitals or anything else bad or unpleasant.

- **Will we be angels?** (Children with disabilities are sometimes referred to as angels, so it's natural for them to ask this question.) We were not angels before we were born, and we won't become angels when we go to heaven. We will be ourselves.

- **Will we have scars in heaven?** Probably not, because our bodies will be glorious resurrection bodies. The scars Jesus had on His resurrection body, which He showed to Thomas, might remain for all eternity to remind us of what He did on the cross (see John 20:27). However, if we will have scars in heaven, we know that they will be perfect and beautiful, without any pain to go with them.

- **What will we do there?** We'll see God and Jesus, and we'll spend time with them. We'll eat, play, work and hang out with our families and friends, only it will be way better than it is here on Earth!

- **How can I know if I'll be going there?** Never pass up an opportunity to bring a child into the Kingdom! Make sure you're comfortable with how to lead a child with a disability to Christ (see "Five Ways to Present the Gospel" on p. 91).

Children can feel eager to tell friends about the hope of heaven. When we get excited about something, we tell everybody who will listen to us what it is that has us so jazzed. It seems like that's all we can talk about. When a child affected by disability learns the truths about heaven, you can bet that child will be excited! It just might become the child's favorite topic. Encourage the child to share with family and friends the hope of eternity.

Death and Dying

Children are sad when people they know and love die; they miss them. This is only natural. You can comfort the child by explaining that Christians who have died are now living in heaven. We wouldn't want them to come back to Earth, because they are now living in a perfect place and aren't experiencing pain or sadness anymore. And we'll see them again when we die and go to heaven. Thinking about dying is scary, but we know that because we love Jesus, the moment we die, we'll be in heaven with Him.

Having that hope can give us courage when it comes our time to die. And God knows when the right time is (see Psalm 139:16).

Salvation

Do children with developmental disabilities who appear to not understand salvation go to heaven when they die? We can't know the inner workings of some children's minds, and we must teach as if they understand, always trusting that God will do what is truly right.

Talk often about heaven. For children with disabilities and their families, heaven is sometimes the favorite subject. Sing songs about heaven, and together read books about heaven (see suggestions below). Show them how excited you are about eternity.

We want to assure children of the glorious hope of heaven, where there will be no more pain or prosthetics, disease or disability, worrying or wheelchairs, sorrow or suffering of any kind. God will wipe away all of our tears for all of eternity. Hallelujah! Let's take as many people there with us as we can!

*Joni Eareckson Tada, *When God Weeps: Why Our Suffering Matters to the Almighty* (Grand Rapids, MI: Zondervan Publishing House, 1997), p. 202.

An Angel Party

The angels are having a party! Have students draw a picture of the angels rejoicing in heaven over each sinner who repents (see Luke 15:7).

Books

- *Wait Until Then* by Randy Alcorn

- *Tell Me About Heaven* by Randy Alcorn

- *Someday Heaven* by Larry Libby

- *Tell Me About Heaven . . . I Think I'm Forgetting* by Janet Clowes-Johnson

- *Big Topics for Little Kids: Tell Me About Eternity* by Joel Anderson

- *What Is Heaven Like?* by Beverly Lewis

- *Grandpa, Is There a Heaven?* by Katherine Bohlmann

- *Heaven for Kids* by Randy Alcorn

- *Heaven Your Real Home* by Joni Eareckson Tada

- *Heaven* by Randy Alcorn

Activity Page: What the Bible Says About Heaven

What is going to be changed? (Read Psalm 30:5; 2 Corinthians 4:17; Philippians 3:20-21; Revelation 22:2-5.)
Write your answers on the pictures of straw and gold.

God Takes Our Pain On Earth...

And Changes It To...

Glories In Heaven!

What won't be in heaven?
(Read Revelation 21:4.)

No more _____

No more _____

No more _____

No more _____

No more _____

What is going to be the best part of heaven? (Read Revelation 5:13.)

_____

Who can you invite to go to heaven with you? _____

_____

What's taking so long? (Read 2 Peter 3:9.)

Jesus wants everyone to _____ before He returns to take us to _____ so that His house will be full!

Tips: Ideas from People Who Didn't Quit

Agatha Christie (1890-1976), possibly the best-selling mystery writer of all time, had a learning disability.

I, myself, was always recognized . . . as the "slow one" in the family. It was quite true, and I knew it and accepted it. Writing and spelling were always terribly difficult for me. My letters were without originality. I was . . . an extraordinarily bad speller and have remained so until this day.

Agatha Christie wrote 80 novels and short story collections and over a dozen plays. (http://www.dyslexia center.org/ar/000045.shtml)

Nelson Rockefeller (1908-1979), forty-first vice president of the United States, forty-ninth governor of New York, businessman and philanthropist, had dyslexia. He had this to say:

I was one of the "puzzle children" myself—a dyslexic. . . . And I still have a hard time reading today. Accept the fact that you have a problem. Refuse to feel sorry for yourself. You have a challenge; never quit!

(http://www.dyslexiacenter.org/ar/000045.shtml)

Actor **Christopher Reeve** (1953-2004) was paralyzed in 1995 in an accident that injured his spinal cord.

I think a hero is an ordinary individual who finds strength to persevere and endure in spite of overwhelming obstacles.

After his accident, Reeve went on to act, direct, produce and write movies, and lobbied on behalf of people with spinal cord injuries. He also founded a foundation to fund research and help people with disabilities and cofounded the Reeve-Irvine Research Center. (http://www.quotationspage.com/quote/34109.html)

Harriet Tubman (1820-1913) had epilepsy. A woman of great religious faith, Harriet escaped slavery and became an abolitionist.

Every great dream begins with a dreamer. Always remember, you have within you the strength, the patience, and the passion to reach for the stars to change the world.

(http://thinkexist.com/quotation/every_great_dream_b egins_with_a_dreamer-always/346539.html)

Fanny Crosby (1820-1915) was blind, but Fanny didn't think her blindness was something awful. In fact, when she was eight years old, she wrote this little verse:

*Oh, what a happy child I am,
although I cannot see!
I am resolved that in this
world contented I will be!
How many blessings I enjoy
that other people don't!
So weep or sigh because I'm blind,
I cannot—nor I won't.*

Fanny Crosby went on to write over 8,000 hymns. (http://www.eaec.org/faithhallfame/fanny_crosby.htm)

Nick Vujicic, popular world evangelist, is 25 years old and has no arms or legs.

Psalm 108:13 says, "With God we will gain the victory, and he will trample down our enemies." Even if those enemies are circumstantial irritations that are meant to frustrate and deplete our resolve to do God's good pleasure, press on and be encouraged in the tasks, big or small, that God places into your hands to do! Do them as unto Him and for His glory!

Nick has preached to over two million people around the globe. (http://www.lifewithoutlimbs.org)

Franklin Delano Roosevelt (1882-1945), four-time president of the United States, used a wheelchair. He once said,

We must scrupulously guard the civil rights and civil liberties of all citizens, whatever their background. We must remember that any oppression, any injustice, any hatred is a wedge designed to attack our civilization.

This quote from President Roosevelt appears on a wall at the FDR National Memorial, where a life-sized bronze statue shows Roosevelt sitting in his wheelchair. (http://www.inclusiondaily.com/news/special/fdr.htm)

Don't Quit

When things go wrong as
they sometimes will,
When the road you're
trudging seems all uphill,
When the funds are low
and the debts are high
And you want to smile,
but you have to sigh,
When care is pressing
you down a bit,
Rest if you must,
but don't you quit.

Life is queer with its
twists and turns,
As every one of us
sometimes learns,
And many a failure
turns about
When he might have won
had he stuck it out;
Don't give up though the
pace seems slow—
You may succeed with
another blow.

Success is failure
turned inside out—
The silver tint of
the clouds of doubt,
And you never can
tell how close you are.
It may be near when
it seems so far.
So stick to the fight when
you're hardest hit—
It's when things seem worst
that you must not quit.

—Anonymous

Don't Quit

When things go wrong as
they sometimes will,
When the road you're
trudging seems all uphill,
When the funds are low
and the debts are high
And you want to smile,
but you have to sigh,
When care is pressing
you down a bit,
Rest if you must,
but don't you quit.

Life is queer with its
twists and turns,
As every one of us
sometimes learns,
And many a failure
turns about
When he might have won
had he stuck it out;
Don't give up though the
pace seems slow—
You may succeed with
another blow.

Success is failure
turned inside out—
The silver tint of
the clouds of doubt,
And you never can
tell how close you are.
It may be near when
it seems so far.
So stick to the fight when
you're hardest hit—
It's when things seem worst
that you must not quit.

—Anonymous

Don't Quit

When things go wrong as
they sometimes will,
When the road you're
trudging seems all uphill,
When the funds are low
and the debts are high
And you want to smile,
but you have to sigh,
When care is pressing
you down a bit,
Rest if you must,
but don't you quit.

Life is queer with its
twists and turns,
As every one of us
sometimes learns,
And many a failure
turns about
When he might have won
had he stuck it out;
Don't give up though the
pace seems slow—
You may succeed with
another blow.

Success is failure
turned inside out—
The silver tint of
the clouds of doubt,
And you never can
tell how close you are.
It may be near when
it seems so far.
So stick to the fight when
you're hardest hit—
It's when things seem worst
that you must not quit.

—Anonymous

I'm Not Sick—
I Have a Disability!

A cheerful heart makes you healthy.

Proverbs 17:22, NIrV

Health: You Can't Catch a Disability

Can you remember how you felt the first time you saw someone with crippled limbs, groaning and drooling in a wheelchair? Did you cross the hall or the street and try to keep your distance? If you were a child at the time, you might have felt fear and wondered if that could happen to you.

Disabilities are not communicable. The only way to get Down syndrome, cystic fibrosis, muscular dystrophy or spina bifida is to be born with the condition. Genetic predisposition can lead to diabetes, retinitis and instances of gradual hearing loss. Other disabilities are the result of spinal cord injuries, serious accidents or severe illnesses. Maternal alcohol and substance abuses are at the root of other impairments. Researchers are still working to find the causes of many disabilities, such as multiple sclerosis, fibromyalgia and autism.

Even when the fear of catching a disability is put to rest, children may still tend to shy away from someone with special needs. Conversely, they may become too nosy and blurt out the wrong things. Usually, unnamed fears come to the surface when children observe neurological disorders in particular.

Helping Children Face Their Fears

As a teacher, you can dispel your students' fears toward children and adults with disabilities. Children pick up your attitudes and actions. If you show fear, embarrassment or pity, your children will learn the same thing. But if you build relationships and encourage *all* children to see their commonalities, they'll focus on the many ways they are alike. Before this can happen, however, children's natural curiosities about disability must be addressed. Let children know it is okay to ask questions. And don't be afraid to give them straightforward, truthful answers. This will dispel misinformation and build respect.

Remember that simply labeling a child's disability does not provide information. "Billy acts this way because he has Down syndrome" is not a helpful or very informative statement.

Answering Children's Questions

Here are some questions you might hear and some meaningful answers you could give:

- **Why can't Amy walk?** Amy's muscles are not as strong as yours.

- **Why can't Tommy talk?** The part of Tommy's brain that helps him with words doesn't work quite right. How can we help him show us what he wants without words?

- **Is Sheri still a baby because she wears diapers?** Sheri can do some things like a big girl, but that one area is giving her extra trouble.

- **Is Joey crazy?** No, Joey has autism. His brain does not work exactly like yours and mine, which makes him act different from other people. But you should see how smart he is with puzzles!

- **Why does Latisha look like that?** Sometimes babies are born different. Have you noticed that no two trees look exactly alike? That's the way it is with people.

Be sure to respond to what is really being asked. When appropriate, urge children to ask their questions directly to the child with the disability. Say, "Maybe José would like to tell you himself."

Talk with parents about how they explain their child's disability, and find out what their child prefers to tell others. When disabilities are not visually apparent, a child may want to control the flow of information. Remember, friends usually want practical information, not medical jargon.

Health: Interviewing Parents

The most important people in a child's life are the parents. They are the experts on their child's communication and way of thinking. Your initial contact with parents is crucial. During a parent interview, you not only gather information about the child, but you also have an opportunity to alleviate concerns by assuring that your church will be a safe place where their child is welcomed regardless of his or her disability.

Questions to Ask

- **What can you tell me about your child?** Parents have different comfort levels regarding how much information they are willing to share. Allow the parent freedom to give as much detail as they prefer. Parents who recently learned that their child has a disability are still trying to assimilate all the information they have received. They may be experiencing one of the normal stages of loss or grief: denial, anger, bargaining, depression and acceptance. Our job is to walk beside them during the process, not bombard them with questions they are not ready or able to answer. On the other hand, seasoned parents who have spent years fighting for their child's needs will be more open to share many details.

- **What type of communication does your child use?** Even children with little vocal language have some form of communication. Do they use sign language, picture communication devices, gestures or sounds? Ask parents to share information on the meaning of specific gestures, word approximations or other communication.

- **What behaviors might we encounter, and what is the best intervention? Is your child a runner, or does your child hit or bite?** When a child has severe behavioral issues, it may be necessary to make a plan to gradually assimilate him or her into the classroom environment. Have the parent attend the first few sessions to help the volunteers understand how to best help the student. Parents frequently experience rejection. Make sure the parents know that their child is wanted and that you are willing to work with him or her.

- **Do we need to be aware of any medical needs? Does the child have seizures, a feeding tube or use oxygen? Is the assistance of a nurse required?** Discuss how parents can be contacted in case of emergency.

- **Does your child need assistance with self-help skills such as toileting or feeding?** Clarify any church policy regarding toileting, especially with older students.

- **Does your child have sensory sensitivity issues?** Find out if the child might be bothered by the flickering of fluorescent lights, the sound of the air conditioner or being touched.

- **What else would you like to tell me about your child? What are your child's strengths? What does your child like to do?** Give the parents the opportunity to share the positive characteristics God has given their child.

Placement Options to Discuss

Explain the options your church offers, and make a decision together, based on what's best for the child.

- Inclusion with a buddy

- Inclusion in a class with younger students

- Partial mainstreaming—part-time in a self-contained special needs class and part-time in a typical class

- Self-contained special needs class

Consider trial placement in a self-contained class. After a few weeks of getting to know the student and observing his or her reactions, you'll be better able to determine the best placement.

Don't rush to place a child with severe medical or behavioral needs before having the necessary buddies or nursing support available. The experience will be better for all concerned when everyone is prepared. And always follow up with the family and teachers on a regular basis to make sure everyone is happy with the placement.

Forms: Sunday School Special Needs Assessment and Church Intake Team Log

Sunday School and church forms are not as detailed as those used for respite care or camps. During church activities, parents are usually on campus or nearby. Parents are inundated with paperwork and will appreciate your sensitivity to using short forms when appropriate.

Sunday School Special Needs Assessment

Date _____

Student's Name _____ Birth Date _____

Parents' Names _____

Parents' Address _____

Parents' E-mail Address _____

Phone (home) _____ (cell) _____

Backup Emergency Person and Phone Number _____

Siblings' Names and Ages _____

School Student Attends _____

Specific Type of Disability _____

    Diagnosis _____

    Diagnosis in Lay Terms _____

Is your child on medication? _____ yes _____no

If yes, what types of medications? _____

Does your child have seizures? _____

    Medical and/or plant allergies? _____

    Food allergies? _____

Does your child need assistance with eating/drinking?

_____

Does your child need help with using the restroom/personal hygiene? _____

Communication Skills _____

Reading Level _____

Writing Level _____

What are your child's strengths? _____

Weaknesses? _____

    Special gifts or talents? _____

Describe your child's understanding of God/relationship with Christ. _____

Describe your child's past Sunday School and/or church experience. _____

_____

What activities does your child enjoy most? _____

_____

Does your child have any phobias or fears? If so, what are they? _____

_____

Does your child display any behaviors that might disrupt a class? If so, what do you normally do to help control these behaviors?

_____

_____

What do you consider to be your son's or daughter's greatest challenge in social settings? _____

What kind of support has been successful for him or her?

_____

Any additional information we should know? _____

_____

Church Intake Team Log

All forms should be on file with the children's director. This card can be completed on a weekly basis or as needed for communication with the parents, teachers and directors.

Child's Name _____

Intake Form Received by _____ Date _____

Initial Communication with Parent _____

Team Member _____

Recommended Classroom Adaptations _____

_____

_____

Communication with Parent _____

Recommended Follow-Up _____

_____

Health: Medical Policies and Procedures

Students with special needs have a variety of medical issues ranging from seizures and tube feedings to allergies and drug side effects. It is essential that churches develop a policy on how medical procedures and emergencies will be handled. Dispensing medication and tube feedings are not normally done during church hours, but such procedures may be required at respite events or camps.

What questions should a medical policy answer?

- **Who will dispense medications and perform medical procedures?** It is strongly recommended that whenever possible, parents or medical professionals dispense medications or perform medical procedures. Ahead of time, determine who will perform the procedures at a church event.

- **How should medications be packaged?** All medications must be appropriately labeled. Prescription medications should be in the original bottle from the pharmacy, clearly labeled with the name of the recipient and clear dosage information.

- **Will teachers be allowed to give over-the-counter medications?** Make sure specific medications and brands are listed. Students may have allergic reactions to certain brands or flavors, so be specific.

- **Is there a signed release form from a parent or guardian to give medication to a child?** Have a release form signed when the child registers.

- **Where will the medications be stored?** Be certain that all medicines and supplies are in a locked cabinet out of children's reach.

- **What is the emergency plan in case a child has a seizure?** Parents need to be contacted in all situations. When a child is prone to seizures, ask the parent in advance how quickly emergency services should be called. Always err on the side of safety.

- **What is your church's wellness policy?** Students with special needs may be medically fragile or prone to illness. Have a policy in place for all students and volunteers, stating that children should stay home when experiencing a runny nose, fever, vomiting, diarrhea, cough, rashes or other contagious conditions.

Review your medical policy with professionals who can determine if it covers all necessary medical and legal issues.

How do different medications affect a child?

Medications can affect a child's behavior, alertness and appetite. Some possible side effects include fatigue, restlessness, increase or decrease of appetite, drooling, tics, fixated staring and obsessive behaviors such as tapping or picking at fingers. Regular communication with the child's parents or caregivers is crucial. You need to understand how medications affect your student to better understand his or her behaviors. Side effects can change as the child gets acclimated to the medications; get regular updates from parents. It is also important to report any changes you observe in behavior. This information helps lead parents and doctors to determine if a medication is helpful or hurtful. Often doctors ask parents to refrain from telling a teacher about a change in a child's medication for a period of time in order to see if the teacher notices changes in behavior without having pre-expectations. Parents appreciate this useful feedback.

How can you support children using medications?

Students with special needs take a number of medications for a variety of reasons. Medications for attention-deficit/hyperactivity disorder, seizures, anxiety or depression are common. It is important not to judge or look shocked by the drugs a child takes. Too often, people freely give opinions without understanding the individual situation. Parents need to trust you with medical information, and they expect it to be kept in confidence.

You may be seen as an expert in a child's life and asked your opinion about certain medications. Don't give specific medical advice. Refer parents to appropriate websites or to other people who may have experience in that area. Join parents in praising God for these drugs that help heal children and give them a better quality of life.

Medical Policies

Medications

The staff and volunteers cannot administer any medications or treatment other than basic first aid. Children who are medically fragile must be assisted by parents or assigned caregivers.

In extreme cases of allergies or asthma, arrangements will be made with written instructions from the parents.

Safety Procedures

Volunteers use a new pair of latex gloves for each child and every instance of handling blood or bodily fluids and when changing diapers. Latex-free gloves will be available for use with children who have latex allergies.

Volunteers will wash hands after accompanying a child to the toilet, after assisting a child with wiping his or her nose and before food preparation.

Illnesses

For the health and safety of all children, families, volunteers and staff, we ask parents to refrain from bringing their child to church if they have any of the following symptoms and/or illnesses. Sick children will not be admitted into class. If a child develops or displays symptoms after admittance, volunteers will contact a staff person immediately. Parents will be contacted to come and pick up the child. A child being treated for an infection with antibiotics must be on the drug for at least 48 hours before admittance to a classroom or program.

Fever Greater than 99°
Runny Nose
Questionable Rashes
Cough
Diarrhea
Impetigo
Active Chicken Pox
Measles
Mumps
Conjunctivitis (Pink Eye)
Lice
Ringworm

Confidentiality

Parents are responsible for sharing information with our staff if their child has a diagnosis of immunodeficiency or hepatitis B. Information is available only to those staff and caregivers who need to know in order to protect the child against other infections.

Form: Accident/Illness Report

Church Office Notification Injury Report

Name, Age and Gender of Child Who Was Injured _____

Address/City/Zip _____

_____

Phone Number _____

Date and Time of Accident _____

Describe in detail how the child was injured. _____

_____

_____

Describe the child's injuries and what action was taken to treat the injuries. _____

_____

_____

How and when was the parent notified? _____

_____

_____

Please list names and phone numbers of witnesses to the accident. _____

_____

_____

_____

_____

Additional Comments _____

_____

_____

Your Name, Address and Phone Number _____

_____

Health: Caring for a Child's Restroom Needs

Every family celebrates when a child learns to "go potty"! For the average child, this happens between two and three years of age. For some children with disabilities, however, going potty can be a lifelong struggle.

There are a few roadblocks to toilet training children with special needs:

- A child may have balance, coordination or physical challenges that restrict independence.

- A child may not be mentally able to process the necessary information to do the toileting tasks.

- A child with severe hearing sensitivity may be afraid of the sound of a toilet flushing or the noise made by electric hand driers in public restrooms.

- A child with body awareness problems may be unable to accurately sense when he or she needs to use the restroom.

Social pressures that play a part in the progress of typical children—wanting to be a "big" girl or "big" boy—may not work with children with special needs. The routine of wearing a diaper feels much more secure than changing to and carrying out an unfamiliar, complex task. Even when children have learned to use the toilet at home, they may not easily adapt to using the toilet in the new church environment.

Get Information from Parents

Ask parents to fill out a restroom questionnaire with information about their child (see form on p. XYZ). This form should include toileting schedules, language that is understood by the child, and any fears about toileting. With this information in hand, teachers will be able to familiarize themselves with each child's routine.

Post a Picture Schedule for Toileting

Since many children with special needs are visual learners, posting a picture schedule for restroom procedures is helpful. Schedules help children organize, sequence and stay focused on the task while establishing a routine. The sense of completing a task is a strong motivator for many children, especially those on the autism spectrum. A visual icon depicting "what happens when I'm finished" is a very important part of the schedule; the icon reassures children that the activity that was interrupted will still be available upon their return from the restroom.

Sample Picture Schedule for Restroom Procedures

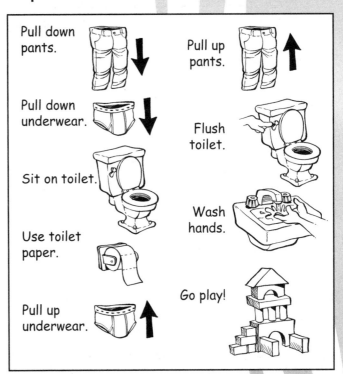

Pull down pants.

Pull up pants.

Pull down underwear.

Flush toilet.

Sit on toilet.

Use toilet paper.

Wash hands.

Pull up underwear.

Go play!

Show Children Respect

If a child requests a parent to aid with toileting, honor that request and give the parent a pager if this is a common occurrence. Be discreet, and respect any sense of modesty. A church might designate a family restroom, so parents are able to assist their children.

Establish a Restroom Policy

A clear policy should be communicated to all church staff regarding procedures for helping children in the restroom. For example, a child over the age of five who has an accident should be changed by her parents unless there is written permission for a specific worker to assist. Only female workers should attend to children in the restroom. You should also have in place a restroom policy checklist to be used by staff when a child is helped with toileting (see form on p. 158).

Because tangible rewards are often crucial for success, it is important to cooperate with any reward system that has been set up by a child's parents. Remember to praise children, even for small steps of progress toward their goal of independent toileting.

Forms: Restroom Questionnaire and Restroom Policy Checklist

Restroom Questionnaire

Toileting Guide for _____

Child's Birth Date _____ Male or Female (circle)

Does your child have any balance, coordination or physical challenges that impede his or her ability to toilet independently? _____ Yes _____ No

If yes, explain. _____

_____

Does your child have sensory issues or fears that could affect his or her toileting (i.e., fear of flushing, noise of hand driers, etc.)? _____ Yes _____ No

If yes, explain. _____

_____

Is your child on a toileting schedule? _____ Yes _____ No

If yes, explain. _____

_____

Which terms should the staff use to indicate going to the restroom ("potty," "teetee," "tinkle," etc.)?

_____

Does the child use an object, picture or sign to communicate his or her toileting needs?

_____ Yes _____ No

If yes, explain. _____

_____

Does the child need more time to process what is being said? _____ Yes _____ No

Should teachers look for body signals from the child? _____ Yes _____ No

If yes, explain. _____

_____

Restroom Policy Checklist

❑ Did you have the parents take their child to the restroom right before dropping him or her off?

❑ Did you check for Pull-Ups® and an extra change of clothes if the child is in training?

❑ Did two female staff accompany the child to the restroom?

❑ Was the door left ajar?

❑ Did staff wash their hands before and after attending to the child?

Safety: Addressing Child Abuse

Children with special needs are at greater risk of child abuse due to the stress experienced by the adults in their lives. The abuse is often mistreatment and neglect during the early years, because parents don't understand their child's developmental needs, and a child with a communication disorder may seem unresponsive. Finding suitable child care can also be difficult, causing fatigue and depression in parents who may also be plagued by financial struggles.

Abuse has also caused children to become disabled. When Patrick's father came home drunk and angry, he was in no mood to deal with his son's colic. He violently shook Patrick until his tiny brain was damaged. Although Patrick was born normal, he grew up as a slow learner and never graduated from high school.

Studies reported by the National Research Council in 2001 indicate that the rate of abuse among children with disabilities ranges from 22 percent to 70 percent. Another study found that children with disabilities are 3.44 times more likely to be abused in some way compared to nondisabled children. And another study found that children with developmental disorders are 4 to 10 times more likely to be victims of crime than nondisabled children.*

What is neglect?

All children need food, water, clothing and shelter. Children should not be ignored or left alone for long periods of time. Children need proper medical care that includes support to grow physically, mentally and emotionally. When these basic needs are not met, that child is being neglected.

What is abuse?

There are three types of abuse: physical, sexual and emotional. Physical abuse includes hitting, shaking, shoving, kicking, punching, beating or biting a child or holding a child's hand under hot water or against anything hot or extremely cold—anything that causes a child bodily harm. It also includes leaving a child with an abuser or allowing a child to be tortured. Sexual abuse includes touching a child inappropriately, fondling a child's genitals, using a child for profit or sexual arousal or allowing anyone to commit a sexual offense with someone younger than 18

years of age. Emotional abuse includes the use of degrading language, threats, name calling or belittling.

What are some signs of abuse?

- Physical injuries including unexplained bruises, welts, broken bones, burns
- Aggressive or withdrawn behavior
- Unusual fears
- Craving for attention
- Wary of physical contact
- Destructive to self and others
- Poor social relations

How can we help prevent the abuse of children with disabilities?

Education is key! Parents, caregivers, teachers and even the children themselves should be trained to recognize abuse and take action. By promoting a greater awareness of the problem, more people will take steps to support these families. Encourage parent groups in your community to build relationships with local agencies serving victims of abuse. And find ways to give parents a break.

How should abuse be reported?

If you suspect a child is being abused, take it seriously and follow your church policies. Document your observations and use proper reporting procedures (see "Suspected Child Abuse Report" on p. 160). Every state has mandatory reporting laws of which church leaders should be aware. If you suspect that a volunteer is abusing a child, you have a moral obligation to take action. Inform your church Sunday School director and church pastor. They will contact the local department for child protection services. It is vital to everyone involved that you keep the information confidential.

If a student tells you about abuse, stay calm and listen. Offer emotional support and remind the student that he or she is not at fault. Do not promise that you will not tell anyone. Pray together. Then be ready to commit the situation "to the governing authorities" and to do what is in the best interest of the child (Romans 13:1).

*Studies quoted in Leigh Ann Davis, "Abuse of Children with Cognitive, Intellectual and Developmental Disabilities," *The Arc*, April 2004. http://www.thearc.org/NetCommunity/Page.aspx?&pid=1649&srcid=217 (accessed June 7, 2008).

Form: Suspected Child Abuse Report

Date _____

Name of Child _____ Age _____

Address _____

_____

Phone _____

Name of Parent or Guardian _____

Name of Person Filing Report _____

Name of Person Receiving Report _____

Nature of Suspected Abuse (physical, sexual and/or emotional) _____

_____

Indications of Suspected Abuse (including physical signs and course of events where necessary)

_____

_____

_____

_____

_____

Action Taken (including date and time) _____

_____

_____

_____

The above information will serve as a guide and will be necessary if a formal report is filed with the police or appropriate government agency. All information received is to be kept strictly confidential.

Signature of Person Reporting _____

Phone Number _____ E-mail _____

Signature of Pastor _____

Safety: Playground Dos and Don'ts

The playground is a wonderful place for children to learn social skills and problem solving while having fun. However, it is often a place where the child with a disability feels left out or inadequate. Don't leave a child out because of your own fear or inconvenience—be creative!

Develop Ways to Include Children with Special Needs

- **Brainstorm with parents and teachers ways to include the child in play activities.** James used a wheelchair but wanted to play kickball with his classmates. Instead of rolling the ball to James to kick, the teacher modified the game by gently tossing the ball to his hands, and he batted it away. His friends took turns pushing him around the bases, which created fun interaction with his peers.

- **Provide enough supervision to keep a child safe while allowing him or her to have as much independence as possible.** Kayla falls easily, so she needs an adult to hold her hand while she walks across the blacktop to the grassy area. However, once she is there, she likes to sit on the grass and play with her friends independently. Kayla's adult buddy respects her wishes and helps her again when it's time to get up and walk back to class.

- **Identify situations to avoid.** Is there too much noise? Is the student sensitive to the sun, or does the student have allergies to pollen or bees? Are large groups overwhelming?

- **Help students navigate social situations, learn how to take turns and play appropriately with others.** David, who has Asperger's syndrome, has difficulty reading social cues. When his friends try to joke with him in the same friendly way that they do with their other peers, David doesn't understand and becomes angry. The volunteer can help David learn how to interpret those situations appropriately.

Help Peers Include Children with Disabilities on the Playground

- **Inform students about a disability, and then help them find common ground.** Children fear the unknown. Often children with disabilities are excluded because their peers just don't know how to interact with them or what to expect. Jason, who is hard of hearing, wanted to make friends. He would go up to someone and start signing and talking in a voice that was difficult to understand. The other students backed away, because they didn't understand. A volunteer explained that Jason has difficulty hearing, so he looks at lips and uses sign language. He also loves playing basketball and would like to be friends. Once the peers understood, they were eager to be Jason's friend. In fact, Jason taught them some sign language and his new friends think he's cool.

- **Use Buddies.** Have students take turns being the special friend or buddy during playtime. The buddy can be responsible for pushing the wheelchair, helping to catch a ball or just hanging out. Spending time together encourages a relationship that goes beyond just helping.

- **Be a helper, not a doer.** The goal of a helper is not to do an activity for a child but to assist the child in accomplishing the task as independently and safely as possible.

Create Alternatives for the Child Who Can't Go Outside

Some children will not be able to go outside for various reasons, including health concerns or an inability to handle large-group activities. Do you have an alternate indoor play area with appropriate activities and/or equipment (small trampolines, soft balls, an obstacle course for wheelchairs, etc.)? Make sure you have extra adult supervision to help you during playtime—both indoors and outdoors. Allow a few classmates to stay inside to interact with the child so that he or she does not feel left out.

Make Sure the Surroundings Are Safe

- **Are there safety hazards that need to be fixed or repaired?**

- **Is an adult aware of what the child is doing at all times?**

- **What precautions need to be taken?** A child who falls frequently or has seizures may need a helmet. A student who puts everything in his or her mouth may need to stay away from the sandbox or have a buddy.

- **Is there metal equipment that could burn a child if it gets too hot in the sun?** Children with low pain tolerance aren't always aware that equipment like a slide may become too hot to use.

- **Is there appropriate fencing or barriers to keep safe children who have a tendency to run off or climb?** Robby loved to climb and was able to scale a fence in no time. His teacher made sure that there were always adults stationed right next to the fence.

- **Are there any poisonous plants or trees in or near the playground that would be harmful if eaten or swallowed?**

- **Do you have an emergency plan?** Carry a two-way radio or cell phone when out on the playground in case of medical or behavioral emergencies. Make sure there are always at least two adults supervising, even if there are only one or two students present. You never know when an emergency situation might arise.

Take Precautions and Make Adaptations

 • Look for obstacles the child may not see. Provide a buddy to guide the child and make him or her aware of the surroundings.

 • Assign a friend to tell the child when the bell rings or when the teacher is talking. Learn a few basic signs to assist in communication, and teach them to the volunteers and peers.

• Be aware of the sensory environment. Is this situation going to be overwhelming? Is there too much noise? Is the reflection of the sun irritating the child with sensory sensitivities? Will the student be better off inside with a small group? How does the child process information? Explain directions clearly, using as few words as possible and allowing the child time to process the information.

 • Make expectations clear. Show the students the boundaries; don't just tell them. Demonstrate appropriate behavior or how to play a game.

 • Prepare to deal with behavioral outbursts. What situations trigger behavioral outbursts? Do you have a behavior plan with clear expectations, rewards and consequences? (See "Using Visual Behavioral Plans" on p. 193 for more details.)

• Do peers know the appropriate etiquette of helping someone in a wheelchair? It is appropriate to ask first before pushing a person's wheelchair as it is an extension of a person's body and needs to be respected. Give guidelines on not making quick turns, pushing too fast or rushing over doorsills or curbs.

• Is the playground accessible to wheelchairs and walkers?

Make Adaptations to Allow Accessibility

- Ramps for children who use wheelchairs or walkers and for other students unable to use stairs

- Accessible ground surfaces such as rubber tiles, shredded rubber or wood

- Swings that have adaptable child seats or a platform for wheelchairs

- Tricycles with hand controls or special alterations

- Water or sand tables at wheelchair height

- Shaded areas for those with heat or sun sensitivity (small pop-up tents work well when there are no shade trees)

Two important purposes of play are to encourage interaction between the child with special needs and his or her peers and to provide the opportunity to increase the social maturity of all the children. Creating a safe and accessible environment is the starting point for the development of wonderful relationships that are beneficial to all.

Safety: What to Do When a Child Has a Seizure

Some of the children who participate in your special needs programs will be prone to seizures. Parents should alert you to this possibility on their child's application and during the interview process. Knowing about the possibility will allow the staff to be well prepared in advance, will save the child embarrassment and will calm the fears of his or her classmates. Following a seizure, many children are able to return to normal activities after only a brief rest. This, however, does not pertain to a first-time seizure. In this case, a child should be evaluated by a doctor or taken to the emergency room.

A seizure occurs when there are abnormal electrical discharges in the brain. A seizure is usually characterized by a brief period of unconsciousness, even though the person's eyes may be open, and may be accompanied by one or more of the following symptoms: muscle spasms or convulsions, brief stares, loss of bladder control, and what may appear to be a temporary halt in breathing.

Research shows that 3 percent of all children will have a seizure before the age of 15, and half of those will be febrile seizures (related to fever). Children who are developmentally delayed are more likely to have febrile seizures as are siblings of children who experience seizures. According to the National Institute of Neurological Disorders and Stroke, 50 percent of children with cerebral palsy will have seizures.* And epilepsy is a disorder that is defined by chronic seizures.

There are three types of seizures: febrile (caused by fever), absence and tonic-clonic. In an absence seizure (formerly called a petit mal seizure), a child will display a short loss of awareness, signaled by staring or eye blinking, but will not show convulsive movements as in a tonic-clonic (or grand mal) or febrile seizure.

Other reasons for seizures include infections, metabolic disorders, drugs, medications, poisons, head injuries, brain tumor and stroke.

Talk to all the children before a seizure happens. Assure them that if a classmate has a seizure, the adults know what to do, and the children can help by calmly following directions and by praying for the child. Be prepared to inform the children's parents about what occurred in class and let them know that the student is okay. In this way, parents hear the whole story, not only the half their own children may tell them.

Caution and Prevention

Outdoor activities can cause greater risk for children who experience seizures. For example, if the church sponsors a pool party or takes children swimming at camp, added measures must be taken with a child who may have a seizure while in the water. This child could drown unless he or she gets immediate help. If a child's seizure results in a fall, his or her greatest risk of injury is falling on hard surfaces such as bathroom tiles or concrete. Children prone to seizures also should never bike alone.

Children with febrile seizures may outgrow them. For other children the seizures continue and require medication. Medication may lessen the incidence or severity of seizures or may eliminate them.

A good resource for information about seizures is *Child with Seizures: A Guide for Parents, Teachers, and Other Professionals* by Kutscher L. Martin. Two websites with more information are http://www.emedicinehealth.com/seizures_emergencies/article_em.htm and http://www.ninds.nih.gov/disorders/epilepsy/epilepsy.htm.

*"Cerebral Palsy: Hope Through Research," *National Institute of Neurological Disorders and Stroke,* February 7, 2008. http://www.ninds.nih.gov/disorders/cerebral_palsy/detail_cerebral_palsy.htm (accessed June 22, 2008).

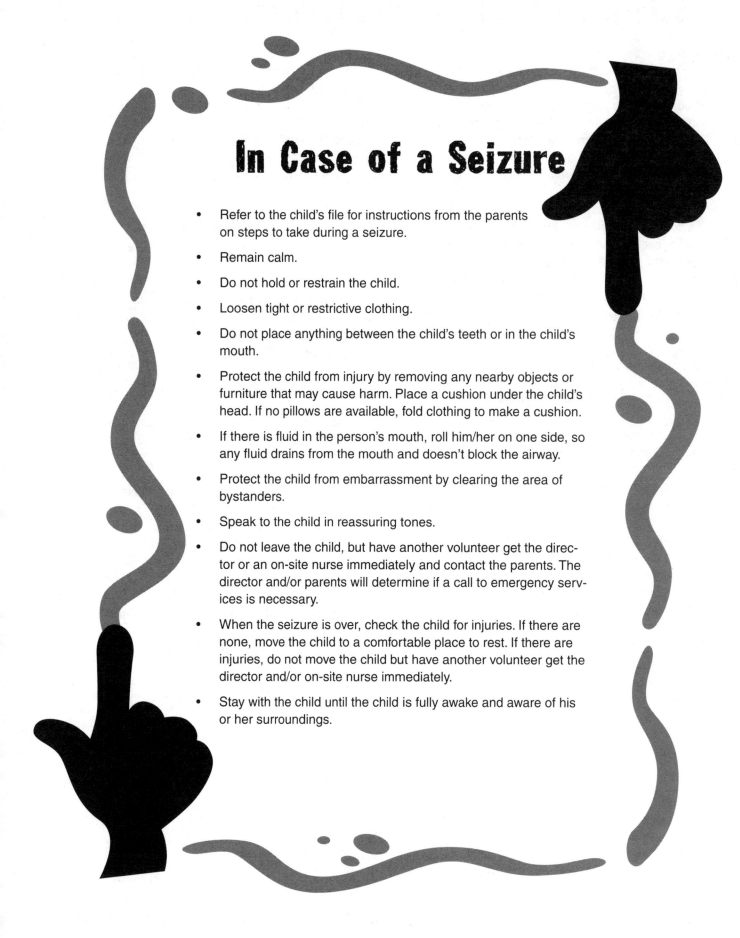

In Case of a Seizure

- Refer to the child's file for instructions from the parents on steps to take during a seizure.

- Remain calm.

- Do not hold or restrain the child.

- Loosen tight or restrictive clothing.

- Do not place anything between the child's teeth or in the child's mouth.

- Protect the child from injury by removing any nearby objects or furniture that may cause harm. Place a cushion under the child's head. If no pillows are available, fold clothing to make a cushion.

- If there is fluid in the person's mouth, roll him/her on one side, so any fluid drains from the mouth and doesn't block the airway.

- Protect the child from embarrassment by clearing the area of bystanders.

- Speak to the child in reassuring tones.

- Do not leave the child, but have another volunteer get the director or an on-site nurse immediately and contact the parents. The director and/or parents will determine if a call to emergency services is necessary.

- When the seizure is over, check the child for injuries. If there are none, move the child to a comfortable place to rest. If there are injuries, do not move the child but have another volunteer get the director and/or on-site nurse immediately.

- Stay with the child until the child is fully awake and aware of his or her surroundings.

Safety: Allergies and Treatment

With his chubby cheeks coated in peanut butter, Caleb's mom couldn't help laughing at her toddler as he smeared it on his high-chair tray. But her laughter turned to panic when Caleb went from giggling to wheezing and a rash appeared on his face. His mother quickly called the pediatrician, telling the doctor that Caleb had eaten nuts and even peanut butter before. Caleb recovered after a trip to the emergency room. His reaction was caused by his skin's contacting with the peanut butter oil, proving that food allergies can emerge at any time.

When it comes to food and other allergies, an ounce of prevention is worth a pound of cure. Teachers must have open communication with parents to ensure the safety of at-risk children who react to the slightest contact with nuts or the myriad of other allergens found in basic foods.

The number of children facing life-threatening food allergies increased significantly over the past five years. Food allergy prevalence increased 55 percent during this time, as reported by the Massachusetts Department of Education. The American Medical Association estimates 30 to 40 million Americans have some type of allergic condition. Although any food has the potential to cause an allergic reaction, these eight foods account for 90 percent of all reactions: peanuts, tree nuts, milk, eggs, soy, wheat, fish and shellfish.*

Characteristic Symptoms

Statistics, however, are just numbers on a page until you look into the face of a child going into severe anaphylactic shock. "Anaphylaxis" is a body's hypersensitivity to some causative agent; "anaphylaxis" also signifies anaphylactic shock. Anaphylactic shock is the mild to severe and potentially deadly systemic reaction of the body when it comes into contact with the agent to which it is hypersensitive. Characteristic symptoms include:

- **Skin**—Hives, swelling, itch, warmth, redness, rash

- **Breathing**—Wheezing, shortness of breath, throat tightness, cough, hoarse voice, chest pain and/or tightness, nasal congestion and/or hay fever-like symptoms, trouble swallowing

- **Stomach**—Nausea, pain and/or cramps, vomiting, diarrhea, itchy mouth/throat

- **Circulation**—Pale or blue color, poor pulse, unconsciousness, dizzy or light-headed, low blood pressure

- **Other**—Anxiety; feeling of impending doom; red, itchy or watery eyes; headache

The symptoms may occur alone or in any combination. Reactions usually begin within minutes of exposure, but reactions may be delayed. Sometimes symptoms appear to resolve themselves, only to recur or progress a few hours later. The most dangerous symptoms are low blood pressure, breathing difficulties, shock and loss of consciousness—all of which can be fatal. In about a third of the cases of anaphylactic shock, symptoms are delayed for two to four hours.

Proactive Response

Teachers must be trained to respond in the case of a critical allergic reaction and to be proactive in dealing with allergies in the classroom. Many churches are adopting a "nut-free policy" and do not allow dairy products, but this is not enough. Particularly in a special needs class where some children can't effectively communicate, teachers need to be aware of any possible allergies.

All child enrollment forms must ask questions about the child's allergies and about potential safety concerns such as choking and difficulty swallowing. This information should be documented by the church staff and filed for safekeeping, yet it must be easily accessible in the case of an emergency. The classroom director should keep on a clipboard a copy of an allergy action plan for each child (see p. 166) . This plan needs to include the child's picture (in case of new teachers or rotating staff) as well as the parents' authorized response to symptoms and emergency contact information.

Sometimes an allergic reaction requires the administration of an epinephrine shot by a parent, nurse or designated medical caregiver. After the immediate threat ends, the student may need to be transported to the nearest hospital for observation, even if the symptoms appear to have been resolved.

Anyone who's dealt with an allergic reaction knows that the best defense is a good offense. Caleb's mother didn't allow him to paint his tray with peanut butter anymore; in fact, nuts were eliminated from his diet altogether. Better safe than sorry!

*Managing Life-Threatening Food Allergies in Schools (Malden, MA: Massachusetts Department of Education, 2002), p. 8.

Form: Allergy Action Plan

Child's Name _____

Allergic to _____

For these symptoms _____ do this _____

For these symptoms _____ do this _____

For these symptoms _____ do this _____

Trained Staff Members

1. _____

Room _____

2. _____

Room _____

3. _____

Room _____

Emergency Contact Information

Parent Name _____

Phone Number _____

Doctor's Name _____

Phone Number _____

Other Emergency Contact

Name and Relationship _____

Phone Number _____

Parent Signature _____

Date _____

Doctor Signature _____

Date _____

Form: Allergy Action Plan

EpiPen® and EpiPen® Jr. Directions

- Pull off gray activation cap.

- Hold black tip near outer thigh (always apply to thigh).

- Swing and jab firmly into outer thigh until Auto-Injector mechanism functions. Hold in place and count to 10. Remove the EpiPen® unit and massage the injection area for 10 seconds.

Twinject® 0.3 mg and Twinject® 0.15 mg Directions

- Remove caps labeled "1" and "2."

- Place rounded tip against outer thigh, press down hard until needle penetrates. Hold for 10 seconds; then remove.

Second-Dose Administration:

If symptoms don't improve after 10 minutes, administer second dose:

- Unscrew rounded tip. Pull syringe from barrel by holding blue collar at needle base.

- Slide yellow collar off plunger.

- Put needle into thigh through skin, push plunger down all the way, and remove.

Once EpiPen® or Twinject® is used, call 9-1-1 for emergency transport. Take the used unit with you to the emergency room. Plan to stay for observation at the emergency room for at least four hours.

This from was adapted from the Food Allergy Action Plan found at http://foodallergy.org. Please check the website for any additions or changes that may be made after the publishing of this book.

Safety: Addressing Repetitive Behaviors

Repetitive, compulsive behaviors shock the unaccustomed eye. Words like "mental" or "crazy" come to mind, and people naturally recoil out of fear or confusion. A little education will help your staff and congregation overcome their natural fears and step into supernatural compassion.

Repetitive actions are common in Tourette's syndrome, obsessive-compulsive disorder, impulse control disorders, neurological trauma and autism. Of these, two of the most common in children are Tourette's syndrome and autism.

Types of Repetitive Behavior

Many children with Tourette's syndrome or autism will have actions that have no clear purpose to the observer. These self-stimulatory or repetitive behaviors might include:

- Flapping arms or hands

- Flipping fingers in front of eyes

- Saying same words or sounds over and over

- Jumping up and down

- Walking repeatedly in the same pattern around a room

- Clenching muscles or turning in circles

- Rocking while seated or standing

- Repeating movie dialogue or songs

- Banging head

- Spinning objects

- Returning constantly to a specific play pattern or particular toy

Other more subtle behaviors include blinking or eye rolling, tapping fingers and mild hair twisting.

Tourette behaviors stem from tics. A tic is a brief, repetitive, purposeless, nonrhythmic, involuntary movement or sound. Tics that produce movement are called motor tics, while tics that produce sound are called vocal tics. Some tics involve freezing in a position for a few seconds. Even when older children can suppress tics for a while, the tics "have to come out" sooner or later.

Reasons for the Behaviors

Some children engage in these behaviors only when excited or agitated, others when they are bored or worried. Other reasons include to avoid a task, situation or activity; to provide self-stimulation or be self-soothing; and/or to gain attention.

If it's unclear why the behavior happens, consider these questions:

- When and where does the behavior occur?

- What is going on in the setting?

- Who else is involved with or near the child?

Bridges to More Appropriate Behaviors

If a child is repeatedly spinning a toy car, show the child how to roll it back and forth. If a child is flipping repeatedly through a book again and again, sit with the child and point to the pictures.

Since some behaviors are sensory based, examine which of the senses a child is stimulating. If a child shows a desire for *visual* stimulation by flicking fingers in front of eyes or gazing at lights, objects or hands, give the child a prism, kaleidoscope, pinwheel or wind-up toy. If a child shows a desire for *auditory* stimulation by repetitive vocalizations or finger tapping, give the child a music box, a talking toy, or headphones and a tape. If a child shows a desire for *tactile* stimulation by touching objects, clothing or people or placing fingers in his or her mouth, offer the child a variety of textures such as some clay, a beanbag or some plastic bubble wrap.

If a child shows a desire for *vestibular* (balance or equilibrium) stimulation by excessively rocking, bouncing or spinning, provide a rocking chair or a Sit 'n Spin plastic twirling seat. If a child shows a desire for *proprioceptive* (muscles and joints) stimulation by walking on toes, flapping hands or holding head to one side, let the child try wrist or ankle weights; or encourage the child to hang on monkey bars or do gymnastic exercises. If a child shows a desire for *olfactory* stimulation by sniffing or smelling objects, people or clothing, put cologne or aftershave on the child's wrist or arm. If a child shows a desire for *gustatory* stimulation by tasting, licking or putting things in his or her mouth, give the child some gum, mints or hard candy.

Frequently, repetitive behaviors subside, once the condition is understood and a supportive environment is provided—something the church *can* provide.

Ministering to these children over the long haul, however, takes close cooperation with their families. Churches that can enlarge their expectations and redefine ministry will succeed. An uncommon compassion grows when there is a willingness to join children on their life journey.

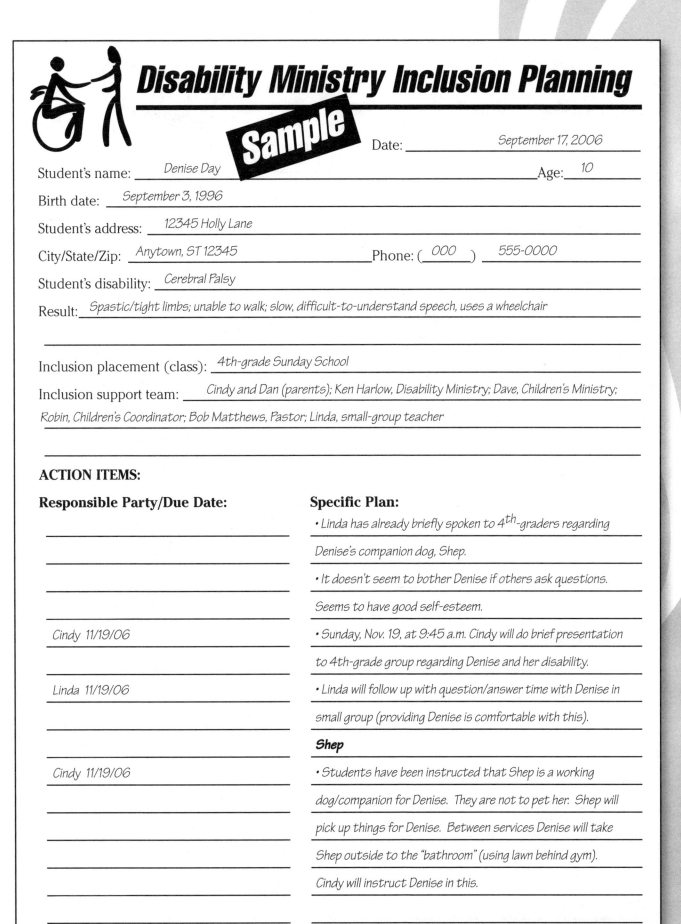

Disability Ministry Inclusion Planning

Sample

Date: _September 17, 2006_

Student's name: _Denise Day_   Age: _10_

Birth date: _September 3, 1996_

Student's address: _12345 Holly Lane_

City/State/Zip: _Anytown, ST 12345_   Phone: (_000_) _555-0000_

Student's disability: _Cerebral Palsy_

Result: _Spastic/tight limbs; unable to walk; slow, difficult-to-understand speech, uses a wheelchair_

Inclusion placement (class): _4th-grade Sunday School_

Inclusion support team: _Cindy and Dan (parents); Ken Harlow, Disability Ministry; Dave, Children's Ministry;_

Robin, Children's Coordinator; Bob Matthews, Pastor; Linda, small-group teacher

ACTION ITEMS:

Responsible Party/Due Date:	Specific Plan:
	• Linda has already briefly spoken to 4th-graders regarding Denise's companion dog, Shep.
	• It doesn't seem to bother Denise if others ask questions. Seems to have good self-esteem.
Cindy 11/19/06	• Sunday, Nov. 19, at 9:45 a.m. Cindy will do brief presentation to 4th-grade group regarding Denise and her disability.
Linda 11/19/06	• Linda will follow up with question/answer time with Denise in small group (providing Denise is comfortable with this).
	Shep
Cindy 11/19/06	• Students have been instructed that Shep is a working dog/companion for Denise. They are not to pet her. Shep will pick up things for Denise. Between services Denise will take Shep outside to the "bathroom" (using lawn behind gym). Cindy will instruct Denise in this.

SPECIFIC CONCERNS/SOLUTIONS:

Responsible Party/Due Date:

Specific Plan:

Responsible Party/Due Date	Specific Plan
Cindy 11/19/06	• Break between services, Denise will take Shep out. Denise will then return to the gym. There is a lot of activity in the gym with hula hoops, jump ropes, basketball, dodge ball, etc. For safety, Denise should observe from sidelines closest to amphitheater. There are usually others watching on sidelines so Denise will not be the only spectator. Note: for safety purposes, keep Denise in the wheelchair at all times.

Communication

•It can be frustrating to you and Denise when she is not understood. Hint: She will usually repeat 3 to 4 times before giving up. Tell Denise it is really important to you that you understand what she is saying, and ask her to please say one word at a time.

Eating restrictions

• None, with the exception of hard candy. (Use discretion.)

Physical Needs

• Typically at school, Denise waits until 1:00 p.m. for bathroom break, so this shouldn't be an issue on Sunday mornings.

Responsible Party/Due Date	Specific Plan
Robin	However, Robin will check to see if she can find 2 adult female
Cindy	teachers willing to be trained in case of emergency. Cindy will
Female Teachers	train them.
ASAP	
Cindy	• Cindy will work with activity time in 4th-grade group in Dec./Jan. Cindy will talk with Denise regarding her participation.
Follow-up	• Denise's inclusion support team needs to start meeting in Feb. to begin plans for her inclusion in family camp this summer.
Ken 2/07	• Early June—Denise's support team needs to meet to evaluate
Ken 6/07	and plan for summer/fall.

Outreach: Special Delivery Ministry

Do unto others as you would have others do unto you. Special Delivery is a unique way to reach children and adults with disability with the gospel message. In this ministry, volunteers deliver packages with gifts from Joni and Friends and from their church. In turn, the volunteers have the opportunity to build relationships and to share the love of Jesus Christ with the whole family affected by disability.

When Jesus spoke of helping the prisoner, the poor, the hungry, the widow, the fatherless, the homeless and the disabled, no one group was singled out for partiality (see Matthew 25:35-36; Luke 14:13; James 1:27). But individuals with physical, mental and emotional disorders seem to rise high on the list simply by their sheer numbers, and the announcement of a child born with a disability or one left disabled due to an injury sets off a chain reaction of dynamic proportion. Challenges can be overwhelming, not only to the child, but also to his or her parents and siblings. Special Delivery is a means of reaching out to these individuals and their families.

Goals of the Ministry

Special Delivery has five main goals:

1. Evangelism through building relationships

2. Crisis intervention with hurting families

3. Prayer support and encouragement

4. Building up the Body of Christ through service

5. Establishing an accessible point of entry for unchurched families.

Volunteers

Special Delivery is a great opportunity to involve first-time volunteers in disability ministry. Volunteers should be sensitive, friendly and sincere. They must learn to let recipients lead the conversation and not to ask questions that children or adults may not be comfortable discussing. Volunteers should be able to do the following:

- Communicate warmth and compassion

- Share encouragement for God's Word

- Be good listeners

- Feel comfortable praying for and with recipients

- Look forward to continuing to help meet the individual's needs

Recipients and Deliveries

Figuring out who should receive a Special Delivery is as simple as putting out the word to church members. When a church member hears about a family who is affected by disability and who doesn't have a church home, the church member simply alerts your church's Special Delivery director, who contacts Joni and Friends to obtain a Special Delivery package. You can also organize Special Delivery teams within your church to specifically minister to those with disabilities in the following venues:

- Rehabilitation hospitals

- Nursing homes

- Group homes

- Independent living centers

- Schools for children with special needs

- Disability organizations

- Church Sunday School classes or programs for adults and children with special needs

Special Delivery gifts can be delivered during an individual visit or as part of a program that includes group activities such as music, speakers, crafts and games. Either way, participants are encouraged to spend quality time with recipients. Remember, the ministry is about developing relationships that will lead to evangelism.

A Special Delivery Story

George and Pat have a real heart for disability ministry. They have volunteered at Joni and Friends Family Retreats for years. Pat is the principal and George is a sixth-grade teacher at a Christian school. When the time came for George's sixth graders to choose a spring service project, he suggested Special Delivery would be a perfect project. His class agreed.

With the help of their area Joni and Friends field office, they received boxes of books, tapes and CDs. The class set up stations in two rooms and packed the items in gift baskets along with teddy bears, note pads, pens, Bible-verse magnets and encouragement cards. At the end of the day, they had assembled nearly 60 Special Delivery baskets.

But the ministry was just beginning. All of the packages were loaded up in vehicles and young people, parents and teachers headed for an area children's group home and a residential facility for youth and seniors with physical and/or developmental disabilities. The class also delivered their youthful joy and energy.

This was the first exposure to disabilities for most of the students, but they did a great job of sharing God's love with those less fortunate. As the end of the day, Special Delivery baskets were gone; but the students had made some new friends, and they had promised to return for more visits.

Special Delivery Letters

Along with the gifts in each Special Delivery package should be a letter from your pastor with the times of your services and an invitation to visit your church. You may also enclose a copy of this special letter from Joni Eareckson Tada:

(For more information on this ministry, visit http://www.joniandfriends.org/fm_gift_outreach.php.)

Dear Friend,

Several decades ago, during the two years I spent in rehab after a spinal-cord injury that left me a quadriplegic, friends and acquaintances visited me at the hospital. Their presence and support meant the world—they simply treated me like a good friend. They shared with me their Cokes, pizza, *Seventeen* magazines, and Beatles albums. Finally, when they opened up their Bibles, they had won the right to be heard. What they had to say was so profound. It opened doors out of my darkness.

I guess you could say those visits were the inspiration for the Joni and Friends Special Delivery program, which partners with individuals, churches and other organizations to provide gifts for you and for others who are affected by disability—gifts that not only brighten your day but also provide insight into the same profound message that brought me out of the darkness of depression and changed my life. It's the heartwarming message of the gospel of Jesus Christ—the One who provides hope in what seem like hopeless situations; light in darkness; and peace, purpose and power for living, even when you can't move your arms or legs.

The friends bringing you these gifts today are cut from the same cloth as those who visited me so many years ago. They want you to enjoy not only these gifts but also their friendship, and most importantly, they want you to grasp the profound message of God's intense love for you. Please listen to what they have to say, and if you have questions or want to talk further, call them at [insert church contact information here] or our local Joni and Friends field ministry office at [insert field ministry office contact information here].

You are loved! By these friends, our team at Joni and Friends, and most of all by the Lord Jesus Christ who provides all good gifts—including the gift of spending eternity with Him! May you know His peace and presence today and always!

Joni Eareckson Tada

Outreach: Ministering to Children in Hospitals

Many families of children with special needs experience long hospital stays. This can create emotional, psychological and financial consequences for the family. These stressors may begin when the initial diagnosis is given, and they may intensify over time. Parents of children who are chronically ill need a caring and supportive environment, yet extended family members are often unavailable, inadequate or exhausted themselves from their busy schedules. Family dynamics can also change when siblings, grandparents, aunts and uncles realize that they may be called on to provide large amounts of patient care. Everyone involved, including the child, struggles with their own fears and questions:

- *Why is this happening to our child?*
- *What exactly is really happening?*
- *Will anything ever be the same again?*
- *How long will the stay in the hospital be?*

Unfortunately, these questions may not be able to be answered with any degree of confidence. And if a child has a disability that affects his or her communication, these questions may go unasked as well as unanswered.

The Road to Recovery

Even when an operation or procedure is declared a success, a child's road to recovery may be arduous. If confined to a bed for weeks at a time, children must recover their balance and learn to walk again. Children who have had surgery related to the digestive tract may have to learn to swallow and eat again. Recurring surgeries and recoveries can take the spirit out of a child and family as they wonder if and when "normal" will ever return. Usually a child's education is also interrupted, and for children with developmental disabilities, the security they derived from their daily routine is stripped away, leaving them with feelings of deep anxiety.

Hope Offered by a Caring Church

Your church can do a great deal to combat a family's sense of hopelessness and relieve some of the difficult problems parents face. You can offer consistent support and maintain a positive attitude toward their child's condition and the medical professionals serving them. This love and friendship, coupled with prayer, can powerfully aid the child's recovery and even help to shorten his or her hospital stay.

Provide Loving Acts of Service

- Offer to clean their house, or pay for bonded cleaning professionals to do the work.
- Offer to do laundry or pick up dry cleaning.
- Help with lawn care and gardening work.
- Send a barber or beautician to cut the child's hair during extended stays.
- Take care of the family's pets.
- Ask to help with medical research. Parents may be lost in the medical jargon. Visit Internet sites or a medical library and photocopy appropriate information to help calm their concerns.

Meet Their Daily Needs

- Show up at the hospital with a home-cooked meal or carry-out food.
- Purchase a hospital meal ticket as a gift.
- Provide a basket with fruit or other healthy foods.
- Make an anonymous donation through your church.
- Give the family coins for vending machines.

Provide Care and Friendship

- Offer to provide child care for siblings.
- Sit with the sick child, so parent(s) can go eat, run errands or go for a walk.
- Pay for a hotel room during an extended stay.
- Provide transportation for visiting family members or siblings.
- Accompany siblings to ball games, doctor or dentist appointments, hair cuts, shopping, etc.
- Provide after-school pickup for siblings.
- Visit the family and play board games or bring movies to watch (make sure there is a player available in the room).
- Show up in a silly outfit or with a nerf gun for unexpected laughs.
- Join them for dinner in the hospital cafeteria or in the child's room.

Make the Most of Christmas and Holidays

- Take a card table, tablecloth, candles and a home-cooked holiday meal to the hospital.
- If the child is well enough, coordinate times for your church groups (Sunday School or Awana Club) to visit, so there is a steady stream of visitors.

- Sing Christmas carols at the hospital.

- On the child's birthday, bring a favorite meal on a tray with a flower or a cake.

- Offer to do parent's shopping for relatives' birthdays or Christmas gifts.

- Give special Easter, Christmas and birthday clothes to wear instead of hospital gowns.

Network Information Updates

- Write e-mails to update friends and church family on the child's condition.

- Set up an online CarePage, a free way for families to stay informed, connected and supported (http://www.carepages.com).

- Make phone calls.

- Set up a prayer calendar.

Provide Help for Out-of-Town Travel

- Arrange for a local pastor to visit the family when an out-of-town hospital is required for treatment.

- Pay for a hotel room during an out-of-town stay.

- Contact an organization like Tyler's Treat to provide help to the family.

Some families have to travel great distances to get the care their child needs, and because they are from out of town, they usually have no friends, family or church to help care for them. Tyler's Treat is a ministry specifically designed for situations in which a family travels great distances for necessary treatment for their child at Cook Children's Center in Ft. Worth, Texas (http://www.tylers treat.org). The goal of Tyler's Treat is to provide a night of respite care for families and primary caregivers of sick children, in an effort to strengthen and support them with prayer, nourishment and rest. Tyler's Treat provides gift cards to the family for dinner at one of the restaurants convenient to the hospital and, in some cases, transportation. Find out if there is this sort of ministry at the place where your family in need is going.

Hospital Gift Bag

Make up a bag to give to the child and his or her family. For children who must a stay in a hospital for an extended length of time, a bag can be made up by a different Sunday School class each month or so. (Use the gift tag patterns on p.175 to complete your bag.) Here are a few suggestions for things to include in the bag:

- Colorful pictures and posters to pin up on hospital walls

- Cheerful cards or posters signed by members of the child's class at church

- An age-appropriate toy or game

- Bible stories on CDs, music CDs or recordings of your church services (bring a player or make sure one is available)

- Gift cards for nearby restaurants

- Crossword puzzle books, or magazines

- Encouraging or fun books to read that don't need to be returned

- Bubble bath for the hospital bathtub (for extended stays)

- Children's or picture Bible

Etiquette at the Hospital

- Check with parents or the hospital for appropriate visiting hours.

- Ask first before touching the child or the child's bed.

- If someone wants to lay hands on the child to pray, the parents may prefer to lay hands on their child and have the others lay hands on them.

- Wash your hands before entering.

- Don't bring anyone with a runny nose.

- Don't question treatment decisions.

- Don't stay too long when the patient seems tired or not up to company.

- Give lots of hugs to caregivers and not too many words.

- Pray with the family before you leave, or look them in the eye and assure them they are being prayed for.

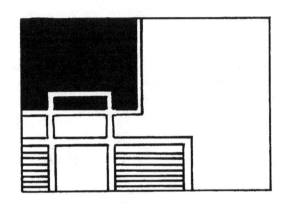

Attendance: Babies and Toddlers with Disabilities

Families of babies and toddlers with disabilities may first experience disability ministry in the church nursery. When we lovingly provide for their child's needs, we can ease the family's intense pain and help them come to terms with their new reality. In our warm welcome, parents can begin to view their child through God's eyes.

If a mother in your church has an adverse prenatal diagnosis, celebrate her child as you would any other. Let her know that you look forward to having her baby in the church nursery. If you learn of a family who has a newborn with a disability, call and congratulate them as with any other newborn. Then ask how the nursery program can best meet their baby's needs. Assure them that you value their little one and believe he or she was created in God's image for His glory.

It's during the toddler years that most children are diagnosed with disabilities that were not apparent at birth. Assure the parents of your love and understanding, and work with them to create a plan to help their child succeed at church.

A Few Basic Considerations

- **Learn to handle specialized medical care and/or equipment.** Some little ones with disabilities will require specialized medical care or equipment. Invite the parents to train volunteers on the use of any equipment. Encourage the parents to stay in the nursery for several weeks until volunteers are comfortable. Keep special equipment safe from other children. Medically fragile children may require a one-on-one volunteer or even a nurse (volunteer or paid) to care for the child during worship. Always welcome parents in the nursery at any time to give medications or special treatments.

- **Listen to parents regarding the care of their child, and don't make assumptions.** Speak often with the parents to learn about changes in care. Unless a parent wants to volunteer in the nursery, allow parents to leave their child with no strings attached. Respite care is expensive and difficult to find, and Sunday morning may be the only time parents have away from their child.

- **Be alert to allergies** (see "Allergies and Treatment," p. 165).

- **Know about sensory integration disorder or dysfunction and how it may manifest itself in children in the nursery.** Find out from parents what therapy or treatment methods are being used. The Sensory Processing Disorder Foundation has a wealth of information to share about research, education and advocacy for this disorder (http://www.spdfoundation.net).

- **Allow the Holy Spirit to minister through you to these little ones with special needs.** Lay the foundation in their lives that God loves them and created them in His image. Make whatever adaptations you can to ensure that they feel safe, secure and loved while they are in your care.

A Few Questions and Answers

- **What do we do if we notice a baby not meeting developmental milestones, but the parent hasn't mentioned anything?** The parent might be in denial, might already know but not be ready to share the information or might not yet see the problems. Prayerfully decide how to handle the situation. Problems will become more apparent as time progresses, and you can inquire of the parent how to handle a specific need without making any value judgments.

- **A boy with Down syndrome is biting other children. How should we handle this?** Generally, you would discipline him according to your nursery policies, just as you would any other child. Specific issues such as biting, hitting or hugging too hard can be brought to the attention of the parents. Ask them how the problem is dealt with at home, day care or school. A chewy toy could be given to a child who bites, activity redirection could be required in the case of a child who hits, and the hugger could be given a large stuffed toy to hold.

- **A girl with autism screams during check-in. How can we help?** Provide a consistent volunteer to welcome her in a low-key way while her parents are registering.

Attendance: Medically Frail Children

The sign on the building might say "Everyone Welcome." The children's church invitation card might note that all are welcome to attend. It's important to remember, however, that the invitation God offers to us is *not* to a building but to a Body of worshipping believers. There are some children who will be able to enter the building to be with that Body. Other children who are medically frail may only be able to accept that invitation if the environment is specially prepared. Our goal, then, is to be creative as we think of ways for that child to become connected with the Body of Christ in unique ways.

Once again, it's important to remember that a child is so much more than a condition or diagnosis. A child is a complex image bearer of God, created with gifts and needs to be used in God's service. Not only should a church know about the child's condition and unique needs associated with that condition, but leaders also need to remember to get to know that whole child. Does the child have a favorite show on TV? What people make the child's eyes light up when they enter a room? Find out about the ways the child is like every other young one that age. Dwell on those areas as well.

Consider ways that a child might be able to attend church at a building by preparing the environment. Would the child be safe with a trained medical person as part of the experience? Can you find willing volunteers so that parents can enjoy worship time on Sunday? Could the child attend the church building experience if there was a room specifically designed around that child? Think about potential electric wiring needs for equipment, the number of people that could be allowed as part of the environment, and which individuals would need to be trained. Could the room where peers meet accommodate this child if the child's friends and leaders were well informed?

Some children, despite our great creativity, would not be able to spend time in a building with people and the germs they carry. The child may not be able to move or may require equipment that needs to stay in one place. In this case, remember that the church is not a building—it's God's people. If the child can't come to the church building, try sending the church to the child. Would it be possible to train some individuals from church to be caretakers on Sunday morning so that parents can worship at the church building? Consider bringing a small group of people to that child's home. Peers may be able to rotate through that experience so that you can have a small group that can worship, pray, hear a Bible story and complete some kind of craft or story reminder that hangs on the child's wall at home. Be creative. Teach the peers what to expect before you arrive at the home so that they are prepared to see the equipment and condition of the child.

One idea for creating peer connections is to have a prayer bulletin board. Using weekly e-mails and photographs, ask peers to pray for their friend who is at home. Get updates and create a community of care. Encourage peers to send cards or notes to the friend.

A Special Note About Hand Washing and Sanitation

If you do have interaction with a child who is medically frail, remember to use a hand sanitizer and to instruct all visitors or members of that group to use one as well. The parents or caregivers may also suggest asking peers and leaders not to touch that child due to the spread of germs. Keep a wall-mounted instant sanitizer in the environment. Instruct other group members to be considerate and stay home if they have a cold or some other illness.

Tips: Adaptive Products and Product Resources

Products

Easy-Grip Scissors—Right- or left-handed scissors that operate by gently squeezing thumb and fingers or palm of the hand that automatically reopen when pressure is released.

Finger Brushes—Small, medium or large brushes that attach to fingers with soft, flexible plastic wraps for children with motor control difficulties.

Puzzles with Sound—Wood puzzles with a large-knob on each piece for easy handling. When a piece is put in the correct place, a realistic sound is made. Sounds are from farms, zoos or vehicles.

Peanut Balls—Peanut-shaped inflatable balls (Gymnic PhysioRolls) that help children with balance and coordination because they only roll forward or backward. Children can also comfortably sit in the center cradle.

Crazy Straws—Funny straws that give children a way to work on jaw stability, lip closure and suck-swallow-breath coordination. They also make great gifts or rewards.

Cube Chairs—Hard molded plastic chairs shaped like cubes. They offer greater stability for young children with poor coordination, and they can also be turned over and used as tables.

Visual Timer—A clock that tells at a glance how much time is left in a period. This timer gives instant feedback for children with attention-deficit disorders.

Junior Ear Muffs—Ear coverings with a padded headband designed to fit young children with sensory disorders.

Writing Slant Board—A nonslip, smooth surface at the optimal wrist position for a child with limited small-motor skills.

Balance Boards—Round or square plastic boards that help children improve balance by providing side-to-side and back-and-forth movement.

Product Sources

Ableware—Designs and manufactures assistive devices and assessment tools for all ages (http://service.maddak.com/index.asp).

Beyond Play—Focuses on young children with special needs (http://www.beyondplay.com).

Disability Products—Assistive devices and aids for daily living for all ages (http://www.disabilityproducts.com/cgi=bin/disabilityproducts.cgi).

Dynamic Living—Products for all ages to make living at home easier (http://www.dynamic-living.com/index).

The Integrations Catalogue—Specializes in problem solutions for children with sensory and learning disabilities (www.integrationscatalog.com).

Sensory Comfort—Specializes in products for people of all ages who have sensory processing difference (www.sensorycomfort.com).

The Therapy Shoppe—Offers a wide range of therapy products for children (http://www.therapyshoppe.com).

(For other adaptive products, see "The Tactile Toolbox," p. 83.)

Joey's Poem

Don't just see my
legs not running;

Don't just see my
hands not writing;

Don't just see my
mouth not talking;

These broken pieces
are not me.

See instead the
light in my eyes;

See instead the
loving soul;

See instead my
thinking mind;

These inner pieces
are the real me.

—Joey Bishop,
who has cerebral
palsy.

(This poem was published in the July 2001 issue of Exceptional Parent Magazine.)

Joey's Poem

Don't just see my
legs not running;

Don't just see my
hands not writing;

Don't just see my
mouth not talking;

These broken pieces
are not me.

See instead the
light in my eyes;

See instead the
loving soul;

See instead my
thinking mind;

These inner pieces
are the real me.

—Joey Bishop,
who has cerebral
palsy.

(This poem was published in the July 2001 issue of Exceptional Parent Magazine.)

I Mess Up— Like Any Other Kid!

"But, Teacher, can't you give me grace today?
You gave Lester grace three times yesterday!"

God is our refuge and strength,
an ever-present help in trouble.

Psalm 46:1

Behavior: What to Expect

Behavior is an outward form of communication. It's a demonstration of an emotion like happiness, sadness, pleasure, fear, confusion, frustration or anger. It can also be a symptom or characteristic of some disabilities. For example, to shut out sensory overload a child with autism may cover his or her ears and scream. That is a demonstration of a *symptomatic behavior*. Hitting another student to get attention is *inappropriate behavior*. It is essential to be able to distinguish the difference between the two.

Social Inappropriateness

 Social skills are learned behaviors that do not always come naturally by observation.

- Invasion of **Personal Space**—A student may want to stand within inches of your face or body to talk to you, not realizing that that nearness makes you feel awkward or uncomfortable.

  Angela loves to be nose to nose when talking, which makes most people back away. But with help, she has learned to keep an arm's distance, which makes others feel more at ease.

- Inappropriate **Conversations**—A student's conversation may be repetitive, simple or bluntly honest. It can be refreshing to know that a child will always tell you the truth, but the lack of ability to know which conversations are not appropriate in public situations can cause problems.

  To the dismay of her mother, Celeste always says what she is thinking. "That man is fat. He eats too much. He needs to go on a diet." Celeste is communicating what she sees without realizing that her statements may be offensive.

- **Inability to Read Social Cues**—Students who are developmentally delayed or are on the autism spectrum are often unable to pick up facial, physical or emotional messages.

  Greg heard a joke in class. He didn't understand it, but he knew everyone was laughing, so he thought he should, too. But when the teacher gave the class a look that allowed others to know it was time to stop, Greg kept laughing. He was unable to interpret the look on his teacher's face that had changed from "okay" to "stop."

  Ted always laughed when someone got hurt. This made the people around him angry. They thought he was uncaring, but Ted was just using the wrong emotion. He had to be taught the appropriate reactions to different situations.

Obsessive and Repetitive Behavior

Obsessive and repetitive behaviors may bring a sense of calm and control into a child's life, or they may be uncontrollable compulsions.

- **Physical Behaviors**—These may include spinning, rocking, tapping or repetitive routines. Before Joey eats he has to touch the plate and cup, pick them up and put them down, touch each utensil (knife, spoon and fork), and make sure they are perfectly straight and in the proper location. Then he's ready to proceed.

- **Vocal Repetitions**—These may include animal sounds, clicking or one-topic conversations. Brian will talk about trains for hours, using one-word descriptive sentences over and over: "Train." "Engine." "Caboose."

Expressions of Frustration, Anger or Lack of Control

 A child with disabilities may be limited in his or her ability to appropriately express feelings. A sense of being out of control or frustrated may result in inappropriate or dangerous behaviors.

- **Emotional Outbursts**—Students may cry excessively or suddenly start screaming.

- **Hurt Others**—Students may hit, bite, pinch, kick or spit.

- **Self-Injuries**—Students may bang their head or hit or bite themselves.

- **Noncompliance**—Students may refuse to comply with a request or completely withdraw from an activity.

Triggers to Inappropriate Behavior

- New situations or people

- Changes in routine

- Transitions from one activity to another

- Sensory overload

- Pain or sickness

- Inability to communicate

- Changes in medications

Get to know each of your students. Learning what triggers a student's behavior and giving the student effective ways to communicate needs, wants and desires will help the student, teacher and class have a successful experience.

Behavior: Hidden Messages in a Child's Behavior

Behavior difficulties in children are often indicators of fear, inability to communicate, frustration, hunger or pain. Knowing our students helps us to understand reasons for their behavior.

"My senses are on overload."

 For children with sensory processing issues, a simple touch, sound or sight may cause pain or crowd out the ability to focus on other senses.

- Victoria does not make eye contact when someone is speaking to her because she is concentrating on deciphering what she hears without having to focus on what she sees.

- When the air-conditioning comes on, Alan may start yelling and covering his ears in order to cover up the other sounds that are bombarding him.

- Charlie refuses to eat from plastic dishware because he is overwhelmed by the smell of plastic.

"You don't understand me, and I don't understand you."

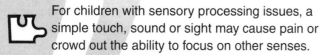 Students with limited verbal abilities may become aggravated when they cannot communicate. Poor behavior may escalate as the child continues to feel misunderstood and confused.

- Brian saw his mother outside the window and knew it was time to leave but was unable to tell his teacher. Brian headed toward the door but was told to sit down. He started to stomp his foot and get angry. Brian felt frustrated because he knew it was time to go, but no one understood him.

- The teacher told Anthony to throw his napkin and cup away and go to story time, but Anthony continued to sit in his chair. The teacher repeated her instructions, becoming frustrated with Anthony's apparent defiance. Anthony didn't mean to be defiant but was trying to interpret the request while being bombarded with more words.

Brian and Anthony both benefit from the use of picture communication books, schedules and emotion charts that allow them to communicate using visual cues.

"I feel helpless; I want to be in control."

 Students who lack control of their environment may feel helpless. Giving simple choices to these children helps them feel secure.

- When Clayton is given a simple instruction ("Please sit at the table"), he often reacts by flailing his arms and screaming. When given a simple choice ("Do you want to sit in the red chair or the blue chair?"), he feels more control over the situation and usually complies.

"I don't feel good."

 Changes in behavior, crying, withdrawal or agitation can be indications that a child is hurting or feels sick. Some students lack the language to explain themselves, while others aren't able to determine where the pain is coming from.

- Melissa is medically fragile and is unable to use vocal or sign language. Those around her need to be in tune to alternate forms of communication. Certain cries and facial expressions indicate that Melissa probably needs medical attention.

"I'm scared." "I'm uncomfortable."

 New situations, new people or changes in schedule can cause fear or anxiety.

- New volunteers were in Sierra's class, and even though she was usually social and happy, she refused to move from her spot on the floor. She felt uncomfortable and needed time to build trust with the new helpers. Sierra's teacher could have prepared her for the change by using social stories or making sure one familiar helper remained in her class.

In James 1:19 we're told, "Everyone should be quick to listen, slow to speak and slow to become angry." Stop to listen to your students before you react. Ask yourself, *What is this child trying to tell me? What can I do to help ease the child's pain or frustration?* Answering these questions will help you respond to children with more understanding and compassion.

Behavior: Treating Children Fairly, Not Equally

There is no one-size-fits-all plan for learning or behavior. God gives each person different strengths, talents and abilities. We must be willing to adapt according to a child's needs. What is best for some is not best for others.

Behavior Guideline Adjustments

Every class has general rules that apply to all students. But some students may need rules adjusted to meet his or her unique needs. In Jonathon's class, the students are not allowed to have food until snack time. Jonathon, however, gets a small goldfish cracker whenever he sits for five minutes without an inappropriate vocal outburst. He is highly motivated by goldfish crackers. The plan works well, and his teacher gradually increases the time between awards. Jonathon may eat before snack time, because it helps him achieve a specific goal.

Appropriate Expectations

It is important to set appropriate expectations for our students based on individual needs. Sitting through 20 minutes of singing and a story may be reasonable for most eight-year-olds, but for Susie, five minutes is a great accomplishment. Allowing Susie to leave to do a puzzle after five successful minutes prevents her from getting frustrated. The teacher will slowly increase the amount of time Susie is expected to participate with others.

Exceptions and Substitutions

Students are expected to participate in all of the daily activities, but some students may need to be excused or given an alternative. Because Jeffrey is sensitive to sound, a helper accompanies him to the office to deliver the attendance envelope during music time. Katie has a learning disability, so she is given a shortened verse to memorize in order to receive a prize.

Helping Peers Understand Fairness

It is natural for children to wonder why someone is being treated differently. It is important to teach children that what is fair and best doesn't always mean things will be the same for all.

Sometimes a student's disability will be obvious, and classmates will easily understand why the expectations for that student are different. Because they have seldom heard Sandra talk, classmates aren't surprised that she gets to use word cards instead of saying her verse.

Some situations, however, are more subtle, and students may not understand why their classmate is treated differently. Johnny gets stickers for sitting still. When a friend wonders why, the teacher explains, "Johnny needs some extra help learning to sit still. You've already learned that. When you need extra help with something I will make sure to help you, too."

Children (and teachers) need to understand that different children require different methods: What works for one won't necessarily work for all. Mark needs to hold a fidget toy to help him concentrate when the teacher is talking, but for David, a fidget toy is distracting.

It is helpful to remind classmates that they are part of a team effort to support and help each member do their best. The child with special needs is an important part of that team and always has something to offer. When students encourage and assist each other, everyone benefits.

Helping Volunteers Have Clear Expectations

Avoid frustration and confusion by making sure that helpers know what is expected from students. Class rules should be clearly posted; and special behavior plans, routines or alterations to the rules need to be written down and made available to each volunteer.

Mark had a substitute teacher for Sunday School. The teacher unknowingly took Mark's fidget toy away because he was unaware that the toy helped Mark concentrate. Fortunately, Mark's friend, David, told the substitute that Mark needed the toy to help him pay attention. Both Mark and the teacher were grateful for David's help.

Behavior: How to Help a Biter

While biting is a typical, mainly harmless behavior for babies and toddlers, biting can be a serious problem if it's exhibited by older children with disabilities. Dealing with a biter requires understanding, patience and time. Incidences tend to increase when children are in group settings and may occur for the following reasons:

- The child's language is limited, so rather than using words, the child uses his or her teeth.

- The child is teething and is very conscious of his or her mouth. A warm body is a good place to try to put new teeth.

- Biting elicits immediate and obvious reactions from adults and other children.

- Biting may satisfy a sensory need for self-comfort.

- Biting is one of the few times the child, not the adult, has power—it is very difficult to prevent because it happens so quickly and often for no discernible reason.

General Information About Biting

- A child who bites is not by nature mean and should not be labeled "bad," "mean" or "a biter." Children generally live up to the expectations of the adults or children around them, so focus on the positive.

- Biting seems to occur in spurts. Weeks can go by without an incident, but the behavior may resurface suddenly.

- Biting is most prevalent between the ages of 15 to 30 months, although it can occur at a younger age or with older children.

- Unless the skin is broken, the wound does not need medical attention. The bruised skin will heal with time.

- If the skin is broken, the wound should be run under water and bandaged with a sterile bandage from a first-aid kit. If the bitten child refuses to be comforted, contact the parents to come and pick up their child.

- Bite wounds can easily become infected, so parents should be encouraged to seek medical attention. If they do not have health insurance, refer them to the business administrator of the church.

Advice for Teachers

- Tell the biter very firmly, "No biting! Biting hurts." Refer to the child's behavior plan for further guidelines (see "Using Visual Behavior Plans," p. 193).

- Comfort the injured child. Tend to wound if necessary.

- In some cases, a biter needs a helper to shadow his or her actions or redirect the child to a special needs classroom.

- Write up an accident/illness report form to give to the parents of the injured child. Do not tell the parents the name of the child who did the biting. Also inform the parents of the biting child about the incident. Both parents will appreciate kindness, compassion and reassurance.

Advice for Parents

- Understand that biting, although unpleasant, is normal at certain ages.

- Believe that ministry volunteers are doing all that they can to help the children (biters and bitees) through the situation.

- Do not ask who is doing the biting. If you know who it is, do not mention the child's name in front of your child or anyone else.

- Never blame or confront the parents of a biting child. They would do anything to stop the behavior and are frequently more distressed than the parents of a bitten child.

- Don't pretend to nibble or bite your own children.

- If you see some children with autism wearing terry-cloth wristbands or soft plastic necklaces, don't call attention to these items. These children experience such high levels of frustration that they bite themselves or others. Biting on a wristband or necklace can relieve stress and prevent injury.

Behavior: Getting a Picture of AD/HD

"If only that parent would discipline that little boy."

"Can't that child just sit still in church?"

Judgmental comments often fly in the direction of parents trying to raise a child with AD/HD. While all parents need advice from time to time, parents of children who have attention-deficit/hyperactivity disorder need special encouragement and understanding. So does the child.

Basics of Brain Chemistry

The human brain is an amazing wonder of God's creation. Literally the nerve center of a human, the brain communicates vital pieces of information through neurotransmitters. Serotonin is a neurotransmitter that helps regulate mood. Chocolate and sunshine may help boost levels and placement of serotonin. Dopamine is the neurotransmitter usually associated with the ability to pay attention. When that particular substance is lacking or insufficient, an individual will struggle in areas related to attention. Medications may help restore dopamine levels in the brain.

Different Types of AD/HD

There are three types of AD/HD:

- **Hyperactive-Impulsive Type**—These children will most often be quite active, have a difficult time moving from one activity to the next and act impulsively. These children behave as if they had a small and powerful engine that keeps them moving. Some people speculate that these children move in order to try and stimulate the neurotransmitters to work.

- **Predominantly Inattentive Type**—These children will not be overly active but will struggle to focus and have difficulty organizing a task. They might be quietly off in another world, while the rest of the group is listening to a story or completing an independent activity.

- **Combined Type**—These children are a combination of the other two types.

Putting AD/HD in Perspective

While children with AD/HD may have areas of struggle, they also have areas of gifting. In addition to whatever other areas of strength God may have chosen for these children, they are also often creative and imaginative.

Such children who think of ideas and solutions that are way outside the box can create energy and excitement in a group of children. Make sure the activity level or inattention of these children doesn't cloud your vision of what an amazing addition they are to your group of children.

Medication Dilemmas for Churches

Most medications that children take to help support the brain's production and placement of dopamine last for 12 hours or less. Some last as few as 4 hours. If a child gets up in the morning and takes a pill at 7 A.M., that medication will be out of that child's system by 11 A.M., 3 P.M. or 7 P.M., depending on the medicine. Most children don't take an evening dose because the medication may prevent sleep or interfere with a good appetite. Some physicians recommend that a child take medication only on school days, while other physicians suggest taking medication consistently each day. The bottom line is that you need to find out from the parents what regimen their child is following. If the children's group meets in the evening, the medication may be wearing off. If the children's group meets on Saturday or Sunday, the child may not be on any medication. At church, children may struggle more to maintain a calm activity level and a high level of attention than in other daytime environments.

Considerations for Support

Try these ideas as you support the needs and use the gifts of a child with AD/HD:

- **Remember the "can't" and the "won't."** Be sensitive that this child may want to sit still but can't do it all the time. The child may want to pay attention and obey the leader of the group but can't do it all the time. Get to know that boy or girl so that you begin to know the difference between poor choices the child is making ("I won't do this") and areas the child will have difficulty controlling ("I can't do this").

- **Set realistic expectations.** If it's not realistic for the child to participate in activities with other children for 30 minutes, then create an expectation that matches the child's level of ability. If the child can participate for 15 minutes, then plan to change activities or ask the child to run an errand in the hallway before tackling the next 15 minutes in class.

- **Offer choices for movement and seating.** "Would you like to sit by the table or kneel by your place?"

"Would you like to sit on the floor and listen, or would you like to listen from the rocking chair?" Intersperse quiet times with actions and movements. Instead of walking to the drinking fountain, offer choices to crab walk or bear walk to that location. Lace your transition times with songs, movements, games or exercises. Instead of making sitting in a chair a consequence, consider offering moving a large pile of books from one location in the room to another a choice.

- **Use the child's gifts.** Think of ways you can plug in that child's gift areas to benefit the group. Perhaps the child has a great vocabulary—check some definitions of words as you tell the Bible story. Perhaps the child is a fast runner—offer games where this child can shine. It's no fun to be in a place where you are always getting in trouble or being singled out for negative reasons. Be specific in using this child's gift areas each time you are together.

- **Use reminders and visuals.** Some children forget instructions and expectations. Find ways to make these visual. Postings of your schedule, steps to follow, or group expectations are constant reminders to the child. Visual postings don't go away; words do.

- **Add an extra pair of hands for redirection and reminders.** Sometimes it's helpful to add another adult or teen to your group to help support the child with AD/HD. Placing a supportive person in the group allows for individualized attention as needed, whether it be to repeat steps, give reminders, take walks, do errands or give quiet correction when a child makes a social error.

While there were no screening tools or diagnostic manuals during Bible times, it's possible that if there had been, Peter might have been diagnosed with the hyperactive-impulsive type of AD/HD. His interactions with Christ and others were laced with impulsivity. Jesus, wisely, had a twofold reaction to Peter: He supported his needs by mopping up some messes and restoring him, and he also highlighted Peter's gifts. In fact, Jesus singled Peter out from the other disciples: "Blessed are you, Simon son of Jonah, for this was not revealed to you by man, but by my Father in heaven. And I tell you that you are Peter, and on this rock I will build my church, and the gates of Hades will not overcome it" (Matthew 16:17-18).

Follow this example of Jesus. Be ready to mop up a few messes. Also be ready to speak into this child's life the gifts that you see. Bless this child. God has a good plan for this little one, and you are part of that adventure.

Behavior: Helping Children Deal with Anger

In the process of raising a son with anger problems, Ann learned much about her own feelings and issues. Relational dynamics that others seem to know instinctively, she found difficult to figure out. She experienced her own rage, but she learned to anticipate it and to walk through the same steps she eventually taught her son.

Today's children need many coping skills. They face disrespect, peer pressure, frustration over failure and social rejection. Their responses to these pressures may include such things as throwing toys, pushing or hitting. As they mature and learn to identify basic emotions, they are better able to express their feelings with words rather than actions. Eventually, they come to understand the perspectives of others and to learn how to solve problems with compromise; that is, unless they have a behavioral disability.

Children with language or impulse control problems struggle with managing negative feelings. They may resort to physically acting out many years beyond what is age appropriate. Children with disabilities face complex struggles to cope with their physical and mental differences. This compounds the children's frustrations and inability to feel accepted by peers in normal relationships.

With God's help, your church can provide an environment that is free from negative peer pressure and from social rejection—a place where all children are encouraged to model Christlike love and acceptance of those who are different.

Solve Problems Beforehand

Ninety percent of classroom discipline problems can be avoided by consistency, scheduling and clear expectations. Knowing when one activity ends and another begins helps alleviate anxiety. Students with special needs can recognize what "finished" or "all done" means for different types of activities. Sound a timer! Fill a box! Complete a puzzle! Turn off the tape player! Let other children line up! These signals show that an activity is finished, enabling children to participate in the transition to what comes next.

Teachers and classmates can model movement to a new activity by taking special friends by the hand, prompting them with sign language or showing a picture card. A five-minute warning that one activity will end and another will begin also helps. Keep each activity in a predictable area in a room. This brings rhythm and calm to the class. Activities that children particularly enjoy, such as art or music, can also be used to reward participation for required tasks such as sitting still to focus on a Bible story.

Share Control

Some bursts of anger are simply expressions of a need for independence. Many children with special needs are overprotected or overcontrolled by well-meaning adults. These children deal with sensory overload, barriers of language comprehension and/or a lack of opportunity to make basic decisions. Letting children make choices may preempt angry outbursts and build better relationships. You will be surprised by how simply asking children which pair of scissors or color paper they prefer can improve their behavior. Many decisions should remain out of children's control, of course; but there are creative ways to build options into the day. Here are some examples:

- Which water fountain would you like to drink from?

- Which swing would you like to sit in?

- Which shoe should we put on first?

- Would you like to write your name or color the picture first?

- Would you like to sit by Billy or Martha?

When given choices they don't like, children may try to add extra options, but stick with the original choices and repeat them once or twice. If children refuse to choose, either make the choice for them, or allow them to do without what is being offered. Learning this principal of sharing control with the teacher is often easiest during snack time when doing without the snack is not a pleasant option.

Show Empathy

Empathize with children's feelings and state the emotion they are struggling to identify, or label. You might try exaggerating facial expressions or using pictures or sign language. Encourage children to practice appropriate expressions of feelings. Teach them to say "I'm angry," "I'm sad" and "I want . . ." [naming the desired item]. Help children practice deep breathing when they are not angry. Later, they will be able to use this technique in order to calm themselves.

Create a place where children can go to calm down when they're angry. This will save embarrassment in front of peers. Go to this quiet place with the angry child, and give the child the chance to be heard. When the child is finished communicating, calmly restate your expectations and return to regular activities if the child is able.

Cooperate with Parents Regarding Consequences

Ask the parents for advice about how to work with their child. If there is a history of anger problems, request that they stay in the classroom and participate during the child's first visit, so you can learn from their example. If a child has a successful behavior plan in school, a church may use that plan as a model. Consistency will cut down on confusion and shows a child that the behavior expected at church is similar to the behavior expected in other settings.

The partnership between the teacher and parents is enhanced when parents take the responsibility of measuring out consequences or rewards, depending on the child's behavior during class. If parents are unwilling or unable to provide consequences and rewards, a teacher can have a prize bag that is only available to children who have met their individualized goals of good behavior. To be effective, rewards must be available only when standards are met. Document problematic incidents and discuss serious behavioral issues with parents. Be watchful for good behavior and new adaptive skills, and report these to parents as well.

Use These Tips

- **Identify the cause of the angry outburst.** This may seem obvious, but surprising triggers may be discovered with a little investigating. This, in turn, may result in unexpected solutions that are much more effective than simply repeating "Stop it!" or "Behave!" Also keep in mind that the phrase "Stop it!" should specify what behavior is to be stopped: running, cutting clothes up, etc. And the phrase "Behave!" should include a specific desired action: be gentle, ask nicely, etc.

- **Understand that appealing to a child's sense of right and wrong may be ineffective or even counterproductive.** Instead, teach thinking skills that help children avoid and resolve peer conflicts, resist peer pressure and cope with emotional stress.

- **Consider adapting curriculum and instructions to alleviate the frustration that is behind the anger.**

- **Be sure to praise children when they appropriately handle their anger.**

Every time a child displays an angry feeling, it is a teachable moment. It gives adults an opportunity to encourage empathy and to teach children that while all feelings are acceptable, not all behaviors are acceptable. (Note: When the teacher sees unreasonable, out-of-control anger in a child not known to be diagnosed with an anger problem, a parent conference is needed to discuss the incident and possible causes. Seizures; head trauma; abuse or exposure to drugs, alcohol and certain chemicals in early life—all may result in a later manifestation of a mood disorder. Parents need to be alerted that medical intervention may be necessary.)

Behavior: Dealing with Meltdowns

Joey crumpled onto the floor in tears. In between sobs, he screamed, "Be nice! Be nice! Be nice!" Sandra was at a loss. She had been nice. As gently as she could, she had told Joey he was going to Grandma's house after church. He usually loved to go. What could possibly be wrong? Joey seemed inconsolable. Sandra conferred with another teacher who helped her walk through the events preceding Joey's meltdown. Suddenly it hit her. She promised Joey a trip to the soda machine for good behavior after Sunday School. Now he thought he had done something wrong and that Grandma's was the destination instead of the soda machine. Sandra stooped down and looked Joey in the eye. "Be nice—*then* soda—*then* Grandma's house," she gently explained. His body relaxed, the tears subsided, and all was right again.

Find an Explanation

Any disability that affects communication can lead to a state of extreme frustration for a child; this, then, may result in a behavioral meltdown. What sets off the meltdown may not make any sense to anyone except the child, but it usually falls into one of the following categories:

- **Desire for Access**—The behavior produces attention and other desired events (i.e., access to toys or desired activities).

- **Desire for Escape**—The behavior allows the child to avoid or escape demands or other undesired events or activities.

- **Need for Stimulation**—The behavior occurs because of sensory consequences (relieves pain, feels good, etc.).

A child may also have physical needs that are not being met, but the child can't tell an adult about them.

To help understand the behavior, a teacher must take a close look at what happens right *before* and right *after* a child exhibits the troubling behavior. The story of Joey and the trip to the soda machine is an example of a meltdown triggered by a forgotten promise. Keep in mind that children remember patterns of adult behavior. If Joey were always taken straight to the soda machine after he had a meltdown, meltdowns would become more and more frequent. Calming a child with a behavior disorder by switching to a favorable activity or by providing a treat will ensure that the unwanted behavior not only will be repeated but also will escalate. Make sure you don't reinforce unwanted

behavior, because a child with special needs will be encouraged by an adult's actions or emotional responses. Even your show of disappointment can be very satisfying to a child. For example, Joann, who has autism, may enjoy Mr. Peterson's face when it gets really red and angry—his full attention may be very rewarding to her.

Teach a Replacement Behavior

The most effective way to lower the incidence of meltdowns is to teach an appropriate replacement behavior.

- **Desire for Access**—Teach the word or sign for "more." Encourage the child to say a single word, to say a part of a word or to point.

More: With fingertips touching,
hands meet at center.

- **Desire to Escape**—Teach the words or sign for "finished" or "all done." Establish sign language or a picture icon that communicates a need for a break. When this system is mastered and relationships established, move to teaching the meaning of the word "then," so a caregiver can say "Story—*then* break" or "Write—*then* snack."

- **Need for Stimulation**—Provide a swing or rocking chair, have foods with a desired texture available, meet visual stimulation needs with kaleidoscopes, etc. Allow a student to have a fidget toy for group times when he or she is required to sit for a long period of time.

A child's comprehension of the word "or" is critical so that choices can become a regular part of communication. Showing a child choices is a helpful first step along the road to eliminating meltdowns. For younger or low-functioning students, much time and practice may be needed before the meaning of "or" is clearly understood. A student may not understand that a choice is being offered, because he or she has never had the experience before. Children with autism and other delays may become stuck in a pattern such as always choosing what is offered last. If this is the case, occasionally offer a preferred item (maybe a piece of candy) first and a nonpreferred item (maybe a cracker) second. Then let the student live with his or her choice. Offer the choice again, in the same order, a few minutes later. Since choices are part of the bedrock of a good behavior program, great effort in teaching this one little word will pay off dramatically in the long run.

Recognize the Signs

Knowing the signs of a looming meltdown can help a teacher be preemptive. Behaviors that might signal that a child needs a break are repetitive behaviors, going limp and flopping by leaning or lying on the floor, pupil dilation, hand flapping, running away, sweating, or picking at hair or skin. These behaviors may not be a red flag for every child, but they're a good place to start when observing a child who is prone to meltdowns.

You cannot talk a child out of frustration, sensory issues or obsessive behaviors. Instead, a clear behavior plan should be outlined in a way the child can understand. Then consistently put the plan into practice, and give it a chance to work, extinguishing frequent meltdowns over time. Check with the child's school to see if there is a behavior plan in place there. Use the same plan, or use the school's plan as a model for your own plan.

When working with a child prone to meltdowns, reaffirm the positive by having a plan to measure progress, even if the progress is in a simple thing. This promotes creative teaching and encourages everyone involved—teacher, child and parent. Keep a journal of small gains, and take pleasure in each one.

Follow a Few Guidelines

- Plan activities that each child can be successful in.

- Plan a variety of activities to prevent boredom.

- Hold all emotions in check, and respond in a calm, straightforward manner.

- Be careful that bad behavior is not rewarded (rewards can include attention, disruption and an emotional rise).

- Make time for unconditional praise, and have fun.

- Remember that many children do much better with directed activities rather than unstructured time.

- Keep track of positive behaviors.

By establishing guidelines for intervention and understanding possible causes, teachers do not have to remain in a state of anxiety. Meltdowns are avoidable, but if they do occur, they do not mean the end of a loving teacher-child relationship. Learn from each incident, and realize that each incident can lead to improved behavior and an even better relationship in the future.

Solutions: Creating a Small, Safe Place

Grace's favorite spot in her first-grade classroom is the book tent. If her teacher doesn't redirect her, Grace would be content to spend the entire day in there. Grace's IQ tests place her at grade level, and she is not particularly shy, so Grace's teacher is puzzled by her behavior. Grace's teacher had hoped the book tent would provide a temporary retreat for her students, not a hangout.

Most classrooms need a quiet place where students can get away. When children with special needs feel overwhelmed by social or sensory overload, a quiet place helps them conquer their fears. Sensory overload can occur when one or more of a child's five senses are overpowered, making it difficult to focus on the task at hand. The term is common in children with autism, but it can also impact children who struggle with attention-deficit/hyperactivity disorder, dyslexia, developmental dyspraxia, Tourette's syndrome, multiple sclerosis and other neurological conditions. Sensory overload comes in many forms and can vary in duration and intensity. The environmental factors that trigger the overload can also vary.

Why a Safe Place Is Necessary

Most of us naturally tune out a great deal of stimulation that bombards our senses from our environment. We learn to focus on the person or task in front of us instead of the people talking in the background, doors slamming, air-conditioning vents blowing, the buzzing of fluorescent lights and chairs sliding. We also fairly easily ignore tactile stimuli such as slight temperature shifts, the feel of changing from metal to plastic chairs, a new outfit with unwashed fabric, and an unexpected touch. Each child, however, may have a different response to the environment and all of its stimuli and may not be able to filter out what's unnecessary, thus becoming overstimulated. A safe place for such children to decompress is necessary.

How to Create a Place of Safety

A small pop-up tent or a table draped with a blanket can create a quiet, dark getaway for any child who feels overstimulated. Students can use this space to be alone. Listening to soft calm music may help them regroup as well. A simple beanbag chair in the corner of the area is usually the only furnishing needed.

How to Use A Safe Place

Students should be allowed the option of going to the safe place whenever they need a break. This safe place should not to be confused with or used as a time-out

location. A teacher may, however, suggest that a child go there to get away and relax. The student may then freely choose whether to go there.

When children with special needs visit a new classroom, they may want to retreat to the safe place and remain there the whole time. Whether this is acceptable (and for how long) depends on the severity of the disability and the resistance of the child. For proper inclusion and learning, the retreat should not go on indefinitely. Meet with parents to decide on a plan to coax the child into fuller participation. If possible, also include the child in setting some rules for the area's use. Place an icon of the tent on a visual schedule, and allow the child to slip away for an agreed number of visits and for only a specified length of time. Setting a timer may be a good idea, because it will remind the teacher and the student when retreat time is over.

Some children may spend more time in the safe place than they spend in class. Check on them frequently to make sure they are okay, but try to slowly expand their class participation over successive weeks. As time away from the safe place increases, eventually just knowing the space is available will have a calming effect.

Explain to classmates that their friend needs a break and will return when he or she can. If nondisabled students want to visit the quiet place, let them each take a turn for a minute at the end of class. This should alleviate their curiosity, and when the area's novelty wears off, the safe place will not be a distraction.

How to Avoid Constant Retreat

There are ways to help students calm themselves without their having to constantly retreat to a safe place. For example, a child with sensitive hearing can wear earplugs or headphones. This may be especially true if your worship service or other church settings are noisy. In some instances, teachers need to experiment with different ways of using their voice. Singing or using silly voices might be a good idea because for some children, even whispering can be irritating. The opposite of this may also be true.

Fluorescent bulbs can be particularly bothersome to students who are visually sensitive. Allow these children to wear dark glasses, or add filters to the lights or change the direction of the lights. Consider using incandescent bulbs or using tabletop lamps to soften light. Some children are sensitive to PowerPoint displays of lyrics during worship, as well as complex backgrounds and moving designs. For these children to participate in the song portion of the worship service, the lyrics could be printed on a plain sheet of paper.

A child's sense of smell can also be overstimuated. Scents as strong as that from vomiting or as benign as that from shaving cream can adversely affect a child. Teachers may need to be careful of using strong-smelling soaps or lotions and of wearing perfume.

A final area to be aware of is touch sensitivity. In your first meeting with the parents, find out if their child likes or avoids touch. If a child is adverse to touch, make sure the rhythm of the classroom is established and a caring relationship is in place before any attempt to touch the child is made. Even then, touch should only be initiated with forewarning to the child and with the child's consent.

The combination of the availability of a safe place and the leader's attitude of general sensitivity to every student's unique needs can strike a balance that allows children with special needs to feel safe and to be better understood by friends at church.

Solutions: Using Visual Behavior Plans

A ministry to children with special needs should be filled with warmth and affection. Getting to that point, however, requires teaching to behave in appropriate ways. A formal behavior plan, which offers children immediate tangible rewards for good interaction with others, is the first step on that journey. After children learn to work well for immediate gratification, they can slowly be taught to behave well for delayed rewards. The author of Hebrews 12:11 says, "No discipline seems pleasant at the time, but painful. Later on, however, it produces a harvest of righteousness and peace for those who have been trained by it."

When tangible rewards are always coupled with praise, children behave well simply for the joy of pleasing others or because it makes them feel good inside.

Getting Parents' Cooperation

A child's behavior plan will be more effective when parents and teachers work as a team. This visible cooperation allows a child to see that a teacher's authority is backed by Mom and Dad. But even when this kind of cooperation is not in place, the visual behavior cues and plans introduced in this section may still be successful. Ask parents about their child's school behavior plan. If you can duplicate the school plan in your class, children will benefit from consistency, and they'll experience less confusion about what to expect at church.

Choosing a Visual Plan

There are two main ways of visually presenting behavior plans: (1) the color-level system and (2) the visual schedule. Both of these methods clearly communicate expectations and are simple to understand.

1. The Color-Level System

In a color-level system, a teacher assigns a level of color according to a child's behavior:

- **Green**—great behavior and cooperation

- **Yellow**—struggling to comply and perform

- **Red**—defiant and disruptive

Teachers give children color-coded stickers to correspond with their behavior levels. Stickers given after each activity encourage good behavior and can be placed on a "My Good Behavior Record" (see sample on p. 195). At the end of the day, one color sticker is given denoting the child's overall behavior. Then parents follow through with a positive or negative consequence. If parents are unable to do this, a teacher can have a collection of tangible rewards from which the child can choose.

2. The Visual Schedule

The Visual Schedule uses graphic symbols, or icons, to communicate expectations. Icons provide increased predictability, which helps decrease a child's anxiety about what is occurring in his or her environment. (To enhance their understanding, some children need actual photographs instead of line drawings or symbols.) This system can be combined with a color chart on which the words are replaced with pictures. Here is an example of this system applied in a church setting:

Name _____ Date _____

Play Time		Hold a favorite toy during next activity.
Bible Story		Candy Treat
Sing and Praise		Pick a song.
Craft		Help pass out snack.
Snack		Extra Cracker
Cleanup		Candy Treat

Overall Color [ ]   Overall Reward [ ]

Green
Good job!

Yellow
Try again.

Red
Oh no!

Defining Good Behavior

The object of a behavior plan is to recognize good behavior and reward it. Children themselves must also understand what constitutes proper behavior. If their ability to communicate is complicated by disabilities, teachers must clearly explain what is expected. Behaviors may need to be modeled repeatedly, or children may need to be physically guided through what is expected.

Mrs. Flynn knew that Anthony's participation would be greatly improved if he could learn to sit quietly. She had never seem him sit in a chair for more than a few seconds, so she decided to reward him for every minute he could keep his bottom in the seat. She showed Anthony a sitting-down icon, modeled the behavior and praised Anthony when he copied her. She set her watch to beep after one minute, sat near Anthony and continued to praise him until the timer went off. At that point, she quietly slipped him a tiny piece of candy and reset her watch. Anthony quickly caught on. The next week Mrs. Flynn set her watch for one and a half minutes and found Anthony tolerated the longer wait well. Mrs. Flynn continued to lengthen the time between rewards until Anthony would remain in his seat the entire 10 minutes of story time. Mrs. Flynn could now save a single piece of candy for the end of the story. She reported the success to Anthony's parents, who were amazed and hopeful that more good behaviors would follow.

This intensive level of instruction can be very satisfying because we see children constantly make small but measurable gains. The initial goal should be carefully chosen and supported with an eye on a child's future success. Goals should be age appropriate and attainable for the child. Here are some examples of initial good behaviors:

- Sitting still in a chair
- Keeping hands to oneself
- Sharing a toy with another child upon request
- Signing or saying "Please" for a desired item
- Signing or saying "No" instead of throwing a tantrum
- Using the appropriate volume when speaking in class

Rewarding Good Behavior

Finding meaningful, effective rewards for children can sometimes be difficult. The two most important principles to remember are (1) the reward must be meaningful to that particular child, and (2) the child should not have access to that particular reward in any other way. It does no good to promise a child a soda if he or she has no interest in it or if he or she gets one every day anyway.

Adults must carefully plan how to structure rewards. An icon schedule is good for younger children who need visual cues and prompt pay off. Behavior contracts work well with older children who can read. A token system works for children who can count, can understand a token-exchange system and can deal with delayed gratification. Ask children what rewards are meaningful to them. Sometimes you can determine what is important to a child by watching what he or she chooses to play with during free time. (Motivation assessment scales have been designed for more difficult cases.) Remember, rewards should be reinforcing but not so large that the child becomes easily satisfied with them. Here are some examples of possible rewards:

- Listening to music
- A star on a chart
- A toy from a treasure box
- Collectible cards
- Stickers
- A small piece of candy (especially if behaviors have to be rewarded quickly and often)
- Being a special helper
- Serving snacks

Scheduling the Reward

When you initiate the use of a reward system, you must make it easy for children to get immediate rewards for good behaviors. Once children start to experience success, you can space rewards further apart. But at first, children must know that rewards are attainable and easy to achieve. Later, they will learn to work harder and harder to earn prizes.

Once children understand how the visual system you've chosen works, just whispering the color that defines a child's current behavior can be effective for praise and/or correction. "Good job! You are doing green right now." "Uh oh, you're going to yellow." "Very sad—that's red." Eventually, the use of colored stickers may be discontinued as children understand the system without needing the concrete object.

Teachers should have high, yet reasonable, expectations. When a child's reward can be delayed until the child is picked up by his or her parents, your praise will be enough to ensure many good interactions during class. Recognize that one difficult day with numerous negative consequences (or lack of rewards) can be followed by many good days. Stay encouraged.

Form: My Good Behavior Record

Name _____ Date _____

Subject/Activity/Job	What Color?	Comments

Overall Color [ ] Overall Reward [ ]

Green
Good job!

Yellow
Try again.

Red
Oh no!

Activities	Rewards

Solutions: Calling People to Pray for Special Needs

True, whole prayer is nothing but love.
St. Augustine

Serving children with special needs is a heart-expanding ministry because it calls on us to "rejoice with those who rejoice, and weep with those who weep" (Romans 12:15, *NKJV*). Its very nature drives us beyond human resources and into the throne room of a merciful God—One who is in control of every situation. While we can individually intercede for these families, Jesus promises even greater power in community prayer (see Matthew 18:20). That's why a prayer coordinator is an important part of your team.

What a Prayer Coordinator Does

A prayer coordinator encourages others to pray for children and families in your disability ministry in many ways:

- Writing and distributing simple prayer guides using Bible promises to lift up the needs of the children and volunteers

- Asking people to volunteer to serve on a special needs prayer team and to attend regular prayer services

- Visiting small groups in your church once a quarter to encourage them to pray for outreach to families with disabilities

- Leading children in prayer for parents, caregivers, teachers and medical teams who serve children with special needs

- Praying with those who serve in disability ministry and for new volunteers

- Starting an e-mail prayer list and sending weekly updates

- Reminding pastors to pray for children with disabilities and their families regularly during worship services

- Leading others in sending notes of encouragement to those being prayed for

- Writing stories about answers to prayers, to include in church newsletters

- Visiting homebound people with disabilities for a time of prayer with them and their caregivers

Who Will Pray

Most Christians will pray for those with disabilities if they are given a plan for prayer. "The Word of God is the Christian's true prayer book," says Joni Eareckson Tada. "The secret to receiving answers to prayer lies in how we use God's Word during prayer time. That's why it's always a good idea to pray next to an open Bible. I often find myself praying in the book of Psalms."

God has also given many people with disabilities a prayer ministry that reaches around the world. They have time to intercede for others, and as you supply them with the names and needs of families in your community, these prayer warriors will be faithful to ask for God's blessings.

How to Pray for Those Who Suffer

- Ask God to give them grace and peace (see Numbers 6:24-26, Philippians 4:6-7).

- Ask God to reveal Himself to them (see Ephesians 1:16-17).

- Ask God to send others to support them (see Ecclesiastes 4:9-10; Galatians 6:2).

- Ask God to bring healing to them (see Mark 1:32-34; James 5:14-16).

- Ask God to provide for all their needs (see Matthew 6:28-33; Hebrews 4:16).

- Ask God to show them His glory in the outcome (see John 9:1-3; 2 Corinthians 4:15-18).

How to Pray as a Family

The following recipe for family prayer was written by Pat Verbal:

Mix ample amounts of love with listening to each other.
Stir together trust and obedience.
Blend with the softened hearts of caring families and friends.
Break the Word carefully; add a little at a time.
Stir well with love.
Cool doubts and fears.
Let faith *rise* in a warm place.
Spread forgiveness evenly;
Garnish well with hope, and
Sprinkle liberally with encouragement.

Solutions: A Prescription for Praise

When you shower children with affirmation, you give them a glimpse of God's unconditional acceptance. It is music to their ears, because buried deep in the hearts of children with special needs is an alternative message: "You're not good enough! There's something wrong with you!" But God's Word says children are a gift, "a reward from him" (Psalm 127:3). He warns us to treat them with care and respect, so they will come to know they are precious in His sight (see Matthew 18:5-6).

Build a Child's Self-Image

Self-image is always shaped by interactions with others. When children are overwhelmed with limitations and restrictions, they may lack a sense of self-achievement and self-worth. But words of praise given to children after they reach small attainable goals restore a child's spirit. Recognition has a powerful effect on students' attitudes and is vital in helping children reach their potential.

Make Praise Genuine

To be effective, praise needs to be realistic and genuine. "You were so kind to pick up the book for me." "Your poem paints a great word picture." Children know when they've not done their best or done a bad job. So be specific regarding their actions rather than their appearance, which is something they have little control over. (Too often girls are praised for their pretty eyes or curly hair.) Avoid value judgments such as "You're a good child" or "You're so nice." Children might view false praise as a way to manipulate their behaviors and give up. Here are some other things to remember about praise:

- **Children love the sound of their own names.** "Harry, you always let others go first in line!"

- **Children want you to notice their smallest attempts to help others.** "Rosy, I like the way you shared your markers with Lyn."

- **Children who are affirmed will learn to appreciate the talents of others and return the praise they receive.**

- **Thanking God for children in prayer is a form of praise.** "I praise the Lord for having you in my class today."

- **Praise can happen anywhere:** hallways, playgrounds, classrooms, kitchens, parking lots, etc.

Use Several Forms

Praise can come in many forms: notes, phone calls, e-mails, a song, gifts, conversations, etc. Don't hesitate to use them all. And be creative. Here are a few imaginative ways to get you started on your own list of ideas:

- Sandwich Praise—This is a great way to motivate children: (1) give a compliment, (2) give one instruction, and (3) follow the instruction with a word of encouragement.

- Tree of Praise—Decorate a bulletin board with a big paper tree that has lots of paper branches. Put a basket of cutout paper leaves under the tree on a small table. Tell children to write a word of praise about someone on a leaf and stick it on the tree.

- Tap and Run—Practice giving quick, affirming pats on the head or shoulders as you say "Way to go!" Remember that physical contact with students is best given quickly rather than with a lingering touch.

Proper Touching

Do	Don't
Hold a hand.	Kiss or ask for a kiss.
Put arm on shoulder.	Extend hugs or tickles.
Pat head or back.	Touch in bathing-suit zone.
Hold chin.	Carry or sit older child on lap.
Focus on feelings.	Be alone with a child.
Comfort crying.	Give body contact.

Gather Resources

Search your library and the Internet for praise ideas to keep at your fingertips. On the Internet, Positive Promotions is one of many companies that makes products for encouragement. Their 101 Ways to Praise Kids Bookmark is a colorful bookmark that has printed on it 101 phrases to say to children to make them feel great about themselves and their achievements (http://www.positivepromotions.com).

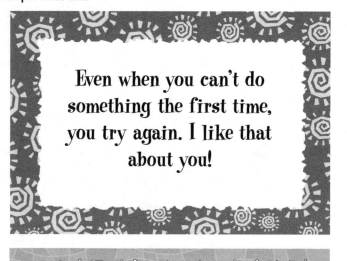

Even when you can't do something the first time, you try again. I like that about you!

Outstanding Student of the Day!

You enjoy helping others. That is just what Jesus would do!

You make others smile by just being YOU!

You made a GOOD choice today! That made me HAPPY!

You are FUN to be around! Keep it UP!

Thanks for finishing the TASK. Didn't that feel GREAT!

YOU have the BEST IDEAS! Thanks for sharing!

Solutions: Coming Alongside Parents and Counselors

The church should always be the place where families feel acceptance, encouragement and unconditional love. But often parents of children with special needs feel rejection and isolation. They are subjected to stares and comments from unknowing strangers and even well-meaning friends. Families are sometimes turned away from the church due to the church's lack of knowledge about how to help. When families are rejected by the Body of Christ, sometimes they feel rejected by God as well.

It may be difficult to know what to say to a family dealing with a disability. One father of a son with developmental delays said,

> I was tired of all the clichés at church. People told us how God promised to never give us more than we could handle. Or they said we must be special parents because God gave us Brian. We just needed friends to ask how we were doing or how they could help. We wanted people to pray with us, to listen, and get to know Brian. We just needed people to be there!

Brian's parents did not need advice from people about things they don't understand. What they did need was church members to come alongside them and be willing to be available and help as needed.

How do you help the parents?

Helping children with disabilities be successful members of the church should be a team process. Linda feared bringing her son Timmy to church due to his autism and severe behavioral disorders. Linda and her husband felt more comfortable taking turns staying home with Timmy. The director approached the family, letting them know that they wanted Timmy to participate. They had a meeting during which the parents discussed their concerns; and the director and teacher spent time getting to know Timmy, including his likes and dislikes and what triggered his meltdowns. A plan was created and Timmy was slowly introduced to the Sunday School class. The first few weeks were difficult, but eventually Timmy made it through an entire morning, and Linda and her husband attended church together. Most importantly, the family knew that the church valued Timmy.

- **Communicate.** Develop relationships with parents so that open communications are encouraged. When a child has difficulty in class, don't judge parents. Ask them for insights on how to help the student through the specific issue. When you know the events in a child's life, what type of day the child had, changes in medications or other factors, you can better understand the child's behavior and be more effective.

- **Devise a plan.** Work with parents to make a plan that benefits both the student and the family. When should parents be called to intervene? How should specific behaviors be handled? Are there other people who can be called for assistance? Sunday mornings may be the only time parents can be refreshed and spiritually fed. Learning to manage behavioral, emotional and physical needs of a student, with as little parental intervention as possible, allows parents a much-needed break. Be sure you and the parents are comfortable with the plan.

- **Provide encouragement.** Assure parents that you want their child to be a part of the church, and together you will do what you can to make it work. Make a point of emphasizing the positive things their child is doing. You don't have to have all the answers; you just need to be willing to try.

How do you support the family?

- **Be available.** Become a friend to the family. Be willing to listen to their triumphs and tragedies. Share their joys and their dejections. One mother said she doesn't need people at church to fix the problem but just to be there and listen.

- **Start support groups.** Provide a place where families can come together for prayer, networking and encouragement. Knowing that you're not alone is itself encouraging.

- **Provide respite care.** Being parents of a special needs child is a 24-hour-a-day job, and it is often difficult to find babysitters who can handle the needs of their child. A respite event allows families the time necessary to have a complete conversation, spend time with the child's siblings, shop or even take a nap (see "Giving Parents a Respite," p. 123).

What should you do about counseling?

Families of special needs children often experience emotional, marital, financial and other stress factors. If your church is unable to provide pastoral or family counseling to help families deal with these issues, encourage parents to seek out a Christian professional.

When should you encourage a family to visit a counselor?

Pastors and ministry leaders are often trained to handle crisis situations and spiritual-growth issues but are not always equipped to provide the level of assistance necessary for a family affected by disabilities. It is appropriate to encourage parents to visit a counselor if any of the following occur:

- Parents seek your advice for dealing with their long-term problems.

- Parents clearly appear overwhelmed, are extremely upset and are experiencing unhealthy effects of stress or confusion.

- You sense that a child is in danger and needs more medical or professional help.

Be prayerful and sensitive when approaching the subject of counseling. You need to have established a good relationship with parents before you give them advice. Once you know the family, share your observations and concerns with your pastor and seek his or her advice and support.

Every church should keep an updated list of four or five counselors to recommend to families. This list should include only the names of those counselors whose spiritual stance and moral character the church feels comfortable with. Recommending only one counselor can cause legal issues if he or she fails to perform in an ethical manner. In any case, many churches choose to carry liability insurance.

Can the church help a family with the cost of counseling?

Most churches have funds to help people in special situations. Each church will have a policy regarding how this money is distributed. Often distributions are handled on a case-by-case basis. If you feel that a family needs assistance, discuss the situation with your pastor who will be able to help you follow the appropriate channels.

Is it okay for a special needs director or teacher to accompany a parent to a counseling appointment at their request?

A parent may ask you to be a supportive person at a counseling appointment. It is important, however, that all parties agree ahead of time to such an arrangement. The parent needs to contact the counselor prior to the meeting and gain his or her permission.

Prior to any appointment, discuss with the family what expectations they have of you. Are they inviting you to be an extra set of ears to help them understand and process information? Do they want you to share your insights or ask questions? Maybe they just need help managing their child while they have the opportunity to talk without interruption. Remember, this is a team effort and all parties are working together to help the child and their family.

Why do you pray?

Prayer is a great support for families affected by disability. On a regular basis, ask the families how you can pray for them, and follow up on those requests. Letting families know that you're praying for them reminds them that you care.

Can-Dos for Frazzled Teachers

With the help of Jesus Christ . . .

I **can** do all things through Christ (see Philippians 4:13).

I **can** teach children with special needs to obey (see Matthew 28:20).

I **can** be light to a child in darkness (see Matthew 5:14).

I **can** be a coworker with Christ (see 2 Corinthians 6:1).

I **can** find grace and mercy in time of need (see Hebrews 4:16).

I **can** bear much fruit (see John 15:16).

I **can** believe that all things work for good in families affected by disability (see Romans 8:28).

I **can** accept God's appointment and seal to serve in special needs ministry (see 2 Corinthians 1:21-22).

I **can** be a personal witness for Christ (see Acts 1:8).

I **can** be a minister of reconciliation for families hurt by the church (see 2 Corinthians 5:17-20).

I **can** approach God freely and confidently as I pray for my students (see Ephesians 3:12).

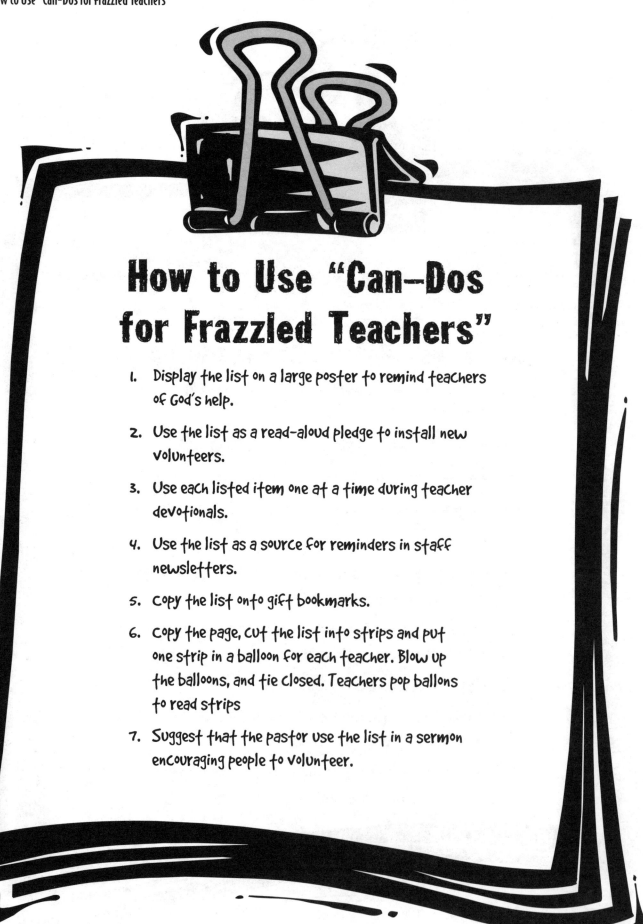

How to Use "Can-Dos for Frazzled Teachers"

1. Display the list on a large poster to remind teachers of God's help.

2. Use the list as a read-aloud pledge to install new volunteers.

3. Use each listed item one at a time during teacher devotionals.

4. Use the list as a source for reminders in staff newsletters.

5. Copy the list onto gift bookmarks.

6. Copy the page, cut the list into strips and put one strip in a balloon for each teacher. Blow up the balloons, and tie closed. Teachers pop ballons to read strips

7. Suggest that the pastor use the list in a sermon encouraging people to volunteer.

Can-Dos for Children

I can take turns.

I can say "Please."

I can share with others.

I can pick up toys.

I can use words when I am angry.

I can say "I'm sorry."

I can wait in line.

I can wash my hands.

I can say "Thank you."

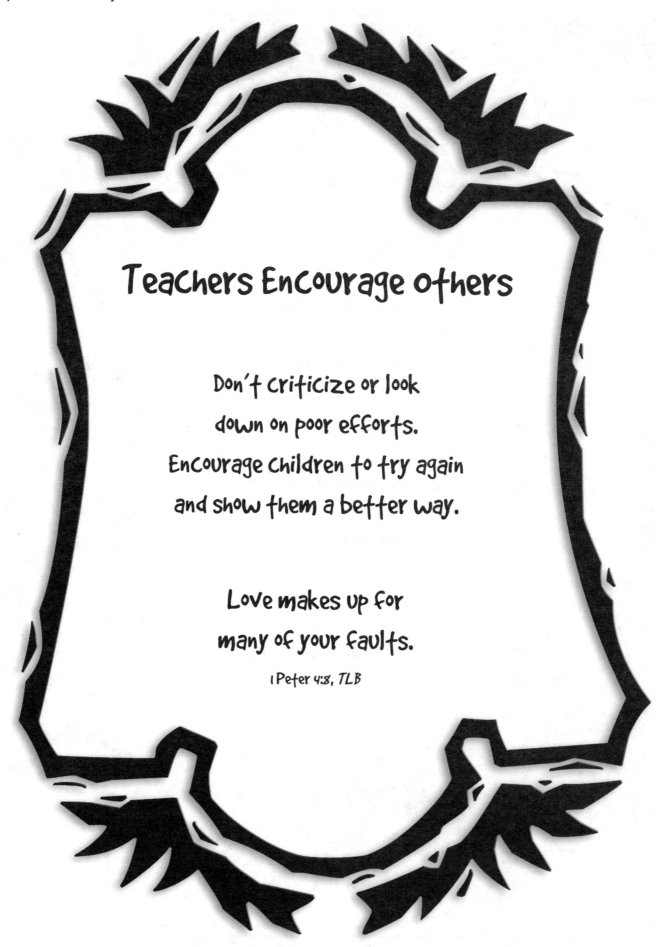

Teachers Encourage others

Don't criticize or look
down on poor efforts.
Encourage children to try again
and show them a better way.

Love makes up for
many of your faults.

1 Peter 4:8, TLB

I Know God Can Use Me— No Matter What!

Make the one who's been left out your special friend.

Do to others as you want them to do to you.

Luke 6:31, *NIrV*

Discipleship: Creating a Faith-Journey Scrapbook

Jesus grew in wisdom and stature,
and in favor with God and men.
Luke 2: 52

The story of God's people is one story—from creation to the twenty-first century. God is not finished with His story because He continues to write it on the hearts of our children. Every newborn baby is a promise of hope. Every Christian is a vessel of God's message. Every step of faith our children take should be applauded and recorded.

Doctors keep physical growth records on children to evaluate their health. Schools keep test scores on children to measure their progress against the age-level norms. What do we do at church to help children understand spiritual growth? One thing we can do is to encourage them to keep a Faith-Journey Scrapbook.

Many children with special needs are concrete thinkers who learn best through repetition and review. A scrapbook is a tangible record of how people have reached out to them. It's a way of tracking the faith steps they have taken and to set goals such as counting their blessings or serving the poor. For children with developmental disabilities, a scrapbook that is filled with pictures and places they are familiar with can become a treasured possession.

All children enjoy knowing that the adults in their lives are paying attention to their efforts. Joni Eareckson Tada tells this story of a preteen she met:

> While speaking at a church, I noticed a preteen sitting on the front row, trying her best to look disinterested. This was one troubled little girl, obviously depressed by the severe scoliosis in her spine. When the service was over, I learned her name was Amber. She had been brought to church that morning by her neighbor.
>
> It wasn't long before Amber began to feel right at home at church. Part of it was due to the kindness of her neighbor. But much of it was the way her Sunday School teacher reached out to her, making sure Amber's special needs were well addressed. And the best part? Amber opened her heart to Jesus, and now her parents are attending church!

Any child like Amber benefits from a Faith-Journey Scrapbook because becoming a Christian is a new experience for the whole family. Many times children with disabilities have little or no church background on which to build. When their teachers use this tool to disciple them, their decision to serve Christ is reinforced and a log of their progress is made.

A Faith-Journey Scrapbook can be filled with many things:

- **Personal Items**—Notes of encouragement from teachers and friends, a born-again birth certificate, a welcome letter from the pastor, etc.

- **Art**—Drawings of Bible verses they have memorized or lessons they've enjoyed.

- **Photos**—Pictures with their teachers, pastors or classmates; pictures of special events such as camps, Vacation Bible School, field trips, pool parties, etc.

- **Favorite Songs**—Sheet music or sign-language charts of songs by Christian artists, from musicals they have participated in, from choir events, etc.

- **Favorite Bible Verses**—Drawings of what the verses mean to them, awards for learning verses, stories of how God used a verse, etc.

- **Prayers**—Praise poems, drawings, prayers copied from Scripture or prayed for family and friends, bedtime favorites, etc.

- **Baptism or Confirmation Certificates**—A list of people who attended, notes of congratulations, etc.

- **Service Projects**—Class projects, mission projects, stories of how God used their talents to help others, etc.

This scrapbook can be an excellent tool to help children share their faith story with family and friends. Encourage parents to keep their child's Faith-Journey Scrapbook displayed on a special shelf and to urge them to add new pages as their child takes greater steps of faith.

Sample: Faith–Journey Scrapbook

Danny's Faith-Journey Scrapbook

Sample: My Faith Is Growing!

As you grow in your faith, put the date in front of the statements that are true.
Add stories and pictures to your scrapbook with these headings.

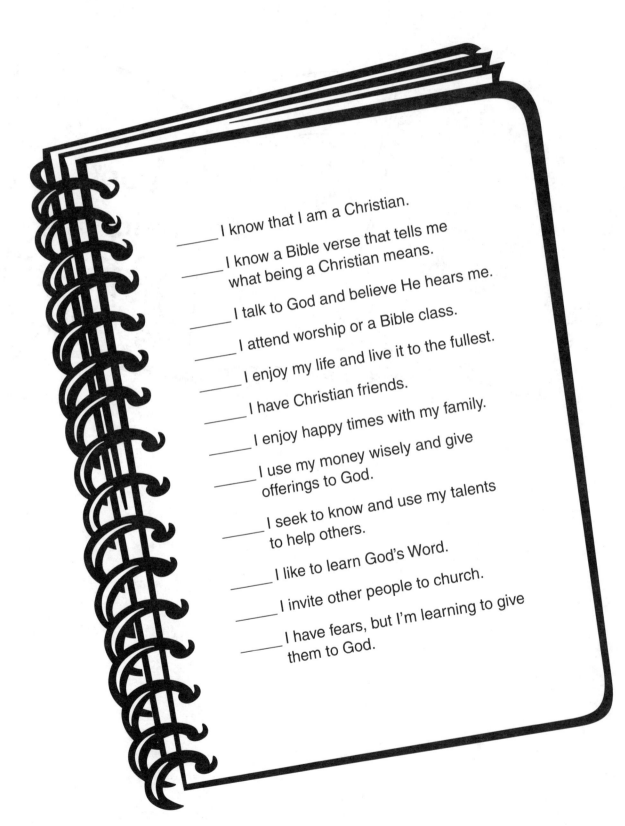

_____ I know that I am a Christian.

_____ I know a Bible verse that tells me what being a Christian means.

_____ I talk to God and believe He hears me.

_____ I attend worship or a Bible class.

_____ I enjoy my life and live it to the fullest.

_____ I have Christian friends.

_____ I enjoy happy times with my family.

_____ I use my money wisely and give offerings to God.

_____ I seek to know and use my talents to help others.

_____ I like to learn God's Word.

_____ I invite other people to church.

_____ I have fears, but I'm learning to give them to God.

Discipleship: Sharing in the Lord's Supper and Baptism

*Never underestimate the power of
God's Spirit in the heart of a child.*
Pat Verbal

During a monthly luncheon for directors of special needs ministries, one director brought up an issue dealing with her church's tradition of first Communion: "Each spring we offer a class for third graders, and this year we had two kids with autism," said Julie. "During our rehearsal for the service, several parents of nondisabled children told me that they didn't think the girls with autism should get certificates of confirmation since they couldn't complete the required work." Julie could hardly believe her ears. She tried to picture herself telling the parents of those children that their daughters would be left out. It would be too cruel—and it would be wrong.

Julie said that she quickly prayed for God's wisdom to respond to these misguided parents. Then she asked them if she could share a verse with them. She read aloud Luke 18:17 (*TLB*): "For the Kingdom of God belongs to men who have hearts as trusting as these little children's. And anyone who doesn't have their kind of faith will never get within the Kingdom's gates." Then the parents understood.

Learning Church Catechism

- The average age for children's catechism, new believer or junior church-membership classes is 8 to 10 years old. Children with physical disabilities or behavioral disorders will likely keep up in class.

• Children with learning disabilities or developmental/cognitive disorders may need to have the curriculum and schedule adapted to their level of understanding and their attention span (see "A Basic Guide for Curriculum Adaptations," p. 72). If Bible memory is required, see "Ten Ways to Teach Memory Verses" on page 92.

• Lessons can be prepared in Braille or recorded on tape for children with visual or hearing impairments.

Some churches hold separate classes for children with special needs, and some churches give these children extra help between classes. Most parents are happy to help in these areas.

Sharing the Lord's Supper

In order to make the first participation in the Lord's Supper meaningful to children and their families, children should be well prepared. Here are several suggestions:

- Tell children the story of Jesus and the disciples at their last meal together as recorded in Mark 14: 12-26, and share Paul's instructions for the Lord's Supper, given in 1 Corinthians 11:23-29.

- Let children observe a service where the congregation is sharing the Lord's Supper.

- Help children make picture books about the Bible stories and/or what they saw in the worship service they visited. Put words they may be unfamiliar with under the pictures.

- Invite the person who will serve the Lord's Supper to speak with the children to help them feel comfortable with him or her.

- Guide the children on a walking tour of what they will do during the Lord's Supper.

Remember that children who have difficulty swallowing have an easier time with Communion bread if it is crumbled into a teaspoon of juice.

Preparing for Baptism

Most children with special needs don't mind getting wet, but some may have difficulty getting into a baptistry, if that is used by your denomination.

• Children with wheelchairs, walkers or leg braces may be comfortable being carried into the water by a parent or trusted friend. If a child is medically fragile, consider adapting the method of baptism and sprinkling or pouring water over the child's head instead of having the child get in the pool.

• Those with visual impairments may need someone to guide them to dressing rooms and in and out of the water.

• Sensory issues in children with autism may cause a child to fear being baptized and to withdraw from the experience altogether. Assure parents that it is okay for their child to decide not to be baptized, even if the decision is made at the last minute. This can be difficult for parents, especially when extended family members have traveled a distance to celebrate the child's baptism. But any child who is pushed to participate and thus has a bad experience may reject going to church altogether.

As with the Lord's Supper, children need to be prepared for baptism. Here are several suggestions:

- Tell the children about Jesus' baptism as recorded in Matthew 3:1-17 and Jesus' command to be baptized in Matthew 28:19-20.

- Let the children watch a baptismal service.

- Guide the children on a tour of the baptistry and changing areas.

- Let the children try on a baptismal robe.

- Guide the children on a walking tour through the steps of the baptismal service.

Families will appreciate all that you do to include their children. A nice certificate for their first Lord's Supper or baptism, along with photos, makes a wonderful gift. They're also a nice addition to a child's Faith-Journey Scrapbook (see sample form below).

If you send or deliver Sunday School lessons to children who are homebound due to their disabilities, take the Lord's Supper to them monthly or quarterly. If they accept Jesus as their Savior and express a desire to be baptized, work with your pastor to give them that opportunity at home. Jesus' words recorded in Matthew 28:19 included children with special needs: "Go and make disciples of all nations, baptizing them in the name of the Father and of the Son and of the Holy Spirit."

Form: Lord's Supper/Baptism Participation Record

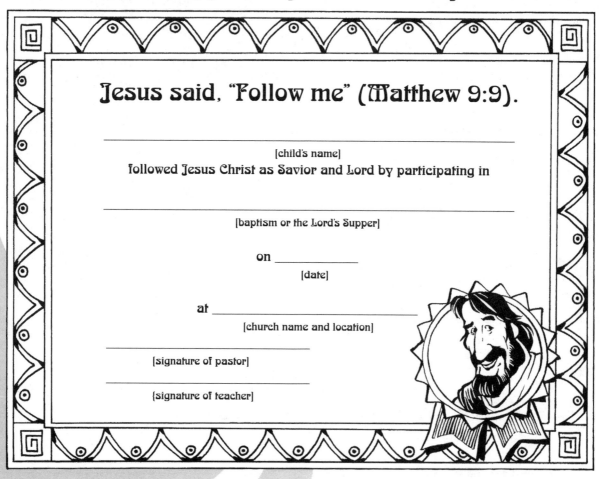

Jesus said, "Follow me" (Matthew 9:9).

_____

[child's name]
followed Jesus Christ as Savior and Lord by participating in

_____

[baptism or the Lord's Supper]

on _____
[date]

at _____
[church name and location]

_____
[signature of pastor]

_____
[signature of teacher]

Discipleship: Talking and Listening to God

Amy's greatest prayer for her son Jack and his twin brother, Sam, is that they know Jesus as their Savior. But she is not sure how much Jack understands because he has autism. When he was diagnosed at age three, he was almost non-verbal. Jack still struggles but currently attends a Christian school with typical first graders.

"One of my favorite things in the world is to hear Jack pray," says Amy. "He has such a sweet spirit. I'm amazed at the things the Lord brings to his mind in prayer. Lately, Jack has been praying spontaneously for family members in the car on the way to school—especially for his grandfather who has been in the hospital. Jack's prayers are unprompted and all his own."

Here are some examples of Jack's prayers:

> Dear God,
> Thank You for the food.
> Thank You for Jesus.
> Amen.

> Dear God,
> Thank You for Papa and for Alex.
> Please help them feel better and come home.
> Amen.

Amy and her husband are working to expand the special needs ministry at their church. "Our church is wonderful. It's a tremendous blessing that Jack has buddies to help him while we attend church," says Amy. "Our church prints an amazing resource every week for families called *The Scrolls*. We use the prayer activities with both our boys."

You will discover that children with disabilities can teach adults a lot about prayer. They naturally seem to understand that it's okay with God to pray short prayers, using simple words. It's also okay to shout praises and dance around the room or lie in the grass smiling at God as they pray.

Try asking the children in your special needs class how they would like to talk to God. You'll be surprised by their creativity. To get you and your class started, here are some ideas that have worked so well that they've become favorites in some classes:

- **Crayon Prayers**—Have everyone pick a crayon. Tell children to take a minute to think about what that color reminds them of. Then tell them to pray a sentence prayer about that person, place or thing. "Thank You, God, for my grandma's purple apron."

- **A Prayer Walk**—Lead children on a walk through your church, praying at each door (e.g., Sunday School classes, pastor's office, kitchen, custodian's room, etc.). "Thank You, God, for playground swings!" This is an interactive way to engage concrete thinkers in meaningful prayer.

- **Prayer Promises**—Create prayer posters using promises from God's Word, and hang them in your class. For example: "His ears are attentive to their prayer" (1 Peter 3:12). "Don't worry about anything; instead, pray about everything; tell God your needs and don't forget to thank him for his answers" (Philippians 4:6, *TLB*).

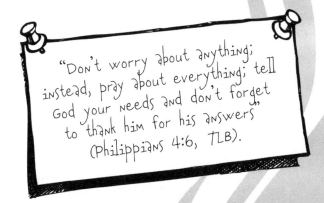

"Don't worry about anything; instead, pray about everything; tell God your needs and don't forget to thank him for his answers" (Philippians 4:6, *TLB*).

- **Song Prayers**—Pick a Bible verse and make up a song about it. Explain that the book of Psalms is full of songs. The children may know "This is the day the Lord has made" from Psalm 118:24. In Old Testament times, Jewish worship leaders who sang or chanted prayers were called cantors, and still today, cantors sing or chant prayers in Jewish religious services.

- **Prayer Posters**—Tell children to draw pictures of things they're thankful for or cut them out of magazines to make prayer posters. Place them around the room as prayer guides for several weeks.

- **Mission Prayers**—Have the class adopt a child with a disability who lives in a third-world country. Keep his or her picture posted and send class letters saying the class members are praying for the child and his or her family. Children with special needs might not understand how far away the child lives, but they will relate to the needs he or she faces.

- **Prayer Journals**—Children who are able to write or draw can create their own prayer journal. Cut four 8 1/2x11-inch (21.5x28-cm) sheets of paper in half twice to form 4x5 1/2-inch (10.6x14-cm) pages, punch two holes on the short side and tie with yarn for a binding. Tell the children that each page represents someone who is important in their lives, such as a family member or a friend. Put one person's name on each sheet. As you use the journals for several weeks, children can write a short prayer, praise or Bible promise on each page for that loved one. When they take the journal home, tuck in a note to parents, encouraging them to use the prayer journal during family prayer at home.

- **Prayer Pictures**—Encourage children to bring a family picture to class. Decorate a bulletin board with pictures placed around the edges. In the center, post written or drawn prayers for each family. Let children work together. Take a photo of each child standing in front of the bulletin board, and send the photo home in a handmade frame.

Every church can provide a nurturing environment of faith, love and spiritual growth for children with special needs. In his book *Transforming Children into Spiritual Champions*, George Barna writes, "The transformation of children into spiritual champions may not happen even if we devote our best resources to the task, but the possibility is worth the risk."*

*George Barna, *Transforming Children into Spiritual Champions* (Ventura, CA: Regal Books, 2003), p. 135.

Discipleship: Discovering Each Child's Unique Gift

Children are a blessing from God. God through Solomon has told us that "Sons are a heritage from the Lord, children a reward from him. Blessed is the man whose quiver is full of them" (Psalm 127:3,5). Notice the lack of adjectives describing children as healthy or smart or beautiful or athletic or artistic. We can see, therefore, that *all* children are a blessing, including those with disabilities. We can also be assured that each child brought into this world has a gift to share and a purpose in life.

Using Everyone's Gifts and Talents

God has given natural gifts and talents to everyone, and while some people have more abilities than others, the important thing is not how much talent one has but how it is used. (Remember how the master reacted in the parable of the talents in Matthew 25:14-30.) Many people make assumptions that children with disabilities do not have much to offer in the way of gifts, and others do not want to take the time or effort to discover those gifts. As leaders in disability ministries, one of our main jobs is not only to discover these gifts but also to encourage children to use them for the glory of God.

Various Scripture passages make it clear that all Christians are supernaturally endowed by the Holy Spirit with gifts that are meant to edify the Body of Christ. First Corinthians 12:6 says that "God works all of them in *all* men" (emphasis added); and verses 7-11 of the same chapter tell that God has given spiritual gifts to each one. These Scriptures do not indicate that spiritual gifts are given only to healthy, nondisabled Christians, so we must believe that Christians with disabilities have gifts to share with the Body of Christ. In fact, it is vital to the health of the Body of Christ that the weakest members are allowed and encouraged to serve (see 1 Corinthians 12:22).

Looking for Each Child's Abilities

It's easy to look at the obvious disabilities children have and what they cannot do, but it's a bit harder to train yourself to *start looking for their abilities*. Actively watch and listen for gifts in these children. Get to know each child, in class and outside the classroom (see "Visiting a Child's Weekday World," p. 60). Talk to the parents and discuss their child's strengths and abilities, finding out what they enjoy and like most. Refrain from comparing children with one another, even if they have the same disability. Each

child is unique, as is the severity and manifestation of each disability. Provide opportunities in the classroom for a variety of activities, and watch for what excites each child. Make use of art, music, movement and sharing activities in your lessons. Ask yourself which activity is each child's strongest. Which activity does he or she get the most enjoyment out of?

- **Provide varied activities, even when you might not see a child participating enthusiastically.** Children with special needs may resist new experiences and need to become accustomed to them before they tolerate them. Acceptance follows tolerance, and finally enjoyment may come. One child who initially resisted art projects due to sensory problems has become a teenage artist at a studio for outside artwork, bringing in several hundred dollars for each painting sold. Avoid limiting experiences for children with disabilities based on perceived weaknesses or inabilities. Amazing gifts and talents may emerge when least expected.

- **Consistently teach God's Word** to children with special needs, to show them His love and to allow the Holy Spirit to work. Teach the fruit of the Spirit (Galatians 5:22-23), and pray that it takes hold in their lives, growing, blossoming and bearing in God's timing. Watch how these children affect others by demonstrating the fruit. Is one student in your class always gentle in his or her interactions with others? Is another one ready to share toys or other materials? Does a girl with Down syndrome show a tender heart by comforting those who are upset or crying? As they exhibit these traits, encourage them with positive reinforcements such as smiles, hugs or verbal praise.

Remember that each child's unique gift might not be apparent at first glance. Watch for their natural gifts and talents and see how God is using them to affect others, remembering that the gift of one child should not be compared with that of another child. Do people's faces smile when Kathy greets them with a grin and a hug? She might have the gift of encouragement. Have you noticed that Jill is faithful in bringing an offering of money for Jesus? She may have the gift of giving. Do Bryce's prayers touch your heart and bring tears to your eyes? He might be a prayer warrior.

What about a child who is nonverbal?

Although the gifts of nonverbal children might be a bit more difficult to discern, nonverbal children certainly *do* have gifts. Two true stories will serve to illustrate this fact. Hollie's grandparents took her in as an infant when her mother decided she couldn't care for a child with such severe disabilities. Neither grandparent was a Christian, but because of Hollie, they began seeking reasons and answers and hope. Hollie never spoke a word in her short life and rarely left her bed, yet she is the reason that two people accepted Jesus Christ as their Savior. Hollie's grandfather even went on to use his gift of evangelism and led countless others to the Lord.

Another young woman, one with autism, had not been able to communicate until she started using a method called facilitated communication, an augmented communication strategy. She was then able to tell her mother that she had had a relationship with Jesus and a deep prayer life for many years. Up until that time, no one knew that she had such gifts of faith and prayer.

What about a child who exhibits difficult behaviors?

Sometimes it's hard to see the gift in a particular child. Some children with special needs have such difficult behaviors that it's easy to forget they were created in the image of God. Sometimes the drooling, bad teeth, peculiar smells or strange noises make it hard to look past the unlovely. When this occurs, ask yourself these questions: *Is this child still a gift of God when he . . .* [finish the question with the child's particular behavior]*? What is this child trying to communicate?* Look into the child's eyes and ask what Jesus would see. Remember, God created this child for a purpose; and He promised that in all things, He works for the good of those who love Him, who have been called according to His purpose, even though the good and the purpose may never become apparent this side of heaven (see Romans 8:28). Perhaps God's purposes involve teaching you patience with those who are very different, or having others observe as you show love to a child they view as unattractive.

Different Packages Bulletin Board
(an activity to highlight children's gifts):

Create a bulletin board with gift packages of different shapes, sizes and colors. (Or have children design their own packages as an art project.) At the top of each package where the bow would go, glue a picture of the face of each student in your class. On the outside of each child's package, highlight some of their talents and gifts.

Title your bulletin board "We All Come in Different Packages!"

Discipleship: Creating an Individual Christian Educational Plan

One special area of inclusion for children with special needs is Christian education. For the most part, children with various physical disabilities—paralysis, cerebral palsy, blindness, deafness and so on—can take part in a church's Christian educational program once some minor modifications are made. Special consideration, however, is needed for including children with developmental/cognitive disabilities. Each of these children is unique, with his or her own blend of education proficiency and rate of skill development.

In special education programs that are developed in today's public schools, each child with a developmental disability has his or her own individualized education plan (IEP); each child's file is written to include details about his or her level of disability, a list of skills to work on, medical needs, necessary therapy and other useful information.

How do you create an individualized Christian education plan?

With the help of a child's parents, your church can create something similar for each child with a developmental disability: an individual Christian education plan (ICEP). For each child, develop detailed information about the child: extent of disability, medical needs, list of goals, etc., and include a copy of the evaluation form filled out by parents (see form on p. 216). Some skill goals from a child's school plan can be added along with objectives that help the student learn about God's plan through His Word.

In addition to helpful information about the child's skill goals, the plan should also include what the child has already accomplished in his or her steps of faith.

Dr. Jim Pierson created a list of lesson aims for children with such developmental disabilities as mental retardation, Down syndrome, fragile X syndrome, fetal alcohol syndrome and hydrocephaly. These aims remind us that children do not come to church to be babysat but to learn many things:*

- Who God is

- Who God's Son, Jesus, is

- Who the Bible heroes are

- Old Testament and New Testament events

- To sing Christian choruses and hymns

- How to pray

- To have relationships with peers

- Their strengths and self-worth

- To be responsible for their behaviors

- To accept Jesus as their Lord and Savior

Who should help with an ICEP?

Everyone at church who works with a child with a developmental/cognitive disability should have some input in developing the child's ICEP, including the parents, and all should be aware of the plan's finalized version.

During the first few weeks that the ICEP is put into action, you'll want to monitor the results to ensure that the plan is working. You may find it necessary to make adjustments. Once the plan is running successfully and the child is progressing, have semiannual evaluations with parents to get their input.

It took Yaling several months to learn the song about the books of the New Testament; but when she did, she received five notes, two balloons and a plate of cookies from her friends. Teachers and volunteers practiced with her at Royal Hearts Club (a midweek class for children with disabilities in Yaling's community), during Sunday School and in children's church. When Yaling met her goal, everyone felt they, too, were winners. Her parents were so proud that they asked Yaling to sing for their Bible fellowship class, and she never missed a word!

Progress may be slow, but having a goal will help everyone stay focused on God's love and power in the lives of children who relish every victory.

*Jim Pierson, Exceptional Teaching: A Comprehensive Guide for Including Students with Disabilities (Cincinnati, OH: Standard Publishing, 2002), p. 29.

Form: Evaluation for an Individual Christian Educational Plan

Student's Name _____

Type of Disability _____ Age _____

Parents/Guardians_____

Address _____

Home Phone _____ Cell Phone _____

E-mail Address _____

Student's School _____ Grade _____

What assistance does the student receive at school? _____
_____

How long has the student been attending this church? _____

Do you (student's parents/guardians) attend? _____

What church programs does the student regularly attend? _____
_____

Does the student attend adult worship? _____

What is the student's favorite thing about church? _____
_____

Does the student talk about God or ask questions at home? _____
_____
_____

What goals do you have for the student at church? _____
_____
_____

What modifications does the student need in the curriculum used at church? _____
_____
_____

As a parent, how are you involved in your child's Christian education? _____
_____
_____

How would you like to be involved in your child's ICEP at church? _____
_____
_____

Additional Comments _____
_____
_____

Service: Wheels for the World

The Joni and Friends' Chair Corps volunteers specialize in turning dreams into realities by collecting used but restorable wheelchairs in communities throughout the United States. By networking with local media outlets, businesses, hospitals and civic organizations, Chair Corps folks get into the trenches in their communities to pluck wheelchairs from the most unlikely places. Each chair has a story behind it, and each story finds its happy ending on the joyful face of the one who receives the chair. It's why the Chair Corps is the Dream Team of Joni and Friends.

How Wheelchairs Are Found

It is estimated that before a wheelchair reaches its final destination overseas, 300 pairs of hands have touched it along its journey of love. One of those pairs could be yours. Look for working or repairable wheelchairs around your community (individuals who no longer need their wheelchairs, thrift stores, etc.). Many hands belong to the truckers and shippers who pick up donated wheelchairs and transport them to storage facilities, where they will await their turn for restoration. Inmates in numerous correctional facilities across the United States work diligently and with pride to renew donated wheelchairs to sparkling, like-new condition—perfectly restored for someone waiting overseas for a miracle.

One prisoner who is serving a life sentence in jail is glad to be part of the Chair Corps: "Before when I reached out, it was to take things or hurt people. Now I feel like I've reached halfway around the world through these bars to help someone. I'm giving them something better in life."

Join in praying for those who repair, transport and deliver thousands of wheelchairs overseas each year.

Who Receives Wheelchairs

Wheelchairs are shipped to China, Cuba, Romania, Ghana, Thailand and India, among others countries. Wheels for the World teams of disability specialists fit each wheelchair to the recipient and provide training in its use and upkeep. Recipients also receive a Bible and the message of God's love in their own language. Speaking and teaching teams help local churches and communities understand the needs of disabled people and how they can help. Whenever possible, construction teams are sent to help improve accessibility in churches, homes and communities.

Who Can Volunteer

"I became a Chair Corps volunteer at the age of 71," says Frank Costello. "Just knowing that each wheelchair can provide the gift of mobility gives my life new meaning every day."

Team members like Frank are people who want to experience the living God working through them and who are not confined to limitations of their own understanding. They are people who commit themselves to the One who wants to use all of us to express His healing love to the world.

Although money is donated for chair shipments, raw materials, and supplies to restore wheelchairs, most volunteers who travel to distant lands with deliveries pay their own expenses; but donations are needed to sponsor some volunteers.

Who Can Donate

If you would like to help JAF raise funds, one of the best ways to do that is to help us get the word out. *The Prison That Set Me Free,* a powerful DVD about the ministry of the Wheels volunteers at Angola Prison in Louisiana, is available from Joni and Friends (order "Episode #2" from http://www.joniandfriendstv.org. God is changing lives in Angola Prison, and prisoners are serving God even behind bars. The movie is inspirational!

Join our praise to God for over 46,000 wheelchairs that have been donated in over 80 countries. To learn more about Wheels for the World, visit www.joniand friends.org/pg_wheelchair.php.

Service: Wheels for the World Projects

Gospel Bracelets: Share the Message of Salvation

Joni and Friends Wheels for the World teams use gospel bracelets to share the good news of Jesus Christ with children and adults around the world. And they need help to make the bracelets.

Each bead on the bracelet stands for a part of the message of salvation. Each gospel bracelet ends up on the arm of someone who lives thousands of miles away, someone who may be hearing about Jesus Christ for the very first time. Everyone who partners with Joni and Friends and Wheels for the World helps to share the good news of Christ all over the world.

Materials

- Cotton (or satin) cord or leather lace cut into 15-inch (38-cm) lengths

- One each of five different-colored pony beads: gold (or yellow), black, red, white and green

- One fancy bead (heart, fish, etc.)

Directions

1. Tie a knot about 6 inches (15 cm) from one end of the cord or lace.

2. String the pony beads in the following order: gold, black, red, white and green. Then tie a knot at the end of the beads. The five beads should end up centered on the cord or lace with the two knots as "bookends."

3. Hold both ends of the cord or lace together and run them through the fancy bead, both going in the same direction.

4. Tie one knot in the two ends of the cord or lace so that the ends can't slip back through the fancy bead. The fancy bead should slide back and forth so that the bracelet size is adjustable.

Packaging

Package the bracelets in a mailing bag or a box. It is not necessary to bag them individually. Enclose your church's name and address in the package. Mail the bracelets to Joni and Friends, P.O. Box 3333, Agoura Hills, CA 91376. Thank you for helping us share the message of salvation!

Pennies from Heaven: Sponsor Wheelchairs and Change Lives

The Pennies from Heaven mission project will support Joni and Friends Wheels for the World, which provides wheelchairs to people with disabilities all over the world.

A group may sponsor one wheelchair at $150, a portion of one wheelchair or many wheelchairs. The children's work to collect their coins will bear much fruit for those in need of mobility.

Getting Students Excited and Involved

Your group can adopt Pennies from Heaven as part of your Sunday School class, Vacation Bible School or camp mission project.

- Talk enthusiastically with your group about the value of this mission project and ways they might raise money—your enthusiasm will be contagious. Then help children set a goal. The goal will depend on the size of your group and the duration of the project.

- Brainstorm with your group various ways they can earn money to donate, or decide on a group project (bake sale, snack bar, window washing, etc.) to raise money.

- Have a special offering at your Sunday service. In addition to asking the children to bring offerings, you may wish to plan a special offering for this project during a regular church service. This could take place the Sunday after your event closes. Have the children explain the project and take up the offering to match what they have already collected.

- Create a Pennies from Heaven poster to track progress. Use a cartoon wheelchair with a happy smile drawn on the back of the chair. Move the chair up to reflect the rise in money collected. The children will enjoy watching the chair move towards their goal. If you are sponsoring multiple chairs, use several chairs to track your success.

Sending the Donation

1. Make checks payable to Joni and Friends. Write Pennies from Heaven on the memo line.

2. Include a card with your church's name, address, phone number and contact name.

3. Mail your check to Joni and Friends, Attn: On A Roll for Jesus, P.O. Box 3333, Agoura Hills, CA 91376.

4. A thank-you letter and a picture of a wheelchair recipient will be sent to your group.

Activity Page: Color Wheels for the World

Service: Preteens On a Roll for Jesus

Looking for a project for preteens? Challenge them to lead a day camp, VBS or children's church service and teach younger students about disabilities. Under adult supervision, preteens can teach from *On a Roll for Jesus! Mission: Unstoppable* published by Joni and Friends. Be sure to include preteens with disabilities on the team. Finding ways to use their abilities is the whole point of this event. The lessons in the book have two goals: (1) to teach disability awareness and (2) to engage students in a mission project to raise money for wheelchairs that are donated to people overseas.

We often hear that today's children are self-centered, always wondering, *What's in it for me?* This service project will open the eyes, minds and hearts of boys and girls to give them compassion for people with disabilities, including their peers. As preteens serve others in meaningful ways, they begin to understand that what Jesus said is really true: "It is more blessed to give than to receive" (Acts 20:35).

Preteens are looking for authentic ways to experience faith and to be part of a team. What better way to help them find this than to challenge them to become leaders and teachers? Public schools have discovered this and partnered preteens with younger students to help build reading, science and math skills. This project will help preteens see how the Bible can make a huge difference in their world and to others around the world by giving them new perspectives and others life-transforming hope.

Curriculum Overview

This curriculum takes students on a special assignment—a mission possible! They will learn that God is unstoppable. Nothing can get in the way of His love for us; as it says in Psalm 100:5: "For the Lord is good and his love endures forever; his faithfulness continues through all generations."

Day 1–Physical Disabilities

Lesson: Four men bring their disabled friend to Jesus (Mark 2:1-12)
Bible Verse: Psalm 139:14
Worksheet 1: "Being a Friend"
DVD 1: "Wheels for the World"
Activities: Dressing-Self Relay, Softball Throw, Wheelchair Ride

Day 2–Hearing Impairments

Lesson: Jesus heals a man who could not hear or speak (Mark 7:31-37)
Bible Verse: Psalm 145:7

Worksheet 2: "Crack the Code"
DVD 2: "Wheelchair Collection and Guatemala Stories"

Day 3–Vision Impairments

Lesson: Jesus gives sight to two blind men (Matthew 20:29-34)
Bible Verse: Psalm 119:105
Worksheet 3: "Can You Picture It?"
DVD 3: "Wheelchair Restoration and Romania Stories"

Day 4–Learning Disabilities

Lesson: Jesus tells the parable of the good Samaritan (Luke 10:27-35)
Bible Verse: John 13:34
Worksheet 4: "Line Up the Clues"
DVD 4: "Wheelchair Distribution and China Stories"

Day 5–Including People with Disabilities

Lesson: Jesus tells the parable of the great banquet (Luke 14:15-23)
Bible Verse: Luke 14:21,23
Worksheet 5: "Disabilities: Fact or Fiction?"
DVD 5: "Mission Accomplished!"

Preteen Participation

Preteens will enjoy decorating the classroom with posters and dressing up as detectives in trench coats and hats. Offer a training session during which they'll learn to tell Bible stories, teach memory verses, correct worksheets and lead music. Some preteens may prepare crafts ahead of time for children who need assistance, plan and shop for snacks, choose games and help with cleanup.

You'll be surprised at how faithful preteens can be when you give them specific assignments and supply them with resources. However, preteens still need adult help with classroom supervision and with sticking to a schedule.

For more information on what is included in the curriculum, visit the Joni and Friends online store at www.joniandfriends.org/store_product.php?product_id=1151.

Service: Hosting a Disability Talent Show

Putting on a talent show for families involved in your disability ministry is a great way to celebrate all abilities. Children with disabilities can shine in the spotlight right along with their siblings, and families will value the fact that all performances are cheered and encouraged.

Venue and Personnel

Choose your venue with accessibility in mind. Make sure your stage has a ramp and that seating for your audience is wheelchair and family friendly. An experienced accompanist and a creative emcee can be valuable assets to the show. Recruit stagehands to set up for each performer, and gather a technical crew to run the audio and video. Begin your celebration by singing worship songs, and distribute rhythm instruments and ribbon wands, so everyone can participate.

Publicity and Event Details

Advertise your event within your own ministry, and depending on how large you want it to become, consider including other ministries in your church. Inviting local disability organizations to participate could also be a great outreach. Require all acts to preregister, listing their names, talents, titles and needed equipment (CD player, a chair, a music stand, etc.). Make sure everyone knows the time limit for each act, so the pace of your show will move smoothly.

Fellowship and Remembering

Host a reception after the talent show. Either provide refreshments or have each family contribute a plate of goodies. After the show, hearts will be softened, and people will enjoy visiting. Ask a volunteer to record the talent show, and send commemorative DVDs to participants a few weeks later. Families will appreciate the memento, and the DVD will keep the excitement going.

Participation

Be creative in finding ways for everyone to perform if they so desire. Allow children with performance anxiety to bring prerecorded DVDs of their talent to play during the show. For young artists, scan their artwork into a computer, and proudly show it on the large screen for all to see. If a child's talent is playing Nintendo, hook up the console so that everyone can watch him or her play a game. Encourage everyone to join in the fun, and get ready to be amazed by the different talents you will discover, and to praise God as you celebrate each child's ability!

Bryce, a teen with spina bifida, has severe performance anxiety. No one even suspected that he had a savantlike ability for playing jazz rhythms on a drum set. When a DVD of his playing was shown at a talent show, he received a standing ovation.

When Raymon, a young man with muscular dystrophy, heard Brandi, who has Down syndrome, sing a worship chorus for the talent show, he was inspired. He realized that God accepts worship from a pure heart and doesn't judge people on their ability. For the next year's show, Raymon was the first to sign up.

Cathryn, who uses a wheelchair due to a rare degenerative genetic disorder, surprised her family by planning a dance with two friends. For the grand finale, her friends lifted her from her chair into the air. Cathryn raised her arms in victory, and there was not a dry eye in the auditorium.

Abel, who is often in the shadow of his older brother who has special needs, had his moment to shine solo on the stage while he jumped up and down the stairs on his pogo stick to the music of his favorite Christian rock band.

Service: Sharing Joni's Story

God uses stories of children and adults with disabilities as a witness to those who don't know Jesus as their Savior. Challenge children to write their own stories and pray for an opportunity to tell others how much they love Jesus.

To help children get started on their own stories, copy and distribute *Joni's Story for Kids,* a brochure that in easy-to-understand language tells about Joni's life, talents and ministry (available on the CD-ROM). Give the children extra copies to share with friends. This brochure is also available at http://www.joniandfriends.org/store_product.php?product _id=1173.

Then, as children show interest, assist them in writing or telling their own life stories.

Joni was born on October 15, 1949, in Baltimore, Maryland. She was named Joni (pronounced Johnny) after her father. Growing up on a large farm was great fun! She and her three older sisters, Jay, Kathy, and Linda, so enjoyed playing … and fighting … in the hayloft!

Her family was the athletic type, always up for a game of tennis, hiking, or outdoor exploring. Joni and her sisters just loved to ride horses. And by the age of seven, she was entering and winning horse-jumping competitions.

Joni became interested in art at an early age while watching her father as he painted at his desk in the evenings. And her first memory of writing was in third grade when she wrote and illustrated *The Three-Legged Pig.*

If she wasn't riding horses, Joni was drawing them. She drew this picture when she was only six.

When Joni was 15, she accepted Christ at a Young Life Camp in Virginia. Everything in her life looked bright and beautiful. A couple of years later she graduated from Woodlawn High School, where she received many athletic and academic awards. Joni had a boyfriend, a family she adored, faith in God, and so many exciting plans for her future. Six weeks later, in a matter of seconds, everything changed dramatically.

The water was murky, still, and cool as Joni dove into the shallow Chesapeake Bay on July 30, 1967. She hit her head on the sandy bottom and broke a bone in her neck. She almost drowned! It was the last time she would have feeling in her body, from her neck down to her feet. Later, during the two years of her rehabilitation, she was angry, hurt, and confused. If God loved her, how could he have allowed

this? But through hard work in physical therapy, constant encouragement from friends, and reading the Bible, she accepted that God had a completely different plan for her life.

It was very hard on Joni not to be able to move. She felt like fighting God and giving up. But He helped Joni understand how much He loved her.

In Therapy Joni started painting with her mouth, and later showed her artwork in local art shows. After a local television program highlighted her work, the producers of The Today Show called to ask if she would appear with Barbara Walters for an interview. After that, things kind of exploded. A publisher asked if she would write a book—she called it *Joni.* The Billy Graham film ministry produced the movie *Joni,* her life story. This resulted in thousands of letters from disabled people which inspired her to begin the ministry, Joni and Friends.

Joni at her easel painting "The Light of the World" for a Christmas card.

Joni didn't lose her talent when she became disabled. An artist's talent is not in her hands, but in her heart. Joni uses her mouth to draw and paint, and it took her many years of practice to control the pencils and brushes. Try writing your name with your mouth sometime!

Has anyone ever told you not to chew on pencils? Well, Joni can't help it. After a day of drawing, her pencils look like they've been to an alligator zoo!

One Sunday morning during a church service Joni was distracted, so she decided to pray for the dark-haired man in front of her. Weeks later at a party, she was introduced to Ken Tada. Wait a minute, she thought, I know him. She asked him to turn around so she could see the back of his head—he was indeed the same person she had prayed for earlier! Two years later, in 1982, they were married. After teaching high school history for 32 years, Ken retired and now works at Joni and Friends. He loves to play racquetball and to fish in the ocean. Joni and Ken enjoy camping in the Sierra Mountains

Ken and Joni

of California. And although they do not have any children of their own, they are continually blessed by the many children God brings into their lives.

Joni's van has special equipment that lets her drive with a mouth stick and with one arm in a steering mechanism to maneuver it—no steering wheel here! When she's not driving to work or church, she's enjoying butter-almond ice cream, books, music, and her miniature Schnauzer, Scrappy.

Even though she's disabled

Joni can do many things. She has written many books and is an international speaker, a singer, an artist, a radio broadcaster, and the president of Joni and Friends. Joni encourages those who have disabilities and trains leaders in churches to reach out to disabled people. She enjoys telling people everywhere how good God has been to her and how wonderfully He has directed her life.

Joni travels all over the world and meets lots of people. She loves to talk with them about the peace that God will give to everyone who believes in His Son, Jesus. **Thank you for praying for all that Joni and Friends is doing to share God's love!**

To learn even more about Joni, contact us at:

Joni and Friends
INTERNATIONAL DISABILITY CENTER
PO Box 3333 • Agoura Hills, CA 91376
(818) 707-5664 • Fax: (818) 707-2391 • TTY: (818) 707-9707
Website: **www.joniandfriends.org**
For current locations of our growing number of
U.S. Field Services and **International Field Services**
please visit **www.joniandfriends.org**
then click on "Field Ministries".

110906

Joni's story ...for kids

AWANA Clubs: Projects for Cubbies (Preschoolers) with Special Needs

Most parents hope their children will develop a desire to serve others—and this includes parents of children with special needs. Serving gives all children a sense of accomplishment and self-worth. Service projects also teach children to work well with others to finish a task.

Cubbies are preschoolers who can learn that by serving others, they demonstrate their love for God. Most children with special needs can understand this concept; others may not. But even Cubbies who can't appreciate this deeper motivation can see that kindness brings smiles to the faces of the people they help.

A service project for Cubbies should be a concrete experience. When they put money in an offering jar, they may not associate it with helping children living in India. A child will, however, understand getting a pat on the head from a leader after planting flowers in the church yard.

Guidelines

Guidelines for working with Cubbies with special needs are similar to those for working with any preschooler:

- Plan several small service projects rather than one long, complicated project. When projects take too long to complete, tired, cranky children are the result.

- Plan projects that take place at church.

- Recruit adult helpers who understand the children's abilities. Involve parents, if possible.

- Throughout the project, praise preschoolers for doing a great job.

- Hand out service awards to honor Cubbies' work (see the samples on p. 230). Encourage lots of cheers and applause from the audience. Simple rewards go a long way in building self-esteem in children with disabilities.

- In some cases, have helpers who will take a child by the hand and actually do the project while bragging on him or her for working alongside.

- During the task, repeat phrases that define what children are doing. "God wants us to be kind to others." "We show God's love to others." "God sees the good job you are doing."

- If the project is serving people, be sure the people are sensitive to children with special needs. Only take

children into positive environments where they will be appreciated.

- Encourage parents to do service projects with their children at home.

Project Ideas

- Make encouragement cards for people at church who are hospitalized or homebound.

- Clean up the room after the club meeting (straighten chairs, pick up trash, erase boards, etc.).

- Visit a senior adult class at church to present a mini-musical or skit.

- Bring supplies from home for Christmas boxes for needy children.

- Draw big pictures for the pastor, maintenance crew or other staff members.

- Plant flowers in a bare area around the church. This can be a great project for special needs children who may have difficulties with coordination. Dropped seeds may yield flowers in unexpected places.

- Pass out supplies to children; and collect and put away classroom crayons, scissors and papers.

- Help teachers set up lesson materials before class.

- Help hold visuals during the lesson.

- Organize toy, book or supply shelves.

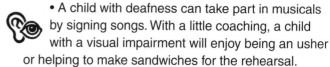

AWANA Clubs: Projects for Sparks (Kindergarten–Grade 2) with Special Needs

Sparks with special needs enjoy stories about heroes in Scripture. Read Bible biographies to them about Miriam, Mary and Martha, Lydia, Moses, Samuel and Paul. Sparks are also inspired by adopting a service motto ("We care! So we share." "God loves me. So I love you!" "Can I help you?")

 Some children need extra help with memory work. Challenge them to say the motto to a specific beat or with emphasis on a particular word. One leader taught students to pump one leg up and down or to rotate their arms in a circle while reciting. These actions help Sparks stay focused.

Sparks are beginning to understand what helping people in other countries means. Tell them exciting missionary stories, emphasizing that missionaries are people who serve God wherever He sends them.

Guidelines

When planning service projects for Sparks, follow these guidelines:

- For service projects that require travel, recruit one adult per child. All drivers should have proper insurance. In some states, Sparks still need car seats. Leaders should carry for every child permission forms with parental contact information and signatures.

- Plan projects according to your group dynamics. Some special needs children have difficulty in strange situations and can be disruptive. If this is the case, limit projects to things such as picking up trash on the church grounds or in a nearby park. Use wisdom in visiting places such as nursing homes or hospitals.

- These children get excited about doing simple things, so don't overplan. One song sung during worship can be an over-the-top experience.

- Divide your group into smaller groups when appropriate. For example, suppose you plan to visit the homes of three shut-ins and deliver gift bags and cards. Children who are uncomfortable in a social situation can make cards. Children who are overly active can put together gift bags. Children who are at ease in social situations can actually visit in the homes.

- Encourage parents to do service projects with their children in their neighborhood. Create a name for the effort ("Good Neighbor Week," etc.). Afterward, have families report back to the club what they did to serve others, and give all family members a loud round of applause.

- Whatever the service project, think of ways that all the children can contribute according to their ability.

  - A child with deafness can take part in musicals by signing songs. With a little coaching, a child with a visual impairment will enjoy being an usher or helping to make sandwiches for the rehearsal.

  - Children with physical disabilities may need extra help to follow through with a task. But don't be surprised if their good-natured willingness to serve adds more creative ideas to the project.

Ask parents for their support, and answer their questions. Parents of children in wheelchairs may be asked to drive if the project involves going a distance away from the church. If you need to use a church van or bus, make sure it is equipped for wheelchair transport and has adequate insurance coverage.

Project Ideas

- Put on a play for a small, supportive audience. Recruit older teenagers to do speaking parts while children act out the drama.

- Clean up bookshelves or toy shelves in the classroom, wash tables and chairs and wipe off the white board.

- Plant seeds in a flower or vegetable garden.

- Bake cookies and deliver them to shut-ins. Sparks need a lot of adult supervision in a kitchen. Divide them into smaller groups for safety.

- Set up chairs for club meetings.

- Write to missionaries or draw pictures for them.

- Paint wooden blocks for the church nursery.

- Give a special offering for Bibles for hospitals and homeless shelters or for new classroom chairs.

AWANA Clubs: Projects for T&Ters (Grades 3–6) with Special Needs

Rachel is a T&T clubber who has quadriplegia and can't use her arms or legs. She loves attending Awana Club. One summer her club volunteered to manage the church Web blog, which was written for younger children. The T&Ters planned what to say and posted it on the website. At the bottom of the post, they asked a question for readers to answer and send to the church. Children who answered a certain number of questions over 10 weeks were invited to an end-of-the-summer event. Rachel helped write the blog and kept track of the children's answers. She was a vital part of the team.

T&Ts with Physical Disabilities or with Visual or Hearing Impairments

Some adults equate physical impairments with learning disabilities. But many of these students keep up with their peers. They enjoy writing e-mails, text messaging, drawing, playing instruments and teaching younger students. Children with visual or hearing impairments need help adjusting to new situations, but they can do it quickly.

Avoid talking down to these students. Don't do for them things that they're capable of doing for themselves. If you aren't sure what they can do, ask first! Often, T&Ters with physical disabilities exude kindness and gentleness toward others. They understand because they've felt different—they know what it's like to stand out. Their personalities can be sweet and giving. But at this age, they are also becoming their own individual. As you keep them interested in the club, you'll keep them focused on God's divine plan for their lives.

T&Ts with Emotional/Behavioral Disorders or with Learning Disabilities

Teach these students that we help others because Jesus commanded it, and He set the example for us. To be a follower of Jesus, we must obey Him and not spend all our time thinking about ourselves. T&Ters with special needs can easily fall into this pattern. They may be overly concerned about what others think, and they need to understand that worrying won't bring them joy and peace.

Students with learning disabilities such as dyslexia or emotional/behavioral disorders such as AD/HD do best when they know what to expect. Spend several club meetings planning, discussing and rehearsing a project before you go somewhere to serve. These students also have a low-frustration tolerance. Plan projects that you are sure they can complete with minimal complications. They like immediate results. For example, if you're collecting money for a project, tape a picture of the goal on the wall and add a symbol for every dollar you raise.

Remind students that good manners are required on all trips because they are representing Jesus and their church. Inside voices are always the rule.

In every service project, let the clubbers shine. Notice everything they do and praise them. If there is an adult or teen in your church who has a disability, invite that person to join the group for a service project. T&Ters will be impressed by their example and respond in kind.

Project Ideas

- Pray for our military and make cards for soldiers. Plan a trip to meet soldiers as they return from service at a local airport and to welcome them home by telling them, "Job well done. Thank you!"

- Do jobs at church (pass out bulletins, collect the offering from different Sunday School departments, etc.).

- Have three or four students at a time go with you to serve meals at a soup kitchen or a homeless shelter.

- Collect school supplies for needy children. Your group can involve the whole church in filling backpacks and donating them to a local charity.

- Have girls start a Locks of Love group. Locks of Love makes hairpieces for children who have lost their hair for any medical reason. Challenge students to research how long their hair must be, how it should be cut and where to send their Locks of Love. Take lots of pictures for a bulletin board.

- Raise money for the Make-A-Wish Foundation.

- Make a quilt for someone special (pastor, teacher, etc.). Students can draw on quilt blocks and ask volunteer quilters in your church to sew them together.

Many children with disabilities won't have the patience to do hand quilting, but some might surprise you.

- Make Christmas gifts for needy families. T&Ters will especially enjoy trying different crafts (clay pottery, bread, wood projects, photography, etc.).

- Adopt a local park and pick up trash there once a month. Ask the parks department in your city for their cooperation, and they will probably be happy to support your efforts by providing bags and empty trash containers.

According to Matthew 13:31, Jesus said, "The kingdom of heaven is like a mustard seed, which a man took and planted in his field. Though it is the smallest of all your seeds, yet when it grows, it is the largest of garden plants and becomes a tree, so that the birds of the air come and perch in its branches." Jesus wanted us to know that small projects can reap large results: Children in God's service can make a difference in the world!

Service: Hosting a Disability Fair

Hosting a disability fair serves many purposes:

- It's a service to the disabled population in your community, providing an opportunity for networking with local disability organizations and vendors (see "Working with Local Disability Organizations," p. 62).

- A fair is a very effective way to present your special needs ministry and attract new members.

- Most importantly, it's one more way to present the gospel. Luke 14:23 says, "Make them come in, so that my house will be full." A disability fair is an ideal event to attract to God's house families affected by disability.

Venue Checklist

- **Spaciousness to Maneuver Wheelchairs**—Large crowds can be frustrating for people who use crutches, canes, walkers and wheelchairs.

- **Plenty of Accessible Parking**—Temporary disabled parking may need to be created.

- **Handicap-Accessible Restrooms Nearby**—Portable, accessible restrooms can be rented if additional facilities are needed.

Exhibitors

Decide whether you will charge a fee for exhibitors and what you will provide in each space (one table, tablecloths, chairs, a canopy if held outdoors, etc.).

Make a list of exhibitors to invite:

- local disability organizations and support groups
- other Christian groups with disability ministries
- speech, occupational and physical therapists
- car and van conversion vendors and wheelchair seating specialists
- group homes and respite care programs
- home health-care stores
- sports and arts groups
- lawyers specializing in special needs issues
- after-school programs and camps
- marriage and family counselors

And remember to set up a booth highlighting your own disability ministry!

Publicity and Event Details

Getting the word out will generate excitement. Send your invited exhibitors announcements about the disability fair that they can display in their offices and/or copy and send to their staff, their membership and other parties who would be interested in attending the fair. Publicize through radio and television community ads.

Create a way for attendees to register as they enter the event. This will give you a list of names with contact information for future mailings and events. Consider giving each person a goodies bag as they arrive at the fair. Have a sign-language interpreter available throughout the day. Ask children and families from your own ministry to volunteer to help run the fair.

Special Touches

Go the extra mile to make your event stand out in the disability community. Show people that God's love for them is extravagant. Provide free or low-cost refreshments—those with disabilities often live on limited incomes, and offering food is a big attraction and help. Think about having a massage therapist provide free massages, a hair stylist provide free haircuts and a cosmetologist provide facials. Offer a prayer counselor, a family therapist's services and an evangelism booth.

Entertainment and Workshops

Be creative and make use of the many resources in your community.

Showcase local performance groups in the center of your exhibit hall. A children's choir can sing and sign a song. Artists who are disabled can display their artwork. Dance teams or drama clubs that include children with disabilities can perform.

If you are ambitious, provide workshops throughout the day, drawing from your exhibitors as workshop facilitators. A lawyer can make a presentation regarding special needs trusts. A respite facility can give a caregivers workshop. A disability minister can discuss meeting the spiritual needs of those with disabilities.

Your disability fair can be a valuable service to families affected by disability; and they will look forward to it every year. Pray that individuals and families will be attracted to God and drawn to your disability ministry because of your event.

Sample: Service Award

Many children with special needs love hats. Copy the following award and give it to students along with a crazy hat for a job well done!

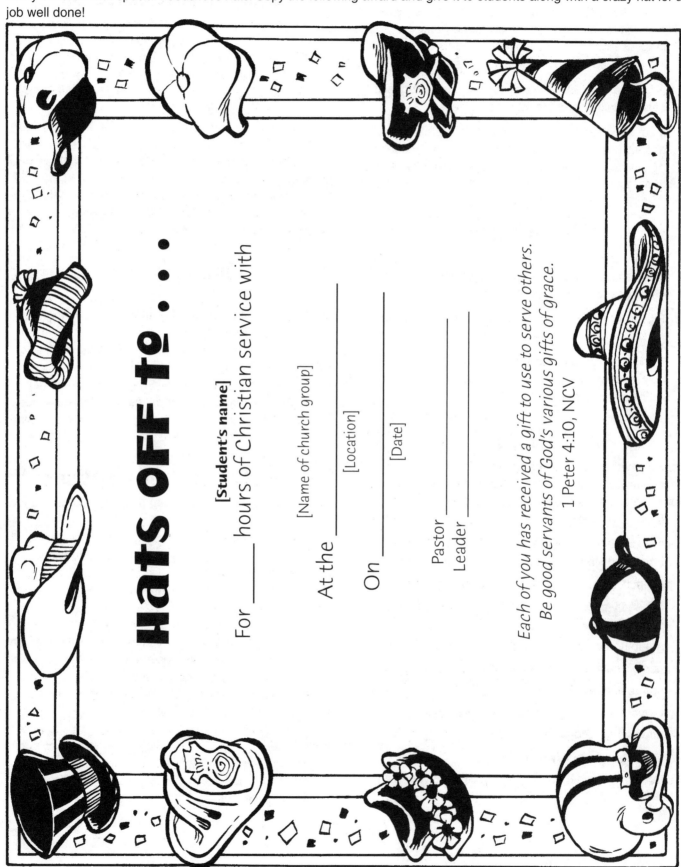

Hats off to . . .

[Student's name]

For ____ hours of Christian service with

_____
[Name of church group]

At the _____
[Location]

On _____
[Date]

_____
Pastor

_____
Leader

Each of you has received a gift to use to serve others. Be good servants of God's various gifts of grace.
1 Peter 4:10, NCV

[Artist Willson Kantz is nine years old and has autism.]

Activity Page: Be a Good Servant

Anyone who wants to be important among you must be your servant.
Matthew 20:26, *NIrV*

In each box, draw a picture showing how you can serve God at home, at school, on the playground, at church, in a store and a friend's house.

I CAN BE A SERVANT AT . . .

Moments That Inspire a Lifetime

Arlene was born three months premature with a hole in her heart and multiple disabilities. Doctors said she wouldn't survive, let alone eat, walk or talk. By age two, Arlene had mastered eating and talking. She had tendon surgery to release her hamstring at age four and soon afterwards she pulled herself up to stand and took six independent steps, without her walker! Only parents of children with special needs can understand the intense emotion that surrounds such a feat! Someday Arlene will walk up to those doctors and show them that God is the One in charge!

—James, Missouri

Our six-year-old daughter has never developed beyond infancy. She is very tiny and has never done anything age appropriate . . . until last week. She lost her first tooth and has three more loose teeth. Just like a normal six-year-old. It's funny to see our family so excited about something so small to most people.

—Kathleen, Washington

My son, Jordan, has autism. He didn't talk or give us eye contact. Before we left on a visit to his grandparents' house, I purchased nighttime Pull-Ups® [Huggies Potty Training Pants] but forgot to pack them. That evening Jordan had some chocolate milk. Using sign language, he asked for more. I mumbled something about forgetting the Pull-Ups and how I didn't want him to wet the bed. He continued to sign "more." When I refused, he looked me in the eye and said, "I . . . want more (still signing "more") . . . m-i-l-k." As you can imagine, Jordon got more milk!

—Jennifer, Virginia

At 26 weeks gestation, Sarah was born weighing 1 pound 10 ounces. After 75 days in the neonatal unit, she finally came home at 4 pounds 7 ounces. Such a joy! She received early intervention services but was discharged at age one because she'd met her developmental goals. Just before she started kindergarten, Sarah got pneumonia and began having seizures. She has had multiple surgeries to correct a curve in her spine, but she continued to keep up with her peers in public school. In sixth grade, Sarah was inducted into the National Junior Honor Society. We praise God for how He has blessed our daughter. She is an inspiration.

—Allen, New Mexico

I have two sons with special needs, but they complement each other very well. Christopher keeps Sammy physically active and mentally stimulated, and Sammy brings out Christopher's personality. They're always together playing cars or building forts in the backyard! Eight-year-old Christopher is visually impaired and attends a school for the blind. Sammy has Down syndrome and is our social butterfly. Everyone loves him, especially his kindergarten classmates. Outside of school, they are involved in Pioneer Clubs at church and swim two or three times a week at the YMCA. Just as they're always thinking of one another, Christopher and Sammy think of others, too. And that makes a mother proud!

—Kristin, California

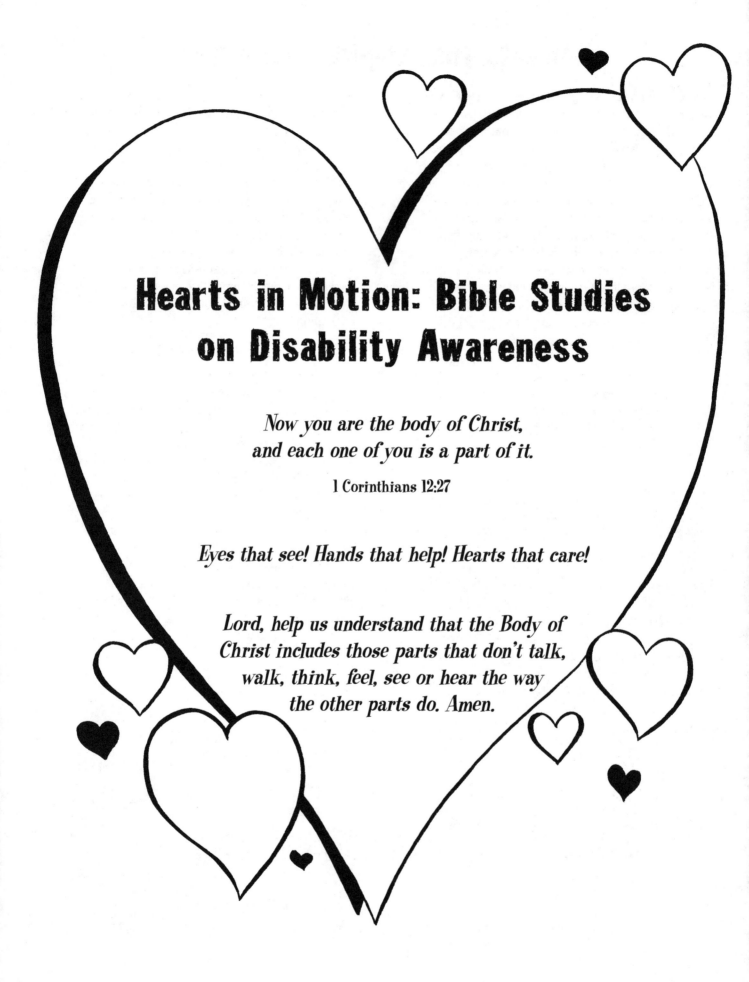

Hearts in Motion: Bible Studies on Disability Awareness

*Now you are the body of Christ,
and each one of you is a part of it.*

1 Corinthians 12:27

Eyes that see! Hands that help! Hearts that care!

*Lord, help us understand that the Body of
Christ includes those parts that don't talk,
walk, think, feel, see or hear the way
the other parts do. Amen.*

How to Use the Bible Studies

As you spend time in this study of God's Word, you will not only learn how to impact the lives of children with special needs, but you will also be drawn closer to the Lord Jesus.

For Personal Devotions

- Pray as you open each study and always close in prayer.

- Follow the instructions, and don't skip any questions.

- Answer the questions honestly, reflecting on your own experiences.

- Jot down any thoughts in the margin for further reflection and study.

For Small-Group Study

Each lesson includes three objectives followed by a group activity guide. Use these activities to help participants examine their own attitudes about people with disabilities and to encourage thoughtful discussion. Be sensitive to individuals who have family members with special needs. Do not assume parents are willing to share their child's story. Always ask for their permission in advance.

For Other Options

- A half-day parent-teacher seminar on disability awareness

- A four-week elective Bible study during Sunday School, midweek classes or home-group gatherings

- A source for articles and quotes for parent-teacher newsletters or staff notes

Lesson Overview Chart

Lesson 1: Open Our Eyes	**A. Know God's View of Disability:** "The Lord does not look at the things man looks at. Man looks at the outward appearance, but the Lord looks at the heart" (1 Samuel 16:7).	**B. Learn the Attitude of Jesus:** "Your attitude should be the same as that of Christ Jesus" (Philippians 2:5).	**C. Exhibit the Proper Motivation for Service:** "Filled with compassion, Jesus reached out his hand and touched the man" (Mark 1:41).	**Group Activities:** • Identify Proper Attitudes and Motivations • Role-Play • Pray Together
Lesson 2: Lend a Hand	**A. Learn How to Minister:** "Our people must learn to devote themselves to doing what is good, in order that they may provide for daily necessities and not live unproductive lives" (Titus 3:14).	**B. Build Genuine Relationships:** "Jonathan said to David, 'Whatever you want me to do, I'll do for you'" (1 Samuel 20:4).	**C. Show True Compassion:** "Carry each other's burdens, and in this way you will fulfill the law of Christ" (Galatians 6:2).	**Group Activities:** • Dealing with Common Difficulties • Who Do You Know? • What Are Your Spiritual Gifts? • Pray Together
Lesson 3: Help at Home	**A. Understand the Impact on Families:** "Please swear to me by the Lord that you will show kindness to my family" (Joshua 2:12).	**B. Be Sensitive to Feelings:** "Be completely humble and gentle; be patient, bearing with one another in love" (Ephesians 4:2).	**C. Take the Initiative:** "In everything I did, I showed you that by this kind of hard work we must help the weak" (Acts 20:35).	**Group Activities:** • Plan of Action • How Could You Respond? • Pray Together
Lesson 4: Spread the Word	**A. Know Your Church's Role:** "Therefore encourage one another and build each other up, just as in fact you are doing" (1 Thessalonians 5:11).	**B. Identify Your Primary Goal:** "Therefore go and make disciples of all nations, baptizing them in the name of the Father and of the Son and of the Holy Spirit" (Matthew 28:19).	**C. Learn the Benefits of Disability Ministry:** "They gathered the church together and reported all that God had done through them" (Acts 14:27).	**Group Activities:** • Church Evaluation • Increase Disability Awareness • Share Testimony • Pray Together

Lesson 1: Open Our Eyes

A. Know God's View of Disability

The Lord does not look at the things man looks at. Man looks at the outward appearance, but the Lord looks at the heart.
1 Samuel 16:7

Allowing our ideas, thoughts, and perspectives to be shaped by Scripture is essential to seeing people who are affected by disability the way God sees them.
Joni and Friends

When Shannon and Doug learned they were expecting their first child, they were excited and thankful for the Lord's blessing of this new life growing inside of Shannon. At 19 weeks, they went for a sonogram, and doctors detected an abnormality. Shannon and Doug's faith in the Lord was strong. As they requested prayer for their baby, they also added, "We know God hears our prayers. We're trying not to worry over what only God can control." They soon discovered that their baby was a boy and named him Andrew.

Shannon's pregnancy was closely monitored throughout the remaining months, and each sonogram revealed the abnormality. Nevertheless, the young couple's faith in God and their love for their precious baby never wavered. At Andrew's birth, the abnormality was evident: He was born with a cleft lip and palate. Doctors watched him carefully those first few weeks.

Today, baby Andrew is home and thriving. His parents never tire of telling everyone how grateful they are for the joy Andrew brings into their lives every day.

God creates us from conception. Our impairments are not a surprise to Him. Read Psalm 139:13-16 to see how Scripture describes God's work in forming us before birth.

- The Bible says that we are _____ and _____ made.

- God's Word says that His works are _____.

- God's eyes saw our _____ bodies.

- He _____ all of our days before they came to be.

Though we might not recognize God's wisdom and purpose in disability, we can trust that God is in control.

We can and must also trust in God's perspective. In our society today, we tend to give high praise to those whose appearance is flawless. Name some physical attributes that people are likely to idolize, and list ways we go about trying to attain those attributes.

_____

_____

_____

_____

Unfortunately, few of us recognize that our outward appearance is the least of God's concerns when He looks at us. Read 1 Samuel 16:1-13 to get a good picture of how God views us. God chose David as the next king of Israel, based on his heart—a heart that was faithful to the Lord.

When our hearts are fully surrendered to God, He displays His power and character through us. Read John 9:1-3. When asked if the man was blind because of his sin or the sin of his parents, what did Jesus say?

_____

_____

God chooses the weak so that He might show His strength through their lives. When we look at boys and girls with special needs, our focus should be on what God can do—not on what these precious children cannot do. Read 2 Corinthians 12:9. What does God say about His power? _____

_____

When we recognize His work in those affected by disability, God is glorified.

For Thought: Read 1 Corinthians 12:22. What do you think this verse means? Give an example. _____

_____

_____

_____

Lord, open my eyes that I may see those with disabilities as You see them. Amen.

Lesson 1: Open Our Eyes

B. Learn the Attitude of Jesus

Your attitude should be the same as that of Christ Jesus.
Philippians 2:5

Accessible hearts enable us to reflect
Christ's love and compassion.
Joni and Friends

Becky was sitting in the church service, listening to the children's choir sing their Easter musical. The children were all dressed up in their Sunday best, and they were standing in orderly rows on the stage. To the far left was Jason, an 11-year-old boy with autism, singing at the top of his lungs. Although terribly off-key, Jason knew all the words to the songs, and he sang them with gusto. Becky kept staring at Jason, feeling embarrassed at the boy's overzealous performance. At one point, he started singing too early, and the other children were quiet. Becky thought this boy's behavior was ruining the performance. As the musical came to an end, the choir leader gave Jason a proud smile and a thumbs-up. Grinning from ear to ear, Jason returned the thumbs-up. Afterward, Becky watched as the boy's family and friends gathered around him and congratulated him for doing so well. Becky was surprised and humbled by the affirmation the boy received from his church family.

Healthy relationships with persons affected by disabilities in your church and community begin with a positive attitude and a willing heart. Read Philippians 2:5. Whose attitude should we mimic? _____

Positive attitudes toward disability are often fostered by accurate information and personal experience with disability. Jesus often associated with the lame, the sick and other outcasts. He showed compassion to the weak because He took the time to know them and understand their circumstances. Jesus was humble enough to love those whom no one else would love.

Attitudes of hostility, apathy or embarrassment may be influenced by fear, negative experiences or lack of understanding. What are some negative reactions you have seen toward disabled people? _____
_____

We do not have to respond to people who are disabled in a negative way. Read 2 Timothy 1:7. "God did not give us a spirit of _____, but a spirit of _____." Because of God's love in our lives, we need to take some

time to learn about disability so that we can relate with a positive attitude to those affected by disability.

When our hearts are willing, we can replace negative attitudes with Christlike ones. How does Romans 12:2 tell us that we can do this? _____
_____

We can renew our minds in relation to disability by focusing on His view of others and letting God fill our hearts with His love for them. "God has poured out his love into our hearts by the Holy Spirit, whom he has given us" (Romans 5:5).

For Thought: Read the following passages to see some of the ways that Jesus showed compassion:

- Matthew 9:36-38—He had _____ and prayed for _____ .

- Matthew 14:14—He _____ the sick.

- Matthew 15:32,36—He _____ the hungry.

- Mark 6:34—He _____ them.

Think about ways you can show compassion toward people affected by disability.

Lord, fill my heart with love for people with disabilities so that I will show them compassion the way Christ did.
Amen.

Lesson 1: Open Our Eyes

C. Exhibit the Proper Motivation for Service

Filled with compassion, Jesus reached out his hand and touched the man. Mark 1:41

As we move past these attitudinal barriers and misunderstandings, we'll discover the joy of caring for someone simply based on the preciousness of their souls.
Joni Eareckson Tada

Tyler is a 17-year old boy with multiple disabilities. He was born with Sturge-Weber syndrome and has a port-wine stain over 50 percent of his body, severe seizures, developmental delays and glaucoma. Tyler is also profoundly mentally retarded. During a hospital stay when Tyler was 12 years old, Tyler's parents, Tim and Melanie, began to notice the other families around them who were experiencing extremely difficult times. Besides having very sick children, many families were struggling with insurance hassles, job responsibilities, fatigue and lack of support. Overall, Tim and Melanie noticed that many of the other families seemed to be feeling hopeless. On the other hand, Tyler's family had learned joy in the midst of their trials and struggles from knowing the peace that comes from God's love. Overcome with sympathy, compassion and the desire to share their joy, Tyler's mom and dad formed a ministry called Tyler's Treat, which provides prayer support, Bibles, cards and food for families with children with special needs who have had to travel to Ft. Worth, Texas, to receive treatment at Cook Children's Center.

Before any ministry can be successful, we must have the proper motivation. What are some motives we might have for helping those affected by disability? _____
_____
_____

Our primary motivation must be our loyalty to God and obedience to His Word. Jesus said, "If you love me, you will obey what I command" (John 14:15). What are we commanded to do in John 13:34 and in Ephesians 4:32? _____
_____

These passages help us understand that our motive for ministry does not necessarily reside in our feelings toward people but in our loyalty to Christ. In everything that we do, especially when we are serving others, we are "working for the Lord, not for men" (Colossians 3:23).

As servants of God, we must show kindness to all people. Read the story in 2 Samuel 9. What did King David want to do? _____
_____

In spite of his disability (Mephibosheth was "crippled in both feet," verse 3), Mephibosheth was treated kindly by the king, who was true to his stated goal. "So Mephibosheth ate at David's table like one of the king's sons" (2 Samuel 9:11).

We serve others because we love the Lord. But we also serve because "Christ's love compels us" (2 Corinthians 5:14). Read 1 John 4:7-21. What was God's greatest act of love for us? _____
_____

Christ's love *for* us is great, and His love *in* us is great. Therefore, we love others with the love that He has given us. In 1 John 4:12, we are given a description of God's love working in us: "If we love one another, God lives in us and his love is _____."
Because of Christ's love in our hearts, we cannot help but pour out that love on others. His love in our lives causes us to hurt with those who hurt, show compassion to those who suffer, share with those in need and help those who are weak.

For Thought: Think about why you minister (or want to minister) to children with disabilities. What are your motives? _____
_____
_____
_____

Lord, give me a heart of compassion for those affected by disability so that I will reach out to them in love. Amen.

Lesson 1: Open Our Eyes

Group Activity Guide

Identify Proper Attitudes and Motivations

Read the following statements. Check the ones that reflect a proper attitude and motivation. Discuss your answers with the group when everyone has finished the exercise.

☐ 1. It may be difficult to teach children with developmental/cognitive disabilities about Jesus, but I'm going to do my best.

☐ 2. I can't help with disability ministry because I don't know anything about autism.

☐ 3. Jesus loves all children, and I can love those with disabilities, too.

☐ 4. Even though children with AD/HD might appear to be wild and undisciplined, they can be excellent learners.

☐ 5. If I work with the disability ministry on Sunday morning, I don't have to listen to the boring Sunday School teacher in my class.

☐ 6. I want to show the same kind of compassion toward those who are weak that Jesus showed.

☐ 7. I feel sorry for my friend whose child is deaf, so I agreed to babysit for her.

☐ 8. The Church is the best source of social and spiritual healing for those affected by disability.

☐ 9. I believe that my life will be enriched if I spend some time with the little girl in our church who has had to use a wheelchair since being in a car accident.

☐ 10. If that family with the child with a disability needs my help, they'll call.

☐ 11. I wish that lady with the "problem" child would call someone else for a change.

☐ 12. God is glorified when I give up my selfish desires and serve those who need my help.

Role-Play

Ask for three volunteers to play the part of a child affected by a different disability: Blindfold one volunteer. The second volunteer is to communicate by shaking or nodding his or her head or by writing (i.e., is not allowed to talk). The third volunteer is to sit in a chair placed just outside the doorway of the room or in the corner of the room, away from the others in the group. Everyone else in the group, except the leader, is to pretend to be typical children.

During the next 10 minutes, role-play the following activities:

- Ask the "children" to tell the group about their favorite toy.

- Put some blocks on the floor, and have the "children" work together to build a city.

- Make plans to play Grocery Store. Let each "child" decide what role he or she will play in the store.

At the end of 10 minutes, have the three volunteers talk about their experiences, and then have everyone discuss how they felt about the activity.

Role-playing provides a glimpse into what it might be like to have a disability—but only as if we were looking through a peephole. When deafness or a wheelchair is experienced for a brief time, the focus is usually on the imposed limitation. But for children living with disabilities, with the grace of God, inabilities do not have to be in the forefront of daily living. Challenges can present opportunities to be creative within our circumstances and encourage us to depend on the Lord.

Pray Together

Pray that God would dispel any lingering fears or apprehensions that anyone in the group might have regarding disability.

Ask God to help everyone have the right motivation and attitude toward ministering to people with special needs.

Lesson 2: Lend a Hand

A. Learn How to Minister

Our people must learn to devote themselves to doing what is good, in order that they may provide for daily necessities and not live unproductive lives.
Titus 3:14

One of the best ways we can prepare for disability ministry is to learn from those who have been there.

Along with the many other programs in Hal's church, the special needs ministry was invited to participate in a Children's Ministry Awareness Fair. It was held in the church parking lot with hopes of drawing in unchurched families in the neighborhood. There were bounce houses, games and food at the event. Each program director was asked to set up a booth to help people learn about their area of ministry. Hal and his special needs volunteers were grateful for the opportunity to promote this vital area of outreach as well as to identify ways to minister to children with disabilities. They advertised the various special needs programs, including their new special needs class available on Sunday mornings and the monthly Parent's Night Out. An important part of the booth included hands-on activities to help people experience disability. Hal also asked people to complete a survey to identify families affected by disability and their needs. Hal received a number of new recruits, because he lent a hand at the fair.

As people who desire to minister to children with special needs, we must try to understand the unique difficulties children affected by disability have to deal with each day. We need to prepare responses our church and volunteers can make to those needs. What are some ways you can educate your church? _____
_____
_____
_____

Hal used activities such as role-playing to help those at the fair put themselves in another's shoes for a first-hand experience with the difficulties of disability. Jesus did this same thing for us when He left heaven and became a man. He experienced life on Earth as a human being and went through all kinds of human trials and struggles. What does Hebrews 4:15 say about Jesus?
_____
_____

We can learn to respond to the specific needs of children with disabilities by imagining ourselves faced with the same trials and struggles that they encounter in life.

Another way we can learn how to respond to the needs of children with disabilities is by talking with adults who are involved in disability ministry. They can serve as mentors, teaching us the best ways to deal with certain types of needs. In 1 Corinthians 11:1, what does the apostle Paul encourage believers to do? _____
_____

This mentoring model is an effective way of learning to serve in disability ministry. God often uses other Christians to prepare us for doing His work. Proverbs 19:20 tells us, "Listen to advice and accept instruction, and in the end you will be wise." What are some ways you could benefit from the mentorship of a person who has more experience with children with special needs? _____
_____
_____
_____

For Thought: Think about who you might find to mentor you to become an effective minister to children with disabilities. It could be a parent of a child with special needs, a church volunteer or a medical professional. Plan to talk this week to one of them about mentoring.

Lord, help me learn to minister to children affected by disability in the ways they need it most. Amen.

Lesson 2: Lend a Hand

B. Build Genuine Relationships

*Jonathan said to David, "Whatever you want
me to do, I'll do for you."* 1 Samuel 20:4

Disability ministry is to be designed around relationships.
Joni and Friends

Sarah, who was born with cerebral palsy, uses an electric wheelchair to get around. Although she is able to control her wheelchair, she has limited use of her arms and hands. She hunches over the tray on her wheelchair because she is unable to sit in an upright position. Her writing is very shaky, yet writing is her primary way of communicating with others. Sarah can somewhat convey her thoughts through moans and extremely slurred speech. She has successfully completed nine grades thanks to her best friend, Valerie.

Valerie and Sarah sat beside each other in second grade. The teacher asked Valerie if she would be Sarah's buddy that year, and Valerie willingly agreed. Throughout the years, Valerie has enjoyed getting to know Sarah, and she discovered that Sarah is smart and funny. Many times, Valerie has confided in Sarah and sought her wisdom and advice. Their friendship has also been a source of strength, unconditional love and support for Sarah. Ministering to those affected by disability is often viewed as a helping ministry—able-bodied people simply do for individuals with special needs what those individuals cannot do for themselves. Unfortunately, such an approach misses two important opportunities. First, disability ministry is to be designed around relationships. Second, people with disabilities are to be an integral part of the Body of Christ—even in their service to us.

Why do you think people mistakenly assume that it is not feasible to have a mutually satisfying relationship with a disabled person? _____
_____

Read Romans 12:10. It tells us to "be devoted to one another in _____." The last phrase in that sentence implies a mutually satisfying relationship, or friendship. What are some ways that we relate to our friends in our devotion to them? _____
_____
_____

By establishing personal relationships, we are better able to understand what our friends with disabilities need. And they are better able to understand what we need.

Read 1 Thessalonians 5:11. What does developing personal relationships within the Body of Christ allow us to do? _____
_____

This is the integral role that we all—including people affected by disability—are instructed to live out each day in relation to one another. In disability ministry, who benefits from the relationship? _____
What does Ecclesiastes 4:9-12 say happens when two people connect as friends? _____
_____

In a good relationship, two people accomplish more than one, and they help and support each other. They strengthen each other through tough times. God's design for friendship is amazing! When we make friends with those who have disabilities, we receive ministry from them, and we both are blessed.

For Thought: Think of someone with a disability at church. Would you like to get to know this person better? What are some mutual ways that you and that new friend would benefit from a growing relationship? _____
_____
_____
_____

*Lord, lead me to someone who has a disability,
so I can become a true friend. Amen.*

Lesson 2: Lend a Hand

C. Show True Compassion

Carry each other's burdens, and in this way you will fulfill the law of Christ. Galatians 6:2

Empathy . . . will lead us to deeper compassion spurring one toward action, not pity.
Joni and Friends

Lily was almost three years old when she was diagnosed with stage 4 neuroblastoma. Immediately, she underwent surgery to remove the cancerous mass in her abdomen and started her first round of chemotherapy. Over time, she went through rounds of chemo, blood transfusions, stem-cell harvests, bone-marrow transplants and numerous other treatments and procedures. She was in and out of the hospital for several years, and she experienced much sickness, fever, pain, discomfort and weakness. However, she also received an abundance of prayer, encouragement, help, gifts, visits, financial donations and support from her church and friends. No matter what she was going through, she always kept her eyes on Jesus and never lost hope because of the constant care and encouragement she received from others in the name of the Lord.

People affected by disability need others to help carry their burdens. Their distress and difficulty can be emotionally, physically and spiritually overwhelming. What does Paul admonish believers to do in 1 Thessalonians 5:14?

_____

_____

When Paul tells us in Acts 20:35 that "we must help the weak," he also reminds us of Jesus' encouraging words: "It is more blessed to _____ than to _____." Because people with disabilities often have so many needs, they rely on the Body of Christ to come alongside them and help carry their load.

Read Romans 12:6-8. What does the first part of verse 6 say we have? _____
List the ways we can use the gifts mentioned in verses 7-8.

_____

_____

_____ By the abundant grace God gives us, we can help take care of others' needs.

God desires that we give generously of ourselves when we minister to people with many different kinds of difficulties:

- Our ministry to those who have difficulty getting from one place to another could be helping them get where they need to go. According to Mark 2:3, what did the men do for the paralytic? _____

_____

- With patient attention and wise discernment, we can learn to understand those who have a hard time communicating and assist them in conveying their message. According to Matthew 15:10, what did Jesus direct the people to do? _____

_____

- Those affected by disability often have a poor self-image because insensitive people have made them feel like outcasts. What does 1 Thessalonians 5:11 tell us about how to make a big difference in people's lives? _____

_____

- Because the difficulties people with disability confront on a daily basis, they get tired and overwhelmed, and it's not unusual for them to be emotionally and spiritually stressed. Read 2 Corinthians 1:3-4. How has God specifically prepared us to minister to the needs of these people? _____

_____

Fortunately, 2 Corinthians 12:9 reminds us that God's grace is sufficient for us, particularly when we show compassion for those who need God's strength.

For Thought: Think about a person with special needs. How might you help care for that individual?

Lord, use me today to meet the needs of a child, youth or adult with disabilities. Amen.

Lesson 2: Lend a Hand

Group Activity Guide

Dealing with Common Difficulties

Share ideas within the group about how you or your disability ministry team might assist a child with special needs in each of the following areas:

- Social isolation and/or loneliness
- Poor self-image
- Behavior issues
- Finances
- Health concerns
- Safety
- Immobility
- Communication difficulties
- Emotional outbursts
- Hearing impairment
- Fears
- Peer misunderstandings

What could you do for a child in the hospital? A homebound child? A child with a terminal condition?

Who Do You Know?

Name a child you know who has a disability. What are some ways that you could develop a healthy, biblical relationship with that child? What type of help might he or she need from you? In what ways do you think a relationship with that child could be a mutual blessing? Let the group brainstorm, and have the leader write the group's responses on a whiteboard or large sheet of paper.

Identify a teacher, volunteer or caregiver who is already involved in assisting children with special needs. What kind of relationship does that person have with the child? Meet with the caregiver and ask questions about ministering to children with disabilities. How does that person view the child, and how does the child relate in return? What are the mutual benefits of the relationship? What suggestions does the caregiver have about how you might start a relationship with a child with special needs?

What Are Your Spiritual Gifts?

God has given each of us spiritual gifts for the purpose of serving Him and others (see Romans 12:3-8; 1 Corinthians 12:1-11,27-31). What gifts are you using in ministry? How could you use those gifts in a disability ministry? Share your comments with the group, and ask others what gifts they see in you. Which of the following spiritual gifts apply to you?

_____ Prophesying

_____ Serving

_____ Teaching

_____ Encouraging

_____ Giving

_____ Leading

_____ Showing mercy

_____ Wisdom

_____ Knowledge

_____ Faith

_____ Healing

_____ Discernment

_____ Speaking in tongues

_____ Interpreting tongues

_____ Helping

_____ Administration

If you have never taken a spiritual-gifts inventory, visit the Building Church Ministries Gifted2Serve website (http://www.buildingchurch.net/g2s.htm). This is a free online inventory with 125 questions designed to help you learn what your spiritual gifts are. You can also read about each of the gifts and find Scripture references to the gifts. An inventory is also available in C. Peter Wagner's book *Your Spiritual Gifts Can Help Your Church Grow,* along with a wealth of information about spiritual gifts.

Pray Together

Pray for a compassionate heart that desires to help those affected by disability.

Pray for opportunities to develop relationships with children who have disabilities.

Lesson 3: Help at Home

A. Understand the Impact on Families

Please swear to me by the Lord that you will show kindness to my family. Joshua 2:12

Assisting someone with a disability can also make a great impact on others who love and care for him or her. Joni and Friends

During Julie's pregnancy, her doctor discovered that her unborn baby had spina bifida. She and her husband, Jarrod, were faced with a difficult decision regarding early intervention. They decided to go ahead with the surgery, so the pediatric neurosurgeons performed intrauterine surgery to close up the baby's spinal cord. When Caleb was born, he had various impairments as a result of the spina bifida. By the time he was four years old, Caleb had been taken numerous times to the doctor, and Julie had sat through multiple surgeries. It was painful for the family to watch him go through the many painful but necessary treatments he had to undergo.

As a preschooler, Caleb continues to use a catheter and requires daily assistance with routine activities. Julie relies on her two older sons to help care for Caleb. Unfortunately, Jarrod must work two jobs to pay the medical bills, and he doesn't spend much time at home. Having a child in the family with a serious disability is a difficult and ongoing adjustment for the whole family.

When a child is born with a disability or becomes disabled due to an injury, family dynamics quickly change. Family members adapt in different ways to the new and often difficult situation. Many families are able to adjust over time and learn to rely on God for His strength and provision. They discover the true meaning of Philippians 4:13: "I can do everything through him who gives me strength." But some families do not do this.

Read 1 Corinthians 12:26. According to the first part of this verse, what happens when one person in a family suffers? _____

Describe how family members might suffer when one of them is hurting in the following ways:

* A child is in physical pain. _____
_____

* A father is struggling financially because of medical bills.
_____

* A child needs daily assistance with dressing, bathing, toileting, grooming, eating and getting around.
_____

* A child's disability makes it difficult for the family to get out and do ordinary family activities. _____
_____

In spite of the hardships, families affected by disability often pull together and enjoy a bond that many other families may never experience. The second part of 1 Corinthians 12:26 says that "if one part is honored, every part _____ with it." Describe what a family might experience in the following situations:

* A child takes baby steps in the area of development where he or she is delayed._____
_____

* A church member helps meet a need for a child with disabilities. _____
_____

* A doctor gives a good report. _____
_____

* A check comes in the mail for the exact amount of a child's medical bill. _____
_____

Families that together seek the Lord recognize His blessings in the good things that happen every day. Often, families affected by disability are more aware of God's strength, peace and joy in their lives as His goodness shines in comparison to the burdens they face.

For Thought: Think about how you might respond to the sibling of a child with disabilities who is in need of some personal attention.

Lord, show me what I can do this week to impact a family affected by disability. Amen.

Lesson 3: Help at Home

B. Be Sensitive to Feelings

Be completely humble and gentle; be patient, bearing with one another in love.
Ephesians 4:2

Disability can greatly affect the emotional well- being of a family.
Joni and Friends

Annette feels that no one could possibly understand all that she goes through each day with her eight-year-old son, Jordan, who has autism. He has violent tendencies, and Annette frequently gets hurt trying to calm him during his temper tantrums. When Jordan explodes, he throws himself down and repeatedly bangs his head against the floor. Annette is terrified that he will seriously injure himself, so she physically restrains him. Jordan usually calms down within minutes as his mom sings softly in his ear. Because his language skills are underdeveloped, Jordan has difficulty communicating. The family struggles to understand what he tries to say, which frustrates them as well as Jordan.

On Jordan's 10th birthday, Annette's husband became so overwhelmed that he abandoned his family and moved away. Their daughter, Jessica, grew more afraid of Jordan, and she now spends most of her time in her bedroom. The older son, Jonathan, grew unsympathetic and now constantly picks on Jordan.

Where will Annette turn for help and for the peace God wants to bring her family?

Without the arms of a loving church around them, families affected by disability may experience a wide range of emotions, and it is not uncommon for feelings of fear and desperation to be stirred up.

How might parents feel toward God when they have a child with disabilities? _____
_____

As each family member responds with different feelings, each also struggles to understand what the others are going through. The unknown stimulates feelings of sadness, fear and despair. Sometimes family members feel like leaving or actually do flee the situation. Psalm 55:6-8 describes one sort of response to unsettling feelings. What does the psalmist want to do? _____

Due to emotional upheaval, relationships both within the family and with others can be seriously affected. Dealing with a child's needs can cause intense stress on a marriage. Spouses may not agree on what is best for their child or the family. Job 2:8-10 describes the different responses of a married couple when the circumstances of life get overwhelming; obviously, the marriage bond can greatly suffer when spouses don't agree on a major issue.

What did Job's wife say to him in verse 9? _____ _____ Unfortunately, the children suffer when there is tension between the adults in their lives. What are some ways you have seen children act out because of family problems? _____
_____

Fortunately, families who are affected by disability do not experience only negative emotions. Those who trust in the Lord are able to cope better with the stresses and demands of dealing with disability because of God's help. According to the following verses, what can God do for families?

- Psalm 28:7 _____
  _____

- Romans 15:13 _____
  _____

- 2 Corinthians 1:3-4 _____
  _____

With the inner peace that God gives, families are able to manage daily feelings and maintain relationships with grace and dignity. They experience joy in their hearts because of the love and strength the Lord provides each day.

For Thought: Read Ephesians 4:2 and James 4:12. How might you respond to a person who is dealing with a child's disability and who is on an emotional rollercoaster?

Lord, let me be a person who is willing to listen and to encourage families affected by disability. Amen.

Lesson 3: Help at Home

C. Take the Initiative

In everything I did, I showed you that by this kind of hard work we must help the weak.
Acts 20:35

Take the initiative. Don't wait for an invitation; rather, approach the family with an idea of how you'd like to assist.
Joni Eareckson Tada, *Barrier Free Friendship*

Rachel felt tired and overwhelmed with the responsibilities of caring for her five-year-old daughter, Tiffany, who has a chronic illness and is confined to a bed. Tiffany requires constant attention; and Rachel, a single mom, was all alone. She longed to attend church on Sundays, if only to get a break.

One evening, several ladies from a nearby church knocked on her door to deliver a home-cooked meal. Rachel could hardly contain her tears of joy. She appreciated their compassion and instantly struck up a new friendship with these ladies.

A specific plan of action is much easier to respond to. A general statement like "Give me a call if I can help in any way," though sincere, puts a family in a rather awkward position. Do you mean you'll do anything at all? Even laundry? Can the family call on you anytime? Even at night? It is difficult to approach a friend who gives a general offer of help.

Families affected by disability have many needs. Most of the time, however, they will not ask others for help. Why do you think people will not ask for help? _____

_____

Most Christians affected by disability will pray to God and ask for His help (see 1 John 5:14-15). And you may just be the answer to those prayers.

Wouldn't it be a wonderful privilege to be the one God uses to answer the prayers of a family affected by disability? When you seek the Lord, He will show you what He wants you to do. If you are willing, He will show you how you can minister to the child with special needs and his or her family.

Praying for a family is one of the most significant ways you can minister to them. What does John pray for in 3 John 1:2? _____

_____

You can also ask the family what their specific needs are and lift those up to the Lord. Pray about ways you can minister, and take the initiative and do it! Don't put it off, because what the Lord reveals to you may be a need the family has at that very moment. Your assistance and timing may be critical. Read 1 John 5:2-3. What does your obeying God—by doing what He says—mean? What does your obedience show? _____

_____

For Thought: Think about a time when someone blessed your family without being asked.

Lord, I'm listening and watching for Your leading today to help a family affected by disability. Amen.

Lesson 3: Help at Home

Group Activity Guide

Plan of Action

Brainstorm with your group ways you can reach out and help families of children with special needs. Consider how you can meet physical, emotional and practical needs of the family. Have the leader write the group's responses on a whiteboard or large sheet of paper. Your list might include such activities as babysitting, cleaning, running errands, writing cards of encouragement and collecting monetary donations. Consider asking the parents or someone close to the family about their needs. Once the list is complete, identify which items on the list are things you can do anytime you are available, such as cooking a meal that could be eaten that day or frozen for another time. Then look at your calendar, and mark the days and times when you are available to minister to the family. If the time to minister is scheduled, you are more likely to do it. If you have a regular day and time available, let the family know about it, and suggest to them the types of assistance you are willing to offer. "I am available every Thursday from 2 to 4 P.M. I can help you by doing the laundry, running errands or cleaning the house."

How Could You Respond?

Discuss or role-play the following situations and how you could respond to each.

- "Because no one else knows how to take care of our son's needs—even though his routine is quite simple—my husband and I haven't enjoyed a night out together in years."

- "My wheelchair is dirty, and it would be nice to have a shiny set of wheels, but I can't ask my mom or dad to clean it, because they already have too many things to do."

- "We have three children with different disabilities. My life is consumed by their various needs. I wish I had some help on a daily basis, but we just can't afford it."

- "Because of Jenny's physical therapy sessions, our two other daughters aren't able to attend ballet classes. They meet at the same time as Jenny's appointments."

- "Our son will have surgery on his leg next week, and I will be staying at the hospital with him for five days. I don't know how my husband and children are going to get along without me."

- "My heart is broken because of the way the other children in our neighborhood treat my son when he goes outside to play. He has Down syndrome, and they just don't understand."

- "We just got a few estimates for a new concrete ramp we need at our front door for Wendy's wheelchair. It's going to cost a lot more than we thought it would!"

- "Our daughter has severe mental retardation, and my wife is exhausted from taking care of her needs every day. She really needs some social time with other women, but she hasn't been able to make any close friends."

Pray Together

Pray that God will alert you to ways in which you can minister to families with children with special needs.

Lesson 4: Spread the Word

A. Know Your Church's Role

Therefore encourage one another and build each other up, just as in fact you are doing.
1 Thessalonians 5:11

The church . . . is unlike any organization known to man. . . . Its growth, its mission, its destiny— all are unique. When it comes to disability, . . . the church plays a distinctive role.
Joni and Friends

Kimberly and James attended a support group for parents of children with epilepsy and met other parents with whom they had much in common. But when they visited Valley Community Church, people reached out to them with a kind of love and encouragement that they had never experienced.

When their daughter, Christina, began experiencing seizures at school, her classmates treated her like an outcast. Naturally, this broke her parents' hearts. They were concerned that she would grow up without any friends. But at their new church, Christina attended Sunday School and quickly became close friends with Alyssa. As a Christian, Alyssa was sensitive to Christina's feelings and understood that she worries about having a seizure in front of everyone. Alyssa prayed that she and Christina would be best friends forever, no matter what.

Kimberly and James also felt a special connection with the members of their Bible fellowship class. They were able to share their prayer requests concerning their daughter, and the class surrounded them with loving support.

The Church's role in society is redemptive. What does Luke 19:10 say Jesus came to do? _____
_____

Because the Church is the Body of Christ, Jesus brings deliverance through it to those who feel lost and hopeless. The Church must reach out and bring people to Christ, so they can find freedom and salvation.

God's Word says that Christ's salvation is for all people. Who does this include according to the following verses?

- Mark 2:17 _____
_____

- Luke 4:18-19 _____
_____

- Luke 14:15-24 _____
_____

- John 3:16 _____
_____

As people come to know Christ and His Church, they come to know His unconditional love and acceptance, His grace and forgiveness, His deliverance from sin and from hopelessness, and His restoration and blessing. How does this compare with what the world offers? _____
_____
_____

With Christ in their hearts, Christians give to and love and serve others in ways that secular society cannot and does not do. That is why upon encountering the Body of Christ so many people are lifted up, encouraged, changed and healed—if not physically, then spiritually and emotionally.

Individuals whose lives have been changed are able to minister to people who are in need, just as they themselves have been ministered to. Everyone goes through difficult times in their lives, and God works within the Body of Christ to lift them up. What does 2 Corinthians 1:3-4 say God does for and through His children? _____
_____

Ministry within the Body of Christ is reciprocal. When Christians share their concerns and struggles, they can encourage each other by praying for one another, listening without judgment, meeting each other's needs and standing together through tough times.

For Thought: Think of ways that a children's disability ministry might be reciprocal.

Lord, I pray that my church would recognize how we can minister to families affected by disability. Amen.

Lesson 4: Spread the Word

B. Identify Your Primary Goal

Therefore go and make disciples of all nations, baptizing them in the name of the Father and of the Son and of the Holy Spirit.
Matthew 28:19

The only permanent "disability" is that of not knowing Jesus as Savior. All other disabilities are temporary by [comparison].
Joni and Friends

When the Jackson family moved to Austin, they could never have anticipated the warmth and support they would receive from their new church. At first, they worried that they would not find a church that would be able to accommodate the needs of their daughter, Savannah, who has a hearing impairment. However, they found a church that had a well-established special needs ministry. When they first visited the church, they indicated on the visitor's card that their child was deaf. Within a few days, Jan and Robert, a young couple from the church, visited them in their home. To the Jacksons' surprise, Jan and Robert knew sign language and were able to talk to Savannah and make her smile and laugh. Over the next few months, Savannah grew very fond of Jan and Robert as she attended their Sunday School class each week. They shared the love of Christ with her, and Savannah gave her life to Christ. The family also enjoyed the fellowship and friendship of other families dealing with disability.

When any ministry in a church first begins, the leadership must establish a mission statement that expresses their main goal. By reading Matthew 28:19-20, that primary goal will be readily apparent. What is it? _____
_____
In disability ministry, initiating and building up a faith in Christ is crucial for a child. Jesus is well aware that we live in a fallen world where our bodies are imperfect and deteriorating. Our broken lives are the very reason we need to have a relationship with Him. What did the psalmist say in Psalm 73:26? _____

As we minister to children with special needs, we must share with them what the love of Christ does for them:

- John 3:16 _____
- John 10:10 _____
- Romans 6:18 _____

What an incredible experience it is to see a child trust in the Lord, who will never fail him or her, even when the child's body seems to be failing!

Sharing Christ with a child with special needs and leading him or her to faith in Jesus requires people who are passionate about helping others. Read Luke 5:17-26.

- Who were the people in the story? _____
_____

- According to verse 18, what were the men doing?
_____
_____

- What was preventing the men from accomplishing their goal? (See verse 19a.) _____
_____

- How did they finally accomplish their goal? (See verse 19b.) _____
_____

- What did Jesus do for the man? (See verses 20,24-25.)
_____
_____

- How did the man respond to what Jesus did for him? (See verse 25b.) _____
_____

The men who took their friend who was disabled to the Lord were committed to getting him to Jesus. They cared enough to go the extra mile to make sure he saw Jesus, and they found a creative way to get him into the house. That is the kind of people the Church needs to do disability ministry.

For Thought: Think of a creative way to share Christ with a child you know who has a disability.

Lord, speak Your gospel message through me so that children with disabilities will come to know You. Amen.

Lesson 4: Spread the Word

C. Learn the Benefits of Disability Ministry

They gathered the church together and reported all that God had done through them.
Acts 14:27

When we [discover] how rewarding it is to develop relationships with people who are affected by a disability, we will want others to join us . . . [in] this ministry.
Joni and Friends

Garret had never worked with children who are disabled when he volunteered to help with the special needs ministry at his church. At first, he was nervous, but he joined a class where five children were playing in various corners of the room. Within the hour, three of them were sitting next to Garret, listening to him read a book. One particular child struck a chord in his heart.

Ethan was extremely shy, giving Garret a coy smile yet hiding his face every time Garret looked up. The next week when Garret walked into class, Ethan took his hand and led him to the bookshelf, wanting more of Garret's stories. It soon became clear that God was working in Garret's heart through this ministry. His world primarily involved business professionals and a few church acquaintances. But since volunteering, he could hardly wait to be with the children and to give them his love and attention. During a worship service, Garret shared what God was doing in his life, because he wanted the rest of the congregation to experience the joy he had received.

Disability ministry brings glory to God. When we serve Him and obey His commands, God is exalted. God's Word tells us what He wants us as followers of Christ to do for people in our world.

- According to Matthew 28:19-20, what does Jesus command us to do? _____
  He does not want anyone to miss out on knowing Him and having eternal life with Him in heaven (see 2 Peter 3:9).

- Read Matthew 25:31-46. God is also glorified when we care for those who are weak. In verse 40, the King (Jesus) will praise those on His right, saying, "Whatever you did for _____ brothers of mine, you did for me." In verse 41, He will reject those on His left because they refused to help the weak; He will say, "_____ from me."

- In Luke 10:25-37, Jesus told the parable of the good Samaritan, who cared for the wounded man on the roadside. In the end, what did Jesus tell His followers to do? _____

God receives glory when His people obey His Word and do good for others. Not only is God glorified by our good deeds, but also those who minister to people with disabilities are blessed. In Luke 14:13-14, why does Jesus say, "You will be blessed"? _____
_____

Blessings may come in many ways. Those who are disabled can touch our lives in ways we could never have imagined:

- They bring out in us a heart of compassion and love that could only come from Christ (see Romans 5:5).

- Our faith is often challenged and strengthened when we see people affected by disability trusting God with their daily struggles and difficulties.

- When we serve God by serving those in need, we can know that God is pleased with us (see Matthew 25:21).

What are some other ways that individuals with special needs might bless your life? _____
_____
_____

For Thought: Think about a time when a person with disabilities encouraged you.

Lord, help me share the blessing of working with children with special needs with others in my church. Amen.

Lesson 4: Spread the Word

Group Activity Guide

Church Evaluation

As a group, walk through your church and evaluate the accessibility of your church building. Imagine that you have a child with special needs or that you are physically disabled in some way (paralyzed and in a wheelchair or blind or deaf).

- Are the church entrances easily accessible from the parking lot?

- Are doorways throughout the church sufficiently wide and are the doors easy to open?

- Is it possible to get to the nursery or children's Sunday School classes without having to use stairs?

- Are restrooms accessible to individuals in wheelchairs?

- Is there appropriate seating in the sanctuary for people with disabilities? Does your church provide a sign-language interpreter for individuals with a hearing impairment, is there sufficient space for wheelchair users and is the lighting appropriate for those who have difficulty seeing?

- Do ramps have handrails on both sides?

- If your church has more than one level, is there an elevator?

- Does each floor have at least one water fountain that is accessible by people with disabilities?

- Is there easy access to a telephone?

Increase Disability Awareness

As a group, plan several ways to increase disability awareness in your church.

- Conduct a survey to identify which families in your church are affected by disability and to learn what their needs are.

- Sponsor a Disability Awareness Event during which you distribute information about how the church can minister to people and families affected by disability. Also provide an opportunity for interested church members to join the disability ministry of the church.

- Invite a church member whose family is affected by disability to share his or her experiences and insights with Sunday School classes and/or the entire congregation. Invite a Christian who works with people with special needs to do the same thing.

- Form a Bible study group or prayer group for the purpose of learning about disabilities and praying for those in your church who are affected by disability.

Share Testimony

Within your group, have members share testimonies about how God has worked in their lives through disability ministry. Members of your group who have never participated in disability ministry can share about how a disabled person has touched their life or how they have been instrumental in the life of someone who has special needs.

Also ask individuals in the group to share ways they have seen God work in the life of a person affected by disability.

Discuss possible opportunities that people in the group might have to share testimonies about disability ministry with other members of the church.

Pray Together

Pray that the members in your church will be aware of the needs of people and families affected by special needs.

Pray that your church will be ready to respond and minister to those affected by disability.

Real Kids

Stories are bridges that connect our hearts and our cultures.

Pat Verbal

How to Use the Real Stories to Read Aloud

The eight true stories in this section represent the poignant voices of children with special needs such as Down syndrome, cerebral palsy and autism. These children bravely spill out their joys and sorrows in hopes of building bridges to their teachers, their pastors, their peers—to everyone. They want you to know that they are "normal" . . . and yet, so very special!

They hope you will laugh and cry with them as they tell their stories (or as it is told for them) and celebrate their faith in Jesus, who can also meet your every need. But mostly, they long to persuade you with their courage to draw near to them wherever and whenever you meet them. They are tired of feeling discarded by society and by the Church.

In these stories, you will learn that these children follow the psalmist's example of sharing God's faithfulness with anyone who will listen.

I haven't kept to myself that what you did for me was right.

I have spoken about how faithful you were when you saved me.

I haven't hidden your love and truth from the whole community (Psalm 40:10, NIrV).

Will you hear their hearts and cross the bridge to reach children with special needs and their families?

Use these stories in as many ways as you can think of to spread the word. Here are a few ways to get you started:

- Life-application stories in Sunday School, midweek clubs, camps and children's church

- Handouts at ministry fairs to recruit volunteers

- Articles for parent-teacher newsletters

- Devotionals for staff training events

- Examples to inspire your children to write their own stories

Story 1: Madison Atwood Makes Her Father Proud

Looking into the Heart

Who is God? What is God? How did He create everything? These are natural questions every child asks sooner or later. Faith is a difficult concept for adults to grasp, so how can we expect eight- or nine-year-olds to understand it? Yet somehow they do. According to Luke 18:17, Jesus said we cannot enter the Kingdom unless we have the faith of a child. Jeff Atwood wrote a children's book to answer his daughter Madison's questions about God, but she's taught him more than he could ever express about living a life of unabashed faith.

Eleven-year-old Madison has a significant seizure disorder and a mild form of hemiplegic cerebral palsy. She lost the function of about a third of her brain as a result of contracting bacterial meningitis when she was six months old. However, anyone who knows Madison would tell you that she certainly hasn't lost any of her heart and that 100 percent of her heart loves the Lord. Sunday morning worship is the highlight of Madison's week, according to her father.

Jeff laughs when recounting the story of a teacher who called to ask if Madison was a cheerleader, because she walks around with her hands up in the air at school. He explained that she was just singing her favorite praise songs.

"Whatever is in her heart just falls out of her," Jeff said, explaining that Madison has little regard for what others around her think. "It is so honest and pure. She may not have some of the other spiritual gifts, but she certainly has the gift of worship."

Walking by Faith

God used Madison to teach her family to trust Him in spite of circumstances. Jeff and his wife, Annette, served in the children's ministry of their church. Throughout Annette's pregnancy and Madison's initial diagnosis, their church family was incredibly loving and supportive. So Jeff was shocked when the children's minister said the nursery could no longer care for then 18-month-old Madison.

"We were devastated and heartbroken." Jeff said. "We were really involved and had lots of friends. They basically said they wanted us to stay involved, but they didn't have a place for our daughter."

The Atwoods knew they needed a church willing to serve the entire family. God used the situation as an opportunity to prove His sovereignty and plan for something bigger. The children's minister at their new church believed that if God had directed the family to the church, then He could be trusted to also bring the resources and abilities necessary to meet Madison's needs. Jeff said it's a natural tendency to be shortsighted, and many people get nervous around things they're not accustomed to. But difficult situations provide God with an awesome opportunity to reveal Himself.

"The new church didn't really know what to do with Madison either, but the children's pastor had a heart for all children," Jeff said. "He thought about it and found someone to be Madison's helper."

Ten years later, the arrangement to help Madison and to be inclusive of all children has evolved into a special needs ministry called Count Me In. The children with special needs are seen as an integral part of the Body, and as the church prepares to build a new facility, the program's needs have been given high priority.

Focusing on God's Love

Madison's parents have tried to find creative ways to help her learn and deal with her special needs. God has blessed their efforts and turned them into side vocations for both Mom and Dad. Since Madison is a tactile learner, Annette fastened a piece of sheet metal to a wall, so Madison could use magnets. The board was a hit with all children, and following a friend's suggestion, Annette decided to sell a version of it online. Sales have been so good that the website has been successful and now also sells original artwork from both mother and daughter.

One popular painting, *Big Heart, Little Globe*, was a divine accident, according to Jeff. Madison was helping Annette paint a large heart on a canvas, when she dipped her paintbrush into a blue-green color and left a huge glob on the heart. Although Annette's initial reaction was to start over, when she stepped back she realized the glob of paint looked like Earth. With a little fine-tuning, it became a powerful visual of John 3:16. The book Jeff wrote for Madison, *Our Big, Big God*, was published by Little Simon Inspirations in 2007. He wanted to help her understand that God is the creator of everything, and He lovingly cares for each of His creations.

God has shown Himself to be a big, big God to the Atwood family. He used a frightening illness and its repercussions to create a daughter with a heart of gold and has used her to teach others to trust Him and look beyond the obvious.

"God makes all of us different. Some think differently, some can't think as well, some can't walk or run—but God made each of us exactly who we are," Jeff said. "We need to not focus so much on what we see but on the hearts of other people. We can learn so much from each other."

Story 2: Bryce Makes Friends

Bryce Olstad is a young man who has beaten all the odds. At birth, he was given a slim chance of survival. Doctors predicted that if he lived, he would be brain-dead. Yet Bryce is here today to show everyone that he has lived a full and purposeful life in spite of, and because of, spina bifida and being in a wheelchair.

Bryce is an accomplished swing drummer and an expert on all things jazz. He began drumming at age four, using a toy drum set to play along with his dad, a jazz pianist. He possesses an encyclopedic knowledge regarding facts about Native Americans. Bryce is also a studio artist and has sold several of his abstract paintings. He contributes much to his family, church and community. Everyone who knows him enjoys his quirky sense of humor and gentle, caring ways.

Once a week, Bryce's father plays lunchtime music at an assisted living facility. The whole family enjoys accompanying Dad to the facility. While Dad plays, Mom and the kids visit with the residents.

One of the first times Bryce went, he was immediately drawn to an elderly gentleman sitting off by himself. Bryce wheeled his chair next to the man and sat quietly by him. Bryce's mother observed from a distance as they chatted, and she watched as the man offered Bryce some apples and oranges from the fruit bowl in the center of the table.

Suddenly, there was a commotion as several facility employees gathered round, taking pictures of Bryce with the old man. Bryce's mom decided to investigate why these folks were taking pictures of her son. It turned out that this man didn't speak—whatever his condition was, he either couldn't or wouldn't talk—

and he never interacted with people, that is, until Bryce came to visit. Bryce had a profound effect on the elderly gentleman, causing the man to take an interest in his surroundings and another individual for a brief moment. The attendants made a commotion in their eagerness to document this seemingly impossible occurrence.

And that's the type of effect Bryce has on a lot of people. He is drawn to those who are hurting and in need. Whether it's the shoeless, homeless man who slid into the back pew at church or his buddy Jerry who has Parkinson's disease, Bryce takes time to sit and listen to people as they share their feelings. When Jerry had emergency brain surgery, the doctors weren't sure he would survive. One of his last requests on the way to surgery was that Bryce would come see him. Jerry made it through surgery, and Bryce visited soon after.

When Paul, another resident at the assisted living facility, passed away, Bryce's family was surprised to learn that he had requested that any funeral donations be made to the Spina Bifida Association in honor of his friend

Bryce. Bryce's parents never imagined the impact their son was having on the life of this one man who spoke often to his family about Bryce and who often gave little homemade gifts to Bryce. Paul and Bryce visited frequently, including hospital visits when Paul was near the end of his life.

Bryce is always ready to visit people in the hospital. He isn't frightened by the tubes and machines he sees hooked up to his friends. Bryce himself has had almost 30 surgeries and has been in the hospital many times. He's content to sit quietly near a friend's hospital bed, holding a hand or rubbing an arm. Sometimes when patients request no visitors, the patients make sure that the hospital staff and Bryce's parents know that Bryce is an exception. People who know him expect a visit—along with a homemade card—when they are in the hospital.

Bryce is also not frightened when he learns that people he knows are dying. While he's sad, of course, that he won't see them anymore, he's actually very excited that they will go to heaven before him. Bryce has a firm grasp on the concept of heaven, and it is one of his favorite discussion topics.

Once while visiting his grandmother, Bryce expressed sadness that his legs didn't work. Grandma comforted him by talking about heaven and how his new body will be able to run and jump. She joked that her disability was not being able to carry a tune, but in heaven she'll finally be able to sing. Bryce laughed and said, "I'll chase you while you're singing, Grandma." His sorrow eased, and he wheeled off to find something else to do. A while later he quietly came back and said, "Grandma, do you mind if I sit for a while and visit with Jesus first before I chase you?"

Bryce's eagerness for heaven is strong and real, and he's ready to go anytime. What saddens him about death, though, is when he hears of someone who died who didn't love Jesus. He doesn't understand why anyone would not want to live in heaven with the Jesus he loves so much. Once while sitting in church next to his grandmother, the congregation sang the old song "I'll Fly Away." During the chorus, he swooped his hands together in a big motion and shouted, "Come on, Grandma! Let's go right now!" For this child, who has difficulty learning and understanding the world around him, heaven is one concept he clings to, believing in and expecting it with all his might.

So despite doctors who gave Bryce's family no hope at the beginning of his life, he has been used for God's purposes and to His glory. God created Bryce, knitting him together inside his mother. He gifted Bryce with a great personality and with abilities that have encouraged everyone around him on their journey to become more like Christ.

Story 3: Devon's Winning Smile

Like most eight-year-olds, Devon Guerra's bright smile has a few teeth missing. But that is not the first thing people notice when they meet her. What people usually stare at when they see the small girl in a wheelchair is her tracheotomy tube and spastic muscle contractions. However, neighbors in Gilbert, Arizona, who are accustomed to seeing Devon and her family on nightly walks, are drawn to her joyous laughter. Her mom, Traci, calls it Devon's whole-body giggles—they seem to bubble up from deep in her soul.

For a preemie born at 24 weeks, Devon has been incredibly strong through the many surgeries she has endured as a result of having cerebral palsy. Last year she was in pain, but doctors had a difficult time diagnosing the cause. Finally, they found that Devon's hip was dislocated. She underwent major hip surgery and was hospitalized seven times in ten months, missing only five weeks of school. Surgeons also implanted a pump that delivers medication into the fluid around her spinal cord, to help control her muscle contractions.

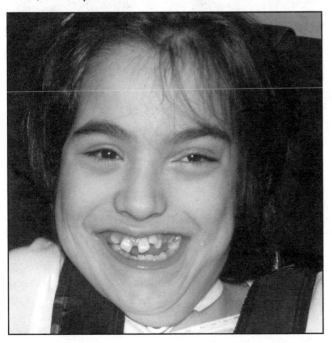

Yet remarkably, Devon's story is not about pain.

Devon's life is about the small everyday events that bring pleasure to the people around her—her parents, Mike and Traci; her school aide, Lorrie; and her sisters, McKayla (age 4) and Rylee (age 18 months). Devon's twin sister died shortly after birth, leaving her parents to cope with grief while at the same time they learned to care for their daughter's disability. They slowly realized that many of their hopes for her would not come true, and they never dreamed she would win an award for the Most Beautiful Smile in her class—but she did! They also never expected her to ride a horse, play in their swimming pool or draw her family to attend a retreat—but she did!

Before Devon was born, her parents rarely attended church. Her disabilities, however, drew them back to worship, and they renewed their relationship with God. Unfortunately, Devon struggled at church because her health did not allow her to attend regularly. When she did go, church seemed unfamiliar to her. She felt left out and sat staring at the other children playing games and eating snacks. So Traci got involved to help her church and others build effective special needs ministries. Early on, Mike and Traci understood that not everyone wanted to be around people with disabilities. They lost some old friends but made new friends at church and through Joni and Friends Family Retreats.

Mike and Traci were nervous about attending their first Family Retreat, which they called Devon's vacation. But they came to realize that they were a part of the disability community, and everyone welcomed them. For the first time, Mike talked to dads with the same issues he experienced, and he was able to share his heart. The love at Family Retreat helped them both understand what God thinks about disability. The retreat was also where Devon rode a horse for the first time. She saw other children like herself, and her excitement grew with each day.

Next to Family Retreat, Devon loves school best. And her very favorite person at school is Lorrie, her classroom aide. Devon is so jealous of Lorrie's attention that she does not like it when Lorrie talks to her classmates. Lorrie helps Devon in her special needs classroom where there are five students with significant multiple disabilities. During music, art and P.E., Devon is mainstreamed into the third-grade class. She loves when Lorrie rapidly pushes her wheelchair in circles in P.E. Before Lorrie retired and became an aide, she worked for a large corporation. Since she and Devon have worked together—for four years now—she says that she now believes this is what she was born to do. Devon might not be able to talk, but her love for Lorrie does not need words.

Devon's parents often wonder what she would say if she could talk. An adaptive communication device, tried in the past, was too difficult to use. Now Devon has an Echo 14 system and is learning to use the switches to give simple answers like yes and no. Who knows the wonderful thoughts she has yet to share? If anyone does, it would be her four-year-old sister, McKayla.

After school, Devon takes a nap and then plays with her sisters. She and McKayla like to have imaginary tea parties. McKayla will ask Devon if she would like some tea, and then she answers for her sister. Devon's face lights up as she tries to form words with her mouth, but no sound comes out. She seems to understand every word as she listens to her sisters around her. She shows them her artwork from school, and they give her hugs and kisses. Big sister Devon even makes crafts for her siblings, who are always delighted to receive her gifts. The three of them enjoy lying on the floor watching TV. To McKayla and Rylee, Devon is a very important part of the family.

Almost every day Devon's smile touches the people she meets, especially those who take the time to get to know her. And it is no surprise when they say they see the love of God in her joyful, innocent eyes. She is definitely doing His work in her world.

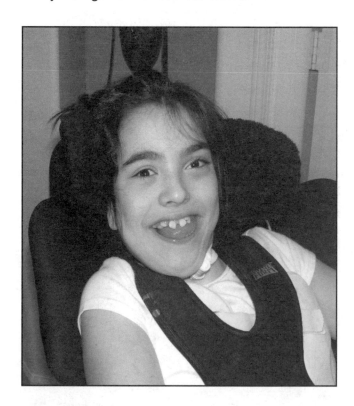

Story 4: My Brother, Willson

by Molly Kantz

My name is Molly Kantz. I live with my mom and dad, whose real names are Arlyn and Will Kantz. I have a brother named Willson who has what is called autism. Before Willson was born, we had a family of four, my Mom, my Dad, my big sister, Grace, and, of course, me! We would play games, dance and my mom would tickle me until I begged her to stop (and then I would beg her to start again).

One day, Mom came home with Willson in her arms. Since I was a one-year-old, I didn't realize that he would make a big difference in my life. Willson acted like a normal baby; he laughed, cried and sometimes he just cooed. But by age two, he had not started to talk like regular toddlers.

At three, his autistic side began to show. Whenever Willson got mad, he would pinch, pull hair and push so hard, you might go flying across the room. Sometimes he did it because he loved me and wanted my attention. But I was a sissy and when he gave me the "I am going to get you" look, I ran to mom.

As Willson turned five, he cried all the time. I think it was because of his disability. I'd cry, too, if I had his problem communicating. My mom says that she has no idea why he did that. Finally, he got better because mom and dad figured out how to use music to help him talk.

It started by Willson talking on a karaoke machine. Soon he was making such good progress that Mom and Dad decided to start a company to help other kids. But the company is a long story; this story is about Willson.

Willson is what they call hyposensitive. That means that he likes to touch everything and to get squeezed. Hypersensitive kids don't want to be hugged or kissed. They don't even go swimming or take a bath, because they're sensitive to water. Since Willson is hyposensitive, he jumps on me, pinches me and squeezes me. He also gets under the covers with me and everyone else, too.

As Willson grew older, Mom heard that changing eating habits might help cure autism. She thought that our whole-wheat bread was the reason. So she changed from our regular bread to this strange bread called garfava bread, which tastes awful. And that's not the worst of it. We had it every day—at picnics, at home and everywhere. It felt good when mom finally switched to good-tasting bread.

Willson loves to play computer games and watch television. His favorite website is pbskids.org. His favorite TV shows are *Bugs Bunny, Snow White, Bambi, Pinocchio* and *Teletubbies.* His favorite computer games are *JumpStart 1st Grade, SmartSteps 1st Grade*

and *Smart-Steps 2nd Grade*, *Living Books* and *My Amazing Human Body*. Willson memorizes everything he sees. But he doesn't like being told no, or hair driers, macaroni and cheese and sound frequencies that he cannot control. Of course, if he can control the sound, he loves it. One day we went on a walk and passed a guy mowing his lawn. Willson covered his ears and ran, because he was afraid of the noise. But he loves the sound of the vacuum, and vacuuming is his hobby. Mom enjoys the clean house.

Willson enjoys going to church. When we stand up to sing, Willson sings out nice and strong. But during children's choir, he sings too loud and is reminded to quiet down. When he listens to the sermon, Willson always gets fidgety.

During his Sunday School, Willson blurts out things that his teachers don't understand, because he can't control his words. Mom started a classroom for kids with autism that has music, Bible lessons, and playtime. It is a fun place for him to hang out.

Willson does have some bad habits. He has pulled out practically all of his eyelashes and all of his eyebrows. He has a big bald spot on his head where he pulled out his hair and ate it. Willson also picks his nose and puts his finger in his ear. Yuck!

Sometimes at night when Willson has a temper tantrum, I lie down with him to calm him down. So now, every night, Willson drags me to his bed, so I'll read Bugs Bunny comic books. Sometimes he pulls me outside to play on the seesaw that he made all by himself. He made it out of an upside-down table and two planks of wood. He also makes me recite lines from *Daffy Duck,* so he can recite the other character.

Now that Willson is nine, he talks more often. He says, "May I have it please?" When we cuddle, he says, "heart," which means "love" to him. Every once in a while he brings Mom the telephone and says "call" so Mom asks, "Who do you want to call?" and Willson says who he wants to call. He doesn't throw his tantrums anymore for no reason.

I am much tougher because of Willson. Not to mention that I can slip out of most anyone's grip. Also I am better at wrestling and can withstand pain. I have amazed my friends with my patience. They call me if Willson is being mean, and I calm him down. I think God put autistic kids on Earth to make us wish for heaven where everything will be perfect. Just like paralyzed people who have never danced before will dance in heaven, kids with autism will be able to tell us their thoughts and opinions.

Even though I wouldn't choose for Willson to have autism, it has been a good influence on me and my family.

I love my brother, even if he does have autism!

Story 5: I Just Needed a Chance

by Sizwe David Mabowe

My name is Sizwe David Mabowe. I am 13 years old. My first name means "the nation." Dad is from Cape Town, South Africa, and Mom is an African-American. I am the true African-American! It was sad when Mom and Dad divorced, but Mommy takes good care of me, and Dad picks me up on occasions.

My Disability

When I was three years old, the University of California, Los Angeles, diagnosed me with autism and mental retardation. I had seizures at least five times a week, cried when Mommy combed my hair, suffered from behavior problems and was very destructive. At age seven, I painted graffiti on a wall inside my church. Pastor phoned and the next thing you knew, I had a bucket of white paint so that I could correct my mistake. After finishing the job, Pastor gave me a bear hug, and a white canvas to draw on the next time I felt creative. Thinking back, maybe he knew I did not know any better. I forget all my wrong behavior, but Mommy's cry for help remains in my mind.

The Los Angeles School District and Westside Regional Center helped a lot. The most exciting part of the Regional Center was summer camp: Disneyland, Raging Waters, barbeques, relay races and basketball—all free of charge! I had a good ole time. Not to mention how helpful it was for Mom, since she was alone. After years of assistance, the echolalia disappeared. I learned language, and my cold glazed eyes turned into moonlight warmth. My temper tantrums reduced, and I began to improve.

Presently, I am in the Ventura County School District. My disability has changed from severe retardation to mild. Mom says God healed some of my disability. As a boy with autism, language, reading, writing and thinking skills are still difficult. I often hear Mommy use the word "cognitive." Go figure! I have no physical disabilities, so it is easier to make friends. I still feel lonely when I cannot keep up with the conversation. I wish they knew special things about me.

My Struggles

It takes time to understand questions that are more than 10 words long. What works better is when people only give me five-word sentences. Usually, I can think through what they are asking me and not get confused. When I am confused, my brain really hurts, and I can't respond to anything. Over time, Mom learned ways to help me. One day, she told me to take my shoes to the room, clean up the bedroom and then come downstairs, so we could begin homework. At that point, BRAIN OVERLOAD, so I sat in my room and did nothing. Although she was a bit upset, Mom realized she had given me too many tasks. I could not think of what to do first and could not find the words to ask her. There are times when homework assignments that may take some kids two hours will take me four hours to complete. My confusion makes me sad sometimes, but it is wonderful when people are patient and praise me when I do get things right. I guess everyone wants to be encouraged.

What Makes Me Happy

My brain feels free when I have fun with my friends playing football, dodge ball and mastering video-game levels. Sometimes my cousins ask me to help them unlock codes, so they can master the games. I have the best time with my family. They treat me like the rest of the kids. I do wonder what it would be like to think clearly like everyone else. I often ask God about my autism, and He answers me through others.

My Sister

Brooke is the best sister I could ever have—but not always. She was ashamed and never told her friends about me. Brooke worried over our mom being alone and the icing on the cake included a brother with special needs. I longed for a close relationship, but she showed no love whatsoever. Brooke screwed up in middle school, so Mom sent her to live with our aunt in Ventura County. During that time, Brooke started missing me and was ashamed for not being more loving. Two years later, Mommy and I joined Brooke in Newbury Park, California. Right away, she realized I changed. She never thought I would get better. Wow! Our relationship soared like a bird in the sky. My sister is finally caring for me with lots of love. Brooke and I play video games, tag (my favorite) and talk about the latest television shows. Now I know she loves me, because I help her to be patient. She is fast, and I am slow. We need each other.

My Faith, My Church, My God

I love Jesus. He has given me the gift to pray. You may not always understand everything I am saying, but the Spirit does, and Mommy is always shouting hallelujahs when I am praying. Often I read my teen Bible and thank God for healing my mind. I attend Lighthouse Christian Fellowship in Newbury Park, California. Two Sundays a month, I am a youth assistant for the kindergartners. We paint, perform plays, read God's Word and sing songs. They love it when I make paper models, especially paper balls and birds of paradise. I am happy when they are excited to see me. I also sing in the gospel choir every three months. One of these days, I will sing a solo. God has given me a voice like an angel. I pray he will use it to bless many people. I am so glad God protects and helps me think, speak and understand.

Story 6: God's Design for Me

by Rachel Yonker

Click, click, click went God's knitting needles the day He created me. He picked out a special knitting pattern for me. He also picked out a one-of-a-kind design for you. Before we were born, God planned how we would look and how we would act. He figured out some things that would be easy for us to do and some that would be hard. Maybe I can meet you someday and talk about you. Today, I want to tell you about me—I'm Rachel.

When I was born, God picked out my blonde hair and blue eyes, and placed me in the Yonker family. I live in a house in Michigan with Mom, Dad and my brother, Nathan. Sometimes Dad drives the car and pulls our camper to Lake Michigan. I like to go camping. My favorite thing about camping is playing on the sandy beach by the big lake.

God's design for me might be a lot like yours. Maybe you like camping, too. My favorite food is pizza. Do you eat pizza? I like to play with my dolls and read books. My favorite places to visit are the park or the store. We may have many things that are the same, but some are different.

God uses building blocks called chromosomes in our knitting patterns. Most people have 46 chromosomes; I have 47. When I was born, doctors told my mom and dad that I had Down syndrome. Down syndrome makes some things easy for me and some things difficult.

One really easy thing for me might be hard for you. I can put the bottom of my foot by my ear and talk on it like a telephone. I can even talk on my other foot at the same time! I am very flexible, but my muscles are not very strong muscles. The muscles in my mouth and tongue are especially tricky, so sometimes people don't understand all of my words. My finger muscles are weak, so I work extra hard to write my name and to stay in the lines when I color. Someday I would really like to ride a bike, but now my leg muscles are too weak. I guess we all have hard things and easy things to do every day. Those are some of mine.

I'm in second grade at Zeeland Christian School. I have lots of friends at my school. Every day I have two buddies who play outside with me. Sometimes I take my dolls outside and give them a ride on the swing. Playing dolls and reading are two of my favorite things to do at school.

Most of my classmates read big words and giant books. I can read, too, but my books are

smaller. My favorite story is called *The Hat.* It is about a girl who loses her hat on a sled. In Michigan, we go sledding at recess during the winter. I try not to lose my hat going downhill with my buddies! I had surgery on my heart when I was little, and sometimes I get very cold outside. My buddies come inside with me.

I go to Haven Church on Sunday and sit with Mom and Dad. Then I go to a room with other kids in second grade. We sing, listen to Bible stories, make crafts and pray. I don't always understand all the words, but my special buddy helps me with important parts of the story. My friends help me when crafts are tough, but I help them, too. I'm a great singer and get excited when the music starts. I like to pray for my friends. Other people don't always know the words I say, but God does. I know my friends at church like me, because they sit by me.

Sometimes at the park or store, people do things that make God sad. He spent time knitting me together before I was born. He made me—Rachel. But when people look at me, they don't see God's work in me. They see that I'm different. People have laughed at me and asked me to go away, because I have Down syndrome. God is sad when people laugh at the pattern He picked out for me. I am like everybody else. God made me, He loves me, and He sent Jesus, so I could be in His family.

I look for times when people run up to me at school or in the park and invite me to play, because that makes God happy. They are glad to be with me and argue over who gets to sit by me or be my buddy that day. When they see me, they don't see Down syndrome. They see Rachel—a girl who loves to have fun, read stories, shop and play with dolls and go swimming at the beach. Friends know I need extra help and that I can help them right back. I can also make them smile with my funny words and jokes. They like God's pattern in me, and I like how God made them, too.

If I visited your church, would you be my friend? Other children like me might visit your church, too. Maybe you have a friend who plays basketball from a wheelchair, because his leg muscles don't work, or someone who uses her fingers to read a Bible with raised dots for letters, because her eyes can't see the words. Whatever God's patterns are for people, you can make God smile by becoming friends and learning to help one another.

Click, click, click! That could be the sound of God's knitting needles making a new friend who He'll send to your church. Will you make God smile?

[The image of God's knitting comes from Psalm 139:13-14. The idea about making God smile comes from His direction in Romans 15:7. Editor]

Story 7: Wakeland Is on the Go

You have heard it said that today's children are overscheduled, but eight-year-old Wakeland Stickens is making up for the lost time he spent in two body casts. The symptoms of his disability resemble cerebral palsy but they are mainly muscular. At the age of three, Wakeland underwent an adductor muscle-release surgery that put him in a cast for 33 days. His parents and grandparents were especially concerned about him after this surgery because he cried so much, and they didn't really understand why. The reason for the many tears became clear when the cast was removed: His body was covered with terrible bedsores.

A few years later, Wakeland's hips began to come out of their sockets, so surgeons cut his femur and hip bones to rotate them into place. He was again put into a body cast—this one from his upper torso to his toes—but this cast he was better able to cope with. In fact, although he had to lie almost flat in a large stroller for seven weeks, he still played water guns with the boys next door! Since the surgeries, Wakeland has been able to give up his walker (except for long walks) and now uses crutches. At home, he walks unaided.

The first Sunday Wakeland walked into his second-grade class with his new crutches, everyone cheered. Mrs. Morton, his Sunday School teacher, says he is one of her most creative students, because his mind is constantly thinking and planning. Once when his class took turns leading "Mother May I?" Wakeland told everyone with pockets to step forward. While his friends were calling for those wearing red or blue, he was thinking about pockets. When Mrs. Morton's husband came to class using a walker after his surgery for bone cancer, Wakeland challenged him to a race.

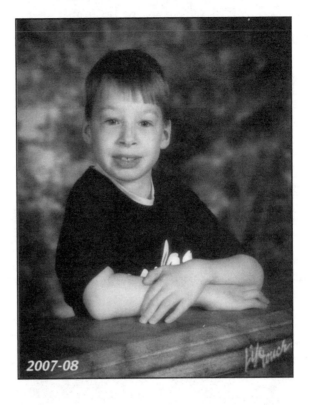

2007-08

Children with physical disabilities like Wakeland's use their mind to stay in the game, and Wakeland is particularly good at it. He did not start talking until the age of three, but he has since learned to be a good conversationalist. His mom, Joanna, said it took Wakeland a lot of repetition to learn everyday routines such as dressing himself. But his favorite activity is wrestling on the floor with his dad, Kyle, and the wrestling has a second benefit: It builds up his weak muscles. Fine-motor skills such as writing are still difficult, so at church, Mrs. Morton assists Wakeland with writing activities.

At Taylor Elementary School in Frisco, Texas, Wakeland is in a functional academic class with a pull-out schedule for music, adaptive P.E., and regular subject classes. Through his school, Wakeland participates in the Special Olympics, which builds his self-esteem and confidence. Sometimes other children make fun of him, because he drools (he wears a bandana that needs to be changed regularly). But he does not let that stop him from serving Jesus wherever he goes. And this cheerful car lover is always on the go! Zoom! Zoom! Zoom!

Wakeland's bedroom walls are covered with posters of cars and trucks, including his favorites: Lightning McQueen and Speed Racer. When he met Antonio on his baseball team in the Miracle League, he invited him over to build Lego cars. Antonio, who has scoliosis of the spine, had surgery to insert a steel rod in his back. But the site of the surgery did not heal and the rod had to be removed. The day after the procedure, Wakeland visited his friend at the Texas Scottish Rite Hospital for Children in Dallas, which is where Wakeland also had his surgeries. And what do you think Wakeland took Antonio? A new Speed Racer!

The Texas Scottish Rite Hospital for Children, which practices a multidisciplinary approach to care, is one of the world's leading pediatric orthopedic centers. Since it was established in 1912, it has treated more than 180,000 children. For the Stickens family, Scottish Rite has been a tremendous blessing by creating a child-friendly environment and meeting their son's special needs. Without this great hospital's free services, children like Wakeland could not reach their full potential.

In addition to making hospital visits, Wakeland ministers in schools and at a mission called Samaritan's Inn. His parents started Retread

Ministry to provide shoes and after-school care for children in low-income neighborhoods. Wakeland is part of the team, playing with children who are homeless or who just need a friend.

Wakeland can't remember a time when he was not in church. His parents were Christians before he was born. And while they feel accepted at church, they admit there are times when they still feel lonely. They wish their church would include Wakeland in more appropriate ways during times of transition or programs in the sanctuary. For example, one Sunday as the children lined up to sing from the platform, Wakeland could not get up the stairs. No one thought to provide a ramp for his walker. Another time, the church planned a Disability Awareness Sunday and invited children with special needs to sit on the front row to be introduced. But during the service, the pastor forgot to acknowledge them. Someone called that afternoon to apologize. It made Kyle and Joanna sad, but not much gets Wakeland down.

Whether playing baseball in the Miracle League, visiting friends at the Scottish Rite Hospital or playing with children in need, Wakeland is usually happy. He has many friends, and more importantly, he knows God loves him. His parents' hopes for him are the same as what other parents have for their children: to do well in school, get a job, have a family and find his passion in his relationship with Jesus. For now, Wakeland's busy lifestyle has great purpose.

Story 8: Keiler's New Wheelchair

To visit Keiler, you must travel by boat and train to Jesus de Otoro, which is one of the poorest cities in central Honduras. You will not need a jacket because this is the warm, humid part of South America. The area is filled with tropical trees, and you can smell the sweet orchids that grow in colorful gardens throughout the region. The people there are mestizo (a mix of European and American Indian ancestry), and most are Roman Catholic. The average family makes less than $1,000 per year, growing crops such as coffee and bananas.

Keiler's Christian school is made of concrete blocks, and there are bars on the windows to prevent theft. You will find him in a crowded, energy-filled classroom where the students speak both Spanish and English. You will not have trouble picking Keiler out because he will be the one sitting in a shiny, sporty wheelchair that he received from Wheels for the World. His classmates will probably be crowded around him, laughing and playing. Keiler is popular among his peers, because he is animated and feisty—but he was not always this way.

Keiler's teacher has known his family since he was a baby. He was born with spina bifida and could not sit up by himself. His teacher said that Keiler used to keep to himself and hardly spoke. No one knew that he had a bright smile. Most of the time, he did not even try to participate because he had to crawl on the floor or be carried. But when he was six years old, a Wheels for the World team came to Jesus de Otoro and fitted Keiler with his first wheelchair. They also told him about the love of Jesus and gave him a Bible. These gifts brought an instant smile to Keiler's face and amazing changes to his life. Sitting upright for the first time, he felt secure and eagerly explored the scope of his new freedom. Instead of feeling ashamed that his father had to carry him to school, he began to look forward to wheeling through the city. People would wave to him as he pushed himself along. It was as though his wheelchair made it possible for him to be truly alive.

Local missionaries came to Keiler's school and built ramps that allow him to move around with ease. Then they did the same thing at his house. Soon, Keiler was racing to the blackboard in class to answer written questions. He played circle games with his friends at recess, moving his wheelchair like a pro. He even began to take an interest in soccer, which is

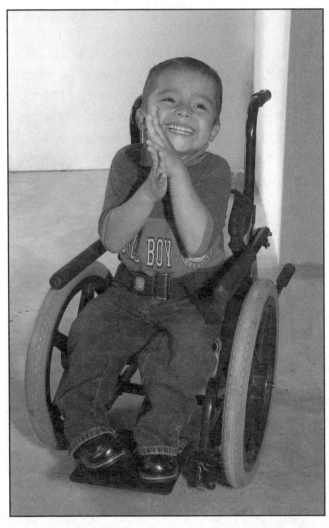

the most popular sport in his country. Everyone was astonished at the impact the wheelchair made on him—he participated in every activity with gusto. Keiler's classmates were equally impressed by how the wheelchair quickly became second nature to him. And as their attitudes toward him changed, Keiler felt more accepted.

Four years later, Keiler received his second wheelchair from his friends at Wheels for the World, because he had outgrown the first one. And his excitement was contagious. It took him only moments to realize that his new wheels were faster and better than his old ones. Wheels for the World mechanics made the needed adjustments, so the new chair fit Keiler just right. And it's easy to see that there are no longer any barriers between Keiler and his classmates. In fact, they line up to take rides in Keiler's chair.

With a wheelchair in their midst, all the children in Keiler's neighborhood have experienced an awareness that comes from love, not from programs. Their fears of people with disabilities have also disappeared. They have leaped far ahead of their parents in understanding. They have begun to shape a new culture.

Keiler's wheelchair has taken him out of the darkness. He is now filled with light and joy. He has touched his whole community, especially his parents, who are no longer shy or ashamed to have a son with a disability. They are proud to take Keiler to town in his wheelchair, and they hold their head up high. Their son has become a bright light revealing God's hand in their lives. And their family verse is now Ephesians 3:20: "Now to him who is able to do immeasurably more than all we ask or imagine, according to his power that is at work within us."

Everywhere Keiler goes, he tells others about the kind people who not only gave him a wheelchair once but did so a second time. These people also did more than just drop off a piece of equipment. These Christians started a friendship that continues with Keiler and his family; and they follow his progress, so he can become all his heavenly Father created him to be.

Wheels for the World intends that children like Keiler will dream, grow and develop as God designed and become bright lights to their communities and change agents in the world.

Disability Awareness

I will pour out my Spirit on your offspring, and my blessing on your descendants.

Isaiah 44:3

Awareness: United States Disability Statistics

How many people with disabilities attend religious services at least once a month?

About 47 percent attend religious services at least once per month, compared to 65 percent of nondisabled Americans.

(Source: The National Organization on Disability. Religious Participation: Facts and Statistics. http://www.nod.org/religion/index.cfm)

How many adults with disabilities seek pastoral care?

About 26 percent of American adults who seek pastoral care have disabilities. At 8.1 percent, people with disabilities are more than twice as likely as nondisabled persons (4 percent) to seek pastoral care.

(Source: The National Organization on Disability. Religious Participation: Facts and Statistics. http://www.nod.org/religion/index.cfm)

How many people in the United States have disabilities?

About 54 million people in America (20.6 percent) live with some level of disability. Of these, 26 million have a severe disability.

(Source: Disability Statistics Center. Frequently Asked Questions: How Many Americans Have a Disability? http://dsc.ucsf.edu/UCSF/spl.taf?_from=default)

How many people need personal assistance?

About 9 million people of all ages need personal assistance for everyday activities.

(Source: U.S. Department of Commerce, Census Brief. December 1997)

How many people in the United States use wheelchairs?

About 1.6 million Americans use wheelchairs.

(Source: Disability Statistics Center. Frequently Asked Questions: How Many Americans Use Wheelchairs and Other Assistive Devices or Technologies? http://dsc.ucsf.edu/UCSF/spl.taf?_from=default)

How many people in the United States use assistive devices or technologies?

Canes are used by about 4.8 million Americans. Hearing aides are used by about 4.2 million Americans. Walkers are used by about 1.8 million Americans. Wheelchairs are used by about 1.6 million Americans.

(Source: National Center for Health Statistics. FASTATS A to Z: Disabilities and Impairments. http://www.cdc.gov/nchs)

How are assistive devices or technologies paid for?

About 48 percent are paid for by the user or with family support; about 53 percent are paid for by a third party (e.g., a government agency or a foundation).

(Source: Disability Statistics Center. Frequently Asked Questions: How do Americans Fund Their Assistive Technology? http://dsc.ucsf.edu/UCSF/spl.taf?_from=default)

How do American women and men differ in terms of disability?

More American women (15.4 percent) than men (14.6 percent) are limited in daily-living activities.

(Source: Disability Statistics Center. Frequently Asked Questions: How Do American Men and Women Differ in Terms of Disability? http://dsc.ucsf.edu/UCSF/spl.taf?_from=default)

How many American children have disabilities?

About 4 million American children under the age of 18 years of age have special needs. Of those needs, 58.4 percent are attributed to diseases and disorders and 41.6 percent to impairments.

(Source: Disability Statistics Center. Abstract 15: Disabilities Among Children. March 1996. http://dsc.ucsf.edu/UCSF/spl.taf?_from=default)

How many people in the United States have visual or hearing impairments?

Over 8 million Americans have visual impairments. Over 34 million Americans have hearing impairments.

(Source: National Center for Health Statistics. FASTATS A to Z: Disabilities and Impairments. http://www.cdc.gov/nchs)

How many people in the United States have speech impairments?

Almost 2.7 million Americans have speech impairments.

(Source: National Center for Health Statistics. FASTATS A to Z: Disabilities and Impairments. http://www.cdc.gov/nchs)

How many Americans have mental disorders or disabilities?

According to a 1990 census, 6.2 to 7.5 million Americans are mentally retarded in some way. Mental retardation is 28 times more common than congenital spinal-cord disabilities.

(Source: The Arc. Introduction to Mental Retardation. www.thearc.org)

How many Americans have spinal cord injuries?

Anywhere from 250,000 to 400,000 Americans live with an injury to or dysfunction of the spinal cord.

(Source: National Spinal Cord Injury Association. Spinal Cord Injury Statistics. www.spinalcord.org)

Culture: Divorce Threatens Families Affected by Disability

Combine the stresses of raising a child with special needs with the trauma of divorce, and you'll get an emotionally numb single parent. Although some newly divorced parents cope admirably with their new circumstance, many others remain overwhelmed or emotionally stuck for years.

No one emerges from a divorce unscathed. Divorce can impair an individual's emotional well-being for years and can produce longer-lasting negative emotions than widowhood. It can administer the greatest emotional pain a parent will experience in his or her lifetime. Divorce radically impacts lifestyle, personal identity, family structure and family roles. And, usually, along with its psychological and emotional trauma comes economic hardship.

Single Parents Need to Connect

A divorced parent's greatest need is to have a variety of healthy, ongoing relationships. Though single parents may also need such things as financial support, special services and therapies, strong friendships within their church can be vital in combating their long, painful, lonely journey.

Be sensitive and respect each parent's unique challenges. Unless you have raised a child with a disability alone, don't say you know how the parent feels. Avoid relating stories of other people's divorces or children. And do not treat the parent like a victim. Instead, encourage the parent to grow and to have confidence in God's promises to help him or her make decisions and move forward.

When Hal's wife left him with their three children, she said she could no longer handle the stress of their daughter's disabilities. Hal felt that he had no choice but to move his family to another state to be near his parents. While the children seemed to handle well their new home and new caregivers, Hal's broken heart over his beautiful wife cast a dark shadow over their lives. Only after four years of counseling and the support of his men's Bible study did Hal recover and become the dad that he felt he was before the divorce.

Single Parents Need Time Out

People who are divorced may come across as extremely upset and emotional. They might struggle to communicate their needs and wants. If you tell them to call you if they need anything, they probably won't. But you can come alongside them with specific invitations involving everyday activities:

- Can we go for a walk together?
- May I pick up something for you at the store?
- When can we meet for lunch?

Although they may decline your invitation, they'll appreciate being asked.

Single Parents Need Perspective

You can encourage single parents by praising their children. Sometimes the daily stress of life causes a loss of perspective. Your positive comments about their child may be a refreshing reminder to parents to enjoy their children just as they are—God's greatest gifts. This liberal praise at church can also remind members that children with special needs are not projects or cases to be solved but human beings with endearing strengths and common weaknesses.

Single Parents Need a Break

Single parents of children with special needs deeply cherish weekly worship services. This break to focus on God is one of the most important ministries a church can give them. *Do not ask these parents to volunteer in the special needs ministry.* Even if they are professionals or therapists working in the field, they are each a parent first. Ask for input and ideas, ask for help in training staff, but do not ask them to volunteer in the classroom. They may feel obligated to help; assure them they are not.

Single Parents Need Balance

Help single parents become educated in using a support system of friends and professionals. Remind them to pace themselves—to focus on running a marathon not a sprint—and to keep a healthy balance. It is scary to have to acknowledge a diagnosis that has no available cure or easy treatment. Remind them of Jesus' promise in Matthew 11:28: "Come to me, all you who are weary and burdened, and I will give you rest." Encourage them to allocate time for rest as well as a variety of activities.

Single Parents Need to Know They're a Blessing

Involvement in ministry and community is not optional for single parents raising children with disabilities. They cannot be allowed to hide, apologize or feel as if they or their child is an inconvenience. After a period of receiving ministry, these parents must be encouraged to discover and use their spiritual gifts to serve the Body of Christ. They may help educate others about children with disabilities or serve in missions, choir, teaching, visiting the elderly, etc. In order to form lasting relationships, the foundation cannot be based on caretaking; each relationship must be a friendship of independent equals. Without proper nurturing, single parents may give in to the role of victim and forget what they have to offer in return. Empower single parents by treating them as equals. No one needs or wants to be on the receiving end forever.

Single Parents Need Practical Ideas

- Offer child care, so parents get needed private time.
- Contribute anonymous financial help.
- Let them vent without attempting to fix or psychoanalyze them.
- Allow for dark humor (tragic, overwhelming subjects being joked about), as this reminds them they can laugh.
- Don't offer platitudes and easy formulaic answers.
- Ask the parent and children to your home for a meal to let them enjoy a family atmosphere.

- Study to gain a working knowledge of the child's disability and to make a connection, but don't make treatment recommendations.
- Remember these families during holidays. Extended family often does not know how to cope either with the dynamic of divorce or the child with special needs.
- Notice and celebrate progress in a child's skills.
- Take nondisabled siblings underwing by making sure they are included and have money and transportation for events geared toward them.

You must come alongside hurting, divorced parents of children with special needs. Through friendship and caring you can powerfully minister to the needs of both children and adults. You can understand the many difficulties facing these single-parent families and reach out to help heal hurting hearts. Feeling the stigma that society applies to those who go through a divorce and to those with a child who has special needs can overwhelm and alienate single parents. As you lovingly work to restore and encourage them, they can reach their full potential. It will take education and effort, but remember that every time a single-parent family walks through the doors of your church, Jesus is saying, "You do not choose me, but I chose you and appointed you to go and bear fruit—fruit that will last (John 15:16)."

Culture: Whatever Happened to the Sanctity of Life?

In order to understand what happened to the sanctity-of-life principle in medicine, we have to consider a bit of Western medical history. There is a long tradition in Western medical ethics that can be traced back to Hippocrates in approximately the fifth century B.C. The traditional Western ethic was informed by an absolute respect for the sanctity of life, and this notion supported the ethics of medicine. In fact, the Hippocratic Oath reads, "I will neither give a deadly drug to anybody who asked for it, nor will I make a suggestion to this effect. Similarly I will not give to a woman an abortive remedy. In purity and holiness I will guard my life and my art."

The Influence of Early Judeo-Christianity

Hippocratic medicine closely linked healing and morality. Hippocratic doctors were concerned with such questions as, Who is a good person? What do good persons do to become good? How does the good person contribute to the good of the society? The Hippocratic Oath was adopted by the Judeo-Christian tradition, and it strongly influenced medicine in the West. In the Middle Ages, as medicine began to be taught in universities, an emphasis on social ethics began to develop. This social ethic informed the ethical codes produced by the American Medical Association from 1847 through the twentieth century.

Ethical codes soon became synonymous with rules for professional conduct. The shift of care to the hospital, the use of ancillary professions and the influence of biological sciences also led to an emphasis on an ethic of competence. At this point, medical ethics quickly moved from a virtue to a utilitarian ethic. Clinical competence then became the center of medical education and even medical ethics. Nevertheless, from the early to the mid-twentieth century, there was still a general consensus that the classical Hippocratic Oath defined the conduct appropriate of a good physician.

The Influence of Modern Science

Modern developments and new technologies in medicine, however, forced society in the 1960s to call for a new ethic. This led to the creation of bioethics, which challenged the sanctity of life because it was no longer clear what is beneficial and what is harmful. Impersonal machines began to separate physicians and patients, and the sanctity-of-life principle was undermined. While physicians appreciated the Hippocratic saying "Life is short, the art long, opportunity fleeting, experience treacherous,

judgment difficult," they seldom seemed bothered by the many new moral dilemmas. This is one of the fundamental differences between the medical ethics of the past and the bioethics of the present.

More and more questions arose in the practice of medicine, and the sanctity-of-life principle was further questioned: Shall we keep someone alive who is in a persistent vegetative state? Is it harmful to experiment on a dying person if it will create better ways of curing disease? Who will pay for those who cannot pay? The growing intricacy and interweaving of medicine with government, commerce and producers of new technologies added to the discord. And professional authority was also challenged at every turn. What began in the 1960s led to a crisis in the medical conscience itself.

What can be done about this ethical mess? New intellectual and spiritual resources are needed to deal with numerous new questions: What is "benefit"? What is "harm"? Who should live? Who should die? Who should have access to scarce resources? Who should decide? The good news is that these questions provide abundant opportunities to share the gospel. When people come face-to-face with their own mortality, the illusion of control is shattered. Where ought people to turn for help concerning the unprecedented choices presented to them by modern medicine? If Christians become a reliable source of information and guidance on these issues, opportunities to share a Christian view of life, meaning, suffering and death will present themselves. Only in this way can we revive and restore the sanctity-of-life principle.

The Theology of Human Life

The Bible makes it clear that all human beings are made in the image of God. After the Fall, this image became deeply marred, but it was never lost. Human beings turned away from God and became His enemies by nature. By the redemptive work of Christ, God graciously restored His image in human beings, making their will and desire one with His. He accomplishes this incredible work through the work of His sovereign grace.

All human life is a gift from God and ought to be cherished for that reason alone. That all human life has value can be seen in the biblical picture of a God who cares for the weakest among us. This revelation ought to guide our treatment of the sick, the disabled, the very young and the very old.

In contemporary bioethics, the value of human life is often measured by quality of life. The lives of the disabled may be considered of lesser value than others. Believers recognize that all human life is of equal worth regardless of capacities, but this does not mean that we never take into consideration quality-of-life issues. But quality-of-life issues must always be weighed and evaluated under the umbrella of the absolute sanctity of life.

A biblical view of justice directs our attention to the weakest and most vulnerable in our midst. Those who practice biblical justice recognize the equal worth of every human being, and they are aware of the requirement that the basic life-sustaining needs of all must be met. Not many think that the praise, thanksgiving and confession that take place in a church service have any connection to bioethical challenges faced on a daily basis. But openly praising God for His creativity in creation, thanking Him for defeating death on the cross, and confessing our lack of interest in helping others all are intimately related to bioethics.

By limiting bioethics to the scholars, we miss an opportunity to show the people of God the connection between bioethics and their faith in Christ.

An effective way to reach out to the community is to provide examples of sound biblical bioethical decision making. Another way to engage society is to challenge popular views in bioethics. There are many ways in which secular and Christian bioethics intersect, and these provide an opportunity to engage Christian apologetics.

The Influence of the Church

The Church ought to speak out against injustice and on behalf of those who cannot speak for themselves. Thus, the Church ought to engage in bioethical decision making, not only on an individual level, but also on social and political levels. The Church is called to be a prophetic voice in all matters pertaining to society and culture. We must go and make disciples of all nations, teaching them to obey everything Christ commanded. This means we also must engage in the debate about bioethics. For in this way, caring for the least and most vulnerable among us—that is, people with disabilities—will be ensured.

References

Jonsen, Albert, R., *The Birth of Bioethics* (New York: Oxford University Press, 1998).

Claydon, David, series ed. "Bioethics: Obstacle or Opportunity for the Gospel?" Lausanne Occasional Paper No. 58, *Lausanne Committee for World Evangelization*, 2005.

http://www.lausanne.org/documents/2004forum/LOP58_IG29.pdf (accessed July 3, 2008).

Culture: Understanding Bioethics

Bioethics can be quite confusing. The experts often use lofty medical terms, which they try to explain in a sound bite. The average person is left with the suspicion that what was said is vitally important, but they are at a loss to figure out what that might be. Sadly, the average pastor might not be able to shed light on the issues either.

Simply stated, bioethics is the study of the ethical implications—in essence, what is morally good and bad—of research and development, especially in medicine. It is an umbrella term that encompasses ethical issues involved with everything from health care to emerging biotechnologies. One area of medicine that has been recently in the forefront over the past decade is genetics.

What the Bible Says About Genetics

The Scriptures do not specifically address such medical technologies as those involved in genetics; nevertheless, the clear scriptural teachings concerning human nature offer at least these important general guidelines:

> To move in the direction of healing in medicine is compatible with the redemptive work of Christ, who, by taking on human nature, affirmed the inherent worth and dignity of all human beings. His overall mission was to reconcile human beings to God by healing and restoring the image of God in them through His sovereign grace.

> Thus medical technologies that take into consideration the inherent dignity of all human beings regardless of abilities and that tend to promote healing may, on the face of it, be considered morally and biblically sound; medical technologies that undermine human dignity by considering usefulness and not the capacity to love may hinder the healing process for some and thus should be considered morally and biblically questionable.

Over the past several decades, there has been an explosion in new genetic technologies. The Human Genome Project (HGP), which was completed in 2001, mapped the entire human genetic code. The HGP gave scientists an abundance of new genetic information, which has raised serious questions concerning patient privacy. The fear is that this kind of information, if not properly protected, could be used for discrimination purposes on many levels. But there is more to be concerned about than merely protecting patient privacy. There has been a plethora of new genetic tests made available, especially to pregnant women, which have raised concerns not only about privacy but also about personhood.

There is a popular view that the essence of who we are can be reduced to our genes. It has been suggested by one Harvard professor that the genome is the "holy grail" of human identity and that it provides the ultimate answer to the age-old command "Know thyself." The enormous advances in genetics have given support to such a materialist view of the human being. According to this view, the concept of personhood can be defined solely by certain physical and mental abilities. If this is true, then personhood can indeed be lost.

A couple of things can be said here. First, the Bible makes it abundantly clear that the human being is a created person who simply cannot be reduced to a physical entity. Since God Himself breathes life into us, what we are has more to do with the soul than the body. As such, His image engraved on our souls cannot be diminished or lost under any circumstances. According to Scripture, we are more than the sum of our parts (see 1 Corinthians 12:12). The soul unifies us and makes personal identity possible.

Second, scientists assume that raw genetic data can answer theological questions. Geneticists are not equipped to answer such questions. When they attempt to do so, they are functioning as theologians or philosophers. For most of them, this is not their area of expertise. The biblical view of humanity is not proven erroneous by those who attempt to define human nature in this way. Nor should we feel threatened by new genetic knowledge. There is nothing that geneticists will ever discover about the human genetic code that will contradict what the Bible teaches.

Genesis 2:7 records that Adam was formed from the dust in the ground, after which the Lord God "breathed" life into him. The word for "breath" is used in the Scriptures for God and for the life He imparted to human beings alone—never for animals. This divine breath gives spiritual understanding (see Job 32:8) and a conscience (see Proverbs 20:27). It can be inferred here that our moral capacity was given by virtue of this inbreathing. It describes the whole person—body and soul—with all its distinctly human capacities. The term "living creature" is used for animals (Genesis 2:19), but "image" never is; neither is "breath of life."

The Dangers of Forsaking the Biblical View of Humanity

Most geneticists have not considered the biblical view of human beings nor have they considered the dangers associated with forsaking such a view. The Bible teaches that human beings are *creatures*; that is, they are wholly dependent upon God. It also teaches that human beings are *persons*; that is, they possess relative independence and are capable of making choices on their own. The Bible clearly teaches both views. The tendency of scientists is to emphasize personhood alone, apart from any serious consideration of creatureliness, and to define personhood merely as the capacity for rational, free choice. This view of personhood is not only flawed but dangerous. For those who can no longer engage in such self-determination, personhood is called into question, and so is human dignity and rights. This ultimately leads to the marginalization of entire groups of people. The "freedom" of those in power takes away the freedom of some who are not. This is tyranny; and no tyrannical society has survived for long.

What True Freedom of the Human Being Is

The Bible reveals the origins of tyranny. It shows that freedom that is exercised apart from divine authority is no freedom at all. It is enslavement, and it will lead to our destruction. It is the ultimate expression of pride, and pride always comes before the fall (see Proverbs 16:18). We see an example of this sort of pride in the devil's words to Christ during the time of His temptation: "I will give you all their authority and splendor, for it has been given to me, and I can give it to anyone I want to" (Luke 4:5-6). This is a picture of self-determination, of freedom exercised apart from divine authority.

In the Gospel of John, Jesus describes the path to true freedom: "If you hold to my teaching, you are really my disciples. Then you will know the truth, and the truth will set you free. So if the Son sets you free, you will be free indeed" (John 8:31-32,36). It is truth that brings freedom. Unfortunately, modern geneticists are more concerned with usefulness than with truth, because they only know half the story. As we communicate our concept of God in this debate about being human, we must be diligent to articulate the biblical view of a human being and the biblical view's implications for modern medicine.

From a biblical standpoint, then, there is nothing inherently wrong with genetic knowledge or genetic testing. Genetic knowledge and genetic testing become biblically problematic only when they are used to call into question the personhood of either mentally challenged adults or unborn children; then they are questionable because justification is sought to deny human rights and dignity. This is precisely what happens with respect to those just beginning life. Psalm 139 teaches that it is God who knits human beings together in their mother's womb (see verse 13). We can apply this truth to embryos created outside the womb as well, because they are still created human persons. We cannot biblically justify putting them into some sort of separate "subhuman" category simply because technology had a hand in the coming together of the sperm and egg.

In sum, Scripture is consistent concerning the human person. This biblical view presents us with clear guidelines concerning the use of genetic knowledge and technologies. But the Church needs to communicate to society the good news that God is in control and is not surprised by genetics or any other medical advance. It is He—God—who gives us the book of life, not the geneticist!

Culture: God's Word on Embryonic Stem-Cell Research

What does God's Word have to say about embryonic stem-cell research (ESCR)? Well, we will not find a scriptural passage that deals specifically with the issue, but that does not mean the Bible has nothing to say about the subject. There are certain timeless biblical principles that are relevant to every aspect of biotechnology. Those principles ultimately involve the protection of innocent human life and the practice of good stewardship. Embryonic stem cells are highly versatile cells from which all the differentiated cells of the human body are derived. When these cells are taken from the human embryo, it is destroyed. From a biblical perspective, then, this research is unethical because it destroys the life of someone made in God's image.

This, however, is not the end of the matter. Many researchers do not accept this argument because it is a religious one—one that is not based on scientific evidence.* In other words, from the researcher's perspective, scientific evidence leads us to believe that embryonic stem cells can cure diseases and relieve the suffering of many human beings who are here now. Therefore, so the research scientist says, we have a moral mandate to engage in embryonic stem-cell research. But is there any scientific evidence that embryonic stem cells can cure disease? The answer is a resounding no!

It is *adult* stem cells that have proven successful in this arena. Adult stem cells do not come from—and so don't destroy—embryos, and for that reason their use is compatible with biblical truth. It is important that Christians understand this important research, because the media will almost certainly not present the whole truth.

Let us consider, therefore, this issue by first examining a short timeline of key dates in embryonic stem-cell research; then we will explore the evidence produced by ESCR. We will also hold adult stem-cell research up to the same light.

Key Dates in Embryonic Stem-Cell Research

1981—Researchers in Cambridge and at the University of California at San Francisco separately isolate embryonic stem cells in mice.

1994—President Clinton bans the use of federal money to create human embryos for the sole purpose of research but permits research on embryos leftover from fertility clinics.

1996—Congress bans federal funding for research in which embryos are destroyed.

1998—Researchers at the University of Wisconsin isolate and grow human embryonic stem cells, prompting patient advocates to urge Congress to lift the ban on federal funding for embryo research.

2000—The National Institutes of Health (NIH) encourages researchers to apply for the first federal grants for research using embryonic stem cells, fueling a debate between pro-life advocates and patient advocates.

July 2001—Pope John Paul II tells President Bush that embryonic stem-cell research is evil and ought to be resisted.

August 2001—President Bush issues an executive order restricting federal funding for ESCR to already existing lines.

February 2004—South Korean scientist Hwang Woo-suk claims to have created stem cells from cloned embryos, paving the way for cell lines genetically matched to individual patients. A second study follows the next year.

November 2004—California voters approve a $3-billion bond measure to fund stem-cell research.

2005—It is discovered that Hwang Woo-suk fabricated data in his stem-cell studies. He faces charges for fraud and misuse of research money.

2006—President Bush vetoes a bill that would have expanded federal support for ESCR.

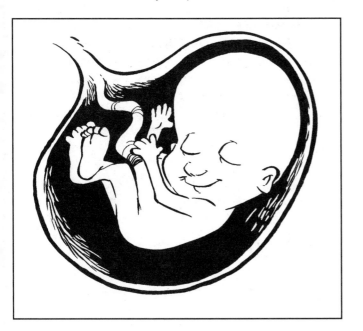

March 2007—The director of NIH tells Congress that he backs an end to the restriction on federal funding for ESCR.

This timeline shows that ESCR has advanced significantly over the past several years, but it has yielded few results and still faces several challenges.

The Results of Embryonic Stem-Cell Research

There have been three main results of ESCR so far: First, there is the constant fear that embryonic stem cells will be rejected by the recipient's immune system. Second, there is the problem that embryonic stem cells form serious tumors when transplanted into adult tissues. Third, research thus far has provided no evidence that embryonic stem cells could be differentiated into normal adult cell types. In other words, embryonic stem cells have not in the least proven to be a safe and effective treatment for disease.

The Promise of Adult Stem-Cell Research

Adult stem cells do not create the moral problems associated with embryonic stem cells, and they show great promise for the future treatment of disease. Adult stem cells are present in human beings of all ages. They can also be derived from placentas and umbilical cords. Obtaining stem cells from these sources does not result in harm to human beings. And there have been several successes in adult stem-cell research.

In August 2005, for example, the *New York Times* reported that making mice furrier had resulted in a discovery regarding stem cells: Dr. Artandi of Stanford University showed that adult stem cells can be activated by an enzyme called telomerase. His findings, published in an article in the journal *Nature,* puzzled some researchers because telomerase is known in a completely different context: it protects against tumors by limiting cell division. The new finding showed that telomerase can actually have two functions: one that promotes growth of new cells that are healthy and one that prevents the growth of bad cells leading to tumors. This insight could lead to new treatments for certain diseases including diabetes.

In March 2006, the *New York Times* reported on a controversial therapy for diabetes. A group of scientists working independently of one another claimed to have discovered that severely diabetic mice can recover on their own if researchers squelch an immune-system attack that is causing the disease. This discovery was actually reported in 2001 by Dr. Denise Faustman of Massachusetts General Hospital, and it raised hopes for people suffering from type 1 diabetes, which is also known as juvenile diabetes and is incurable. The prospect of reversing such a disease would truly be remarkable.

In early 2007, *The Journal of the American Medical Association* published a study that suggested a new way to treat diabetes. Thirteen young diabetics in Brazil stopped taking insulin after being treated with stem cells from their own blood. (The research was done in Brazil because the United States was not interested in the approach.) The experimental procedure has allowed these teens to live insulin free for three years now. More rigorous studies are needed, but this procedure seems to show some promise for the future.

In the late fall of 2007, research groups in Japan and the United States showed that human skin cells can be coaxed into behaving like embryonic stem cells by a process called direct reprogramming. Like embryonic stem cells, these reprogrammed cells are capable of becoming any cell in the human body.

From both a Christian and a scientific perspective, stem cells produced from direct reprogramming offer several advantages. First and foremost, they do not destroy innocent human life. Second, they have a tremendous ability to produce patient-specific stem-cell lines for research on genetic diseases. Third, unlike the theoretical patient-specific stem cells from cloned embryos, these cells are available right now. Fourth, they are simpler to produce than embryonic stem cells.

Adult stem cells hold promise for future treatment of many debilitating diseases. They will help to improve, repair and maintain human life because they cooperate with the body's natural healing capacities. Therefore, though the Bible may not specifically discuss adult stem-cell research, there is no question that this research honors God by protecting human life and by practicing good stewardship.

* Much more could be said about this issue, but it goes beyond the scope of this work. Please contact the Public Policy Center at Joni and Friends International Disability Center for more information.

Culture: How Other Cultures View Disability

"Blessed to be a blessing" is not a cliché for Rhea Tavares. The 32-year-old works as an advocate for children with special needs who immigrate to the United States. She helps families understand special-education laws and ensures access to proper care and resources. Rhea's desire to give back is rooted in her gratitude for her own success in spite of a disability. Rhea was born in Brazil, where physical or mental disabilities are viewed as curses from God or consequences for wrongs done.

When Rhea was born, doctors wouldn't even let her mother, Doraci, see Rhea's disability. The nurses kept the newborn swaddled in fuzzy blankets with only her head full of dark hair and big brown eyes peeking out. The doctors told her mother that Rhea did not have arms and needed to be wrapped up at all times. Although Doraci protested, she left the hospital with a baby she'd only seen from the neck up.

It was Rhea's grandmother who first announced that it was time for Doraci to see her daughter. Her grandma laid little Rhea on the bed and revealed the child's deformities. They were shocked because the still-pink infant did have arms, but the forearms were very short and had one crooked finger growing from each of them.

Initially, Rhea's father blamed himself. He was guilt ridden because for many years he'd said he didn't want children. He saw the disability as divine retribution. Though Doraci went through some depression, she ignored advice to institutionalize her daughter and instead taught Rhea to take on day-to-day challenges and to believe in herself.

"My mother never rejected me. That's why I never gave up," Rhea told *People* magazine in a March 2007 article featuring everyday heroes. She moved to the United States at the age of 16, and for the past 10 years, through the Federation for Children with Special Needs in Boston, she has helped hundreds of Brazilian families who have come to the United States. Many of these families deal with the same language barriers and cultural stigmata she had faced.

"Things have improved in Brazil," Rhea said. "People are promoting awareness now and the inclusion of children with special needs in school. But most of the schools are not prepared to handle children with disabilities."

Although people are starting to get educated, Rhea said misconceptions still exist. For example, certain religious denominations in Brazil still believe autistic children are not disabled but demon possessed.

Crossing Cross-Cultural Barriers

Churches serve an increasing number of immigrant families with beliefs and practices that differ from those of mainstream America. If your church membership is diverse, your teachers must be aware of the mores of the various cultures represented in the congregation. The apostle Paul encourages us in 1 Corinthians 9:22 to be all things to all people in order to bring them to Christ.

According to the National Organization on Disability (NOD), America has 54 million men, women and children with disabilities. Worldwide the number is 650 million people. The Church not only faces logistical facility issues to serve children with disabilities but also must cross cultural barriers to meet the needs of this underserved population. The Religion and Disability Program of NOD has initiated partnerships with seminaries to provide information that equips religious leaders to work alongside children and adults with disabilities. Two of the program's goals are (1) to nurture the view that children and adults with disabilities are created in the image of God and (2) to confront theology that suggests disability is a result of sin or lack of faith.

Although many cultures in developing nations have made strides to disassociate disabilities from supernatural forces, success has not been complete or universal. Some peoples still believe that disabilities are the result of God's anger at a parent for wrongdoing or for breaking a taboo. Some traditional African religions believe a person is reincarnated with a disability as punishment for living a wicked life. The stigma of disability attaches both to the individual and to the family, so a child with disability is seen as a curse or an incomplete person unworthy of life. Families sometimes abandon these children to hospitals or orphanages, or a baby may simply be killed.

Education is the key to changing such deep-rooted misconceptions, and NOD has partnered with the United Nations World Programme of Action Concerning Disabled Persons to recognize nations that have expanded the participation of people with disabilities for economic, humanitarian and social reasons. The Franklin Delano Roosevelt International Disability Award is named for Franklin D. Roosevelt, who spent most of his life in a wheelchair after he contracted polio at age 39. Since the award's inception in 1995, nine countries have been honored for their efforts: the Republic of Korea, Canada, Ireland, the Republic of Hungary, Thailand, Ecuador, Italy, the Hashemite Kingdom of Jordan, and Poland.

Learning Cultural Differences

Church staffs and volunteers need diversity training targeted toward their membership. From a simple handshake to eye contact, different protocols are exhibited by different cultures. The simple act of greeting parents at the door of the classroom is an opportunity to build a cross-cultural bridge. For example, in America, a handshake is considered appropriate, while in South America an embrace is typical, and in Japan a bow is common. A myriad other social "violations" can occur with the offending party being none the wiser. Here are a few examples of cultural variations that need to be taken into account so that no offense is given:

- Personal space varies cross-culturally. The distance Americans feel most comfortable talking with colleagues is approximately three to four feet (.9 to 1.2m). Arabs stand closer, so when members of the two groups converse, Americans may step back to maintain their comfort zone, and Arabs may step closer. Middle Easterners could interpret the move by Americans as an indication that they are cold or uncaring.

- Hand gestures can be misinterpreted. For example, crooking the index finger while the arm is extended toward another person in the United States means "come here," but it is offensive and insulting in some Asian countries, because it is a gesture used to call animals. A thumbs-up sign varies in meaning from "That's great!" in America and Brazil to "Get stuffed!" in Greece. The "okay" hand gesture (thumb and forefinger making a circle while the other three fingers are extended) has a vulgar, insulting connotation in Brazil.

Aside from earning a doctorate degree in cross-cultural communication, how can staff and volunteers begin to effectively serve the different cultures in the modern Church? Training geared toward individual congregations is key, but also important is increasing overall awareness of assumptions and biases. The best approach is to see these interactions as a learning experience and to remember Jesus' words as recorded in Mark 11:17: He said His house would be "a house of prayer for all nations."

Rhea Tavares attends a Baptist church and points to her strong faith as the ultimate source of her success. "My faith in God changed my life forever," Rhea said. "He broke all the barriers and showed me the way. He opened doors that I thought would be impossible to open. God made me capable when people thought I was not because of my disability. He gave me courage and determination."

Rhea now sets out to give back each day, claiming as her life verse: "I can do all things through Christ who strengthens me" (see Philippians 4:13).

Caregivers: Caregiver Burnout

Exploring Canaan was a study on perspective and faith. Twelve men were sent to look at the land. Numbers 13 and 14 tell about the expedition and the final reports of the men. Ten of the men came back and noted the amazing goodness, but they also reported on all of the obstacles. Because of giant people and fortified cities, they encouraged the crowd to anticipate certain disasters and to question why God ever made them leave Egypt in the first place. Caleb and Joshua, however, had a very different report. They saw the same events and people. "Then Caleb silenced the people before Moses and said, 'We should go up and take possession of the land, for we can certainly do it'"(Numbers 13:30). Joshua and Caleb spoke of God's promised intervention and tried to steer the people to see circumstances through the lenses of His power and might.

God makes amazing statements about the worth and value of each individual. He promises in Jeremiah 29:11 that He has a hope-filled plan for each one. God surrounds His children with words like "secure," "loved," "salt and light of the world," "honored" and "indispensable." While those words don't change, it's possible to lose sight of that picture due to the daily circumstances of life. Just like Canaan got mixed reviews, earthly lenses can get clouded with the daily muck of life.

Caregivers of children who have special needs can struggle to keep their lenses free from circumstantial spots. The daily battles with issues like dressing, eating, behavior plans, therapy and/or medical appointments, financial stress from treatment costs and specialized devices, and a host of other issues that crowd the day often steal the vision of who that child is in Christ. Trying to devote time to each family member while meeting the needs of the one child with a disability can be an exhausting prospect. Imagine the mom and dad whose child with autism would not leave the safety of her blanket spread on the living-room floor. The edges of that blanket were her safe boundary, and she refused to leave that spot. All meals, sleeping and living were done on the blanket. For months, one of the parents had to stay in that space with her, as the child's safety and behavior demanded their constant attention. Imagine that being your daily routine.

Some people use the word "burnout" to talk about what happens to caregivers of children with disabilities. Thinking of that time as wearing lenses completely covered with the circumstances of life would also be helpful. The caregiver's perspective is driven by those lenses, and the result is hopelessness and isolation.

Symptoms of Burnout

Some parents find out before or at birth that a child has some form of disability. Others find out over time. A child may have a life-changing accident, and the future changes after one car crash. Many parents and other family members enter into a time of grieving—going through stages that represent an adjustment to that information and of the change in life's circumstances. It's within the first two stages of grief—denial and anger—when intensive care for the needs of a child are needed most, but that is also the time when helping others is furthest from one's thoughts. With no map for this uncharted territory, and facing radical life shifts and new and unexpected emotions, a heavy paste seems to drift over the eyeglasses through which caregivers view the world around them.

Caregivers might begin to withdraw, and family and friends wonder why that individual no longer attends family functions or friendly get-togethers. A congregation member who was active in many areas of the church may no longer attend church functions. Activities that used to bring joy are no longer in the daily planner. Hobbies and interests go by the wayside, while the details of everyday life consume that person's energy and thinking. A caregiver experiencing burnout might feel irritable, angry, hopeless, helpless and/or depressed. Sometimes there also are physical symptoms such as weight loss or gain, disturbed sleep patterns or frequent illness. Whatever the symptoms, the result is the inability to share God's perspective for the child and family affected by special needs, even if that family is their own. Hope gets buried under the ground of circumstances.

Hope for Caregivers

While it may not be possible to radically alter the needs of the child with the disability, there are many ways to alter the lenses through which a caregiver views the situation. The Church can be a powerful force and lifeline in allowing parents, grandparents or other caregivers to see their situation in a new way.

- God expects us to be able to cry with one another and laugh with one another within His Body. Don't skip the crying part. Examine the situation and know what caregivers deal with each and every day. Understand what it may be like to be trapped in the living room with a child who refuses for months to leave her blanket. Think through and imagine the sleep deprivation that comes from administering medical treatments throughout the night while at the same time monitoring the situation for emergencies. Live in the shoes of caregivers who spend months at a child's hospital bedside, wondering if that little one will survive and then discovering that the care needs of that survivor are overwhelming. Know the medical co-pay involved in one therapy session and multiply that number by the numerous specialists involved in that child's life. Understand. Don't, however, wear their circumstance-covered glasses on your face. Keep your Joshua and Caleb perspective while understanding the life of the family.

- As a church, offer to come alongside that family. Consider creating a G.L.U.E. team to surround those daily needs (see p. 139). Use the church community to free up some time for parent date nights, on-call help for emergencies, financial support, transportation, meals, sibling fun-time activities, respite care, or breathing space in a schedule that seems to be suffocating the caregiver. A caregiver may simply need time away to recharge for the daily tasks—it's possible that after the time away, the caregiver will return with completely different eyeglasses. Stay close and monitor those life lenses. Look for times when you can both share the same God-given perspective of that child and the situation. Nurture glimpses of hope and offer "eyeglass cleaner" for caregivers.

- Understand that most situations involving a child with special needs are long-term situations. If your church is expecting to offer support for only a couple of months, they misconstrue the picture of what support is. We are the family of God, so those family members are permanent fixtures in your community. Expect to be involved for a lifetime.

- See the broad scope of the term "caregiver." While we primarily think about parents, look at the additional caregivers in the picture: extended family members, siblings, medical staff, school staff and/or group-home communities, among others. Let the whole group know of your care and support for this family and child. So often God tells us that our acts of love are a powerful witness to the community. Let your light shine to all involved, so they see how the perspective of a Christian is actually played out. May God use your involvement and care to change the hearts and lives of an entire community of people.

Hope: Calling Church Leaders to Disability Ministry

When calling your church leadership to follow the biblical mandate on disability ministry in the local congregation, it is best to begin with the common doctrines that leaders accept and have a desire to apply. The brief discussions here of some of the doctrines offer a reasonable starting place for you to expand from.

God's Kingdom

The kingdom of God is the reign of God over all things. Throughout the Gospels, we see that the coming of the Kingdom means the restoration of all things, more and more, to their intended purpose and the bringing of everything under the authority of the King. The coming of the Kingdom increasingly brings the presence of shalom, which one preacher describes as "Nothing broken. Nothing missing." As the Kingdom progresses, lives are changed, families are changed, communities are changed, culture is changed and even creation is changed. All of life is redeemed.

A theology of the Kingdom also recognizes the "already-not-yet-ness" of the kingdom of God—the hard reality that the Kingdom is truly here in part but will not be here in its fullness until the consummation of history. It means pursuing wholeness in the lives of people with disabilities as agents of the Kingdom. This implies that in this lifetime, shalom can be experienced in part but not in its entirety. The concept of the kingdom of God is a beautiful, far-reaching view of disability in the context of all of life.

Christ's Body

The Pauline metaphors of the Body of Christ provide powerful imagery that supplies an undeniable mandate about the necessity and blessing of diversity in our midst. Very specific examples of varying abilities and gifts are fleshed out at length in Romans 12, 1 Corinthians 12 and Ephesians 4. These passages about the Body of Christ remind us that everyone has spiritual gifts, every person has an important part to play in the Body, none of us has the right to dismiss any other part of the Body and differentness actually promotes oneness. Positive and encouraging descriptions of the Body of Christ provide a wonderful word picture of the inclusive congregational life to which God calls us.

God's Image

The doctrine of the image of God is firmly established in the creation account of Genesis 1, in addition to many other passages (see Genesis 5:1; 9:6; Colossians 3:9-10; James 3:9; among others). The concept of the image of God can be thought of as something we are and something we do. In other words, we are created in the image and likeness of God, and as such we reflect God. The image of God is the basis for human value and, therefore, the basis for respect-based relationships. Imparting a deep sense of worth into the lives of people with different abilities, the doctrine of the image of God is an essential element of disability ministry. When we engage inherently valuable people with disabilities, we image God in the active sense of doing so. We reflect God's character when we embrace those whom society often rejects. As a result, we are doubly blessed—not only by individuals who are God's precious creation in our midst, but also by the ways that God restores His image in our own fractured lives by developing character qualities that reflect His.

Mercy, or Compassion

St. Gregory of Nyssa once said, "Mercy is a voluntary sorrow which enjoins itself to the suffering of another." While living with a disability is not necessarily defined as suffering, there are many aspects of relentless difficulty that often impact the lives of people with disabilities. Mercy, or compassion, calls us to acknowledge those difficulties and to respond to people affected by them. The Gospels are full of examples of Christ's expressions of mercy toward people He encountered. The Church is the hands and feet of Christ on Earth. But acts of kindness offered with attitudes of arrogance are resented by families with disabilities. Mercy is not just entering another's difficulty; it is doing so with honor and respect.

Justice

Throughout Scripture, there are hundreds of references to the word "justice" or a form of that word. Identified as one of God's attributes, justice is near to God's heart. Scripture warns us about injustices committed against the poor and the oppressed. Whether dealing with inclusion issues in the local church or helping to restore social service systems in the community, a disability ministry has as its center biblical justice.

Hospitality

Some congregations have a rich history in the area of hospitality. Hospitality literally means "to love a stranger." It involves welcoming those who are outside of our typical circles and doing so in genuinely loving ways. The Gospels abound with examples of Jesus welcoming and loving those who were marginalized by society.

Evangelism

In the parable of the great banquet in Luke 14:15-24, Jesus told us to go where people are and invite them to church—and don't stop until the church is full. Jesus clearly included people with disabilities in the invitation. If your church leaders are committed to evangelism and discipleship, people with disabilities are one of the world's most unreached people groups.

The Word of God is the truth that transforms lives. The process of change must begin in the hearts of leaders. And it *will* begin when they focus on imparting God's truth to others in ways that the others can understand. Transformation takes time and is a process that involves several things:

- Engaging in the biblical truths of disability ministry
- Explaining the applications of doctrine and theology
- Educating your congregation on real-life issues
- Equipping people with ideas and support
- Encouraging loving action
- Exhorting a higher level of commitment
- Expecting results from one another in your faith community

The peace of Christ calls us to be peacemakers in the Church and in the Kingdom. Disability ministry calls Christians to bring shalom—completeness, wholeness and harmony—to the Body of Christ and the world around us.

The coming of the Kingdom of God in our lives is truly good news—good news that contagiously affects all we do and say. The Gospel of Christ is to permeate our relationships while we pursue the purpose of peace, promote the process of transformation and emulate the posture of the Lord Jesus.

When children and adults with disabilities arrive on the doorstep of your church, will your leadership take a deep breath and say, "Oh no!"? Or will they smile and say, "Here is a breath of fresh air! I can't wait to hear what these families have to share with us!"?

Hope: Advocating for Children with Special Needs

The quiet words of the wise are more to be heeded than the shouts of a ruler of fools.
Ecclesiastes 9:17

What is an advocate?

An advocate is a person who speaks up for, acts on behalf of or supports someone else. Jesus was an advocate who spoke up for those with disabilities. In Matthew 12:9-13, He challenged the injustice of those in the synagogue who cared more for a sheep in a pit than for a man with a withered hand. Jesus powerfully illustrated His values by healing the man's hand, even on the Sabbath.

As a special needs advocate, you can speak up for children with disabilities while demonstrating God's unconditional love. It has been proven time and again that the squeaky wheel gets the grease. But how loudly you squeak will determine how much grease you get.

What do advocates do?

Advocates get involved by addressing discrimination of any kind and encouraging better special education and services. They raise money for research and facility improvements and vote for local and federal policies that make life better for the millions affected by disability. Advocates also build community networks that promote awareness and support family services.

George never thought of himself as an advocate until a parent called him that. He taught the kindergarten class at his church, a class that had in it two students with autism. As George's relationship with their families grew, he became aware of the need these children have for early intervention. That, in turn, led him to notice an ad in his local newspaper about an Easter Seals Walk with Me event in a nearby town.

George discovered that Easter Seals is one of the leading providers of services for people with autism. Every 20 minutes another child is diagnosed with autism, and Easter Seals has many programs to help fight this incurable disorder.* At first, George made an online donation, but he couldn't get the walk out of his mind. He wanted the families at his church to know how much he cared. Eventually, he called a number of friends and asked them to join him on the walk and raise donations. Not only did the walkers from his church raise $3,000, but also they determined to host an event in their town the next year. George became a hero to his students, and the church gained a new family that George met on the walk.

Why do families need advocates?

Parents wear many hats. But along with wearing many hats, parents of children with disabilities need the courage of skilled mountain climbers to scale the huge amount of information they must process. A child's medical file can be inches thick after years of diagnostic tests, medications, therapies and treatments. Along with the medical records come confusing insurance forms and staggering financial costs. Parents (some of whom struggle to balance a checkbook) can become lost in the maze of paperwork and information. They need advocates with experience in medicine, insurance and finance.

The history of education in America has not been kind to children with special needs. Parents have fought for quality educational services in schools, institutions and group homes, but they have not always met with success. Today, an equal education is mandated under the Individuals with Disability Act (IDEA). This law requires schools to evaluate students, create individualized instruction goals and provide appropriate services. An individual education plan is used to monitor the child's performance, but problems arise when school districts fail to provide services. Schools are struggling due to a shortage of special education teachers, therapists and budget dollars. Parents need advocates with experience to help them deal with the system. In some cases, they hire legal advocates who represent their child's interest in a court case.

When Simon's school tried to move the special needs classroom out of the building to a portable trailer, his parents worked with an advocate to block the move. When Molly's speech therapy sessions were cut from three times a week to once a week, her parents appreciated the advice of a friend from church who had faced the same situation with her son. The friend acted as an advocate and was instrumental in restoring Molly's therapy.

Church leaders can compile a list of members with skills that parents might need. A list of parents who have walked the same road is also a blessing to parents who are new to disability issues.

What training do advocates need?

God calls people to advocacy and equips them for the task. He always works with our personal interest to lead us into a ministry. While it's true that lawyers, doctors, therapists and counselors are needed in the advocacy process, caring Christians, especially those who have witnessed injustice, can be strong advocates for disability rights and medical research. Advocates should be well informed on topics and current facts. Many disability associations place updates on local and federal policies on their websites.

Your goal should be to represent others in ways that honor God in word and action. Anger and strife are not part of God's way to help others. Open, honest discussion can bring about lasting change that honors our Savior, Jesus Christ.

How can the church support special needs advocates?

Churches are villages filled with people from a wide variety of occupations, offering a wide variety of talents. Yet families affected by disability feel alone. Our society teaches independence instead of the unity modeled in the Early Church and recorded in the book of Acts. Remember what is said in Proverbs: "If you want to win, you need many good advisers" (Proverbs 24:6, *NIrV*). Churches can encourage advocacy, train advocates and pray for them.

Take a page from the PACER Center as a guide to get you started in your advocacy. PACER Center is a source of information and training for families of children with disabilities. PACER's Health Information and Advocacy Center (HIAC) provides help for families affected by disabilities and complex health-care needs. HIAC provides resources, support, advocacy and information about the health-care system so that families can make better-informed decisions about the many issues affecting them. PACER promotes family-centered care and family and professional collaboration at all levels of health care. To learn more, visit http://www.pacer.org.

*"Autism Services," *Easter Seals,* 2008. http://centralcal.easter seals.com/site/PageServer?pagename=CACN_ps_autism (accessed July 6, 2008).

Caregivers: Loving Mothers of Children with Special Needs

She was late again. She knew it as soon as she got in the car to drive to church. Actually, she knew it would happen when Lisa woke up with an extra dose of morning stiffness and pain from her juvenile rheumatoid arthritis. She knew that this was not the morning to skip the warm bath and morning exercise routine. She knew that everything from breakfast to dressing to making the walk out the door would be slow. Very slow. As she walked into church, she hated how conspicuous she felt. She wanted someone to know what it had taken to get there at all, but she didn't want to be the one to describe it. Instead, she offered a line other mothers use that really doesn't explain anything: "Oh, it was just one of those mornings!"

Mothers of children with special needs get used to routines. So do the children. It's when the routine changes that both mother and child can experience anything from mild frustration to debilitating stress. And everything is different on Sunday. The week of school, homework, medical appointments and any number of physical, medical and/or behavioral interventions often take their toll on a mother's patience and energy. The good news is that the local church can help these moms. The community of faith offers a ready-made occasion to share love and support in ways that other interventions cannot.

Welcome in a Big Way

Target this special family, particularly the mom, with an especially warm greeting. Make her feel that whatever effort it took to get to church was worth it. Be ready to help with bags, equipment, directions or young children so that the mom can make the home-to-church transition a calm and secure one. Support her with extra understanding when she walks in late. Make her feel glad she came, late or not. Thank her for making the effort with a warmth and gentleness that melt unnecessary guilt.

Organize a "Sunday Friends" Group

If you have several families who come with children who have wheelchairs, walkers or other kinds of equipment, consider organizing a Sunday Friends group. Sunday Friends are people who are ready at agreed-upon entrances to be an extra pair of hands and feet for each family as the car is unloaded and everyone gets to where they need to be. Go the extra mile and offer to park the car. Consider regular pairings so that these Sunday Friends are available before and after Sunday School, worship services or any event where extra help makes a big difference.

Remember That a Little Help Goes a Long Way

Food events at church sometimes offer extra complications. It certainly was true for Josh, who could choke on food. Everything he ate needed to be finely cut up or mashed. He had to be watched constantly while he ate to make sure he swallowed properly. Several sensitive moms and dads offered to learn what to do and watch for. With permission, they prepared Josh's plate at church potlucks and picnics. This freed the mom to help her other children, who usually had to wait or fend for themselves. It also gave the mom time to interact with other adults, a luxury she didn't expect to enjoy at a food function. Besides, Josh had a chance to interact with other people besides his family. Everybody won.

Ask First

Always ask before helping the mom or the child with special needs. What may seem like a simple solution to the problem you see may create another problem the mother wants to avoid. Ask simple questions, and ask your questions in ways that affirm how well she handles so many responsibilities. "May I open the door for you?" "May I help her get a drink of water?" "Can I help in some way?" If the mom rejects your help, take it as information that there is more involved than what you understand at the moment.

Help Mothers Make Connections

Often the best way to support a mom raising a child with special needs is to help her connect with others who face similar challenges. Ask a mom who is very open about her journey if you could introduce her to another mom who is on a similar trip. Simply help them connect. What the moms do after the introduction is their responsibility.

Invite the mom to a support group if your church offers this for families raising children with special challenges. If not, consider something as simple as an e-mail group. Find a facilitator who will build the e-mail list and who will e-mail participants for prayer requests. Knowing someone else wants to help goes a long way in bringing much-needed support for a mom.

A note of caution: Be careful about assuming anything. Don't use a label or diagnosis that the parent does not use. If a parent does not openly acknowledge a special need, simply support the struggles he or she does talk about.

Meet to Make a Plan

Meet with a mother or both parents to talk about specific ways to address special challenges while at church. Troubleshoot facility barriers: heavy doors, stairs, etc. Is a mom afraid to leave her child with untrained volunteers? Consider using the nursery paging system to page her when a question arises. Do whatever it takes within the boundaries of your staff's time and resources to address key concerns. Explore the many ideas in this resource to see what person, team or equipment you could add in order to overcome an obstacle.

Sarah had difficulty with fine-motor skills. That included cutting and coloring. After the Sunday School teacher learned what Sarah used at school, the teacher made arrangements to purchase special scissors and larger crayons so that Sarah could enjoy more class activities. What the teacher did to meet the needs of the child met an even greater need of the mom.

Listen So That You Can Pray

Besides addressing the specific needs of the child, look for ways to address the specific needs of the mom. Sometimes you don't have to *do* anything at all. Just listen. Listening will always give you a way to pray. Don't just promise to pray. Stop talking, and pray before separating. Offer your phone number and/or e-mail address as a way to extend midweek encouragement.

Understand that parents of children who face ongoing emotional, mental or physical challenges ride the roller coaster of emotions that place them at one of the stages of a grief cycle that includes denial, anger, bargaining and depression as they work toward acceptance. They need extra doses of understanding and affirmation to move through different phases of loss in emotionally and spiritually healthy ways.

Freely Give Love, Not Answers

Always remember that hope for these mothers will never come from your answers; it will come from your love. Lead with love. Address problem-solving issues with love. This mother didn't come by accident. She is in your circle of care on purpose, because God placed her there. Look for ways to make the church a place of sanctuary for her and her family as they face unique and unpredictable challenges. Then enjoy celebrating small victories together.

Caregivers: Encouraging Fathers of Children with Special Needs

While a man may be surprised to discover that he is going to become someone's dad, he is usually almost immediately filled with pride and optimism. He begins dreaming of a son who will carry on and enlarge his legacy or a little princess who will have only the best. But when he hears the dreaded diagnosis that his and his wife's child has special needs, feelings that he never knew existed can be stirred in the man's heart. His response to the initial crisis and ongoing care may vacillate between love and repulsion. A man tends to fear what he cannot fix, and nothing is more "unfixable" than a lifelong disability.

The Reactions of Fathers

A father's dreams for his child may quickly fade in the blinding reality of a child's special needs. If the disability does not have a clear medical cause, the father may blame himself. If the disorder is an emotional/behavioral one, a father may feel like a bad parent. In some families, there is an unspoken agreement that dad will focus on the siblings while the mom devotes herself to the child with special needs, so the father spends little time with the child with disability. Other fathers simply throw themselves into their work to escape or to earn enough to provide for extra necessities.

Even fathers who are willing to be involved often become discouraged. Too often they are simply lost for one reason or another:

- Educators, physicians and therapists seem to direct questions and instructions to the mother—even when the father is present.

- Appointments and meetings conflict with the the father's work schedule.

- Dad's time spent with the children is often viewed by society as giving the wife a break instead of as crucial, hands-on masculine parenting.

- Men struggle to overcome stereotypes and to understand their crucial parenting role.

These fathers need Christian friends who will come alongside them and share their journey.

The Crucial Role of Fathers

Fathers are indispensable in bringing balance to their families, particularly when faced with the impact of a special needs diagnosis. Mothers may become all consumed with the new medical terms and need their husband's perspective, encouragement and sense of steadiness. Couples

need one another as reminders that they are not alone in all they face. Though a dad's approach may be different from a mom's approach, the mom should be encouraged to step back a little and let the father address the issues.

Life is better for all children when they have a loving father who is involved in their daily lives. With sufficient training, information and support, fathers can learn to be effective caretakers and advocates for their children. When they find this support at church, a personal crisis can become a positive, affirming turning point.

The Lord's Call to True Manhood

Paul wrote to the believers in Corinth:

Brothers, think of what you were when you were called. Not many of you were wise by human standards; not many were influential . . . But God chose the foolish things of the world to shame the wise; God chose the weak things of the world to shame the strong . . . so that no one may boast before him (1 Corinthians 1:26-29).

The Corinthian believers were underrated in the world's eyes. Today, children with disabilities remain underrated. Without the strength and guidance of the Holy Spirit, few men will consider as a blessing a child with disabilities. Often, men struggle with "the weak things." They might not realize that God's hand is drawn to the overlooked and outcast. God's eye is on the meek. When a father devotes his strength and resources to his child, he will shine and stand out as a servant who is blessed by the Lord, interested in the things God is interested in.

There is nothing more rewarding than for the strong to be the hero to the weak. A "guy's movie" is one where justice is served because a powerful defender became the champion of the downtrodden. Having a child with disabilities challenges a man to become a victor, not only in things spiritual but also in practical things, like the eyes of his wife. When a dad wrestles on the floor, talks eye to eye, or jogs pushing a wheelchair, he takes the path of servanthood to greatness.

Fathers' Need of Church Support

Encourage men in your church to befriend children with disabilities and their fathers. Relationships are the best way to increase a man's interest in spiritual things and to see his child participate more in church programs. Be sure to include fathers and their children with special needs on camping trips, sports and recreational events and father-son retreats. Families of children with special needs should receive personal invitations. With extra effort, a supportive learning environment can be created where children with special needs can explore new skills, foster friendships and have opportunities to experience success. This allows their peers to develop compassion and empathy without jeopardizing fun for everyone involved. Ask fathers of boys and girls with special needs to suggest needed adaptations for their children's participation. They'll be glad to help their child. Here is a letter from one such dad:

Dear Coach David,

Joey had a good time at practice tonight. His teammates have warmed to him, and several were quite sensitive to his needs. He has also improved in his basic basketball skills.

When you speak to the referees about Joey's part in games, you might suggest that he could do some throw-ins and a free-throw shot that wouldn't count, as Joey doesn't notice the scoreboard. By the end of the season, Joey may be able to dribble the ball to mid court, pass it to a teammate and then come off as a replacement run-in. For him to meet that goal, he will need to practice it with a specific teammate. That way, he will be able to do it without me being with him on the floor during the game. Perhaps this can be a goal for later in the season.

I've enclosed a line drawing on how I communicate with Joey, since he is not good with words but really "gets" pictures.

Thanks for all you do!

Joe's Dad, Bill

Tips for Including Dads

- Direct your questions about the child to Dad as often as you do to Mom.

- Have a male church member specifically call the dad and ask for his insight into his child's strengths and needs.

- Plan fellowships centered around food and a structured activity or project (men are doers, not talkers).

- Bring in a male speaker and call the event "Coaching for Dads." Avoid using words like "teaching," "helping" or "encouraging," which are associated more with feminine activities.

- Understand that many men may prefer a one-on-one approach to larger groups, so keep the structure of large-group activities informal.

- Encourage a father who has lived with his child with special needs for some time to consider being a coach and mentor to a father new to a diagnosis.

- Be persistent. A father who brushes off an invitation may be in the early stages of grief. If your first offer is refused, check back at a later date.

Be sure your church holds dads up in prayer. Every male in your congregation needs to adopt the model of servant leadership. Because the Christian idea of leadership is not concerned about power, domination or manipulation, a devoted father of a child with special needs is the ideal model for the rest of the Body of Christ.

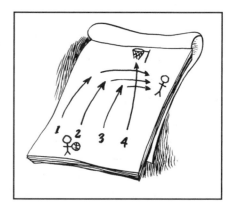

Caregivers: Supporting Grandparents Raising Children with Disabilities

They thought their granddaughter's high activity level and sleepless nights came from displacement issues. Grandparents Jim and Carolyn had reentered the parenting role when their daughter's drug problems escalated to include prison time. After several doctors' appointments and tests, their seven-year-old granddaughter was diagnosed with AD/HD and placed on medication. It was just one more complication to add to an already complicated life.

When the grandchildren had first come into their home, one child was seven months old and the other was five years old. Carolyn knew where the nursery was at church, but she wasn't sure who staffed it and how. She only hoped she stocked the diaper bag with all the necessary paraphernalia. When Granddad started to take the five-year-old to class, he realized that he wasn't sure which one it was. But the challenges didn't just stem from the children's issues. The grandparents experienced changes in their life on every level. They had to get home at decent times. Their Sunday School class never offered child care for any outing, so they couldn't go. No one invited them to a quick restaurant meal anymore. And they were tired. They were always tired.

The 2000 United States Census reported that 2.4 million grandparents headed homes in which their grandchildren lived with them.* The reasons for this high number are as drastic as the decision to make the life change. Death, illness, military service, drugs, abuse or imprisonment remove parents and displace children. Add a disability to the mix and the challenges increase.

Provide Support

How does the church help grandparents like Jim and Carolyn find a supportive place within the community of faith? There are a number of ideas that don't require investing a lot of time, people or money. You start by evaluating how you already handle special needs issues within your church ministry. Then use this new situation as an opportunity to make at least one improvement in the ministry: Take advantage of this challenge and seek to connect intergenerational families. Consider starting a faith-based support group for families of any age who are raising children who have special needs. These once-a-month problem-solving and encouragement groups can offer meaningful support with a minimum investment.

Help the church community understand their role in this family's new challenge. To do that, the church must find a positive way to inform the congregation. Talk to the grandparents and the pastor about praying a blessing for

their blended family. Make sure you don't talk about any details without permission (this includes the reasons behind the family's regrouping and any diagnosis). Simply affirm the grandparents' choice to provide a loving Christian home for their grandchildren. Treat and talk to the whole church as the extended family for this new blended family.

Make the Welcome Public

Consider having your church offer the new blended family a more formal way to share with the congregation their new arrangement. Soon after Kathi and Frank took over raising their grandchildren, they decided to make the arrangement permanent by adopting the children. When the grandchildren wondered if there was some way to make a public commitment at church, they spoke with the pastor and scheduled a ritual of family commitment. The public opportunity to make this legal decision a spiritual commitment was a powerful experience in the lives of the children.

Consider welcoming the children and addressing the grandparents' new role by organizing a family shower. Along with age-appropriate clothing, books and games, compile a *Family Favorites* booklet in which each family shares a favorite place to eat, shop or play. Include favorite snacks, quick meals, family games, outings, etc. Share "Count on Us" coupons from families who offer a movie night, park outing or other fun family event.

Help with Plans and Technology

Make sure you alert all ministry leaders who have a responsibility to work with the new children. Inform them of any disability diagnosis you have permission to share. Help them plan for appropriate adaptations so that the child's first experience is positive. Provide adequate support when there are challenges that the regular class staff cannot address. When Pat found herself raising her grandchildren, one had complicated emotional and physical challenges resulting from an unusual stroke. It took many ministry leaders and volunteers to address the child's emotional outbursts, but they did work it out.

Identify people within the church family who can share support in specific ways. Are there other parents who have experience in any of the new challenges facing these grandparents? Perhaps the parents can explain how to work with an Individualized Educational Plan (I.E.P.) at school, or they can recommend health professionals. They may even be able to share resources or their own expertise with legal and financial issues. And don't underestimate technological challenges. Grandparents may need someone to explain computer safeguards, iPods, cell phones, Gameboys and other types of technology that young people use today.

Provide Respite

Look for ways to offer respite care to multichallenged grandparents. This care could be as simple as offering transportation to and from extra church activities. Encourage other families to include the children with or without their grandparents on a family outing. As the children connect, they may spend time together away from church, even going on overnights with their friends. But what about the child with special needs? Look for specific ways to give these grandparents a break for a few hours a week or for even longer intervals. Also speak with those who lead the Sunday School class that the grandparents attend. Find out how everyone could work together to make it possible for the grandparents to maintain their social connection with people their own age.

Be Aware of Health Issues

Be sensitive to the health needs of the grandparents. As they age, they will face more and more health and energy challenges. The added stress at their age can be a complication that may hasten or introduce serious and sometimes debilitating health issues. That's what happened to one grandmother two weeks before Christmas. Severe pain sent her to the emergency room and eventually to surgery. She was hospitalized for two weeks. Without the help of her church family, everyone in the blended family would have suffered. Friends helped with school transportation, brought meals during her long recovery and even helped with Christmas shopping and provided Christmas dinner. What a wonderful experience of love in action was enjoyed by the children.

Make Meetings Inclusive

Understand that grandparents don't always feel at home in parent meetings. Be proactive and give them a personal invitation by phone or in person. Consider letting the invitation come from another parent who offers to accompany them to the parent meeting. Help these grandparents understand the value of sharing their experience from parenting as well as receiving help and information themselves. From the very beginning, include these grandparents on all communication lists. Also consider wording invitations using inclusive language ("To the family of . . .") so that they don't always confront how different their parenting experience is.

Can the Church make a difference in the lives of grandparents raising grandchildren, especially when one or more of the children have emotional, physical or mental challenges? Absolutely! With simple and compassionate support, the church can offer an intergenerational community of faith where everyone becomes stronger from the experience.

*"A State Fact Sheet for Grandparents and Other Relatives Raising Children," GrandFacts, October 2007. http://www.grand factsheets.org/state_fact_sheets.cfm (accessed July 4, 2008).

Caregivers: Organizations That Can Help

You've heard it said that there is no need to reinvent the wheel. That is also true in special needs ministry. Many creative people have gone before you, and with God's help, they have created programs that will bless the children in your ministry. You can find on the Internet information about specific disabilities and about organizations that serve families affected by disability. While not all organizations offer a faith component, they do model the kind of attitudes and support we want to provide at church. Many churches partner with local chapters of these organizations to expand their service and meet unchurched families. In doing so, they've discovered that many of the people who work for or do volunteer work for these organizations are Christians, and their enthusiasm is contagious.

When you approach one of these organizations, have with you a packet of information about your church and special needs ministry. Consider what you might offer them, not just how they can assist you. As Christians, we're called to look out for the needs of others. Your conversation should leave a positive witness but not come across as preachy. Your purpose is to create a mutually helpful network that will serve everyone for years to come. (See also "Working with Local Disability Organizations" on p. 62.)

The Arc

The Arc is a community-based nonprofit organization that is made up of and serves people with intellectual and developmental disabilities and their families. It has available many different services and supports for individuals and families and has hundreds of local chapters across the nation. The Arc is devoted to promoting and improving supports and services for all people with intellectual and developmental disabilities. Find out more about the Arc at http://www.thearc.org.

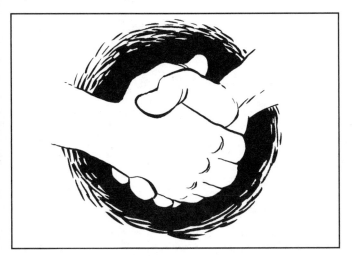

Christian Church Foundation for the Handicapped (CCFH)

Under the leadership of president Jim Pierson, CCFH trains, encourages and makes resources available to people so that they can effectively minister to people with disabilities. To meet the physical and spiritual needs of persons with disabilities, CCFH partners with individuals, churches and other organizations. CCFH's provision of a full range of services for persons with developmental/cognitive disabilities includes job training, opportunities for social interaction, opportunities for spiritual growth and residential homes. The CCFH website is http://www.ccfh.org.

The Miracle League

The Miracle League is a charitable organization that provides all children, regardless of their ability, with an opportunity to play baseball in an organized league. The Miracle League plays its games on specially built fields, custom designed with flat, cushioned synthetic turf that accommodates wheelchairs and other walking assistance devices, while helping prevent injuries. In other words, it provides a level playing field where children with special needs can hit, run and catch just like nondisabled children. During each Miracle League game, every child bats each inning and scores a run. Miracle League team members are assigned buddies who assist them playing the game. Buddies can be business leaders, fellow schoolmates, college students—anyone who wishes to volunteer their time. For more information, visit www.miracleleague.com.

MySummerCamps

MySummerCamps.com is a directory of all sorts of summer camps for children, including over 700 camps for children with special needs. If your church does not hold a camp or if your church camp does not accept children with certain types of disabilities, look at this website to see which camps in your area are open to children with special needs. Make sure parents are also aware of this website, because many parents of children with special needs are more comfortable sending their children to camps that specialize in disabilities. Consider taking a small group of children from your special needs ministry to one of the camps listed, and take along some volunteers—a camp is a great place to train volunteers. Look at the directory at www.mysummercamps.com.

Upward

Upward is an evangelistic sports ministry specifically designed for kindergartners through sixth-grade boys and girls. It promotes character, self-esteem and salvation in every child. Upward offers basketball, cheerleading, soccer and flag football programs and provides opportunities for all believers to become involved in their church's ministries. Upward also provides leadership training to equip church members to coach a team, referee a game, share a devotion, pray for your program and minister to people in the community through relationships developed with those who participate in your program. Learn more at http://www.upward.org.

Sibling Support Project

The Sibling Support Project, through various means, trains people on the creation of support programs for brothers and sisters of people who have special needs. This national effort also provides information for brothers and sisters of people with special needs and for parents and program leaders so that they better understand sibling issues. Their website is http://www.siblingsupport.org.

Handi*Vangelism Ministries International

Handi*Vangelism is a nonprofit faith-based mission that seeks to grow and serve the Body of Christ around the world by sharing the love of Jesus and equipping the Church to share His love with people who have disabilities. They provide training, resources and special events; and they also publish *Increase,* a newsletter with current information on their many ministries for people with special needs. Their website is http://www.hvmi.org.

Rest Ministries Chronic Illness Pain Support

Rest Ministries is a Christian nonprofit organization that serves people who live with chronic pain or illness, and their families. They provide practical, relational, emotional and spiritual support through Bible studies, devotionals, online communities and networks, and other resources and materials. Learn more at http://www.restministries.org.

Hope: Becoming a Disability-Friendly Church

Throughout our communities, we see efforts being made to ensure that people with disabilities have greater access to the world around them. Businesses and offices have set aside parking spaces for people with disabilities. Stores have widened their aisles and sometimes offer shopping assistance for those who are unable to reach high shelves or have available electric carts for those who have poor mobility. National parks offer special hiking paths for blind visitors and sign-language interpreters for people who have a hearing impairment.

Be a Role Model

Even though progress is being made, there is still a long way to go. The barriers, both physical and attitudinal, are still many in number. What is most unfortunate is that people with disabilities have found that churches lag far behind businesses and offices in the efforts to eliminate barriers. The one place anyone and everyone should feel welcome, regardless of his or her mental or physical condition, is the church; yet many churches still are not welcoming people with special needs. You have an opportunity to let your church shine out to the community as a place where people with disabilities are truly welcome. You can serve as a role model to your community.

The best way to determine what your church can do to become barrier free is to take a careful look at the "Accessibility Checklist" (p. 298). As you go through the checklist, you will find ways you can make your church a more user-friendly place for children and adults with special needs.

Joni and Friends is committed to accelerating Christian ministry in the disability community. One of the ways we are doing this is through our nationwide Field Ministry Offices and our Department of Church Relations. If you are searching for advice, resources and training, you can call the field office in your area. They can tell you about local training events, director's groups and new materials. They will also answer your questions, pray for your needs and encourage you along the way. (To locate the closest JAF Field team, visit the JAF website at http://www.joniandfriends.org.)

Sometimes the most helpful thing you can do is talk to leaders who have started disability ministries in other churches. Our Field Ministry maintains a list of these churches, which is also posted on the JAF website.

Provide Financial Assistance

Your church may want to establish a scholarship fund to sponsor leadership training or to pay a family's way to a camp or JAF Family Retreat. From time to time, your church may become aware that a family affected by disability is experiencing a financial crisis. A special fund can help you meet that need and reach them for Christ.

The Christian Fund for the Disabled (CFD) provides one-time grants to qualifying individuals through the churches that are willing to provide matching funds. The CFD is administered through Joni and Friends and its area ministries in the United States. Applications are sent to the CFD committee for review. Grant requests must reflect a practical or educational need relating to a disability concern, or a disability ministry outreach project or program that includes an evangelism component. This foundation simply wishes to contribute financial assistance on a matching grant basis, all with an emphasis on providing ministry, practical assistance and a demonstration of Christ's love to people with disabilities to strengthen or create a relationship between people with disabilities and their local church. (To learn more, visit http://www.joniandfriends.org/resources.php.)

Accessibility Checklist

☐ 1. **Inclusive**—The church's philosophy of ministry is one of inclusiveness.

☐ 2. **Biblical**—The church understands and implements the biblical principles of disability ministry.

☐ 3. **Accessibility**—The church is accessible physically, audibly and visually, or is implementing a plan to become accessible.

☐ 4. **Practical**—The church understands the practical felt needs of children and adults with disabilities and their families and is implementing a plan to meet them.

☐ 5. **Evangelism and Discipling**—The church is intentionally and systematically evangelizing and discipling people with disabilities.

☐ 6. **Assimilating**—The church is assimilating people with disabilities into the church, so the people with disabilities are making up a growing percentage of the congregation.

☐ 7. **Promoting**—People with disabilities hold positions of leadership and service in the church outside the disability ministry.

☐ 8. **Multiplying**—The church is multiplying leaders in disability ministry and sending them to minister within the church and in the larger community.

Hope: The Christian Institute on Disability*

Before I formed you in the womb I knew you, before you were born I set you apart.

Jeremiah 1:5

The Christian Institute on Disability (CID) is the vision of Joni Eareckson Tada, founder of Joni and Friends International Disability Center. It officially opened in 2007 to carry disability ministry into the twenty-first century. Joni is so passionate about this new institute that she wants to share its beginnings with you in her own words:

Dear Friends,

The idea behind the Christian Institute on Disability began in 1982, just after a Down syndrome child with mild complications was starved to death in a hospital. The parents, doctors and the Supreme Court of Indiana said the family had the right to refuse to grant permission to operate. They had the right to starve a child to death. I remember thinking, *The life of every disabled person is now in jeopardy!*

Many people think a civilized society would never condone something as horrible as infanticide. But it's happening, here and around the world. Infanticide is only one small component of a much wider assault on God-given life.

With God removed from the public arena, these are dangerous days for families affected by disability. If this downward spiral is allowed to continue, disabled people—and the personhood and dignity of all human beings—will be systematically targeted. Friends, the situation is urgent and the time to act is now!

God has ordained the Christian Institute on Disability for such a time as this. It is my sincere prayer that you will stand firm with us on the front lines, safeguarding the future of loved ones now and countless generations to come.

Joni

The mission of the Christian Institute of Disability is to impact the Church and Christian and public institutions and societies with a biblical worldview and life-giving truth on issues pertaining to life, dignity, justice and equality that affect people with disabilities.

Core Values

- **Life**—All life comes from God, the creator and sustainer of all things, and is therefore sacred. Issues pertaining to life and death should be approached from an understanding that all individuals have a moral claim to life and God alone has the final decree to end a life (see Genesis 2:7; Colossians 2:15-17).

- **Dignity**—Every individual is created in the image of God and has inherent dignity, value and worth as a person regardless of physical capability and intellectual function. It is the responsibility of Christians and society to protect and advocate for the dignity of all people (see Genesis 1:27).

- **Justice**—The character of God as revealed in Scripture is distinguished by love, mercy and justice. Justice as a theme throughout Scripture compels us as Christians to stand for righteousness and justice in order to correct the wrongs (injustice) that society causes or allows to happen to those affected by disability (see Psalm 37:5-6).

- **Equality**—Every individual is equal in the eyes of God and should be treated as such. Equality means recognizing that all persons, regardless of their capabilities, exist for the glory of God and have been granted different gifts, abilities and life circumstances (see Romans 10:12; 1 Corinthians 12:12).

- **Evangelism**—The Great Commission given by our Lord Jesus Christ in Matthew 28:19-20 mandates that our first and foremost priority in all we do as Christians is to bring all people, including those affected by disability, to a saving knowledge of Jesus Christ through declaration and demonstration of the gospel and to encourage their discipleship, maturity and service in the local church.

Education and Training

Equipping the church for the ministry is at the heart of Joni and Friends, and education and training is a central thrust of the CID where laity, professionals and ministers are prepared for the work of disability ministry. The CID also develops materials and coursework from the grassroots level to higher academia that will allow Joni and Friends to have an impact across the globe in bringing a biblical worldview on disability and the role the Church is to play in evangelizing, including and empowering the disabled.

- **Degree Offerings**—Programs from undergraduate degrees to graduate degrees through partnerships with highly respected and recognized seminaries and institutions of higher learning

- **Certificate Programs**—Certificates with transferable college credits as well as certificates for continuing education

- **Web-Based Education**—Online courses and certificate programs as well as downloadable materials and training videos

- **Training Conferences and Summits**—Expanded national and international training, lectures and seminars, as well as on-site training for churches and institutions

- **Curriculum Development**—Fully developed disability training manuals, church curriculum for awareness, Bible studies and small-group ministry as well as an online e-library with the archived works of Joni Eareckson Tada and other disability-related materials by other authors

Public Policy

Human life can now be copied and replicated, altered and aborted, cloned and euthanized, patented and redefined. It is culture's fundamental fear of disability and suffering that is fueling the maddening pace toward eugenics,

Joni and Friends — CHRISTIAN INSTITUTE ON DISABILITY

Education and Training

Educating tomorrow's leaders for disability ministry through:

- Seminaries
- Universities
- Missions Training School
- Certificate Programs
- Curriculum Development

Public Policy

Shaping culture with a biblical worldview on issues of bioethics and the sanctity of life by:

- Position Papers
- Research
- Journals
- Debates
- Media

Internship

Experiential learning through hands-on ministry:

- Mentoring
- Training
- Equipping
- Empowering
- Discipleship

embryonic stem-cell research and the redefinition of what it means to be human. The Policy Center of the CID will bring together theologians, ethicists, educators, doctors and attorneys to address these hotly debated disability-related issues and present a clear, reasonable and biblically based perspective on these issues.

- **Position Papers**—Compositions on bioethics and the sanctity of life, disseminated to laity and to academic journals, providing a clear and concise biblical view on these issues by utilizing an interdisciplinary peer-review approach; web-based availability and interaction

- **Debate Teams**—Groups of trained speakers, who will respond to secular and humanistic views by addressing bioethics and sanctity-of-life issues in public debates

- **The Advocacy Resource Center**—Source of assistance on social and sanctity-of-life issues and responsible for the creation of a network of organizations, agencies and advocates

- **Research**—Professional and academic contributions and the development of Fellows (Project Teams) for topical and cultural topics

- **Consortiums**—Creation of think tanks of Christian minds coming together through forums, summits and an international congress

Internships

Every year thousands of volunteers serve the disabled around the world in short-term missionary opportunities through Joni and Friends and other disability-related ministries. Outside of this annual experience, volunteers have little opportunity to continue to learn about disability ministry and/or have the opportunity for continued hands-on training. The Internship Department of the CID will provide a structured learning experience whereby interns receive education and training on disability ministry while experiencing hands-on training at the same time. Students from colleges, universities and seminaries will also have the opportunity to receive transferable credits toward a degree for their training and experience.

- **Experiential Learning**—Giving interns hands-on experience while studying in the classroom at the same time will greatly enhance the overall learning experience for students. Training will take place residentially at the JAF Headquarters, virtually via online with a supervisor and through various national and international affiliates.

- **Program Models**—Various models will be structured for flexibility and optimization of resources including two-week to 12-month internship options. Areas of ministry will include local ministry within the church, JAF Family Retreats, Wheels for the World and other international options. In addition, students will have the option of certificate course work for continued education or for credit transfer to a college, university or seminary.

- **Potential Interns**—Candidates will include seminary students, college and university students, training-school students, missionaries, life long learners and JAF volunteers/short-term missionaries.

Join our prayer team and receive regular updates on the projects of the CID; and/or donate to the CID, and "defend the cause of the weak . . . maintain the rights of the poor and oppressed. Rescue the weak and needy" (Psalm 82:3-4).

Information in this article is from "Christian Institute on Disability," *Joni and Friends International Disability Center*, 2006. http://www.joniandfriends.org/institute.php (accessed July 4, 2008).

Hope: Creating Movies for Inspiration

Most children's ministry leaders know that the best way to reach twenty-first-century volunteers and donors is to show them quality movies done in living color. The images of smiling children, grateful parents and joyful helpers can powerfully move people to action. This is definitely true in regard to disability ministry. The children are our best recruiters.

Some churches have the resources to film and edit their own movies featuring families from their church. Movies can be shown in worship, in small groups or at training events to build awareness and dispel fears. Many ministries include movie clips on their church's website.

Check with churches in your community that have disability ministries. Ask them if they have movies that you could preview to get ideas for your church. Also contact colleges and universities in your area that have film departments. You may find students who will use filming your ministry as a school project. Make people aware of the need, because they may have the resources to support your project.

The following movies are available from Joni and Friends (http://www.joniandfriends.org/store.php). They can be used to inspire your staff and congregation or as models to create your own ministry movie.

The Father's House: Welcoming and Including People and Families Affected by Disability (DVD)

Do you need a movie that answers every excuse you have heard about why a person cannot volunteer in special needs ministry? In *The Father's House,* pastors, parents and people with disabilities respond to those excuses by sharing personal accounts of how they have been touched and changed through disability ministry. Ten practical ideas for becoming a disability-friendly church are presented, along with helps to dispel fears and misunderstandings.

In His Image: Special Needs Ministries and the Church (DVD)

This 11-minute movie pulls on your heartstrings. It is an excellent tool for introducing a new disability ministry to your church board and congregation. It was created by In His Image Ministry at the First Church of the Nazarene in Pasadena, California. It begins with the testimonies of some teachers who feel called to minister to children with special needs. It also portrays the fears and hopes of moms and dads who find God's grace in the smiles of their courageous children. As one dad said, "Wouldn't it be great if all children made good grades? And what if, when children played sports, they were all stars? But when that is not the case, it is the struggles that change our lives."

Hope: *Joni and Friends* TV Series Trains and Inspires

In 2007, Joni and Friends accepted a challenge from the National Radio Broadcasters to create its first television series hosted by Joni Eareckson Tada. Programs can now be seen on many TV affiliates around the world and are also available on DVD. These inspiring programs highlight a refreshing, honest approach to people's toughest questions about the goodness of God in a world shattered by pain and suffering. Through dramatic and powerful glimpses into the lives of real people who have endured or are still enduring heart-wrenching trials, Joni and her guests put Scripture to the toughest of tests, showing why God is worth believing and how to trust Him in the worst of times.

Training and Inspiration

Each program of *Joni and Friends* is a half hour of riveting images, soul-stirring stories and proof-positive truths from the heart of God's Word, which will change your life. These beautifully told stories can be used in your church as an addition to Bible studies and/or as training tools for leaders, teachers and volunteers. They may be used for many purposes:

- To inspire your congregation to volunteer to serve children with disabilities

- To provide insightful discussions about the theology of suffering

- To encourage people to donate offerings to special needs ministry

- To reveal God's power to meet the needs of His people

- As useful tools for evangelism of families with disabilities

- As welcome gifts to anyone needing to trust God through difficult times

A Sampling of the Programs

A Family for the Fatherless

William and Debra Hopson are God-honoring parents raising God-honoring children—a high calling in today's culture. But these two have met an even greater challenge: Of their eight children, six are adopted and some have special needs. God calls His people to care for the fatherless, and this couple has responded to the call! Spend a day with the Hopsons, and you'll see the joy they've found in becoming a family for the fatherless.

Not by Sight

At age 14, Brian Bushway's eyesight deteriorated suddenly and for no obvious reason. In a short time, he became blind. During the 10 years that have followed, Brian has faced tough questions and tough challenges. But because of his relationship with Jesus Christ and his desire to serve others, this young man now sees life in a whole new way.

Yours for a Song

Renee Bondi, a music teacher with a beautiful singing voice, was young and in love. But a bizarre accident left her paralyzed, with almost no use of her voice. Would she ever sing again? Would her fiancé still love her, much less want to marry her? What can God do with a body so suddenly and seriously disabled?

See how God's hand upon her life has made her "confident of this, that he who began a good work in you will carry it on to completion until the day of Christ Jesus" (Philippians 1:6).

Emily's World

Meet Emily Shanahan—intelligent, enthusiastic and passionate about her faith in Jesus Christ. Emily lives with the physical limitations of cerebral palsy, but there is certainly no limit to what God has accomplished in her life! Enter the world of this determined, yet unselfish, university student, and see how she has enriched the world of those who know her!

I've Got Questions

A person's attitude toward himself has a profound influence on his attitude toward God, his family, his friends and his future. The amazing story of Nick Vujicic and his ability to live life to its fullest has had just such a dramatic impact on people all around the world. Almost everyone struggles in some way with their appearance, their abilities or their faith. This young man's story will cast fresh light on some of the tough questions faced by us all.

For the complete list of episodes, visit the JAF website at http://www.joniandfriendstv.org.

Goals for _____ (Year) [Sample]

What are the ... things that our ministry needs to do in the coming year?

> "We overestimate what we can do in a year and underestimate what we can do in five years." —Ted Engstrom

Category	Activities		
A. TRAINING OF DISABILITY OUTREACH TEAM MEMBERS	1. Conduct a Disability Discovery Class	2. Conduct a Disability Exploration Class	3.
B. AWARENESS BUILDING FOR THE CHURCH	1. Disability Ministry Sunday	2. Propose CEF curriculum or VBS program	3.
C. OUTREACH EVENT	1. "Special Delivery"	2. Attend and recruit families for Family Retreat	3. Participate in Wheelchair Drive
D. INTEGRATION OF PEOPLE OR FAMILIES WITH DISABILITIES	1. Improve accessibility of Sanctuary	2.	3.
E. RECRUITING	1. Disability Ministry Sunday	2.	3.
F. RELATIONSHIP WITH CHURCH LEADERSHIP	1. Pastor/Elder Breakfast to share plans and ministry	2.	3.
G. PLANNING AND ADMINISTRATION	1. Planning meeting with Disability Ministry/Outreach Team	2.	3.

Disability Ministry Planning Calendar

Year __2007__

Sample

January	February	March
New Year's party for all Disability Ministry/Outreach volunteers and participants.	Begin Wednesday night program for physically disabled.	Wheelchair cleaning day at residential facility.

April	May	June
		One-year evaluation of Disability Ministry/Outreach program. Review Accessibility Checklist.

July	August	September
Start respite care program.	5-day Family Retreat.	

October	November	December

Visual Bible Stories, Songs, Verses and Prayers

The Lord has shown you what is good.

Micah 6:8, NIrV

How to Use Visual Bible Stories, Songs, Verses and Prayers

Visual communication is beneficial for students who have hearing and language impairments, developmental/cognitive disabilities, learning disabilities or a visual learning style. Visual stories and sign-language songs, verses and prayers are a great way to enhance Bible teaching.

Stories

- **Make a Book**—Print out the story and cut out each panel. Make a book out of construction paper or card stock and glue one panel onto each page in the book. Use the fewest number of words when telling the story, allowing the child to focus on the pictures.

- **Make Picture Aids**—Print out the story and enlarge each panel to approximately 8x10 inches (20.5x25.5 cm). Glue each panel onto a piece of construction paper, and laminate each panel. Show only one picture at a time as you tell the story.

- **Teach Sequencing**—Print out the story and cut out each panel. Glue each panel onto a piece of card stock or cardboard, and laminate each panel. Place the pictures in order on a chalkboard tray or bulletin board as you tell the story. After you finish, give the pictures to the students, and let them retell the story by placing the pictures in the proper order. (After you laminate each panel, you could glue the hook side of Velcro onto the back of each panel and then place the pictures on a felt-covered board as you tell the story.)

Songs, Verses and Prayers

Teaching students songs and prayers in sign language increases their ability to learn. Signing enables children to use their visual and physical abilities. It is very difficult to teach children with language difficulties how to say a word, but it is easy to help them form a sign with their hands. For students who don't have difficulty talking, sign language creates another way to help the brain memorize words.

- **Prompting**—When teaching a song or prayer, let the child watch one person do the sign while another helper stands behind the student, gently guiding his or her hands through the proper motions. As the student learns, the prompting can gradually be faded away.

- **Adapting**—For students with physical limitations, it is okay to modify the sign to adapt it to the student's ability. For example, if the student is unable to touch his or her middle finger to the opposite palm when signing "Jesus," it is okay to accept close approximations. The signs are being used to assist the students in learning, so it's important to be flexible and meet individual needs.

- **Simplifying**—Some students will be able to sign every word presented while others may only be able to sign one word per sentence. Choose signs that best represent the concept being presented. If signing "Jesus" "loves" "me" and "know" is too difficult when singing "Jesus loves me this I know," you may have the student just sign "love." It is important to not frustrate the student by requiring too much. Our goal is to help children learn and communicate the love of Jesus one step at a time. It is better to start simple and add more as signing becomes easier.

Song: Jesus Loves Me*

Jesus

loves

me!

This I **know**,

For the **Bible**

tells

me

so;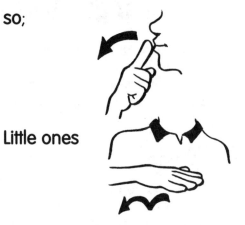

Little ones

to **Him** belong;

They are **weak**,

but **He**

is **strong**.

Yes,

Jesus

loves

me!

Yes,

Jesus

loves

me!

Yes,

Jesus

loves

me!

The **Bible**

tells

me

so.

Story: The Ten Commandments

This story from the Bible is about the special rules God gave to His people.

From Exodus 20:1-17

Moses went to the top of the mountain to talk to God.

God gave Moses 10 very special rules.

There is only one real God.

Our God is not made of wood, stone, gold or silver. He is alive.

God wants us to use His name nicely in prayer, worship and praise.

God wants us to give one day each week to Him.

God wants us to always listen to our mom and dad.

God does not want us to kill, steal or want what others have. He wants us to be kind to others.

God wants us to be faithful to our family.

God does not want us to steal or lie. He wants us to tell the truth.

God wants us to follow His rules because He loves us.

Verses: The 23rd Psalm

The Lord Is My Shepherd

From Psalm 23

The Lord is my shepherd.
God takes care of me.

I shall lack nothing.
God will give me everything I need.

He makes me lie down.
God knows what is good for me.

He guides me in paths of righteousness.
God tells me how to live by giving me the
Bible and prayer.

I will fear no evil.
I don't have to be afraid
because God is with me.

God's rod and staff comfort me.
God will protect and support me.

God prepares a table before me.
God always makes sure I am fed.

Goodness and love will follow me.
God gives me love.

I will dwell in the
house of the Lord forever.
If I follow Jesus, I will go to heaven.

Story: The Christmas Story

This story from Matthew 1 and 2 and Luke 1 and 2 is about how God gave us His Son, Jesus.

God sent an angel to Mary. The angel said, "Don't be afraid. You will have a baby. He will be the Son of God."

An angel came to Joseph while he was sleeping and told him that he and Mary will be married, and Mary will have baby.

Mary and Joseph took a long trip to Bethlehem.

Joseph tried to find a room, but the inn was full.

Joseph and Mary stayed in the stable with the animals.

Jesus was born.

Angels came to the shepherds and told them the good news of the birth of Jesus.

The shepherds found Jesus lying in a manger.

Three wise men followed a star to find Jesus.

The wise men gave gifts to Jesus and worshiped Him.

Prayer: The Lord's Prayer

Our

Father,

who art in **Heaven,**

hallowed

be Thy **name.**

Thy **kingdom**

come.

Thy **will** be done

on **earth,**

as it is in **heaven.**

Give us

this **day**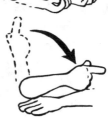

our daily **bread.**

And **forgive** us

our **debts,**

As we **forgive**

our **debtors.**

And **lead** us

not

into **temptation,**

but **deliver** us

from **evil.**

For **thine**

is the **Kingdom,**

and the **power**

and the **glory**

forever.

Amen.

Verse: John 3:16*

For **God**

so **loved**

the **world**

that he **gave**

his one and **only**

Son,

that **whoever**

believes

in **him**

shall **not**

perish

but have **eternal**

life.

Story: The Plan of Salvation

Becoming a Child of God

God loves us and wants us to love Him.

"God is love" (1 John 4:8).

We have all done bad things.

"All have sinned" (Romans 3:23).

So God sent Jesus to save us.

"The Father has sent his Son to be the Savior of the world" (1 John 4:14).

We need to tell God we are sorry for doing bad things.

"If we confess our sins, he is faithful and just and will forgive us our sins" (1 John 1:9).

We need to thank Jesus for being our friend, and we need to tell others about Him.

"If you confess . . . 'Jesus is Lord,' and believe in your heart that God raised him from the dead, you will be saved" Romans 10:9).

Then someday we will live forever with Jesus in heaven. "The gift of God is eternal life in Christ" (Romans 6:23).

Story: **Through the Roof**

This story from the Bible is about how God healed a man and forgave his sins.

From Mark 2:1-12

Many people went to hear Jesus teach.

One man wanted to see Jesus, but he couldn't walk; his legs didn't work.

Four good friends put the man on a mat and carried him to see Jesus.

When they got to the house, they couldn't get inside. There were too many people.

His friends took him up to the roof.

The friends cut a hole in the roof above Jesus.

The friends lowered the man through the roof right in front of Jesus.

Jesus saw that the man had faith and believed in Him. Jesus forgave the man for all the bad things he had done.

Jesus healed the man's legs and told him to get up and walk.

The man walked home, praising God!

Everyone was amazed and thanked God.

Story: The Easter Story

This story from the Bible is about how Jesus died for our sins
and rose again so that someday we can live with Him in heaven.

From Mark 11—16

Jesus healed people and taught them about God.

One day, Jesus rode into Jerusalem on a donkey. The people shouted, "Hosanna! Blessed is the King!"

Jesus ate the Passover meal with His friends. It was His last meal with them.

Jesus went with His friends to a garden to pray.

Soldiers came and arrested Jesus, even though He had never done anything wrong.

The soldiers put Jesus on a cross, and He died.

Jesus' friends buried Him in a tomb.

Three days later, some of Jesus' friends went to the tomb, and it was empty.

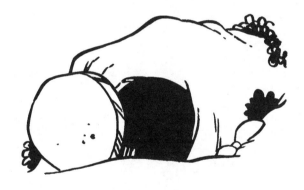

An angel told them, "Jesus is alive again!"

Jesus went to visit His friends and told them to spread the good news about God's love. Because Jesus gave His life for us, we can live again, too!

Index

Joni and Friends Resources

To learn more about these and other resources, visit http://www.joniandfriends.org.

All God's Children
by Joni Eareckson Tada and Gene Newman

This is a handbook for pastors, elders, ministry leaders and any concerned Christians who want to help people with disabilities. It will equip churches for ministry to those who are mentally retarded or have a physical or learning disability.

All Things Possible: Calling Your Church Leadership to Embrace Disability Ministry
by Stephanie O. Hubach and Joni and Friends

Do you have a passion to see people with disabilities and their families embraced and included in the life of the Church? Here is a discussion of the scriptural basis for disability ministry, a thoughtful look at a Christlike posture and purpose that will call your church leadership to action that will transform your church.

Autism and Your Church: Nurturing the Spiritual Growth of People with Autism Spectrum Disorders
by Barbara J. Newman

This resource will enable church leaders to appreciate those with ASD as persons created in God's image, to learn about 5 specific disorders included in ASD, to discover 10 strategies for including people with ASD and to develop plans for ongoing ministry with children and adults who have autism.

The Art of Helping: What to Say and Do When Someone is Hurting
by Lauren Littauer Briggs

All of us want to offer comfort and support to someone in pain or someone who has experienced a loss, but we often can't find the right words, and we end up pulling away and doing nothing at a time when our friend or family member needs us most. Here, the author addresses 30 of the most common heartaches people face, giving examples of creative forms of comfort and support for each, helping to pave the way for the brokenhearted to experience the grace, healing and comfort of a loving God.

Barrier-Free Friendships: Bridging the Distance Between You and Friends with Disabilities
by Joni Eareckson Tada and Steve Jensen

This book shares insights on how friends and relatives can help those who feel limited by their bodies or their circumstances. Writing from her own experiences, Mrs. Tada shows how to build mutually fulfilling relationships based on insights into how Jesus related to individuals with disabilities.

Camp Lean-on-the-Lord
by Diane Monreal

Through camp activities, Bible stories and crafts children learn about God's compassion for all people. They will gain an understanding of autism, cerebral palsy, spina bifida, Down syndrome, learning disabilities and AD/HD. Mission projects provide opportunities for groups to sponsor campers to Joni and Friends Family Retreats. This kit includes a teacher's manual with five lessons, missions project DVD, song CD, and posters.

Children's Ministry Pocket Guide to Special Needs

In this 16-page booklet, you will learn 10 quick tips to reach every child in the classroom. You'll also learn how to identify and connect with children who have special needs and how to reach them with Jesus' love. Included are surveys and tools to guide teachers as they partner with parents and establish action plans that work.

Exceptional Teaching: A Comprehensive Guide for Including Students with Disabilities
by Dr. Jim Pierson

Helping children with special needs reach their full potential has been the lifework of Jim Pierson. In this comprehensive book, he shares his knowledge of the many different kinds of disabilities so that you can become the exceptional teacher.

The Father's House: Welcoming and Including People and Families Affected by Disability

This DVD is a powerful visual teaching tool that presents 10 practical ideas for becoming a disability-friendly church. It will help churches address common fears and misunderstandings associated with beginning a disability ministry.

Give Them Jesus: Evangelizing Children with Special Needs
by Pat Verbal

All children are capable of experiencing God's love in amazing ways. It is never too early (or too late) to tell a child about Jesus. This exciting resource addresses the hard questions children with disabilities ask about faith, and it explains how to present the gospel on their level. It includes discipleship ideas for new Christians, such as how to create a Faith-Journey Scrapbook.

Hearts in Motion: A Bible Study for Disability Awareness— Leader's Manual and Participant's Guide
by Joni and Friends

This four-lesson Bible study raises the level of disability awareness in one's small-group or Bible study class. You'll learn how to view disability from God's perspective and help open the doors of your church by becoming aware and responsive to the needs of people with disabilities.

Helping Kids Include Kids with Disabilities
by Barbara J. Newman

This book includes information for understanding children with special needs, information about specific areas of disability, lesson plans, letters and devotions for families.

How to Be A Christian in a Brave New World
by Joni Eareckson Tada and Nigel M. de S. Cameron

Stem-cell research, cloning, genetic engineering—today's discoveries in biotechnology are occurring so rapidly that we can barely begin to address one ethical debate before another looms overhead. This brave new world brings disturbing implications for the sanctity of life and for human nature itself. Here is thoughtful, passionate and gripping reading about the world that is already here and how to live out your faith with conviction in its midst.

Joni and Friends Television Series DVDs

Hosted by Joni Eareckson Tada, these 28-minute programs highlight a refreshingly honest approach to people's toughest questions about the goodness of God in a world shattered by pain and suffering. Through dramatic and powerful glimpses into the lives of real people who have endured heartrending trials, Mrs. Tada and her guests put Scripture to the toughest of tests, showing why God is worth believing and how to trust Him in the worst of times.

Including People with Disabilities in Faith Communities: A Guide for Service Providers, Families, and Congregations
by Erik W. Carter

This book addresses how faith communities, service providers and families can work together to support the full participation of individuals with disabilities in the faith community of their choice. Topics include the importance of collaboration among faith communities, service providers, families and individuals with disabilities to establish and maintain supports; and specific ideas for including individuals with disabilities in a network of religious groups and service providers to make faith communities more inclusive.

Let All the Children Come to Me: A Practical Guide to Including Children with Disabilities in Your Church Ministries
by MaLesa Breeding, Dana Hood and Jerry Whitworth

This practical handbook is filled with both inspiration and information. Teachers and pastors alike are reminded that God calls us to include all children, no matter the challenge. Packed with wonderfully practical elements, this book has ideas that can be easily integrated into any classroom.

Practical Pathways: Reaching and Training Volunteers for Ministry with Special Needs Children
by Pat Verbal

Children grab hold of your heart and don't let go— that's how God created them. This invaluable resource is designed to help church leaders inspire volunteers in disability ministry. It includes how-tos for presenting volunteer opportunities, training teachers, selecting and adapting curriculum for special needs students and addressing burnout.

On a Roll for Jesus
by Diane Monreal and Joni and Friends

This kit—which includes a teacher's guide, DVD, CD and fun activities to promote disability awareness among children—is a missions project offered through Wheels for the World at Joni and Friends. This program can be implemented through Sunday Schools, VBS, youth groups, midweek groups, etc. Children will participate in giving the gift of mobility and sharing the love of Jesus in a meaningful way.

Responding with Compassion: Ministry Models for Families Affected By Disabilities
by Debbie Lillo

Every family is precious to God, but those affected by disability go to church with unique needs. They look for acceptance and compassion—not perfection. It is okay to start small with one of the ministry models described in this detailed guide. Models include Sunday School, respite care programs, Vacation Bible Schools, parent support groups, sibling workshops, camps and church events.

Same Lake, Different Boat: Coming Alongside People Touched by Disability
by Stephanie O. Hubach

Through both scholarly discussion and heartwarming stories, the author of this book presents a biblical view of disability, along with a call to churches to reform and become an inclusive community for all people.

Special Needs Special Ministry: For Children's Ministry
by Jim Pierson, Louise Tucker Jones and Pat Verbal

This practical guide is filled with examples of how churches became welcome places for children with special needs. It was written by experienced mentors and includes outlines and reproducible materials to build awareness, to create a well-trained staff and to reach out to new families for your disability ministry.

So My House Will Be Full: A Guide for Including People with Disabilities in the Church
by Paul Dickens, Jane Young and Sheena Baird

How do we change our natural responses and actions toward people with disabilities to reflect Christ? You must learn to understand their world, use good manners in their presence and support their abilities to serve the Body of Christ. This training manual breaks this down into a dozen step-by-step lists.

Through the Roof: A Guide to Assist Churches in Developing an Effective Disability Outreach
by Joni Eareckson Tada and Steve Miller

Presenting the why and how-to of disability ministry, this resource helps leaders determine the needs in their congregation and community, explains how to prepare for disability ministry and includes a ministry worker's training course, plus a variety of recommended resources.

When God Weeps: Why Our Sufferings Matter to the Almighty
by Joni Eareckson Tada and Steve Estes

Explore God's hope for all of us through our sufferings with your Bible study group. This kit includes Joni's message tapes on DVD, a leader's manual, a participant's guide and a copy of the book *When God Weeps*.